new home plans for 1999

Cover Plan
Cover Photo by Jeff Garland Photography

Library of Congress No.: 97-99623
ISBN: 0-938708-81-3

Submit all Canadian plan orders to:
The Garlinghouse Company
60 Baffin Place, Unit #5
Waterloo, Ontario N2V 1Z7

Canadian Orders Only: 1-800-561-4169
Fax No. 1-800-719-3291
Customer Service No.: 1-519-746-4169

© Copyright 1998 by The L. F. Garlinghouse Co., Inc. of Middletown, Connecticut. Building a house from a design found in this publication without first purchasing a set of home plans is a copyright violation. Printed in the USA. New Home Plans for 1999 is published at 282 Main St. Ext., Middletown, Connecticut 06457, USA. All photographed plans may have been modified to suit individual tastes.

Plan # 10839 p. 56
Photography by John Ehrendou

Inside Features

- Hot Off The Drawing Board!   6 - 24
  First Time Published Home Plans
- Cover Plan   3
  Focus on Plan No. 99460
- Home Plan Of The Year   118
  An Award Winning Favorite
- Architectual Design   57
  A Home on the Cutting Edge

Ordering Made Easy

- Here's What You Get   248
  Cabinet Plans, Cross Sections & Much More!
- Options & Extras   250
  These Accessories Provide Valuable Information
- Modifications Made Easy   251
  Cut Costs or Add Your Own Special Touches...
- Zip Quote Home Cost Calculator   252
  Obtain a Construction Cost Calculation
- Copyright Information   253
  Legalities Regarding our Blueprints
- How To Order   254
  Shipping Costs and other Pertinent Info

Plan # 99119 p. 50
Photography Supplied by Ahmann Design

Publisher James D. McNair III
Chief Operating Officer Bradford J. Kidney
Staff Writers Debra Cochran/Sue Barile
Cover Designs Judy-Ann Konopka

Chairman of the Board Whitney B. Garlinghouse **Publisher** James D. McNair, III **Chief Operating Officer** Bradford J. Kidney **Editor-in-Chief** Nancy Garlinghouse **Writer** Debbie Cochran **Financial Analyst** Gregg Lafferty **Marketing Assistants** Louise Ryan, Barbara Jones **Operations Coordinator** Susan Barile **Financial Planning & Reporting Manager** Doug DiMora **Financial Planning & Reporting Staff** Beth Grant, Jodi Sciacca **Admin./Pers.Assistant** Laura Bauer **Receptionist** Priscilla Arnold **Design Director** Wade Schmelter **Design Staff** Lisa Mesick, Brian Winslow, Michael Rinaldi, Robert Fortier **Telesales Manager** Frank Shekosky **Telesales Staff** Candace Wilks, Eelise Twomey, Janet Bonet **Information Systems Manager** Ken Mosher **Webmaster** Kevin Daly **Senior Programmer** Robert Reed **Plans Fulfillment Manager** Nina Padilla **Plans Fulfillment Staff** Natalie Ward Copeland, Louie Padilla

All Design, Film, and Printing of this publication is managed by Graphic Productions 860 - 704 - 22200 Middletown, CT. 06457
CEO Ron Poehailos **Art Director** Paula Mennone **Administrative Assistant** Dana Moraci **Senior Graphic Designer** Judy-Ann Konopka **Associate Art Director** Robert Miles Long **Graphic Artist** Grant Copeland **Graphic Designer** Debra Novitch **Art Production Assistant** Josephine Rudyk **Production Assistants** Marla B. Gladstone, Steven Jylkka, Robert Jones **Freelance Assistance** Laura Scott **Account Executive** Oscar Larancuent **Telemarketing Coordinator** Peter Chamberlain

Visit Our Website
http//www.garlinghouse.com

All Website Credit Card Transactions Are Secure With VeriSign Encryption

We Welcome Your Feedback!
E-mail us at: DCochran@garlinghouse.com

Design 10483

INTELLIGENT USE OF SPACE

Lots of living is packed into this well-designed home which features a combined kitchen and dining room. The highly functional U-shaped kitchen includes a corner sink under double windows. Opening onto the dining room is the living room which is illuminated by both a front picture window and a skylight. A lovely fireplace makes this an inviting place to gather. The sleeping area of this home contains three bedrooms and two full baths, one of which is a private bath accessed only from the master bedroom.

Main area — 1,025 sq. ft.
Garage — 403 sq. ft.

Total living area:
1,025 sq. ft.

Refer to **Pricing Schedule A** on the order form for pricing information

An EXCLUSIVE DESIGN By Karl Kreeger

No. 10483
Main Area

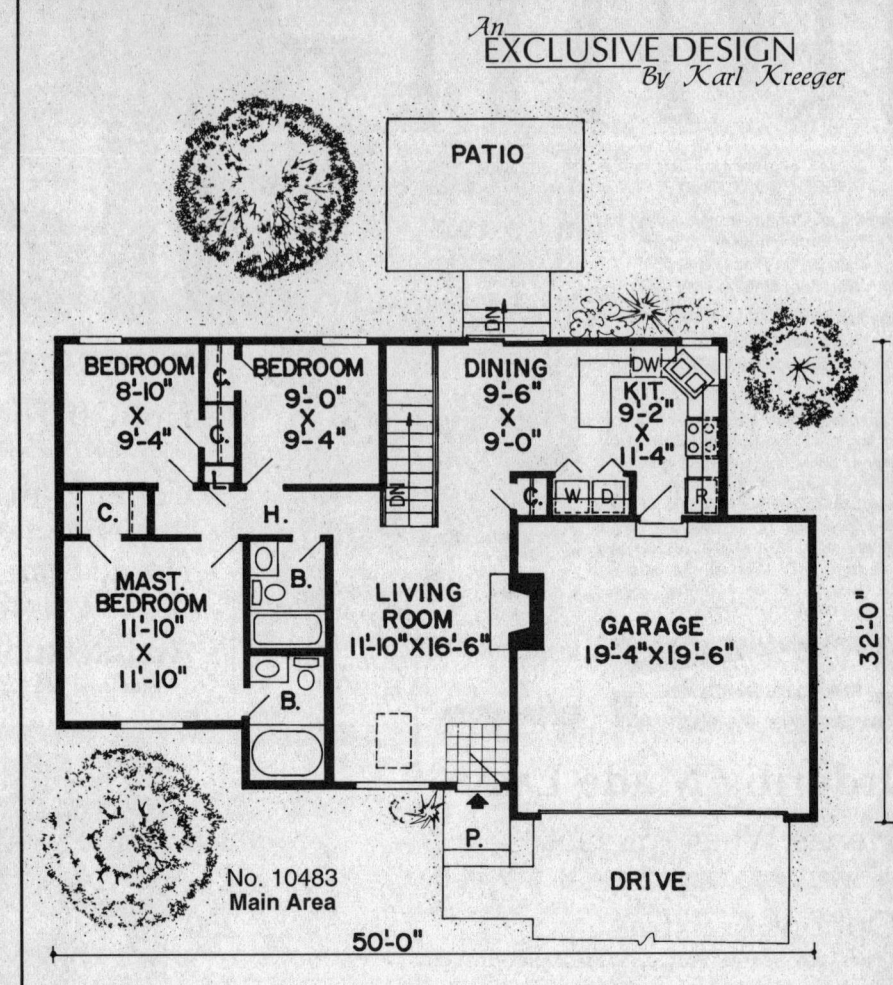

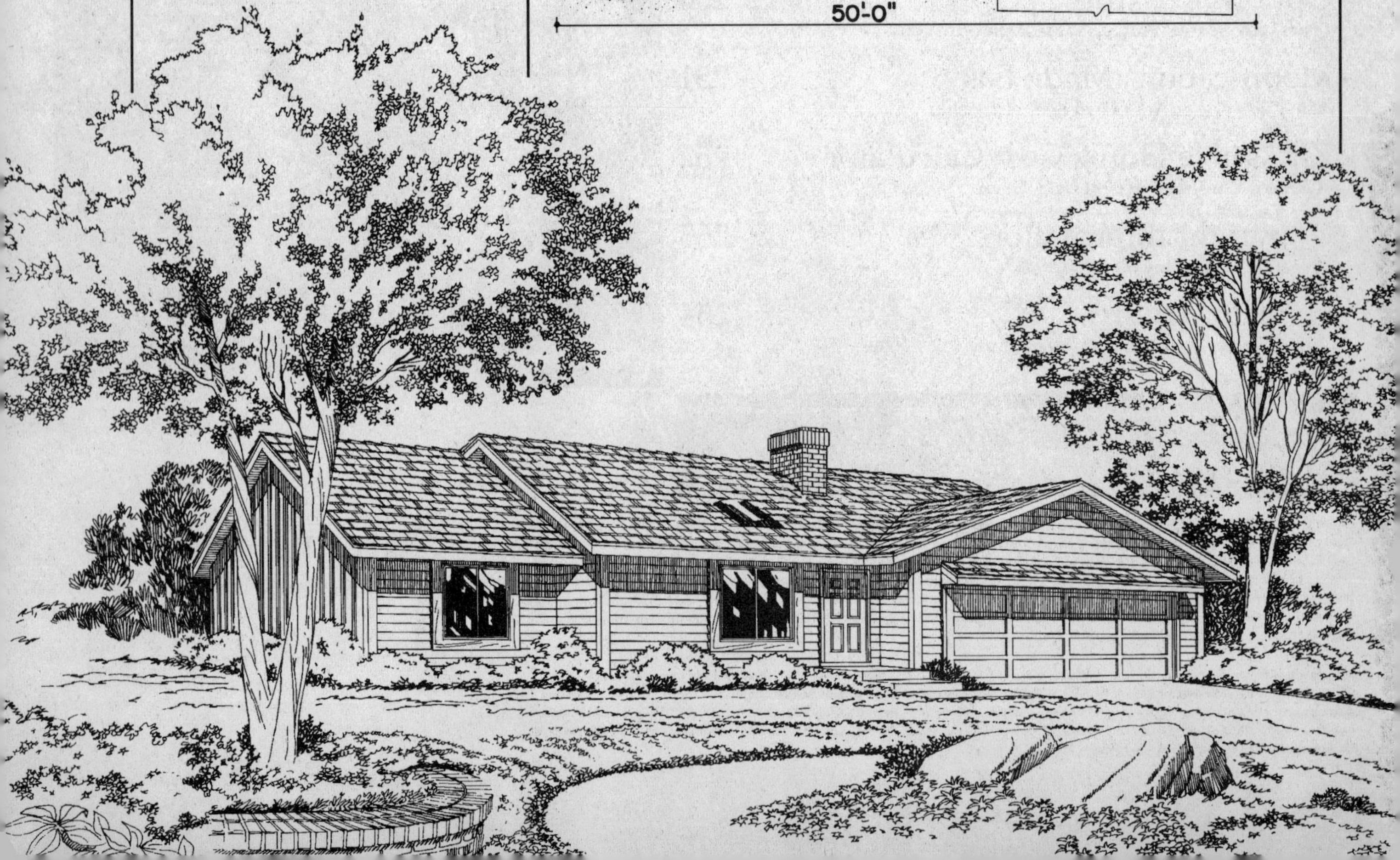

ORDER TODAY! 1 - 800 - 235 - 5700

STATELY LINES ALLUDE TO ELEGANCE

Design 99460

First floor — 2,040 sq. ft.
Second floor — 927 sq. ft.

The dynamic entry views the den, formal dining room and magnificent curved stairway. An upstairs gallery wall with arched openings surveys the elegance below. French doors access the den topped by a volume ceiling. The bayed dinette is highlighted by a unique ceiling detail and outdoor access. The kitchen features an island, a walk-in pantry and abundance of counter space with built-ins. Wooden columns frame the entrance into the spacious volume Great room with spider-beamed ceiling, see-through fireplace, hide-away wetbar and a wall of four arched transom windows to the back. The comfortable hearth room has a another see-through fireplace, bookcases and an entertainment center. The main level master bedroom has well placed bright windows and a decorative ceiling treatment. The sumptuous master bath/dressing area has two closets, a dual vanity, and a roomy whirlpool tub. The comfortable secondary bedrooms include ample closet space.

No. 99460
FIRST FLOOR
© 1987 design basics inc.

Total living area: 2,967 sq. ft.

SECOND FLOOR

Refer to **Pricing Schedule E** on the order form for pricing information

© 1987 design basics inc.

Sunken Living Room Featured

Design 26112

Wood adds its warmth to the contemporary features of this solar design. Generous use of southern glass doors and windows, an air lock entry, skylights and a living room fireplace reduce energy needs. R-26 insulation is used for floors and sloping ceilings. Decking rims the front of the home and gives access through sliding glass doors to a bedroom-den area and living room. The dining room lies up several steps from the living room and is separated from it by a half wall. The dining room flows into the kitchen through an eating bar. A second floor landing balcony overlooks the living room. Two bedrooms, one with its own private deck, and a full bath finish the second level.

First floor — 911 sq. ft.
Second floor — 576 sq. ft.
Basement — 911 sq. ft.

Total living area: 1,487 sq. ft.

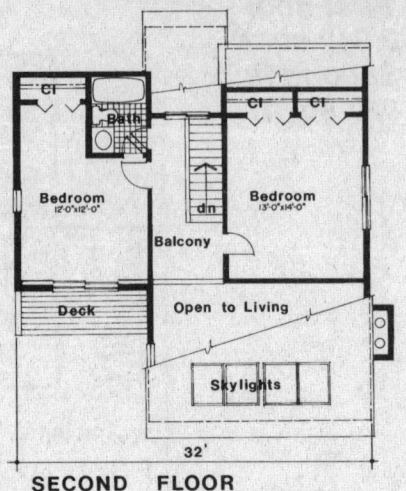

SECOND FLOOR

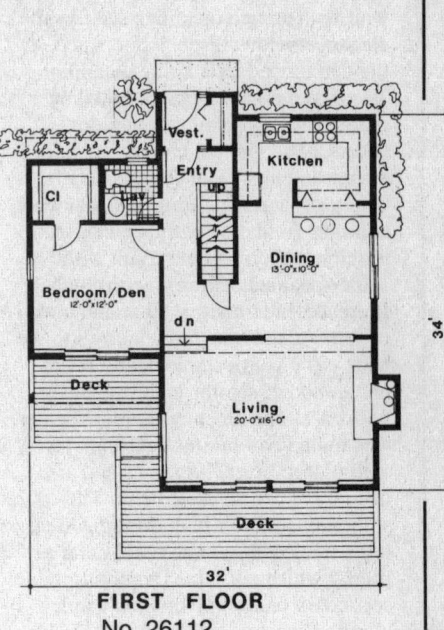

FIRST FLOOR
No. 26112

Refer to **Pricing Schedule A** on the order form for pricing information

ORDER TODAY! 1 - 800 - 235 - 5700

COMPACT COUNTRY COTTAGE

Design 99856

Multi-paned bay window, dormers, cupola, covered porch, and a variety of building materials give this compact country cottage visual impact. The foyer opens to a large Great room, with fireplace and cathedral ceiling, which flows to the open dining and kitchen area. Two front bedrooms, one with bay window, the other with walk-in closet, share an ample bath. The master suite is privately located at the rear with walk-in closet and private bath with double vanity. A partially covered deck with skylights becomes an outdoor room accessible from dining room, Great room, and master bedroom.

**Main floor —
1,310 sq. ft.
Garage & Storage —
455 sq. ft.**

Total living area:
1,310 sq. ft.

Refer to **Pricing Schedule B** on the order form for pricing information

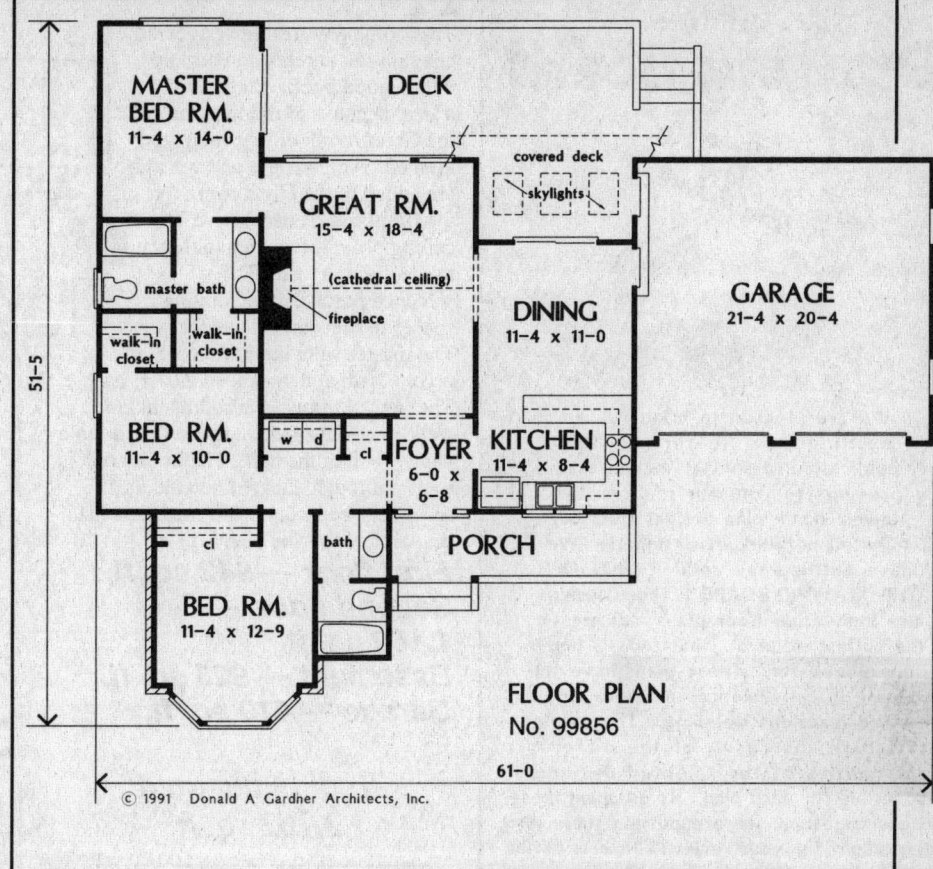

© 1991 Donald A. Gardner Architects, Inc.

Hot off the Drawing Board

We are pleased to bring you an exciting new feature in this publication, a special section that presents to you, our readers, the newest home plan designs from our talented network of designers. We have entitled this section "HOT OFF THE DRAWING BOARD". These designs use innovative floor plans and are on the cutting edge of what today's home buyers look for. These plans have the ultimate in convenience and style not to mention luxurious detailing. The varying styles are the result of the different personalities of the talented designers responsible for each plan. By grouping these designs together, we are putting them into the spotlight for your review. Time is of the essence. Your dream home is waiting to be chosen. Take a moment to thumb through pages 6-24. You may have just found the "key" that opens the first door to your very special home.

HOME SWEET HOME

Design 24728

This home features those special, cozy places to relax and curl up with a good book. Entertaining is a snap because of the location of the Great room, dining room and kitchen. Atmosphere and warmth are added to the Great room by the fireplace. A decorative ceiling provides an elegant touch to the dining room. The screened porch expands living spaces in the warmer weather. The master suite includes a private bath and a walk-in closet. The two additional bedrooms include walk-in closets and share the full, double vanity bath in the hall. The book nook is a special touch, located outside the secondary bedrooms. No materials list is available for this plan.

First floor — 942 sq. ft.
Second floor — 1,160 sq. ft.
Basement — 923 sq. ft.
Garage — 410 sq. ft.

Total living area: 2,102 sq. ft.

Refer to **Pricing Schedule C** on the order form for pricing information

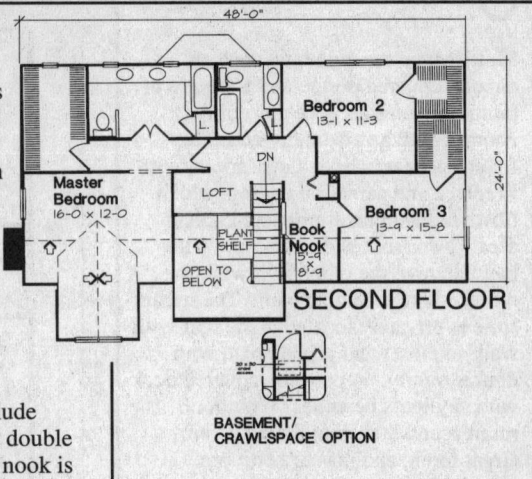

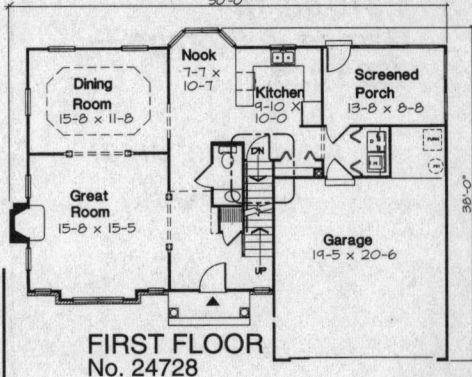

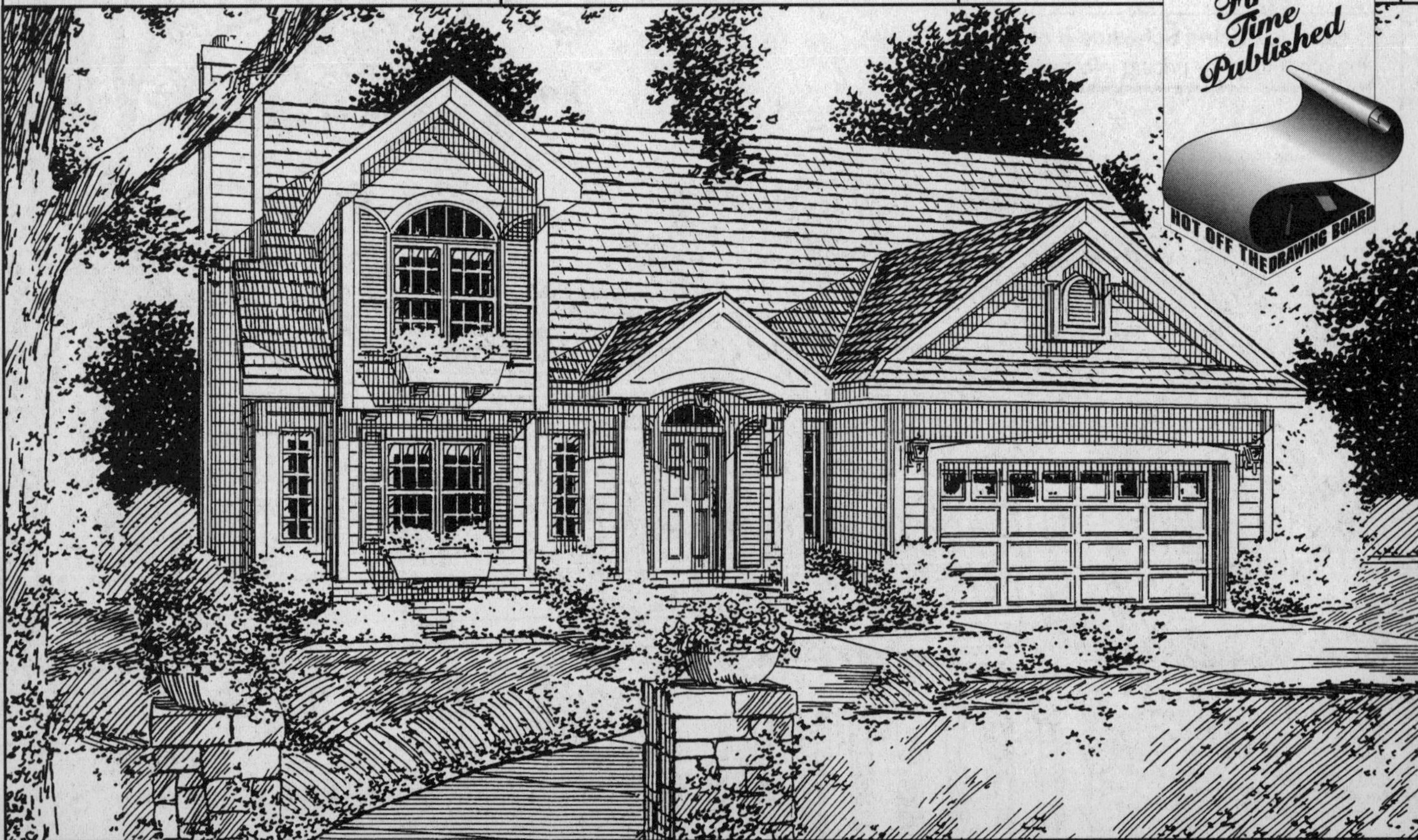

ORDER TODAY! 1 - 800 - 235 - 5700

Design 93442

CHARACTER AND CHARM

This impressive elevation doesn't disappoint in its contemporary floor plan. The dining room has direct access to the kitchen, yet can be made private by the pocket door. The kitchen features a cooktop island, an abundance of counter space and a built-in pantry an adjoining breakfast room, a built-in china cabinet, and a snack bar. The sun room adjoins with the kitchen and the family room. A fireplace and a fourteen foot ceiling highlight the family room. The master suite pampers the owner with a five-piece bath and a walk-in closet. The two additional bedrooms share a full bath in the hall. No materials list is available for this plan.

First floor — 1,626 sq. ft.
Second floor — 522 sq. ft.
Bonus — 336 sq. ft.
Basement — 1,626 sq. ft.
Garage — 522 sq. ft.

Refer to **Pricing Schedule C** on the order form for pricing information

An EXCLUSIVE DESIGN *By Greg Marquis*

FIRST FLOOR
No. 93442

SECOND FLOOR
WIDTH 54'-7"
DEPTH 62'-8"

Total living area:
2,148 sq. ft.

First Time Published — HOT OFF THE DRAWING BOARD

ORDER TODAY! 1-800-235-5700

Design 94251

Balance of Past & Present

A romantic air combines with the clean simple lines of this seaside getaway, set off by stunning shingle accents and a sunburst transom. Horizontal siding complements an insulated metal roof to create a charming look that calls up a sense of 19th century style. Inside, an unrestrained floor plan harbors cozy interior spaces and offers great outdoor views through wide windows and French doors. At the heart of the home, the two-story Great room features a corner fireplace, an angled entertainment center and an eating bar shared with the gourmet kitchen. Columns and sweeping archways define the formal dining room, while French doors open to the verandah, inviting breezes inside. The first floor master suite entices relaxation with a garden tub. Upstairs, an expansive deck captures panoramic views and serves the sounds of the sea to a secondary bedroom. No materials list is available for this plan.

First floor — 1,290 sq. ft.
Second floor — 548 sq. ft.

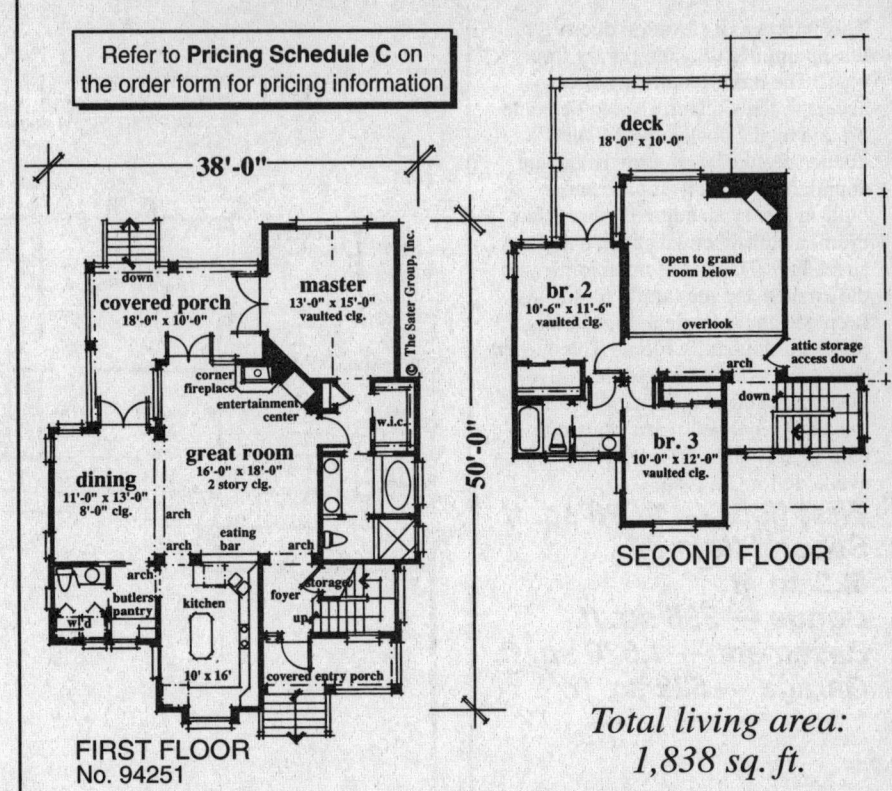

Refer to **Pricing Schedule C** on the order form for pricing information

FIRST FLOOR No. 94251

SECOND FLOOR

Total living area: 1,838 sq. ft.

First Time Published — Hot Off The Drawing Board

ORDER TODAY! 1 - 800 - 235 - 5700

Design 99081

Easy Living Ranch

Distinct exterior features of this home include vinyl siding, a series of gables, a circle top window in the dining room and a protected front door with sidelights. To the left of the foyer is the dining room that has fourteen foot ceilings. Directly behind is the kitchen featuring a serving bar and an adjoining breakfast area with easy access to the Great room. The master bedroom has a tray ceiling and a master bath with a large walk-in closet, dual vanity separate shower and a garden tub. Two additional bedrooms share a full hall bath. No materials list is available for this plan.

Main floor — 1,590 sq. ft.
Garage — 506 sq. ft.
Basement — 1,590 sq. ft.

Total living area:
1,590 sq. ft.

Refer to **Pricing Schedule B** on the order form for pricing information

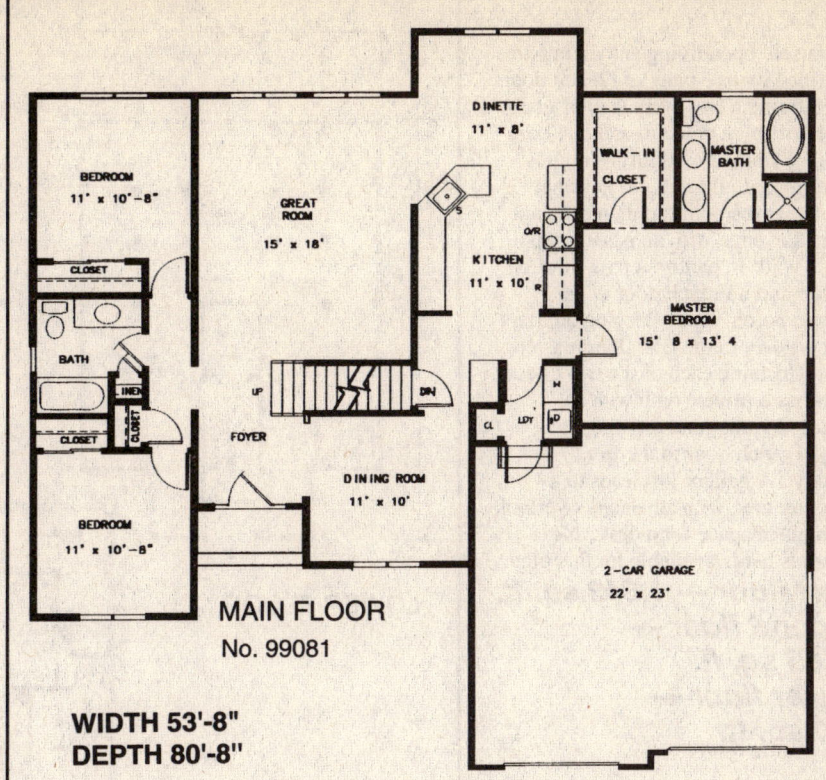

MAIN FLOOR
No. 99081

WIDTH 53'-8"
DEPTH 80'-8"

First Time Published
Hot Off The Drawing Board

POETIC SYMMETRY

Design 94261

The raised, open living and dining area is defined by two pairs of French doors which frame a two-story wall of glass topped off by a graceful arch. A cozy fireplace framed by built-ins invites gatherings of all kinds. A gourmet kitchen serves both family meals and planned events, with an island prep area, a walk-in pantry, a pass-through counter and a French door to the covered porch. Split sleeping quarters offer privacy to the first floor master suite. Upstairs, each of the two guests suites has a private bath with an oversized vanity and dressing area with a French door to the front balcony. A gallery loft leads to a computer area with a balcony overlook and built-in space for a desk. No materials list is available for this plan.

First floor — 1,642 sq. ft.
Second floor — 1,165 sq. ft.
Lower floor — 150 sq. ft.

Total living area: 2,957 sq. ft.

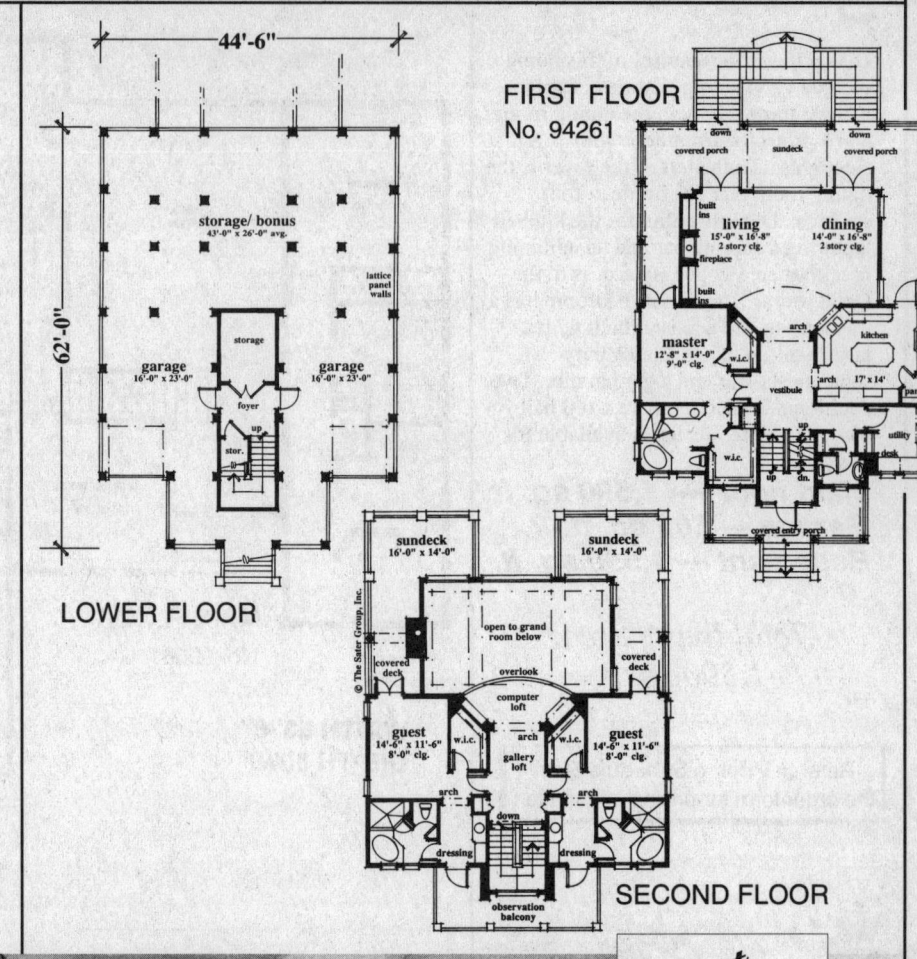

Refer to **Pricing Schedule E** on the order form for pricing information

First Time Published — Hot Off The Drawing Board

ORDER TODAY! 1 - 800 - 235 - 5700

STYLE & VERSATILITY

Design 96494

A traditional hip roof, arched and picture windows, and a barrel vaulted entrance decorate the face of this commanding home, while its spacious, livable floor plan offers style and versatility. The stunning Great room makes a statement with a magnificent cathedral ceiling that highlights rear French doors flanked by windows and capped with transoms and an arched clerestory. A cozy fireplace with space saving built-ins shields the Great room from kitchen noise. With two bedrooms up and two bedrooms down, this home promises privacy for everyone. The secluded master suite enjoys twin walk-in closets, a luxurious bath and a stately tray ceiling in the bedroom. Cathedral ceilings enhance both bedrooms on the second floor, and the first floor study/bedroom provides ample flexibility for any family.

First floor — 1,687 sq. ft.
Second floor — 514 sq. ft.
Bonus room — 336 sq. ft.

Refer to **Pricing Schedule D** on the order form for pricing information

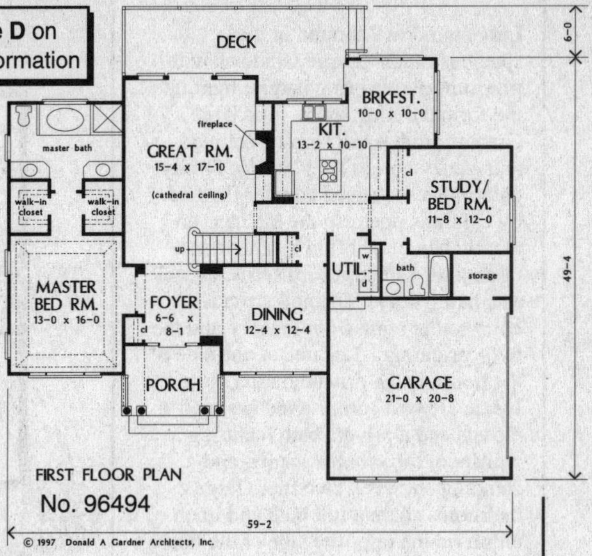

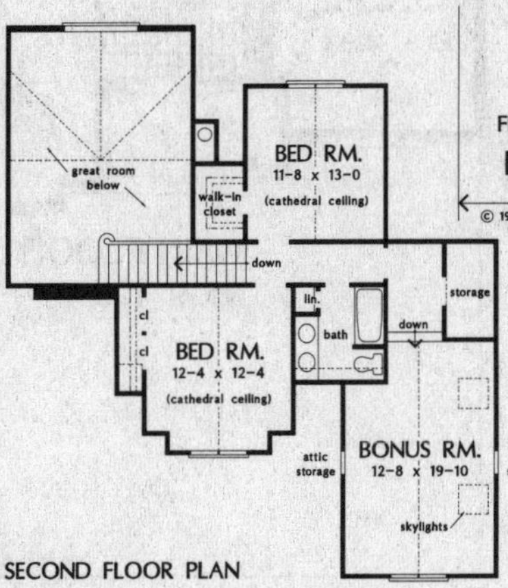

FIRST FLOOR PLAN
No. 96494

SECOND FLOOR PLAN

Total living area: 2,201 sq. ft.

© 1997 Donald A. Gardner Architects, Inc.

ORDER TODAY! 1-800-235-5700

UNIQUE THREE BEDROOM RANCH

Design 97123

Large windows abound in this spacious ranch. Large windows with transoms above bring natural light into the formal dining room. The large Great room has tall sloping ceilings and a cozy corner fireplace for family gatherings. A raised counter flanked by columns opens to the kitchen. In the kitchen, you'll find an abundance of counter and cupboard space, as well as a hall pantry. The hall provides entry to the main floor laundry and the two-car garage. Located at one side of the house is the private master suite. Inside are two corner windows, two closets and a private bath featuring a whirlpool tub, double vanity, and a standing shower. Two more large bedrooms share a full bath and linen closet on the opposite side of the house for privacy. No materials list is available for this plan.

**Main floor —
1,817 sq. ft.
Basement —
1,817 sq. ft.**

Total living area:
1,817 sq. ft.

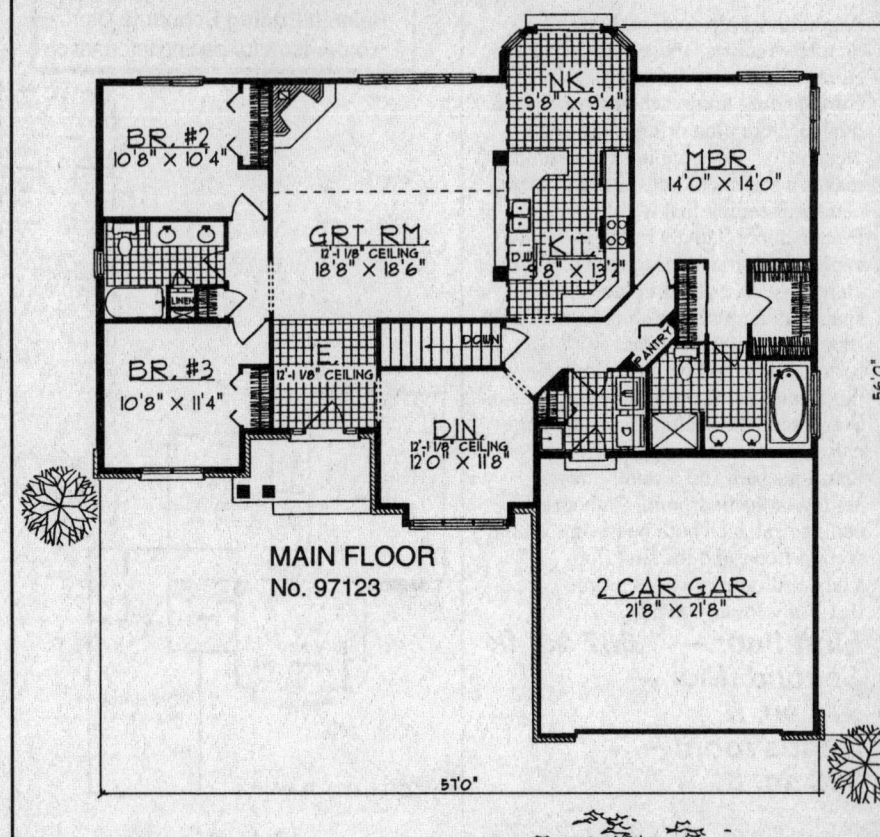

MAIN FLOOR
No. 97123

Refer to **Pricing Schedule C** on the order form for pricing information

First Time Published — HOT OFF THE DRAWING BOARD

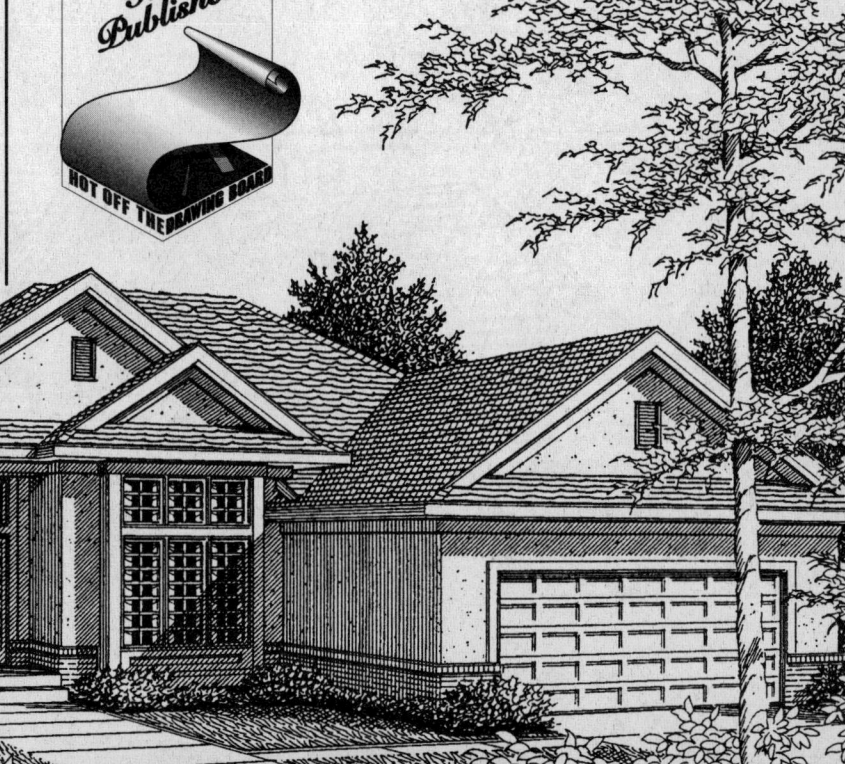

ORDER TODAY! 1 - 800 - 235 - 5700

Design 97203

VAULTED CEILINGS

This home has a smaller square footage with the features of a much larger home. The family room adjoins the dining room creating an illusion of more space. The entire area is crowned in a vaulted ceiling. The breakfast area and the master bath are also topped by a vaulted ceiling. A fireplace adds to be ambiance in the family room. The kitchen has sufficient work space and a French door from the breakfast area to the rear yard. The master bedroom is topped by a tray ceiling. A large walk-in closet is located off the master bath which includes a compartmental toilet, a double vanity, an oval tub, and a step-in shower. A linen closet is located outside the bath. This plan is available with a basement or crawl space foundation. Please specify when ordering. No materials list is available for this plan.

First floor — 1,073 sq. ft.
Second floor — 418 sq. ft.
Bonus — 167 sq. ft.
Basement — 1,073 sq. ft.
Garage — 420 sq. ft.

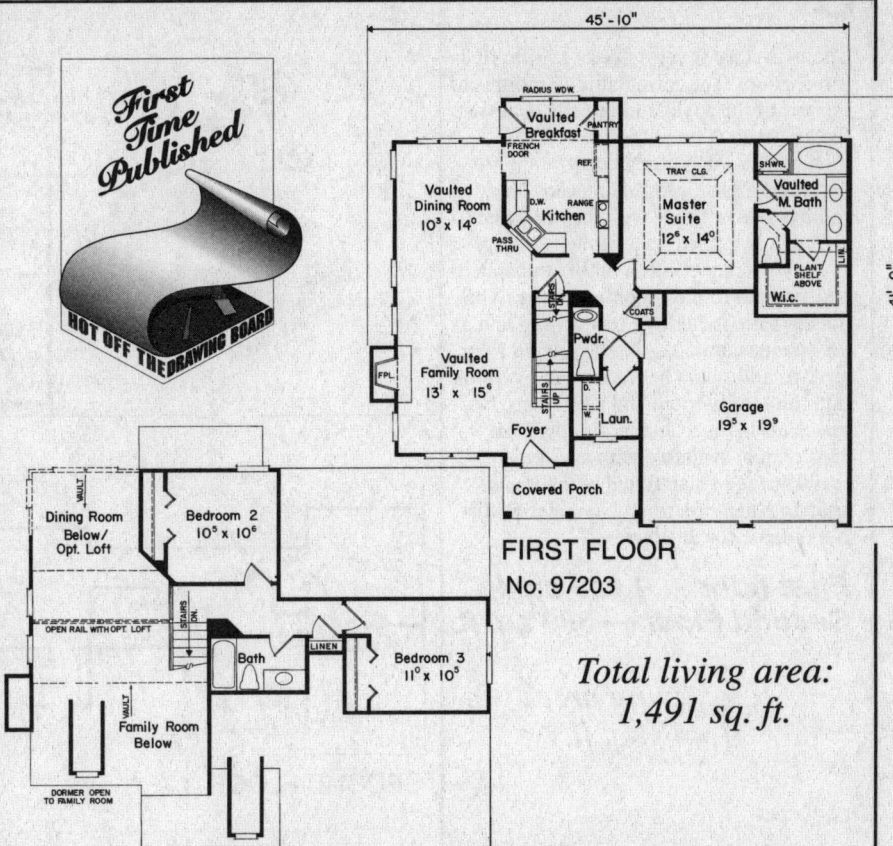

FIRST FLOOR
No. 97203

SECOND FLOOR

Total living area:
1,491 sq. ft.

Refer to **Pricing Schedule A** on the order form for pricing information

ORDER TODAY! 1 - 800 - 235 - 5700

Stylish Smaller Home

Design 97201

The two-story foyer makes a terrific first impression. The formal dining room is to the left of the foyer and directly accesses the kitchen. A breakfast area off the kitchen is a bright and cheery surrounding for informal meals. The family room adjoins with the breakfast area and is topped by a vaulted ceiling. A cozy fireplace adds a bit of atmosphere and warmth to the cooler evenings. The master suite includes a tray ceiling and a private master bath. On the second floor are two additional bedrooms, an overlook into the family room and a full bath. No materials list is available for this plan. This plan is available with a basement, crawl space or slab foundation. Please specify when ordering. No materials list is available for this plan.

First floor — 1,049 sq. ft.
Second Floor — 399 sq. ft.

Total living area: 1,448 sq. ft.

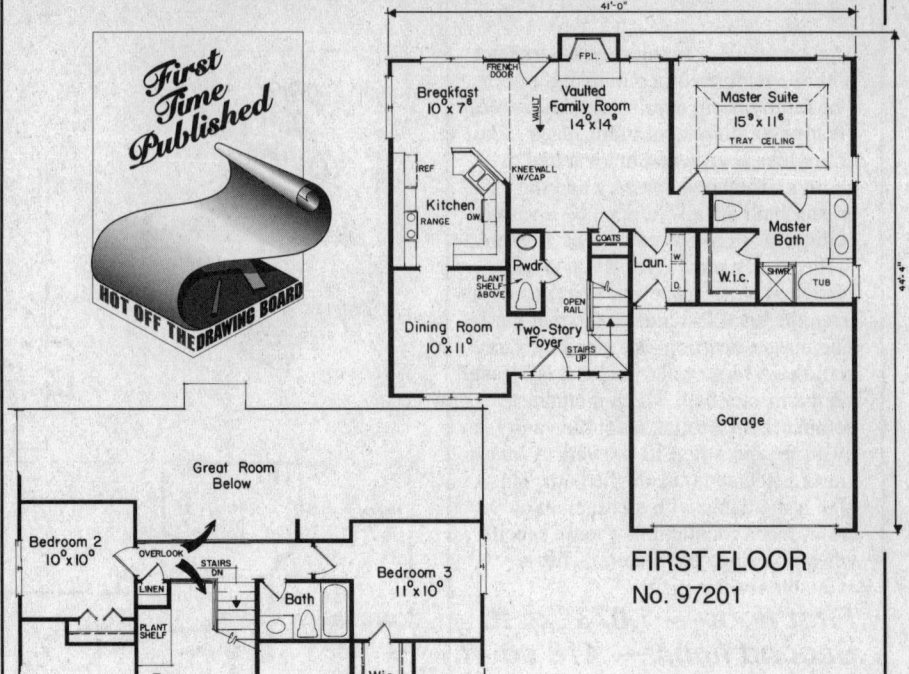

FIRST FLOOR
No. 97201

SECOND FLOOR

Refer to **Pricing Schedule A** on the order form for pricing information

ORDER TODAY! 1 - 800 - 235 - 5700

Many Modern Amenities

Design 97124

This attractive ranch has many modern amenities. The Great room has a vaulted ceiling and a cozy fireplace. Wrap-around counters make this kitchen ideal for busy mornings. The dining room has a cathedral ceiling and allows access to the backyard. A large walk-in closet and spa tub make the master bedroom a private retreat. Two additional bedrooms on the opposite side of the home share a full bath and linen closet. A main floor laundry room and two-car garage add to this fabulous ranch. No materials list is available for this plan.

Main floor — 1,416 sq. ft.
Basement — 1,416 sq. ft.

Total living area: 1,416 sq. ft.

Refer to **Pricing Schedule A** on the order form for pricing information.

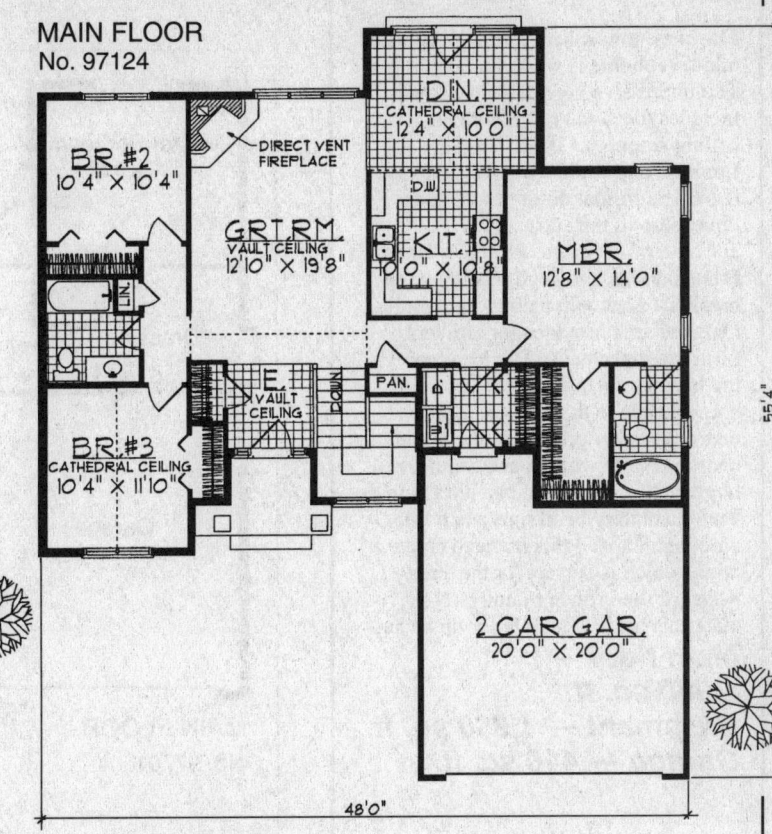

ORDER TODAY! 1 - 800 - 235 - 5700

Cozy Atmosphere

Design 97701

The cozy atmosphere of this delightful one-level home is warm and inviting. The impressive view from the foyer includes the Great room with the ceiling sloping to 10'-6" height, a fireplace and triple windows across the rear. The formal dining room adds dimension to the entry and is conveniently located near the kitchen. French doors, and skylights flood the breakfast area with natural light and a recessed area provides for efficient furniture placement. The location of the laundry room provides step saving convenience to the kitchen. Split bedrooms offer privacy to the master bedroom suite with sloped ceiling, a large walk-in closet and an ultra bath. Two secondary bedrooms and a full basement expand this home to create a home which is perfect for the empty nester or the growing family. No materials list is available for this plan.

Main floor — 1,980 sq. ft.
Basement — 1,980 sq. ft.
Garage — 440 sq. ft.

Total living area: 1,980 sq. ft.

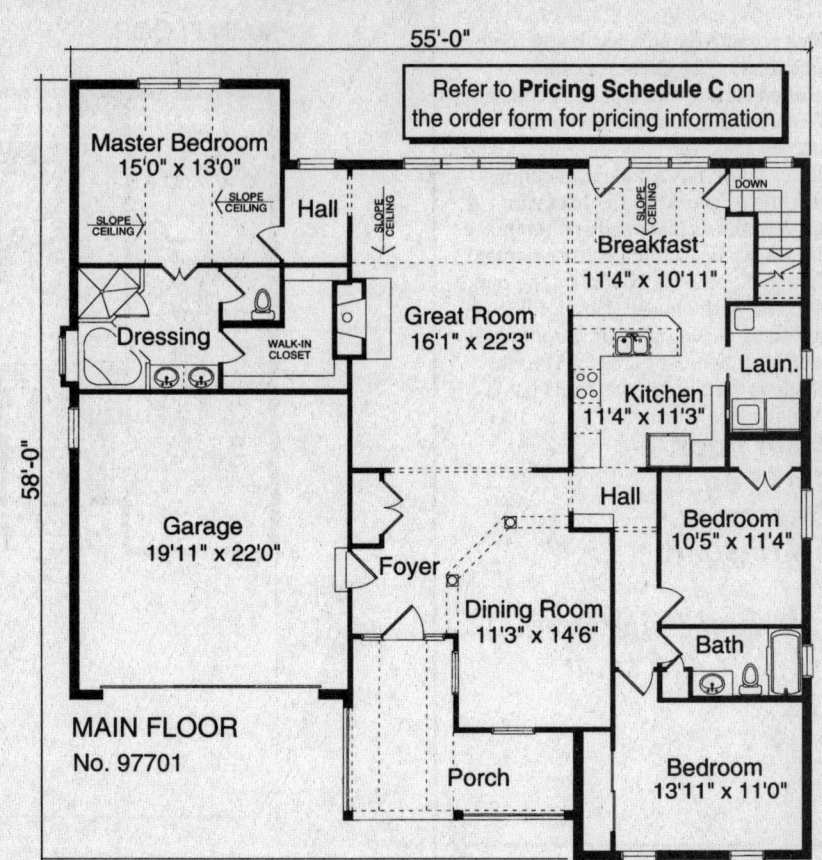

Refer to **Pricing Schedule C** on the order form for pricing information

ORDER TODAY! 1 - 800 - 235 - 5700

Formal, yet Modest Brick Home

Design 98000

A combination of stately arched windows, keystone arches, and a stylish hip roof accents this formidable yet modest brick traditional. Front and rear clerestory dormers embellish both the foyer and the Great room, increasing vertical space and adding light. Interior columns add elegance to the Great room which is heightened by a cathedral ceiling. Designed for efficiency, the kitchen features a pass through to the Great room and is open to an informal dining room with bay window. Positioned for privacy and crowned with a tray ceiling, the master suite lays claim to a private bath and walk-in closet, while two additional bedrooms share a hall bath.

Main floor — 1,488 sq. ft.
Bonus Room — 338 sq. ft.
Garage — 534 sq. ft.

Total living area:
1,488 sq. ft.

Refer to **Pricing Schedule B** on the order form for pricing information

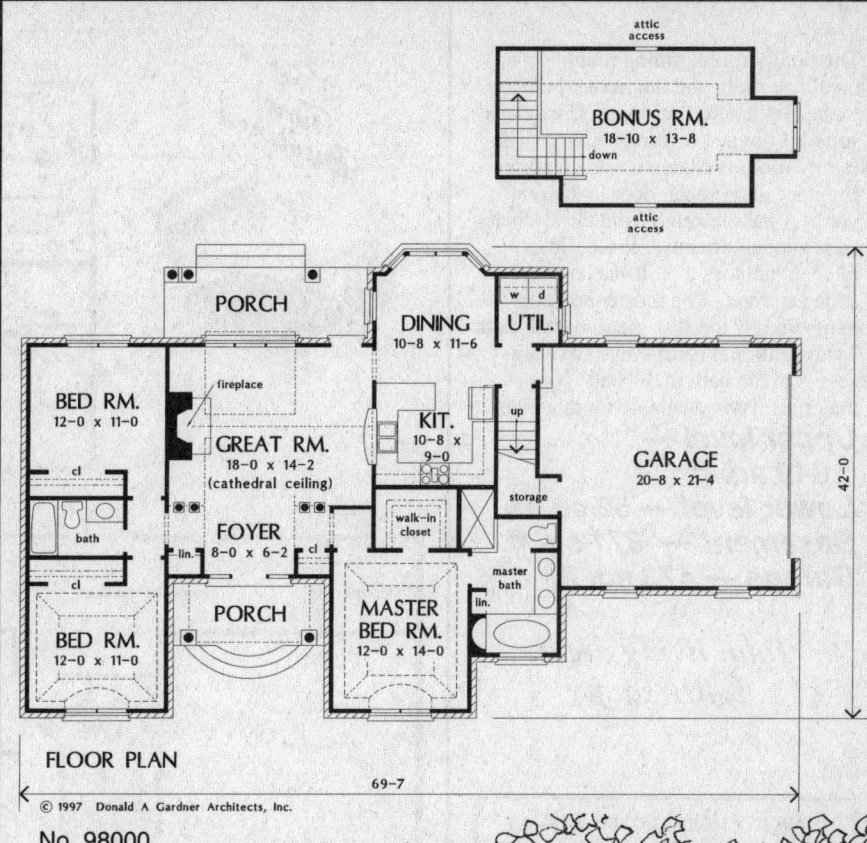

No. 98000

©1997 Donald A. Gardner Architects, Inc.

VAULTED CEILINGS

Design 98487

The family room, dining room, breakfast room and the master bath are topped by vaulted ceilings. The master suite is crowned in a tray ceiling. The family room is expansive and features a fireplace and French door to the rear yard. A pass through from the kitchen adds a touch of convenience. The kitchen includes a built-in pantry for added storage. The master bedroom is pampered by the five-piece master bath. Two additional bedrooms have easy access to the bath in the hall. No materials list is available for this plan.

Upper level — 1,349 sq. ft.
Lower level — 52 sq. ft.
Basement — 871 sq. ft.
Garage — 478 sq. ft.

Total living area: 1,401 sq. ft.

Refer to **Pricing Schedule A** on the order form for pricing information

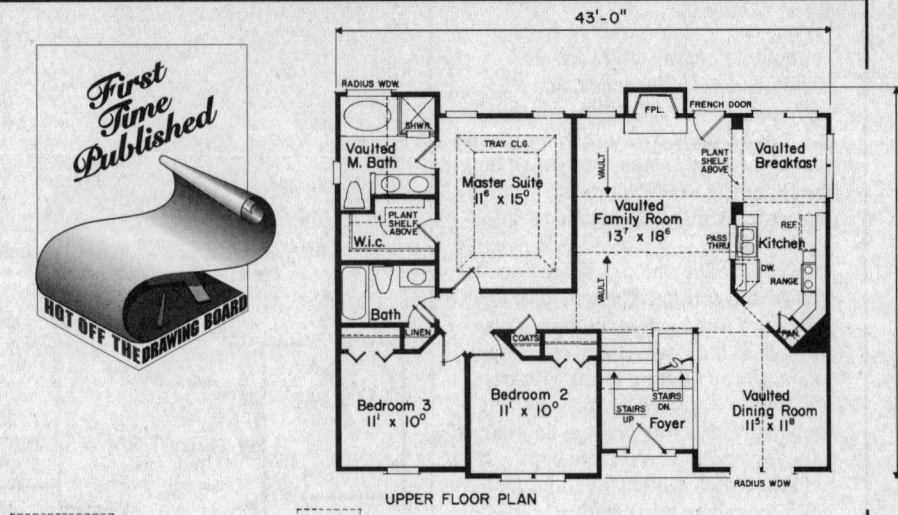

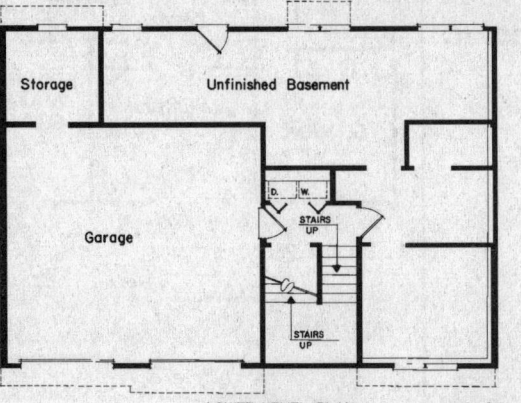

ORDER TODAY! 1-800-235-5700

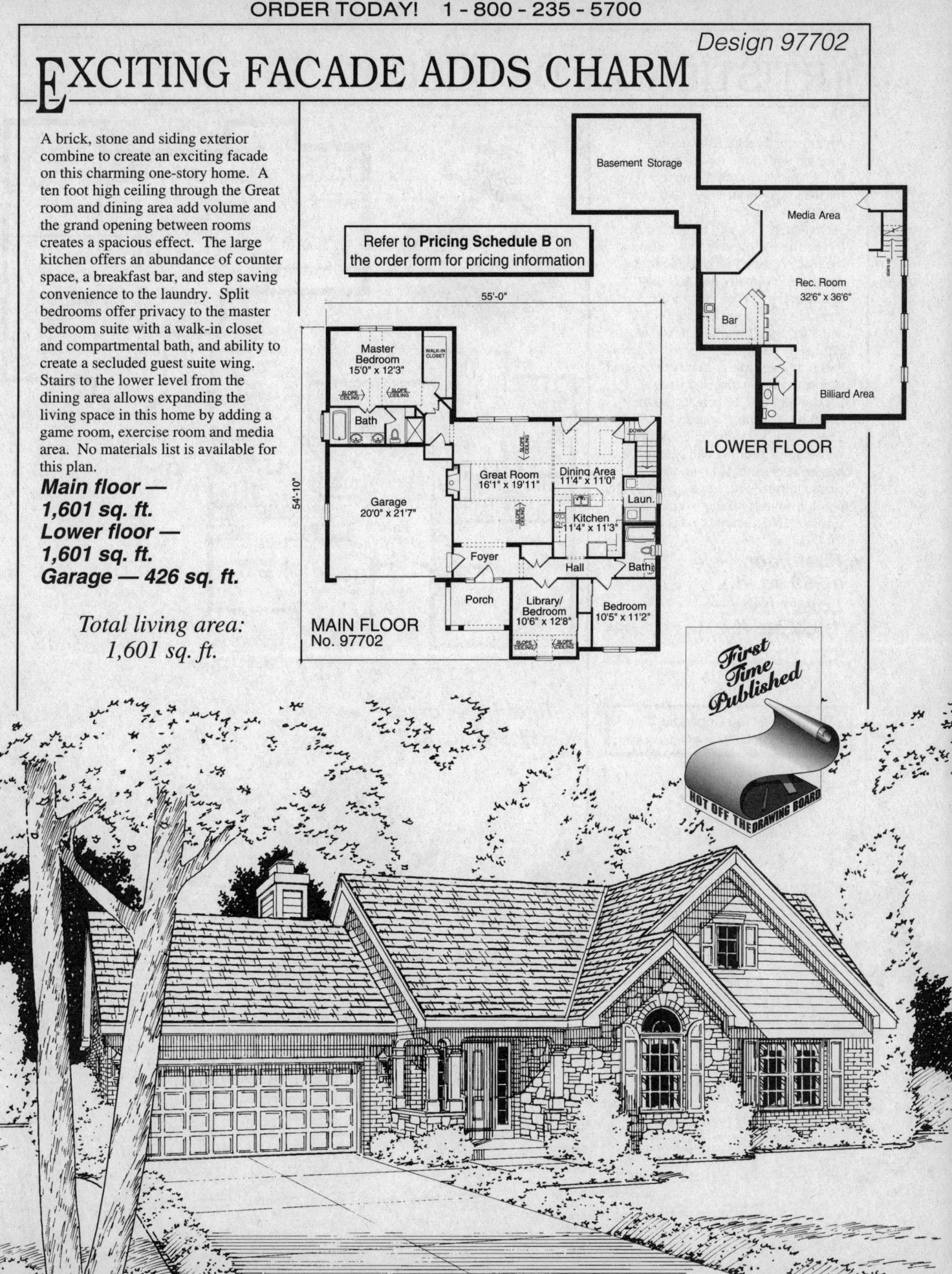

ORDER TODAY! 1-800-235-5700

EXCITING FACADE ADDS CHARM

Design 97702

A brick, stone and siding exterior combine to create an exciting facade on this charming one-story home. A ten foot high ceiling through the Great room and dining area add volume and the grand opening between rooms creates a spacious effect. The large kitchen offers an abundance of counter space, a breakfast bar, and step saving convenience to the laundry. Split bedrooms offer privacy to the master bedroom suite with a walk-in closet and compartmental bath, and ability to create a secluded guest suite wing. Stairs to the lower level from the dining area allows expanding the living space in this home by adding a game room, exercise room and media area. No materials list is available for this plan.

**Main floor —
1,601 sq. ft.
Lower floor —
1,601 sq. ft.
Garage — 426 sq. ft.**

*Total living area:
1,601 sq. ft.*

Refer to **Pricing Schedule B** on the order form for pricing information

ORDER TODAY! 1-800-235-5700

ARTISTICALLY DETAILED

Design 97703

An artistically detailed exterior coupled with large rooms and flexible living spaces creates the perfect home for the empty nester. A grand foyer introduces you to the spectacular Great room, where you will be surrounded by the fireplace and high windows to the rear. A nine foot opening to the dining area visually expands this spacious living area. Extensive counter space, an extra large island, and a pantry allows the kitchen to efficiently fulfill its purpose. A private hall provides orderly family entry, and access to the laundry and stairs. Eleven foot ceiling heights top the Great room, dining area and the foyer. The master bedroom suite is topped with a sloped ceiling and pampers the homeowner with its luxurious surroundings. Entry to a covered rear porch from this retreat is a pleasant surprise. No materials list is available for this plan.

First floor — 1,963 sq. ft.
Lower level — 1,963 sq. ft.

Refer to **Pricing Schedule C** on the order form for pricing information

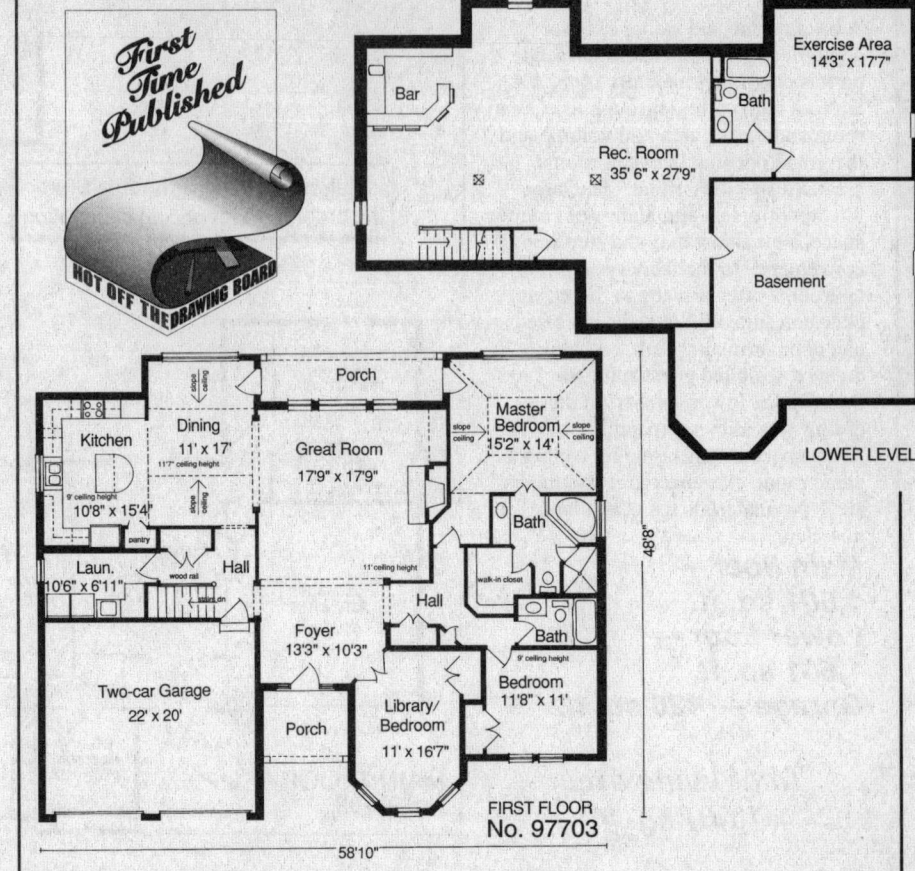

Total living area: 1,963 sq. ft.

ORDER TODAY! 1 - 800 - 235 - 5700

Design 98009

STUNNING FOUR BEDROOM

Large windows with circle tops, a stucco veneer and tile roof, and an open, easy living floor plan all combine to create this stunning four bedroom home. Impressive twelve foot ceilings grace the central common areas of the home as well as the inviting screened back porch. The kitchen, partially enclosed by eight foot high walls, features a useful pass-through to the Great room, keeping the family cook in the conversation. A versatile study/bedroom is adjacent to a powder room with an alternate full bath option. The master bedroom, with elegant tray ceiling, has access to the screened porch, and its private bath features a garden tub, separate shower, and dual sink vanity with knee space. Two additional bedrooms are located on the opposite side of the house.

**Main floor —
1,954 sq. ft.**

*Total living area:
1,954 sq. ft.*

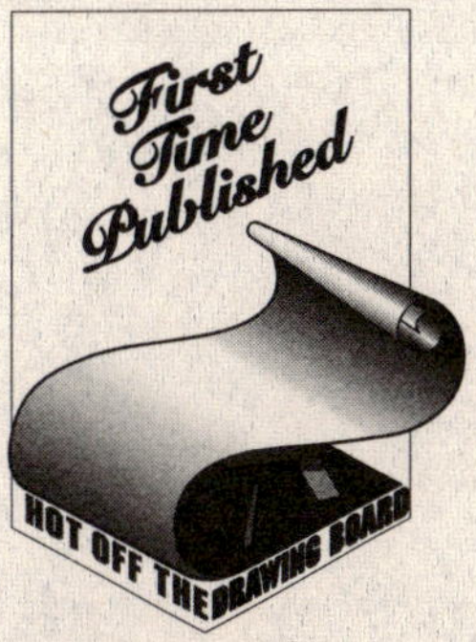

Refer to **Pricing Schedule C** on the order form for pricing information

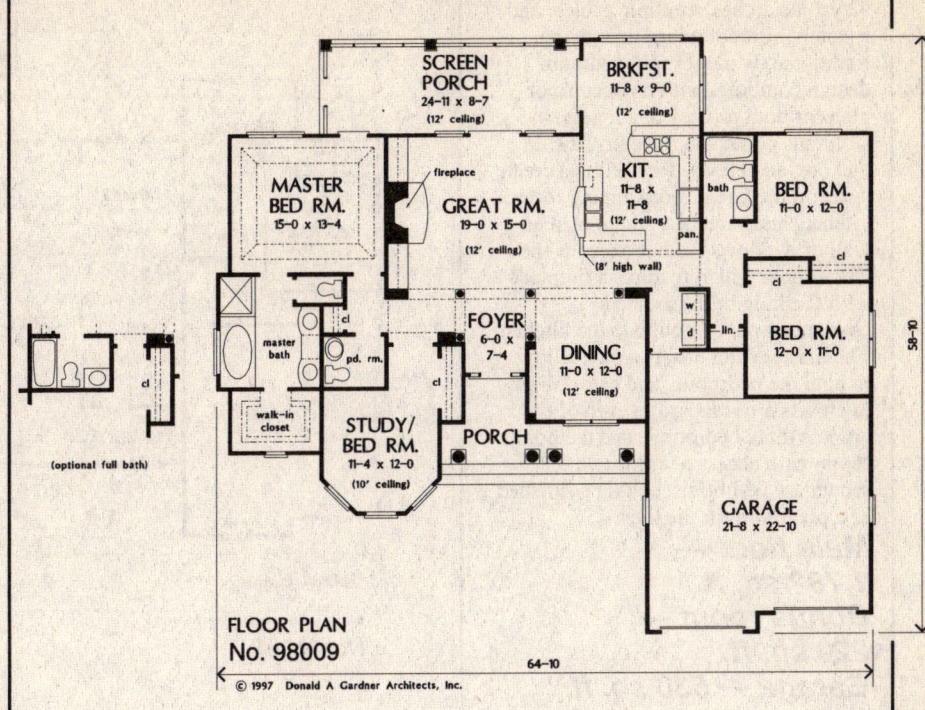

FLOOR PLAN
No. 98009
© 1997 Donald A Gardner Architects, Inc.

First Time Published

HOT OFF THE DRAWING BOARD

©1997 Donald A. Gardner Architects, Inc.

COLUMNS PUNCTUATE ENTRY

Design 98001

Keystone arches, multiple gables, and a stately hip roof adorn this stucco traditional, while its split bedroom design combines with an open floor plan for both privacy and togetherness. Columns punctuate the entry, inside and out, and eleven foot ceilings create space in the Great room, dining room, kitchen, and screened porch. A rear wall of windows further expands the Great room which features a fireplace with flanking built-ins and a convenient pass-through to the kitchen. The master suite boasts a tray ceiling in both the bedrooms and bath. Walk-in closets are standard in each of the home's three bedrooms, and the bonus room, with access near the two secondary bedrooms, could be finished as a playroom for the kids.

Main floor — 1,782 sq. ft.
Bonus room — 229 sq. ft.
Garage — 530 sq. ft.

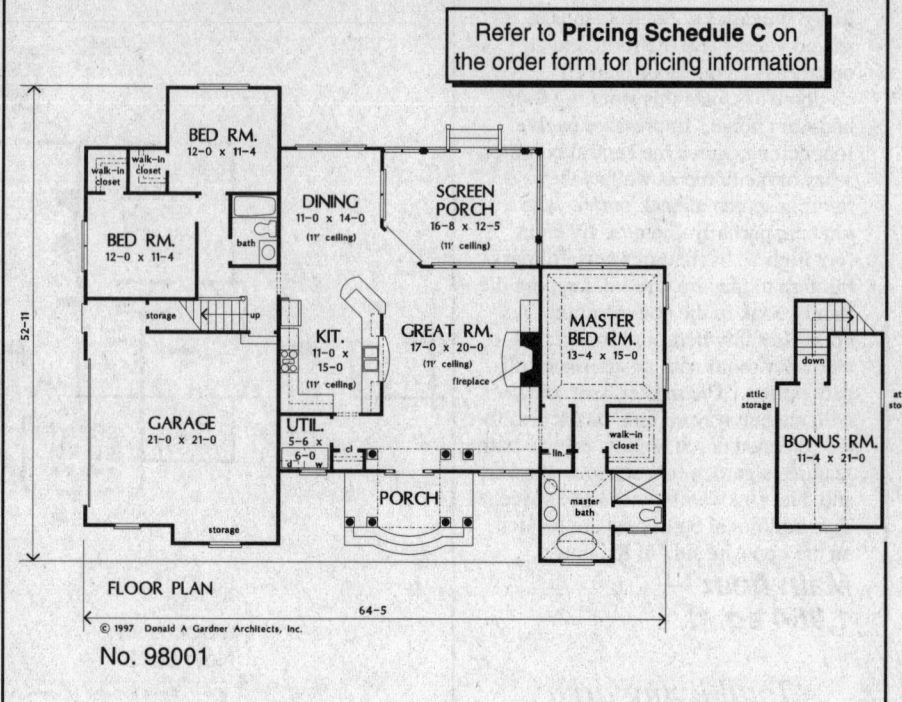

No. 98001

Total living area: 1,782 sq. ft.

First Time Published — Hot Off The Drawing Board

ORDER TODAY!   1 - 800 - 235 - 5700

PACKED WITH OPTIONS

Design 98559

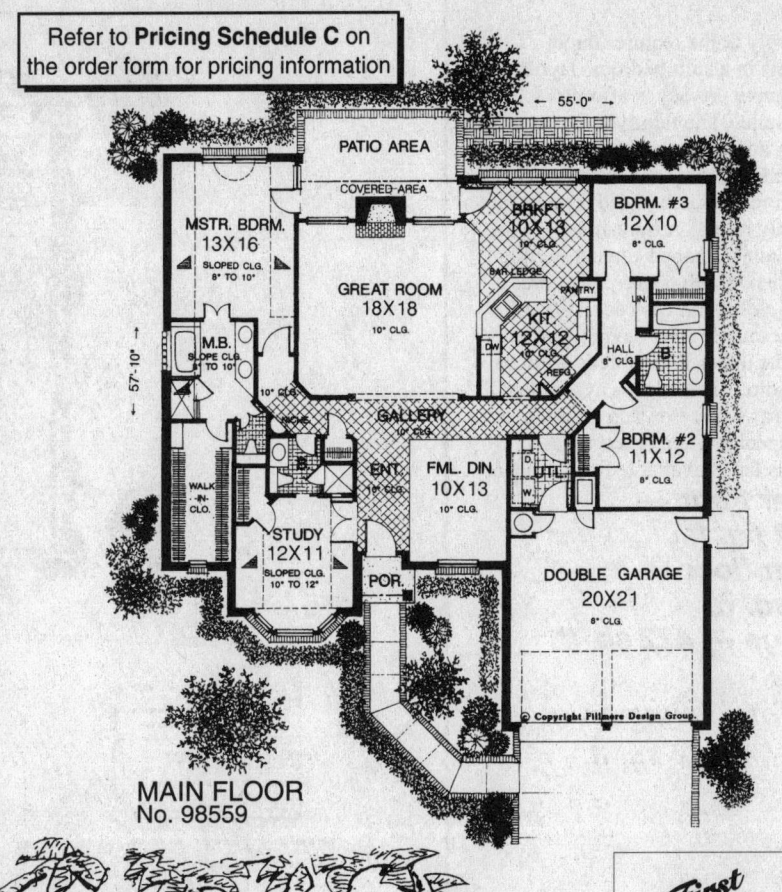

This home features a tiled entry and gallery area. The master bedroom boasts a sloped ceiling and a walk-in closet just beyond the master bath. The Great room is topped by a ten foot ceiling and includes a large fireplace. The formal dining room is also topped by a ten foot ceiling. The kitchen includes a built-in pantry and a bar ledge on the peninsula counter. The breakfast area and the master bedroom have access to the patio area. The front study is topped by a sloped ceiling and has direct access to the three quarter bath. The two additional bedroom are at the opposite side of the home and share the full bath in the hall. No materials list is available for this plan.

Main floor — 2,081 sq. ft.
Garage — 422 sq. ft.

Total living area: 2,081 sq. ft.

MAIN FLOOR
No. 98559

First Time Published — Hot Off The Drawing Board

ROOM FOR EXPANSION

Design 98564

This lovely home features three bedrooms in a split bedroom layout so that ultimate privacy is afforded to the master suite. The family room includes a fireplace and a pass-through from the kitchen. The breakfast area flows from the kitchen and is open to the family room. A built-in pantry and an efficient U-shaped counter highlight the kitchen. Each bedroom features a walk-in closet and easy access to a full bath, the master suite having a private bath. The upper floor houses a future game room. This plan is available with a crawl space or slab foundation. Please specify when ordering. No materials list is available for this plan.

Lower floor — 1,552 sq. ft.
Upper floor — 282 sq. ft.
Garage — 422 sq. ft.

Total living area: 1,834 sq. ft.

Refer to **Pricing Schedule C** on the order form for pricing information

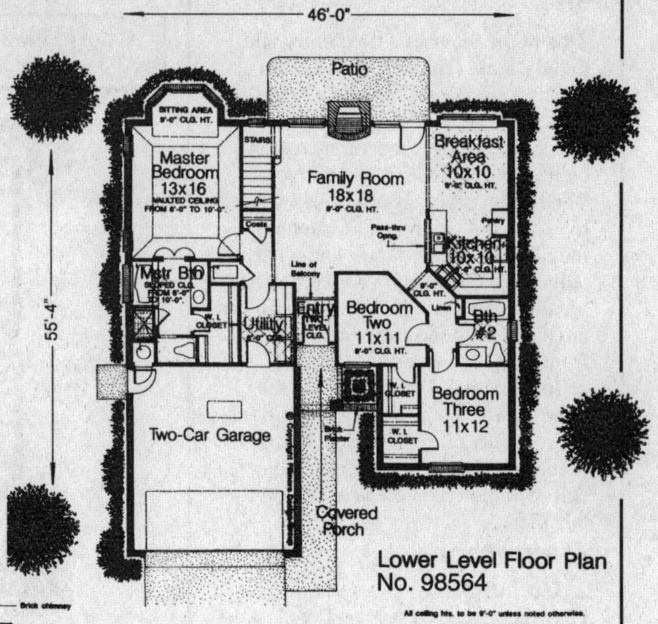

Lower Level Floor Plan No. 98564

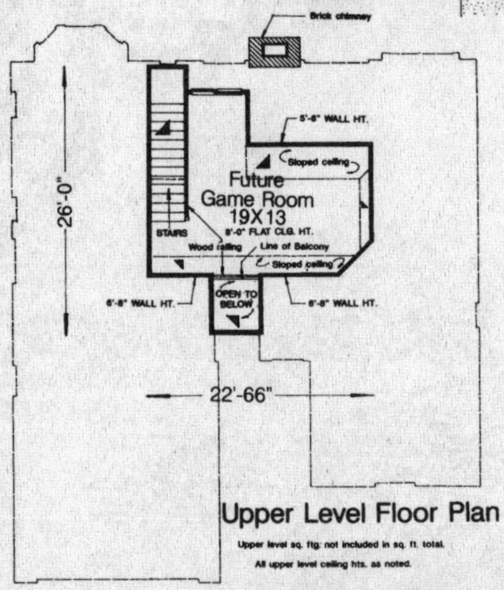

Upper Level Floor Plan

First Time Published — Hot Off the Drawing Board

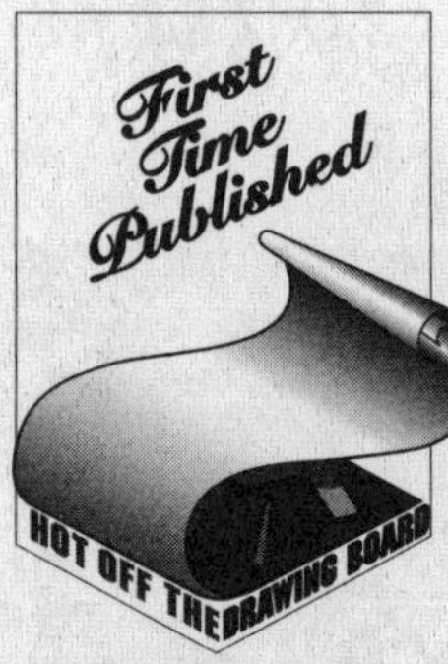

ORDER TODAY! 1 - 800 - 235 - 5700

ONE-LEVEL WITH A TWIST

Design 20083

Here's an inviting home with a distinctive difference. Active living areas are wide-open and centrally located. From the foyer, you'll enjoy a full view of the spacious dining, living, and kitchen areas in one sweeping glance. You can even see the deck adjoining the breakfast room. The difference in this house lies in the bedrooms. Each is a private retreat, away from active areas. The master suite at the rear of the house features a full bath with a double sink. Two additional bedrooms, off in their own private wing, share a full bath and the quiet atmosphere that results from a well thought out design.

Main area — 1,575 sq. ft.
Basement — 1,575 sq. ft.
Garage — 475 sq. ft.

Total living area: 1,575 sq. ft.

No. 20083
MAIN FLOOR

An EXCLUSIVE DESIGN
By Karl Kreeger

Refer to **Pricing Schedule B** on the order form for pricing information

Stylish One Floor Living

Design 93193

This stylish ranch home awaits your family. The columned front porch is a perfect spot to read the evening paper. Once inside you'll find a formal entry with an archway to the dining room. The dining room has a butler's pass directly to the kitchen. The large kitchen has plenty of counter and cupboard space, including an island with a breakfast bar. The adjoining nook has sliding glass doors providing access to the backyard. The Great room has cathedral ceilings and a large fireplace. On both sides are large windows with arched transoms, allowing the warmth of natural light in. There is a guest powder room just off the nook, as well as a main floor laundry with direct access to the three car garage. The master bedroom is your private retreat. Inside you'll find a large walk-in closet, private bath with double vanity, spa tub and, a corner shower. Two additional bedrooms share a full bath. No materials list is available for this plan.

Main floor —1,802 sq. ft.
Basement —1,802 sq. ft.

Total living area: 1,802 sq. ft.

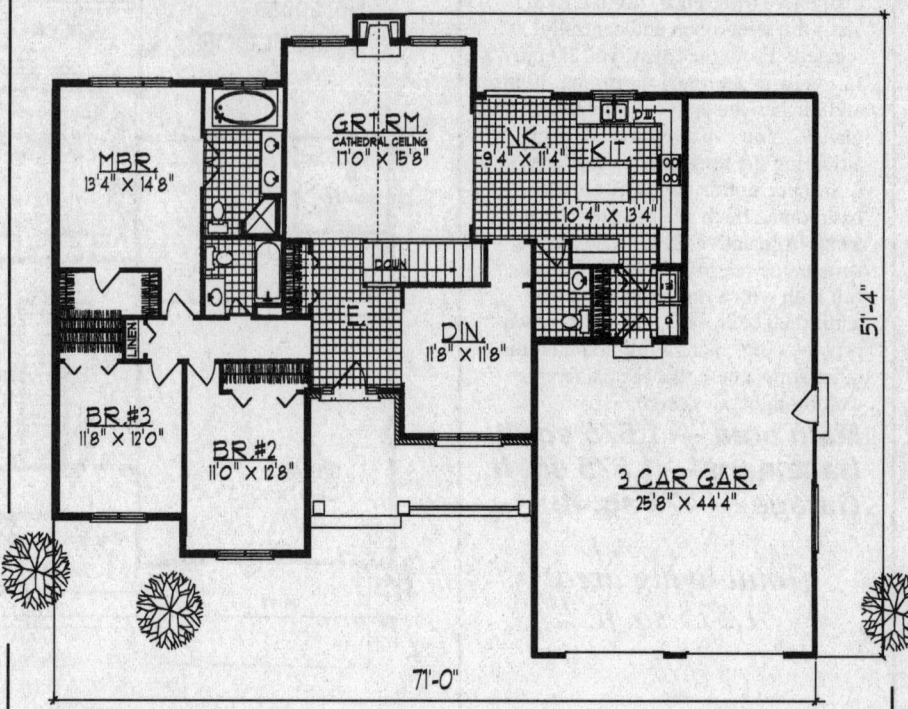

MAIN FLOOR PLAN
No. 93193

Refer to **Pricing Schedule C** on the order form for pricing information

ORDER TODAY! 1-800-235-5700

Small, but not lacking

Design 94116

This home features a Great room, formal dining room, kitchen, dinette, laundry room and three bedrooms using only 1,546 sq. ft. The living room is enhanced by a bayed window viewing the porch and beyond. The Great room adjoins the dining room for ease in entertaining. The kitchen is highlighted by a peninsula counter/snack bar that extends work space and offers convenience in serving informal meals or snacks. The split bedroom plan allows for privacy for the master suite, which features a three-quarter bath and a walk-in closet. The two additional bedrooms share the full, family bath in the hall. The garage entry is convenient to the kitchen.

Main floor — 1,546 sq. ft.
Basement — 1,530 sq. ft.
Garage — 440 sq. ft.

Total living area:
1,546 sq. ft.

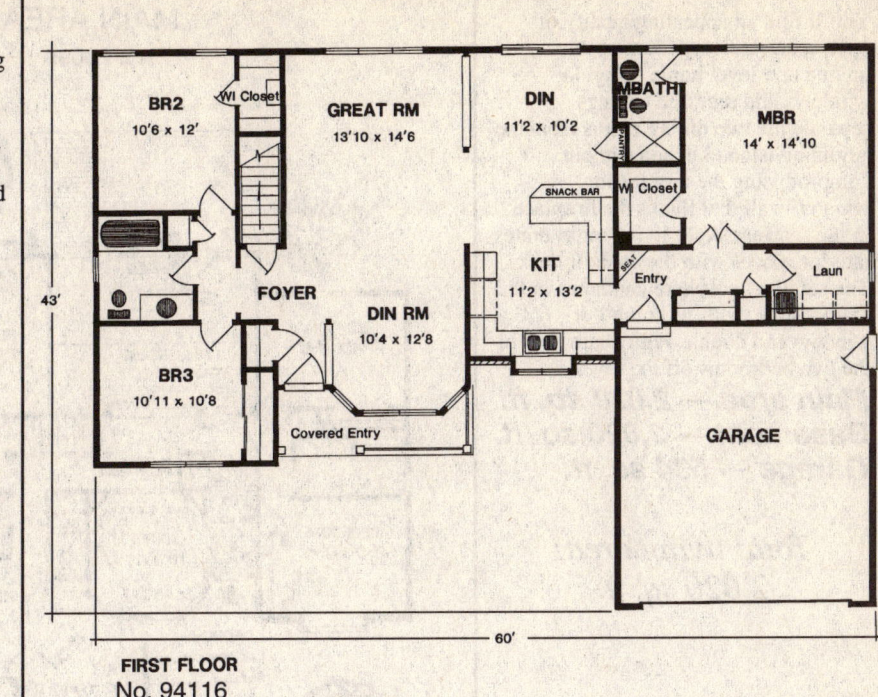

FIRST FLOOR
No. 94116

Refer to **Pricing Schedule C** on the order form for pricing information

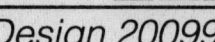

UNIQUE ONE-LEVEL TUDOR

Design 20099

You'll find an appealing quality of open space in every room of this unique one-level home. Angular windows and recessed ceilings separate the two dining rooms from the adjoining island kitchen without compromising the airy feeling. A window-wall that flanks the fireplace in the soaring, skylit living room unites interior spaces with the outdoor deck. The sunny atmosphere continues in the master suite, with its bump-out window and double vanity bath, and in the two bedrooms off the foyer.

Main area — 2,020 sq. ft.
Basement — 2,020 sq. ft.
Garage — 534 sq. ft.

Total living area: 2,020 sq. ft.

Refer to **Pricing Schedule C** on the order form for pricing information

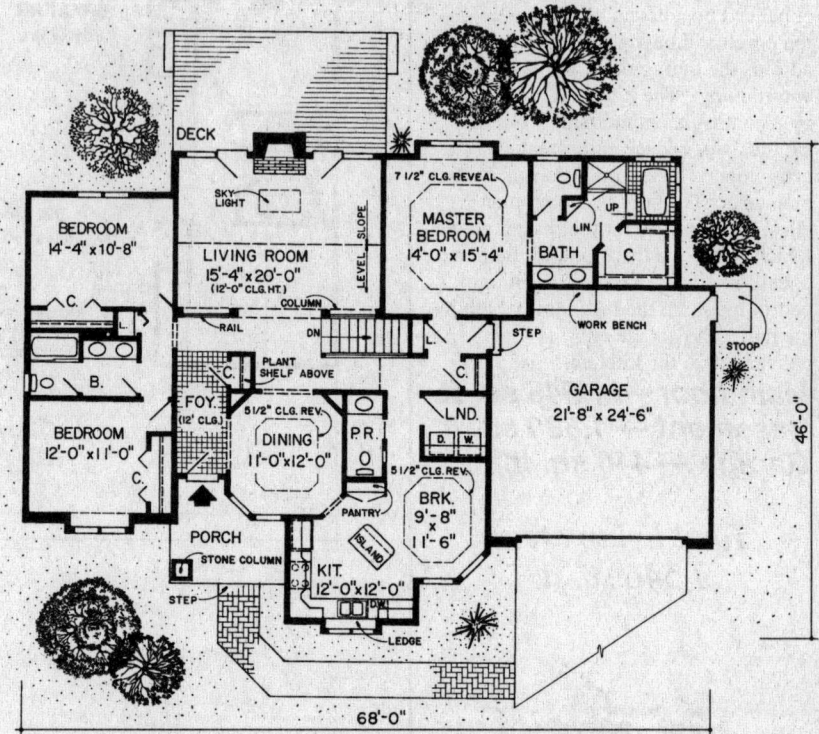

MAIN AREA
No. 20099

An EXCLUSIVE DESIGN *By Karl Kreeger*

Open Spaces

Design 93279

The family room, kitchen and breakfast area of this home all connect to form a great space. A central, double fireplace adds warmth and atmosphere to all the rooms. The efficient kitchen is highlighted by a peninsula counter that doubles as a snack bar. The master suite includes a walk-in closet, a double vanity, separate shower and tub bath. Two additional bedrooms share a full hall bath. A wooden deck that can be accessed from the breakfast area expands living space in the warmer weather. This plan is available with a crawl space or slab foundation. Please specify when ordering.

Main area — 1,388 sq. ft
Garage — 400 sq. ft.

Total living area: 1,388 sq. ft.

Refer to **Pricing Schedule A** on the order form for pricing information

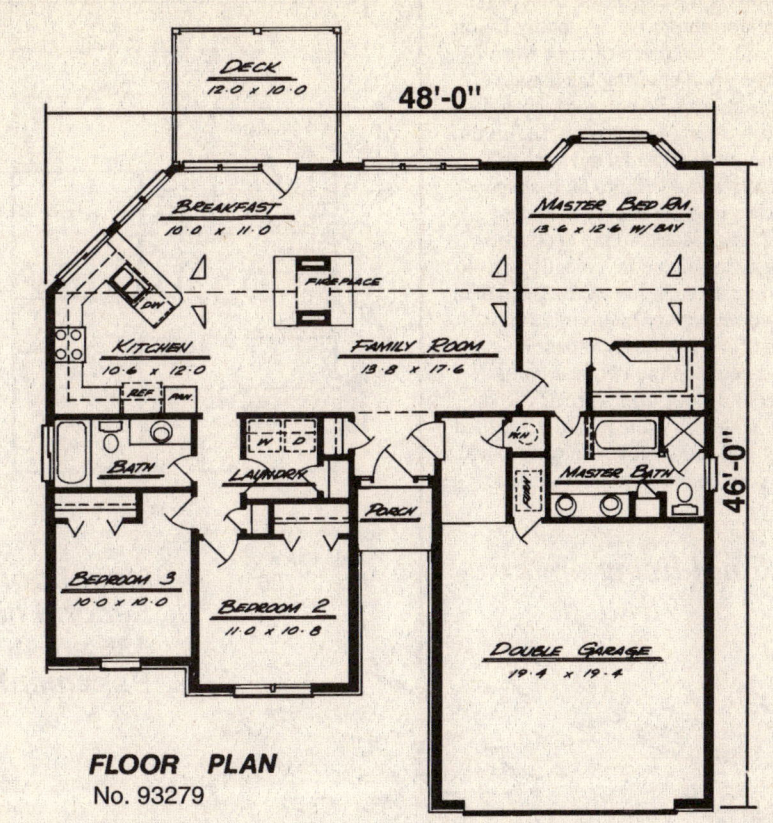

FLOOR PLAN
No. 93279

An EXCLUSIVE DESIGN
By Jannis Vann & Associates, Inc.

ORDER TODAY! 1-800-235-5700

Attractive Dormer and Front Porch

Design 24706

Country styling is evident in this elevation by the use of the front porch and the dormer above. A roomy living room with a fireplace offers a warm welcome upon entering the home. There is also a side entrance through the utility room, keeping tracked in dirt to a minimum. The island kitchen is efficiently arranged into an L-shape and flows into the cheery breakfast area. Direct access to the deck from the breakfast area conveniently adds to the living space in the warmer weather. The two secondary bedrooms are on the first floor. A full hall bath is located between the two bedrooms. The second floor offers privacy to the master suite. A walk-in closet, vaulted ceiling and full double vanity bath add to the convenience and style of the suite.

Total living area: 1,470 sq. ft.

Main floor — 1,035 sq. ft.
Second floor — 435 sq. ft.
Basement — 1,018 sq. ft.

Refer to **Pricing Schedule A** on the order form for pricing information

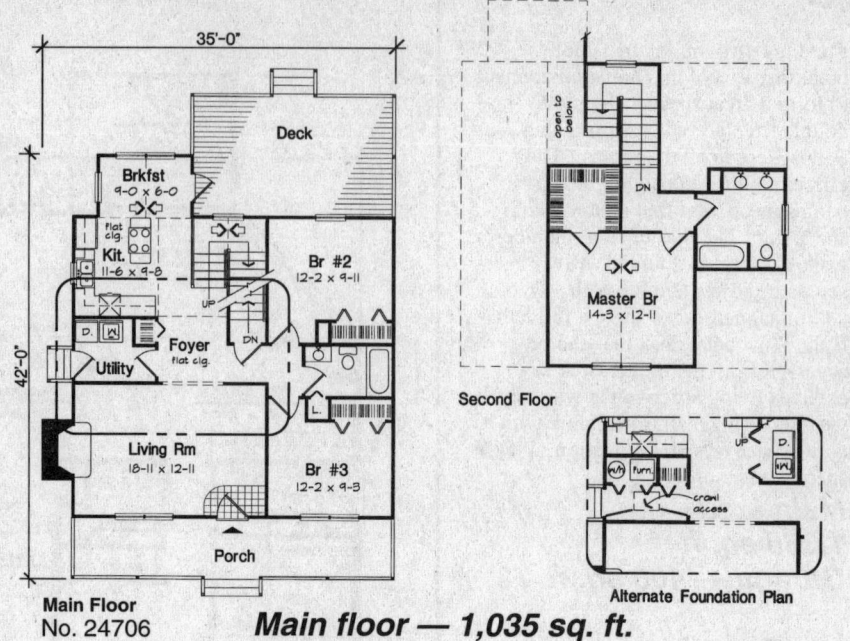

Formal Balance

Design 90689

Here's a magnificent example of classical design with a contemporary twist. The graceful columns that adorn the facade of this one-level beauty also separate interior spaces without walls. Combined with the half-round windows in the living room, they create an open, elegant feeling throughout formal areas. A bow window in the dining room overlooking the deck echoes the classic image. Kitchen and dinette share the open atmosphere, flowing together into a spacious unit that opens to the rear deck through sliding glass doors. The master suite enjoys a private corner of the deck, complete with hot-tub, dual vanitied bath, and ample closets. Two front-facing bedrooms across the hall share another full bath.

Main area — 1,476 sq. ft.
Basement — 1,361 sq. ft.
Garage — 548 sq. ft.

Total living area: 1,476 sq. ft.

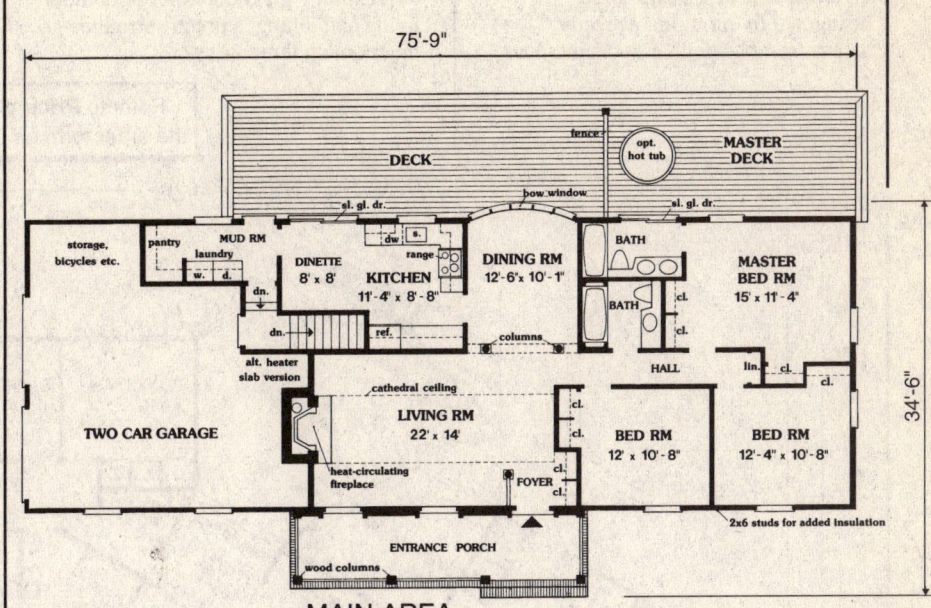

MAIN AREA
No. 90689

Refer to **Pricing Schedule A** on the order form for pricing information

Western Approach to the Ranch

Design 90007

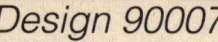

Here is an authentic ranch style house with long loggia, posts and braces, hand-split shake roof, and cross-buck doors. Two wings sprawl at an angle on either side of a Texas-sized hexagonal living room. Directly across from the double-door entrance, a sunken living room is two steps lower and enhanced by two solid walls (one pierced by a fireplace) and two ten-foot walls of almost solid glass (with sliding glass doors). For outdoor living and dining, a porch surrounds the room on three sides.

Main area — 1,830 sq. ft.
Garage — 2-car

Total living area: 1,830 sq. ft.

Refer to **Pricing Schedule C** on the order form for pricing information

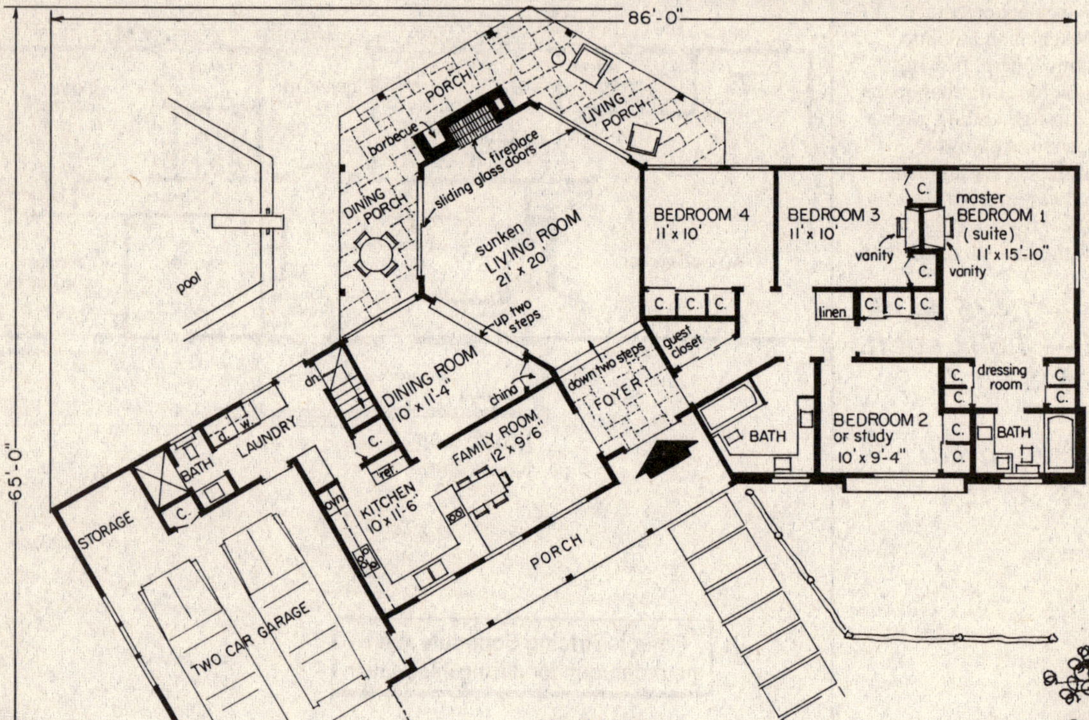

No. 90007
MAIN AREA

A VIEW FROM EVERY ROOM

Design 34047

The impressive facade of this beautiful home hints at the sunny, open atmosphere inside. The two-story foyer, flanked by a private study and formal living room, is dominated by an angular staircase to the bedroom floor. Step past the powder room to the rear of the house, and discover the kitchen of your dreams. Notice the cooktop island, built-ins throughout, and sink overlooking the rear patio. The glass-walled breakfast room, three season porch, and towering fireplaced family room share a backyard view. Upstairs, the balcony overlooking the family room links three spacious bedrooms and two full baths, including the master suite with its private garden tub, double vanity, and room-size closet.

First floor — 1,511 sq. ft.
Second floor — 1,163 sq. ft.
Basement — 1,511 sq. ft.
Garage — 765 sq. ft.

Total living area: 2,674 sq. ft.

Refer to **Pricing Schedule E** on the order form for pricing information

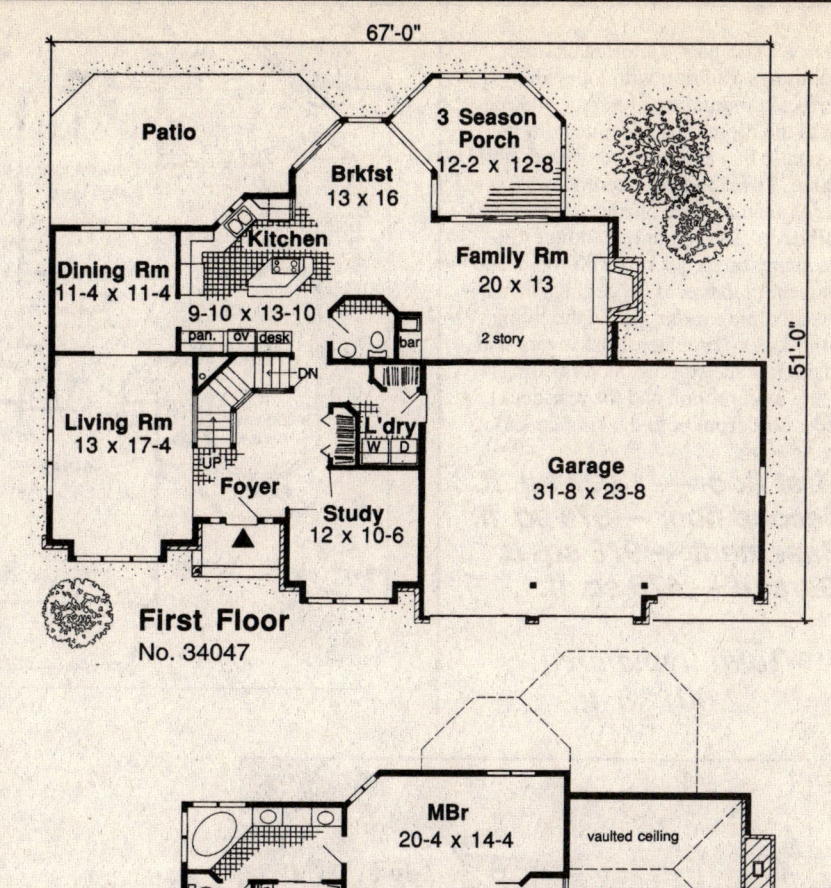

PORCH ADORNS ELEGANT BAY

Design 20093

Here's a compact Victorian charmer that unites tradition with today in a perfect combination. Imagine waking up in the roomy master suite with its romantic bay and full bath with double sinks. Two additional bedrooms, which feature huge closets, share the hall bath. The romance continues in the sunny breakfast room off the island kitchen, in the recessed ceilings of the formal dining room, and in the living room's cozy fireplace. Sun lovers will appreciate the sloping, skylit ceilings in the living room, and the rear deck accessible from both the kitchen and living room.

First floor — 1,027 sq. ft.
Second floor — 974 sq. ft.
Basement — 978 sq. ft.
Garage — 476 sq. ft.

Total living area: 2,001 sq. ft.

An **EXCLUSIVE DESIGN** *By Karl Kreeger*

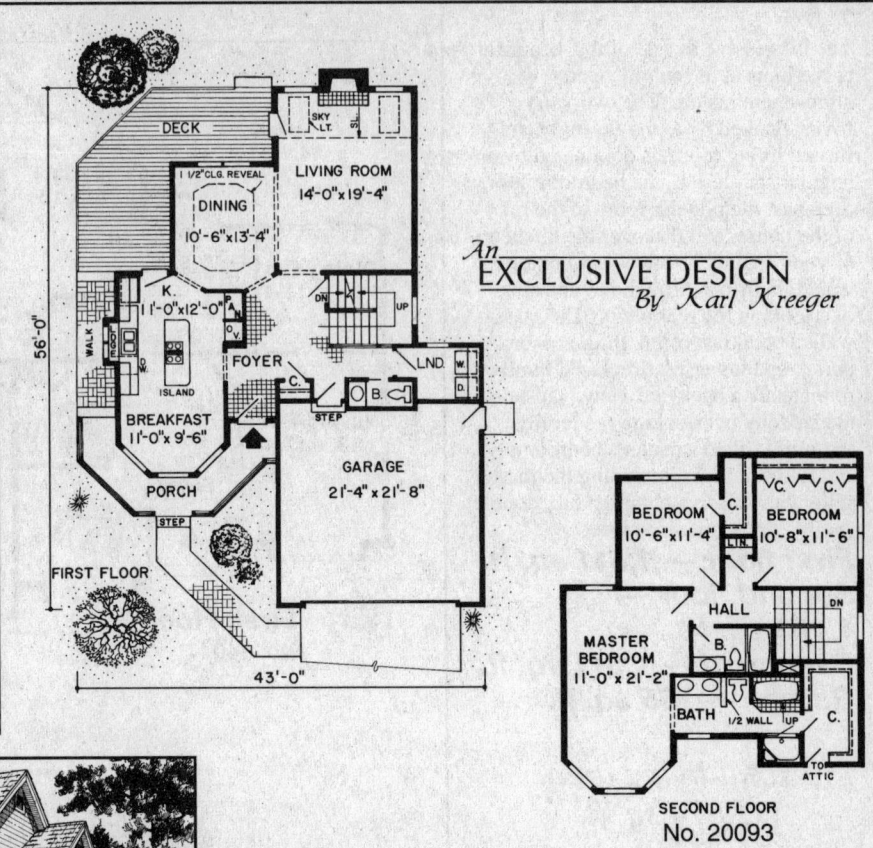

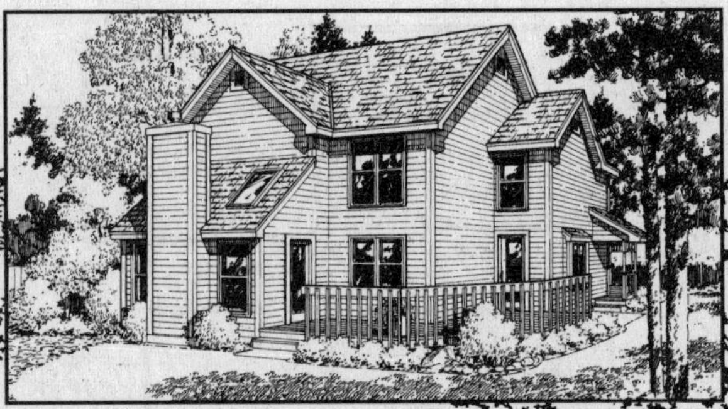

Refer to **Pricing Schedule C** on the order form for pricing information

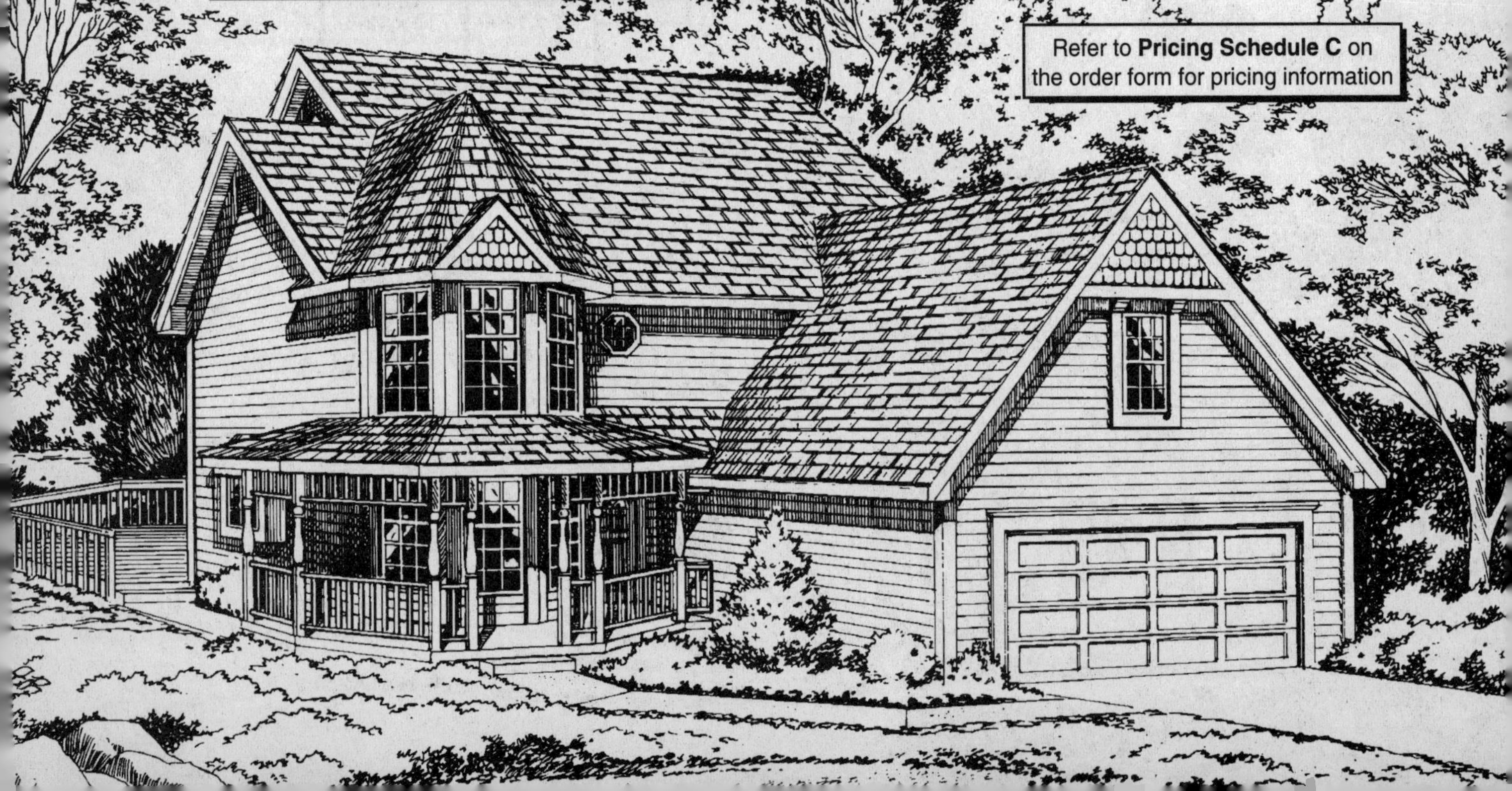

ORDER TODAY! 1 - 800 - 235 - 5700

Design 98518

Memories of Yesterday

Relive those days of yesterday with this charming Victorian home. The covered front porch is perfect for visiting with family and friends over a glass of iced tea and a sandwich. The plant box under the utility room window, as well as the large arched window in the living room, will give a great impression. An angled country kitchen with an island range, and dining area is open to the spacious family room. The family room is highlighted by a large fireplace and wall cabinets, sure to add to a family's enjoyment. Retire to the master suite and two other bedrooms upstairs. Do not overlook the future room space for future family enjoyment. Please specify a basement or slab foundation when ordering. No materials list is available for this plan.

**First floor — 1,447 sq. ft.
Second floor — 1,008 sq. ft.
Garage — 756 sq. ft.**

Total living area:
2,455 sq. ft.

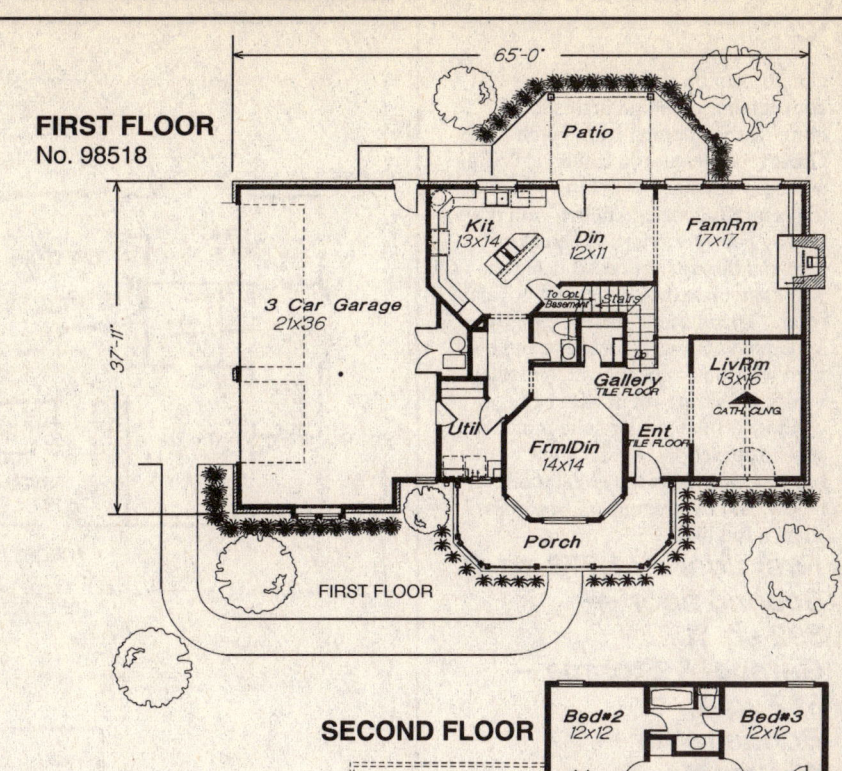

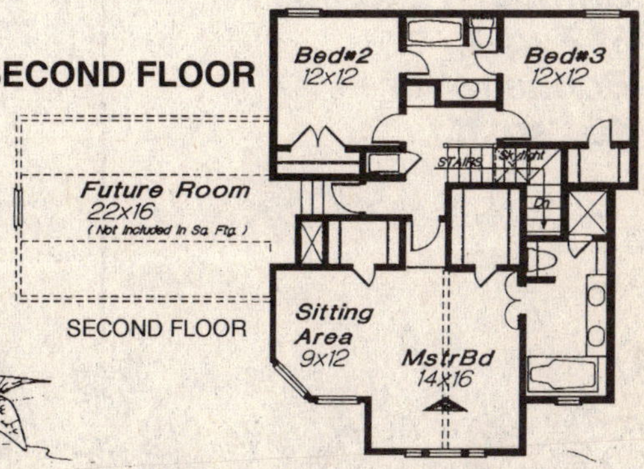

Refer to **Pricing Schedule D** on the order form for pricing information

COUNTRY CHARM & MODERN FEATURES

Design 96459

Country charm and modern convenience combine in this lovely home with wrapping front porch. The Great room features a cathedral ceiling and cozy fireplace with built-ins, and the centrally located kitchen with it's nearby pantry services the breakfast area and dining room easily. Guests will appreciate the convenient powder room. The master suite is elegantly appointed with walk-in closet and bath with whirlpool tub, shower, and dual vanity. A sitting room with bay window off the master suite is a special attraction. Upstairs, the hallway overlooks the Great room below, and two secondary bedrooms share a full bath.

First floor — 1,778 sq. ft.
Second floor — 592 sq. ft.
Garage & Storage — 622 sq. ft.
Bonus room — 404 sq. ft.

Total living area: 2,370 sq. ft.

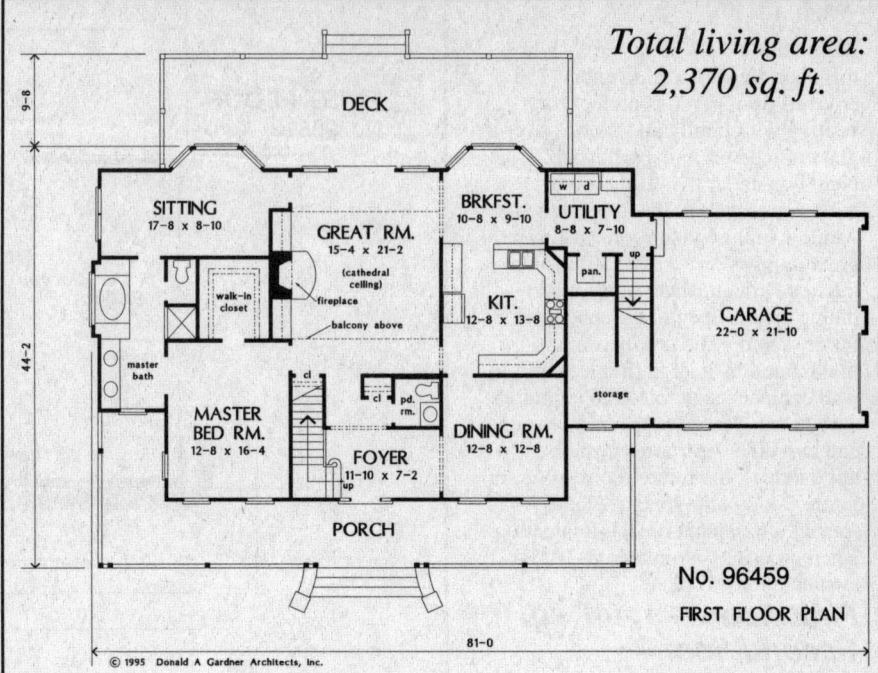

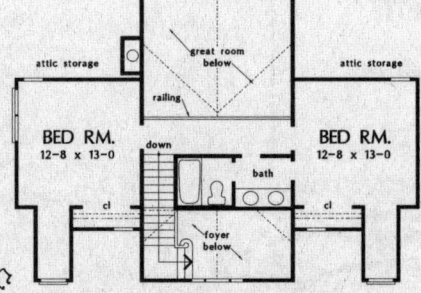

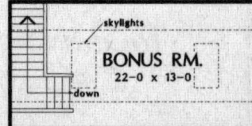

Refer to **Pricing Schedule D** on the order form for pricing information

ORDER TODAY! 1 - 800 - 235 - 5700

Design 98534

STATELY COLONIAL HOME

This colonial home will take you back in time every time you pull into the driveway. Stately columns and arched windows provide a backdrop of luxury and quality that is evident throughout this lovely manor. As you enter, you are sure to notice the elegant angled staircase. A formal dining and living room are to each side of the foyer. The large Great room is visible from the entry and provides a feeling of spaciousness. A unique island kitchen with a breakfast area is sure to satisfy the family meal planner. The large master suite includes a luxurious five-piece bath and huge walk-in closet. The loft area upstairs overlooks the foyer via a wood railing. Three bedrooms and two baths are also located on the second floor. No materials list available.

First floor — 1,848 sq. ft.
Second floor — 1,111 sq. ft.
Garage — 722 sq. ft.

Refer to **Pricing Schedule E** on the order form for pricing information

Total living area: 2,959 sq. ft.

WIDTH 73'- 4"
DEPTH 44'- 1"

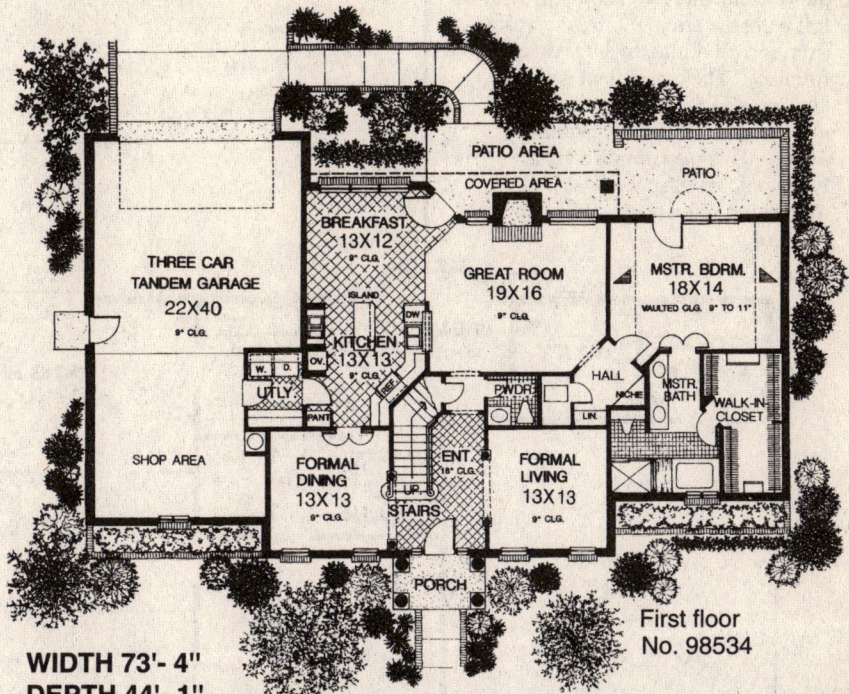

First floor
No. 98534

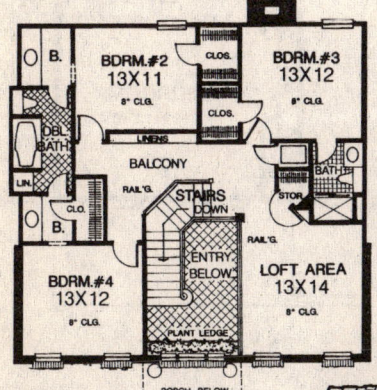

Second floor

FIREPLACE DOMINATES RUSTIC DESIGN

Design 90409

The ample porch of this charming home deserves a rocking chair, and there's room for two or three if you'd like. The front entry opens to an expansive Great room with a soaring cathedral ceiling. Flanked by the master suite and two bedrooms with a full bath, the Great room is separated from formal dining by a massive fireplace. The convenient galley kitchen adjoins a sunny breakfast nook, perfect for informal family dining. This plan comes with a basement, crawl space or slab foundation. Please specify when ordering.

Main area — 1,670 sq. ft.
Garage — 2-car

Total living area: 1,670 sq. ft.

Refer to **Pricing Schedule B** on the order form for pricing information

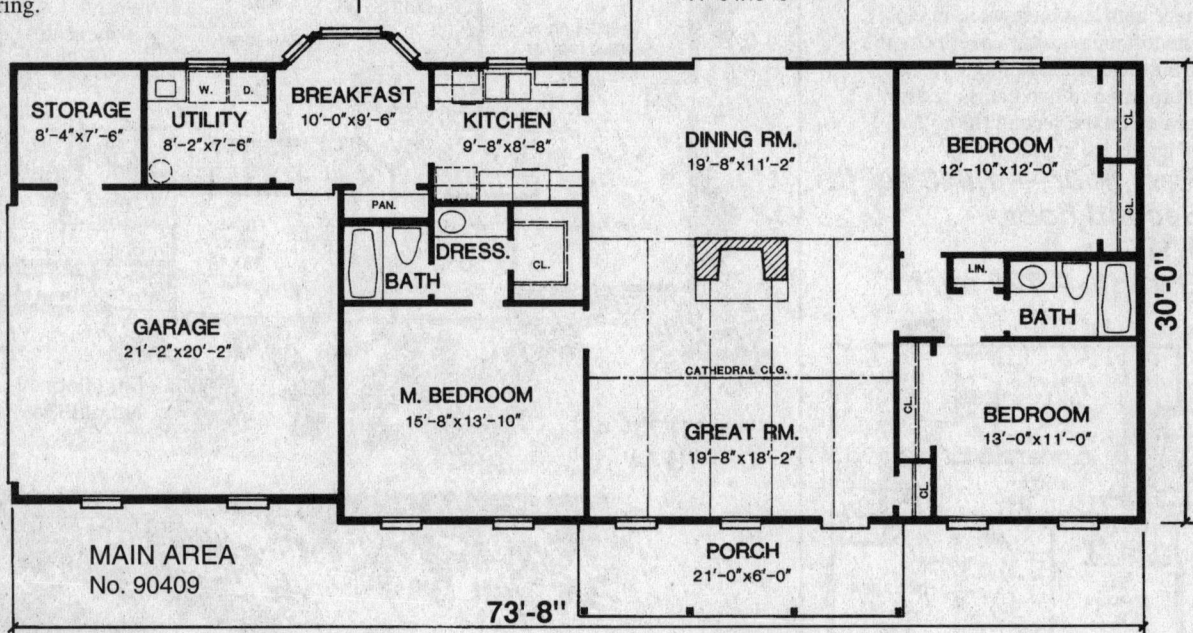

ORDER TODAY! 1 - 800 - 235 - 5700

Design 92552

EUROPEAN STYLE — GEORGIAN FLAIR

The elegant European styling of this home has been spiced with Georgian styling to create a charming design. Arch top windows, quoins and shutters on the exterior, a columned covered front and a rear porch combine to become an eye-catching home. The formal foyer gives access to the dining room to the left and the spacious den straight ahead. The kitchen flows into the informal eating area and is separated from the den by an angled extended counter eating bar. Featuring a split bedroom plan, the master suite is privately placed to the rear. The three additional bedrooms share a full bath in the hall. This plan is available with a crawl space or slab foundation. Please specify when ordering.

**Main floor — 1,873 sq. ft.
Bonus room —
145 sq. ft.
Garage — 613 sq. ft.**

*Total living area:
1,873 sq. ft.*

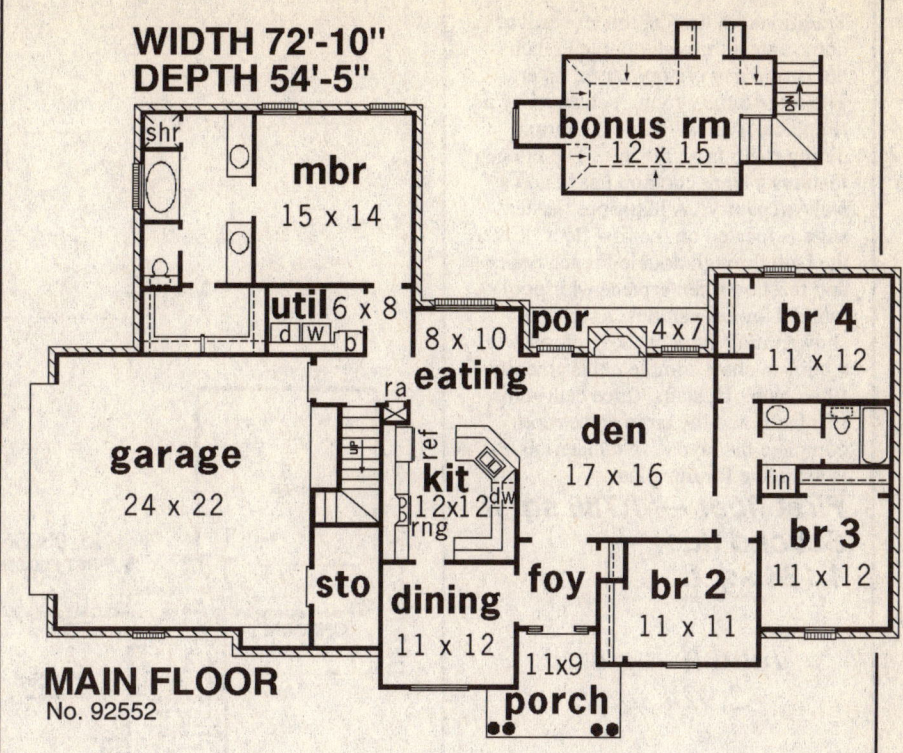

Refer to **Pricing Schedule D** on the order form for pricing information

TRADITIONAL HOME

ORDER TODAY! 1 - 800 - 235 - 5700

Design 93055

Traditional in design, this executive home enters through double French doors into a two-story raised foyer. The large family room, enhanced by a fireplace, is ahead while the formal dining room is on the left. The kitchen features a large cooktop island and a walk-in pantry. A luxurious master suite is located on the first floor. Enter the bath through double French doors and feast on a centerpiece whirlpool tub. His-n-her vanities, a separate shower and a large walk-in closet with a built-in chest complete this amenity filled bath. Upstairs, three bedrooms, two baths and the large game room complete the layout. No materials list is available for this plan.

First floor — 1,788 sq. ft.
Second floor — 1,136 sq. ft.

Total living area: 2,924 sq. ft.

Refer to **Pricing Schedule E** on the order form for pricing information

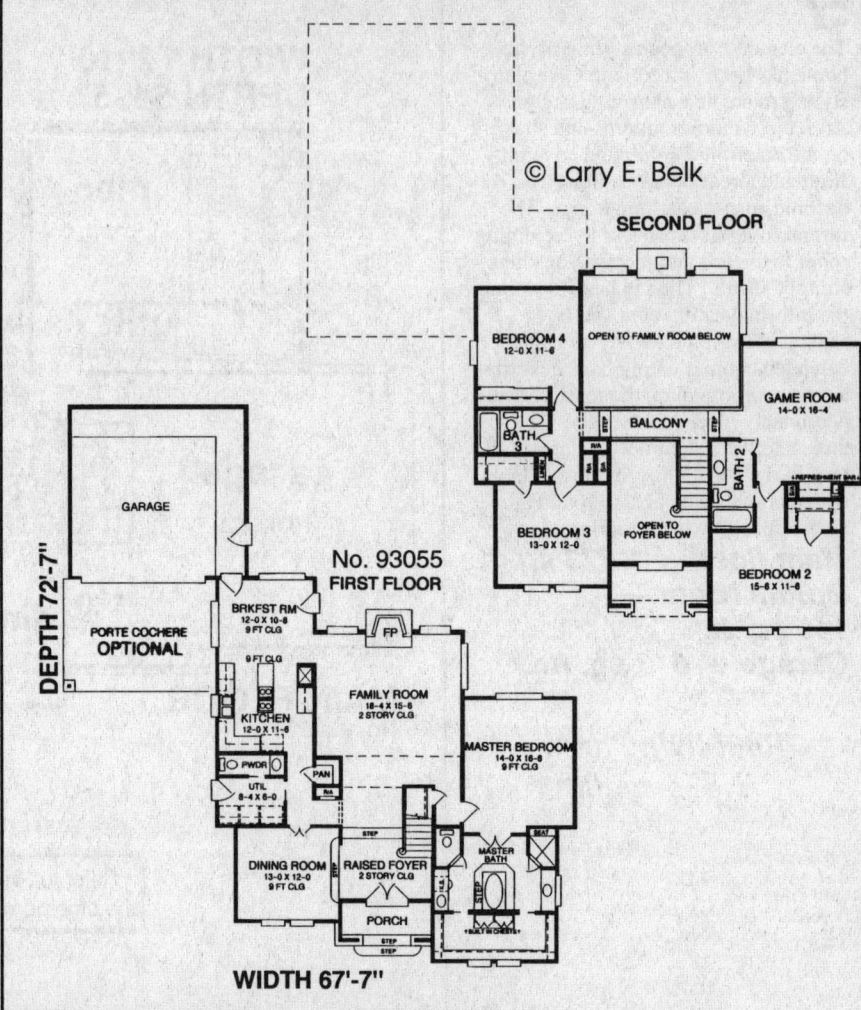
© Larry E. Belk

ORDER TODAY! 1 - 800 - 235 - 5700

Design 98410

Magnificent Manor

The two-story foyer is dominated by a lovely staircase. The formal living room is to the left. The dining room is through an arched opening to the right. The efficient kitchen directly accesses the formal dining room for ease in serving. The breakfast area is separated from the kitchen by only the extended counter/serving bar. The two-story family room is highlighted by a focal point fireplace framed by windows. A tray ceiling crowns the master bedroom while a vaulted ceiling tops the plush master bath. Two additional bedrooms share the full double vanity bath in the hall. This plan is available with a basement or crawl space foundation. Please specify when ordering.

First floor — 1,428 sq. ft.
Second floor — 961 sq. ft.
Bonus area — 472 sq. ft.
Basement — 1,428 sq. ft.
Garage — 507 sq. ft.

Total living area: 2,389 sq. ft.

Refer to **Pricing Schedule D** on the order form for pricing information

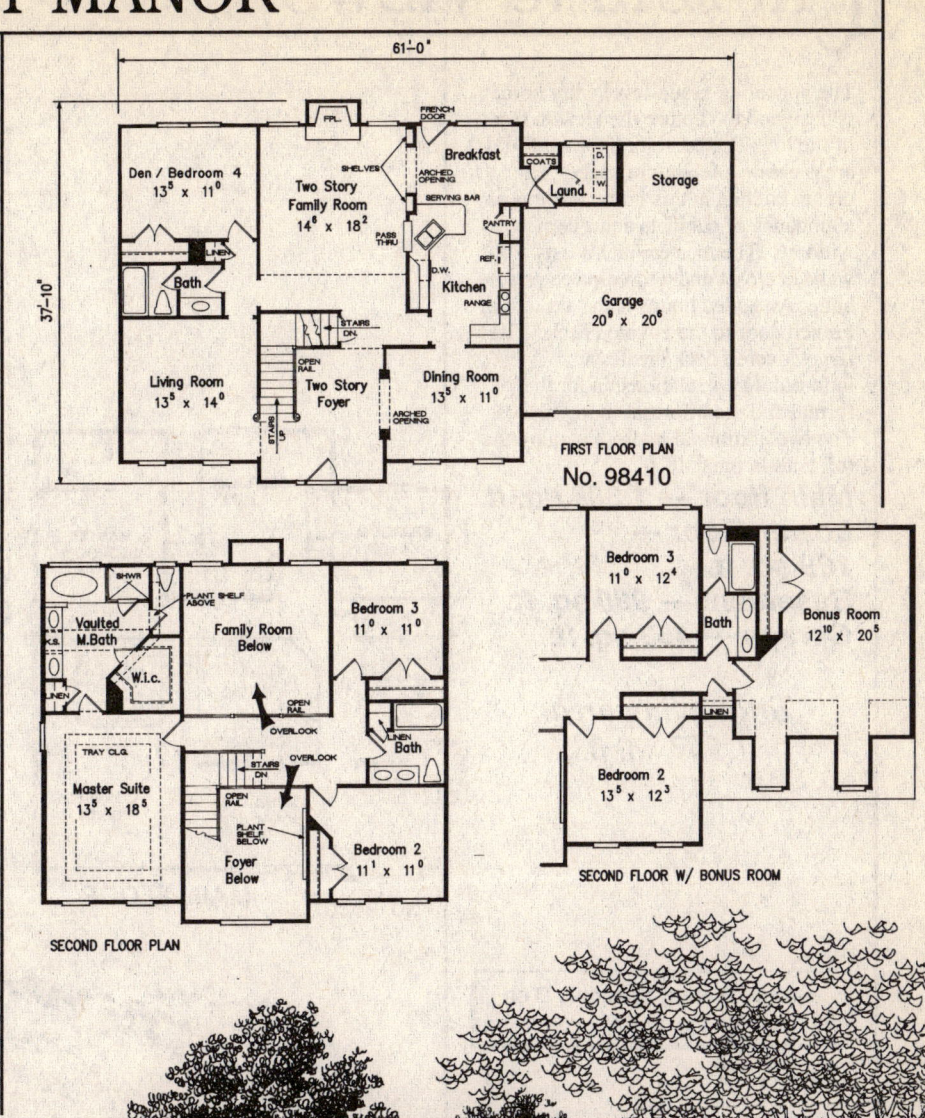

ORDER TODAY! 1 - 800 - 235 - 5700

Design 98801

CAPTURING VIEWS

The appealing grade-level entry home is designed to capture the view in front of the lot. The combined formal living areas create a feeling of space. The dream kitchen in this home features an abundance of cabinets and a corner window. The master suite boasts a walk-in closet and a three-piece private bath. An added bonus is the attractive French door to the covered deck. The large covered deck creates an indoor/outdoor relationship for the formal and the informal living spaces. The two additional bedrooms share the full bath in the hall.

Main floor — 1,388 sq. ft.
Lower Floor — 169 sq. ft.
Basement — 930 sq. ft.
Garage — 453 sq. ft.

Total living area: 1,557 sq. ft.

Refer to **Pricing Schedule B** on the order form for pricing information

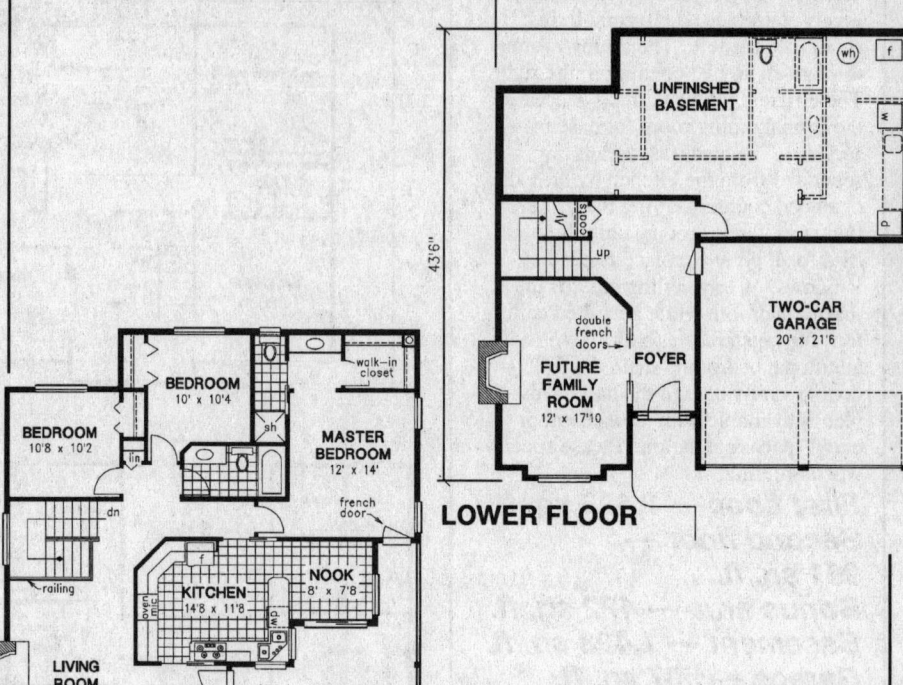

Design 20198

DRAMATIC RANCH

The exterior of this ranch home is all wood with interesting lines. It is more than a ranch home, it has a expansive feeling to drive up to. The large living area has a stone fireplace and decorative beams. The kitchen and dining room lead to an outside deck. The laundry room has a large pantry and is off the eating area. The master bedroom has a wonderful bathroom with a huge walk-in closet. In the front of the house there are two additional bedrooms with a bathroom. This house offers one-floor living and yet has nice big rooms.

Main area — 1,792 sq. ft.
Basement — 818 sq. ft.
Garage — 857 sq. ft.

Total living area:
1,792 sq. ft.

Refer to **Pricing Schedule B** on the order form for pricing information

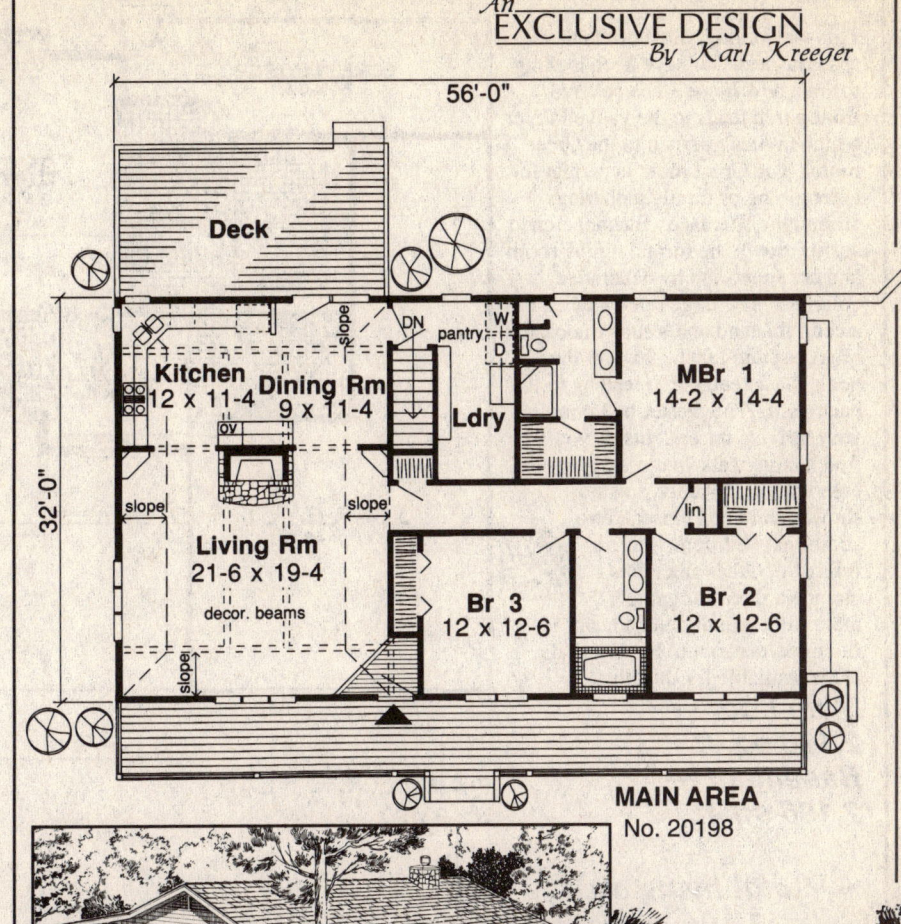

An EXCLUSIVE DESIGN By Karl Kreeger

MAIN AREA
No. 20198

Luxurious Ranch

Design 93190

ORDER TODAY! 1-800-235-5700

This welcoming ranch offers the spaciousness you have been looking for in a new home. The covered front porch leads to the vaulted foyer which invites guests into the Great room. The Great room is perfect for entertaining or family gatherings around the fireplace. Elegant arched soffits crown the formal dining room and are supported by decorative columns. The large open kitchen has a central island and a sunny nook for breakfast and lunch. Just off the nook is a screen porch leading to the back yard. The master bedroom is your private retreat. Inside you'll find a large walk-in closet, private bath with dual vanity, spa tub, shower and linen closet. Two additional bedrooms share a full bath. Other amenities include a three car garage, main floor laundry and a main floor powder room. No materials list is available for this plan.

Main floor — 2,196 sq. ft.
Basement — 2,196 sq. ft.

Total living area: 2,196 sq. ft.

Refer to **Pricing Schedule C** on the order form for pricing information

ORDER TODAY! 1 - 800 - 235 - 5700

Design 34150

Elegant Window Treatment

Consider this plan if you work at home and would enjoy a homey, well-lit office or den. The huge, arched window floods the front room with light. This house offers a lot of other practical details for the two-career family. Compact and efficient use of space means less to clean and organize. Yet the open plan keeps the home from feeling too small and cramped. Other features like plenty of closet space, step-saving laundry facilities, easily-cleaned kitchen, and a window wall in the living room make this a delightful plan.

Main area — 1,492 sq. ft.
Garage — 462 sq. ft.
Basement — 1,486 sq. ft.

Total living area:
1,492 sq. ft.

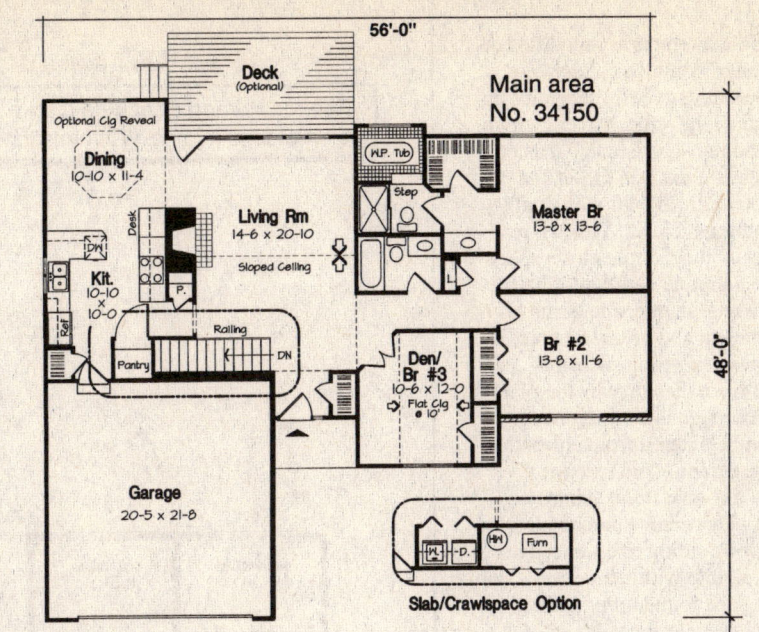

An EXCLUSIVE DESIGN *By Karl Kreeger*

Refer to **Pricing Schedule A** on the order form for pricing information

CATHERDRAL CEILING & A STUDIO

Design 90420

This rustic-contemporary modified A-Frame design combines a high cathedral ceiling over a sunken living room with a large studio over the two rear bedrooms. The isolated master suite features a walk-in closet and compartmentalized bath with double vanity and linen closet. The two rear bedrooms include ample closet space and share a unique bath-and-a-half arrangement. On one side of the U-shaped kitchen and breakfast nook is the formal dining room which is separated from the entry by the planter. On the other side is a utility room which can be entered from either the kitchen or garage. The exterior features a massive stone chimney, large glass areas and a combination of vertical wood siding and stone. This plan is available with a basement, slab or crawl space foundation. Please specify when ordering.

First floor — 2,213 sq. ft.
Second floor — 260 sq. ft.
Basement — 2,213 sq. ft.
Garage — 422 sq. ft.

Total living area: 2,473 sq. ft.

Refer to **Pricing Schedule D** on the order form for pricing information

WIDTH 91'-8"
DEPTH 45'-8"

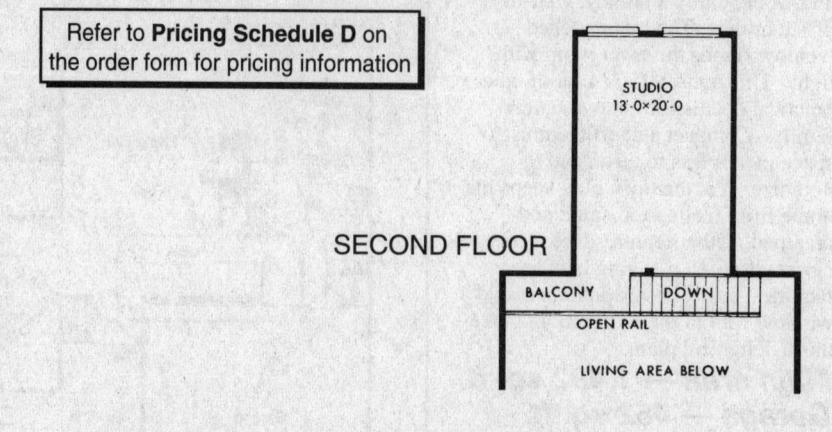

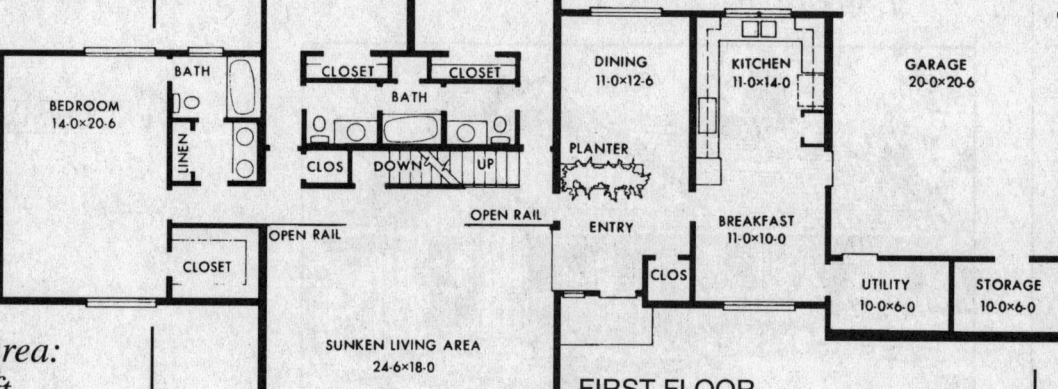

Design 20205

SMALL BUT ROOM TO GROW

This contemporary is perfect for the young family starting out. It has three bedrooms. The master suite has a vaulted ceiling and its own master bath. The secondary bedrooms have ample closet space and share the hallway bath. The fireplace in the living room adds the warmth and atmosphere needed on cold winter evenings. The lower level offers an optional room to be used as a Rec Room or whatever your growing family needs. Although it may be smaller, this home does not scrimp on style.

Main level — 1,321 sq. ft.
Lower level — 286 sq.ft.
Garage — 655 sq. ft.

Refer to **Pricing Schedule B** on the order form for pricing information

MAIN FLOOR
No. 20205

LOWER FLOOR

Total living area:
1,607 sq. ft.

An EXCLUSIVE DESIGN *By Karl Kreeger*

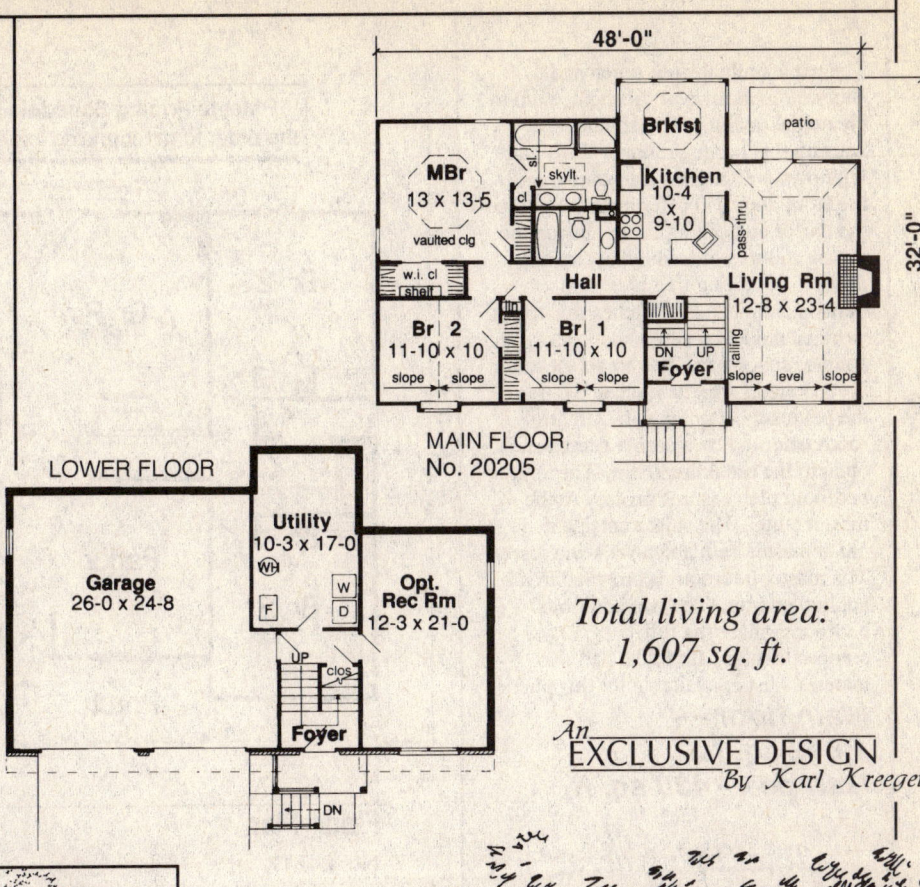

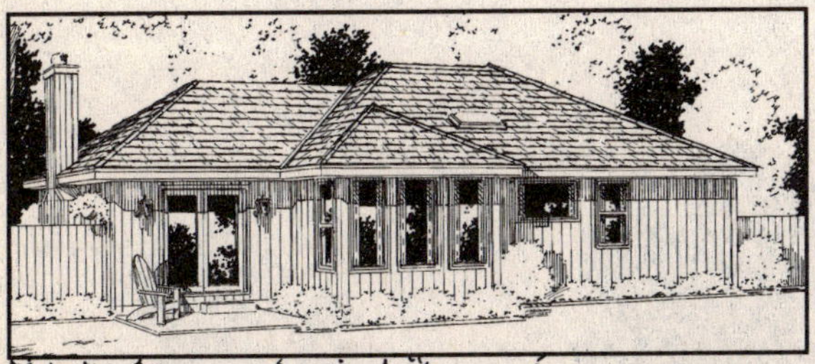

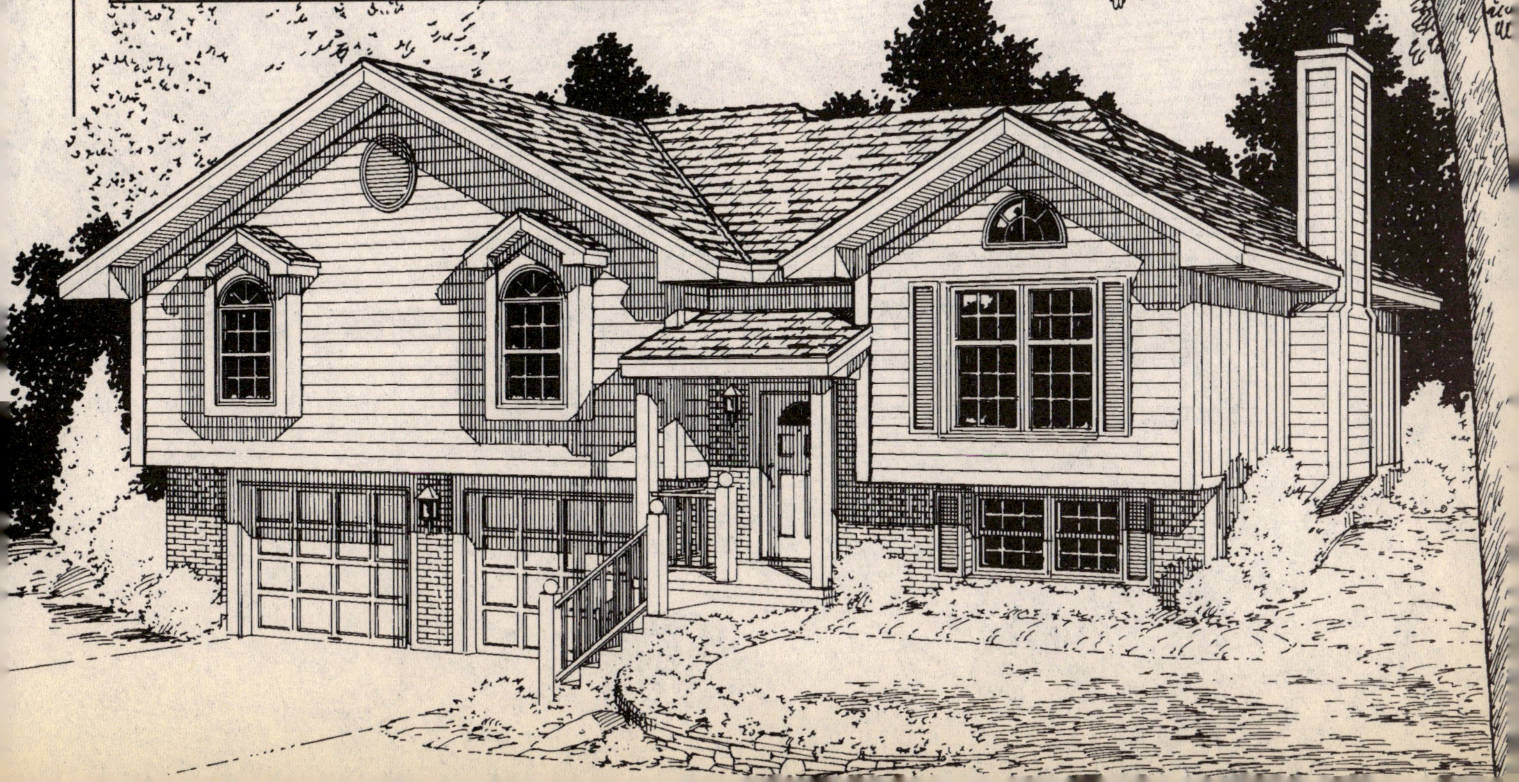

TRIPLE ARCHED FRONT PORCH

ORDER TODAY! 1-800-235-5700

Design 24717

The triple arched front porch and shuttered windows of this home help to create the quaint, old-fashioned warmth this home presents. Two large windows with arched transoms frame the front door and offer natural light to the parlor and dining room. Inside the dining room is graced by an elegant decorative ceiling treatment and a built-in cabinet. The kitchen features a work island and a peninsula counter/snack bar. The breakfast room is separated from the kitchen by only the peninsula counter. The Great room, adorned by a corner fireplace, is open to the breakfast room. The split bedroom plan assures privacy to the master suite. The suite contains a plush master bath and a walk-in closet. The master bedroom is crowned in a vaulted ceiling. The two additional bedrooms share the full, compartmental bath in the hall. No materials list is available for this plan.

Main floor — 1,642 sq. ft.
Garage — 430 sq. ft.

Total living area: 1,642 sq. ft.

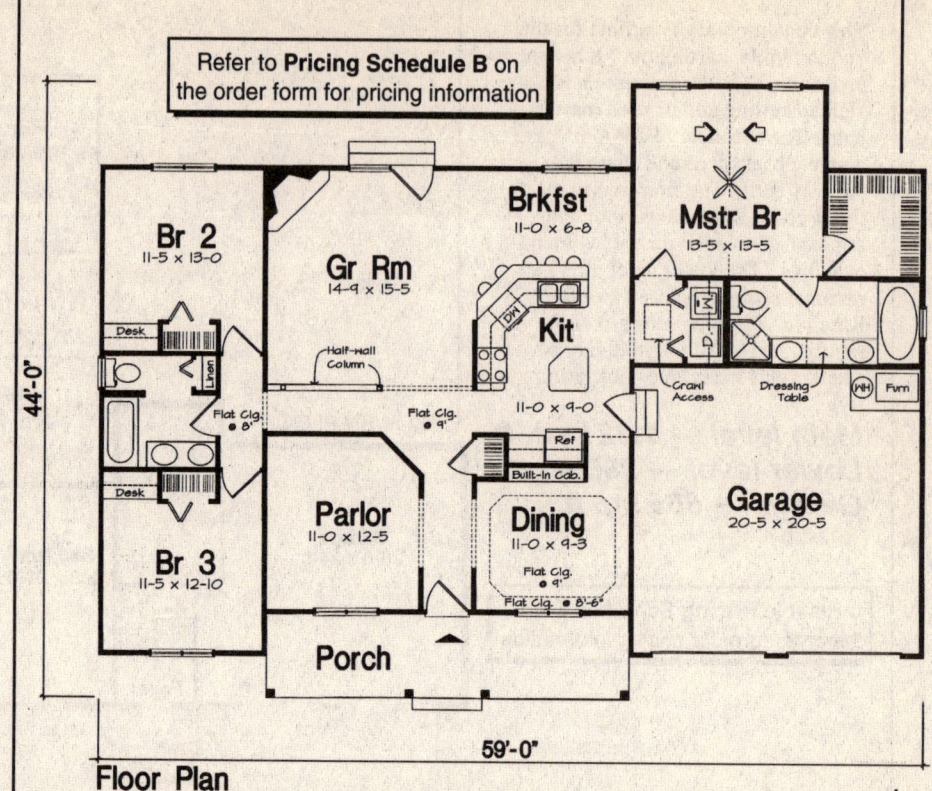

Floor Plan No. 24717

Haven for Empty-Nesters

Design 91340

This transitional design meets the needs and requirements of empty-nesters and the handicapped. It is easily accessible, barrier free, and the hallways throughout are enlarged for maneuverability. From the carport, a ramp leads to the wrap-around front porch that is shaded from the sun by the roof that extends to its very edge. The plan flows from the vaulted Great room through the efficiently-arranged kitchen complete with eating bar. The master suite bedroom with vaulted ceiling also boasts a full private bath and double door wardrobe. The secondary bedroom has a walk-in closet, exits to a private deck, and is served by a full bath that has entrances from both the bedroom and the hall.

Main area — 1,111 sq. ft.
Carport — 2-car

Total living area: 1,111 sq. ft.

Refer to **Pricing Schedule A** on the order form for pricing information

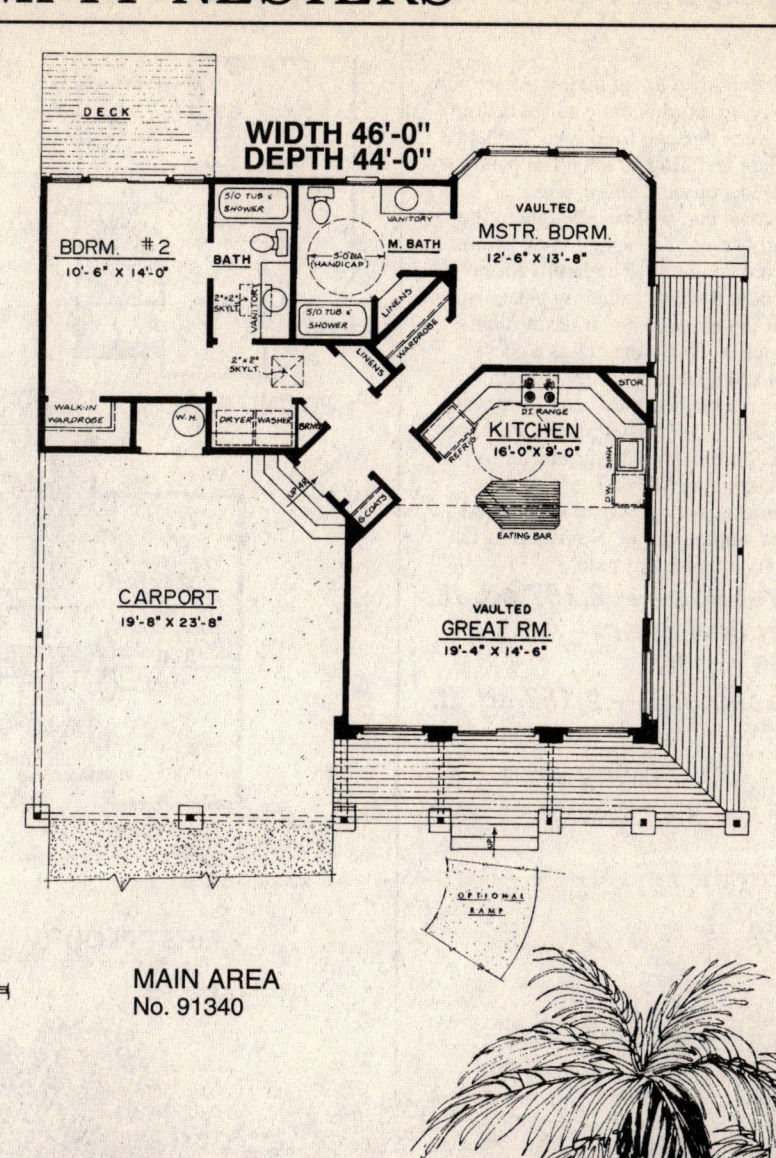

Design 99119

DISTINCTIVE MASTER SUITE

This two-level home invites guests into the living room with a vaulted ceiling and a see through fireplace. The large kitchen featuring an abundant pantry area, lots of work space, and a breakfast bar, will be a delight to the family cook. The sunny nook adjoins the screen porch. The family room provides a warm gathering place with built-in cabinetry and a see through fireplace. Down the hall is a guest bath and a laundry center. The main floor master bedroom has a deep walk-in closet. The master bath is a private spot for relaxation in the spa tub. Upstairs, one finds three large bedrooms with plenty of closets and extra storage space. No materials list is available for this plan.

First floor — 2,157 sq. ft.
Second floor — 956 sq. ft.
Basement — 2,157 sq. ft.

Total living area: 3,113 sq. ft.

Refer to **Pricing Schedule E** on the order form for pricing information

SECOND FLOOR

No. 99119

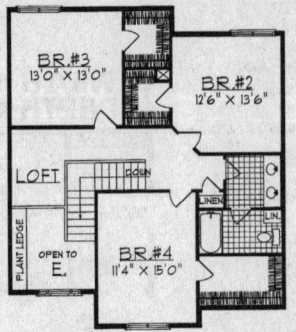

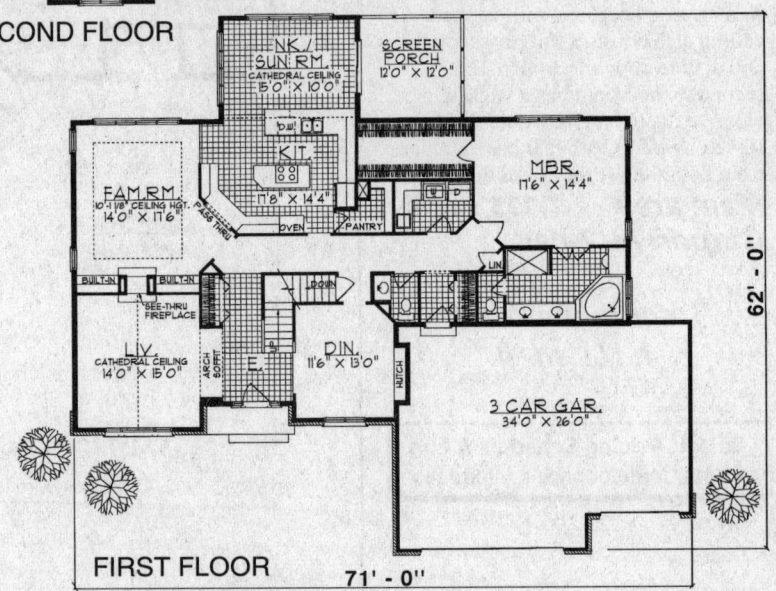

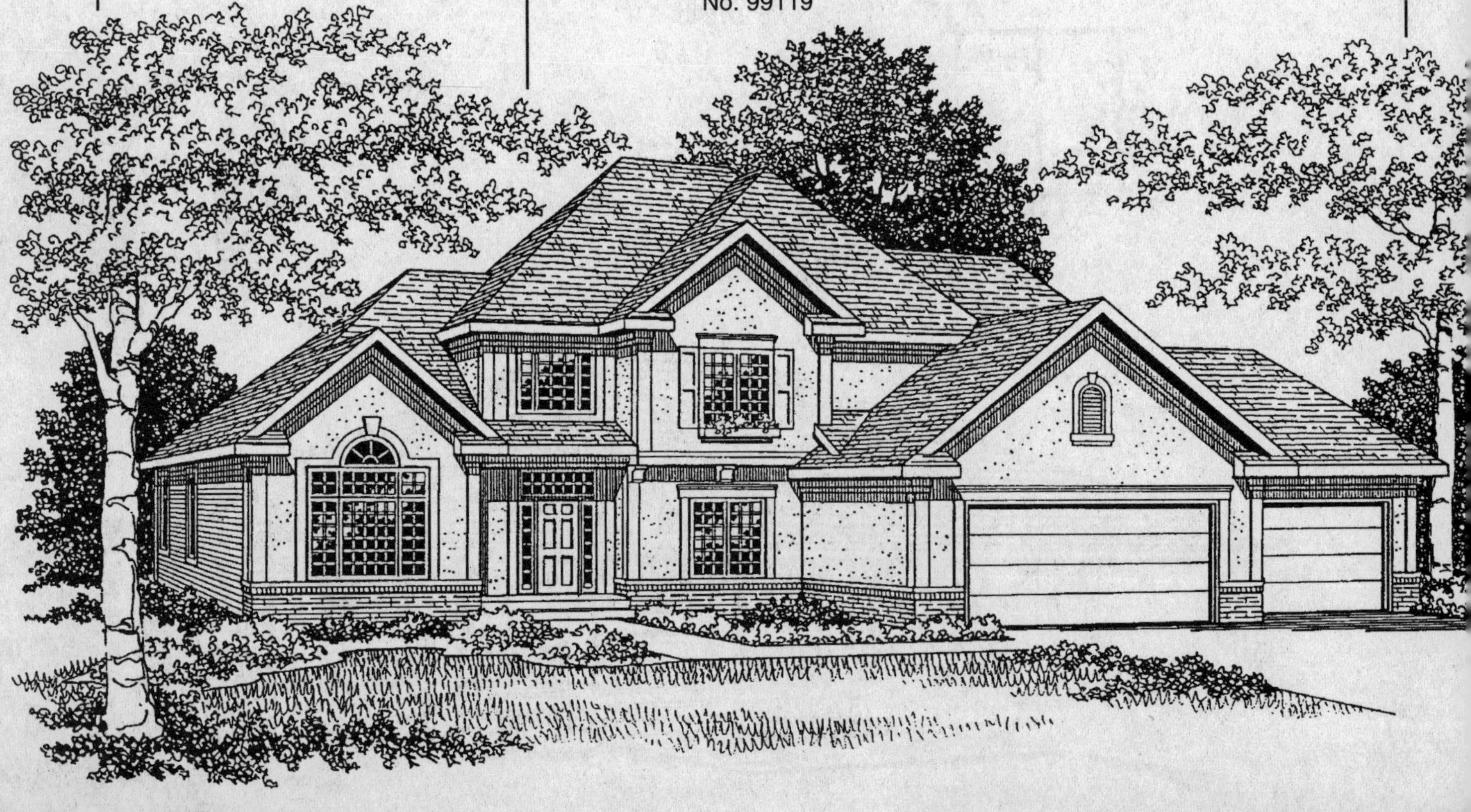

ORDER TODAY! 1 - 800 - 235 - 5700

Design 20087

PRIVATE BEDROOM WING

Don't worry about waking up the kids. They'll sleep soundly in a quiet atmosphere away from main living areas, on a hallway off the foyer of this charming one-level. Sunny and open, the living room features a window-wall flanking a massive fireplace, and access to a deck at the rear of the house. The adjoining dining room boasts recessed ceilings, and pass-through convenience to the kitchen and breakfast room. You'll find the master suite, tucked behind the two-car garage for maximum quiet, a pleasant retreat that includes double vanity, a walk-in closet, and both shower and tub.

First floor — 1,568 sq. ft.
Basement — 1,568 sq. ft.
Garage — 484 sq. ft.

Total living area:
1,568 sq. ft.

An EXCLUSIVE DESIGN
By Karl Kreeger

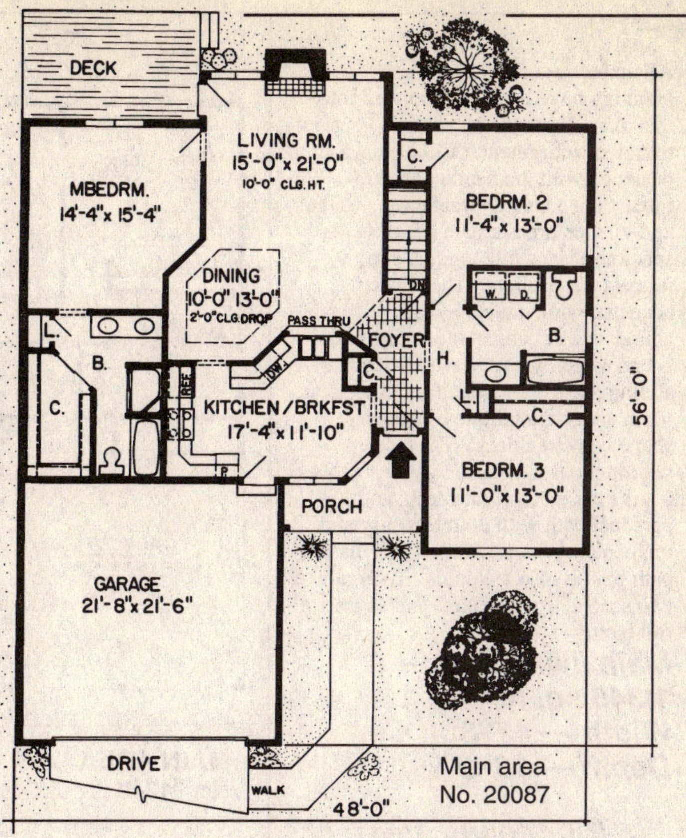

Main area No. 20087

Refer to **Pricing Schedule B** on the order form for pricing information

EASY LIVING DESIGN

Design 91342

All amenities of modern home planning have been incorporated into this plan. Perfect for vacation, year-round, or retirement, this house was designed with the handicapped in mind. The vaulted Great room, dining and kitchen areas create a feeling of spaciousness, while lending to a relaxed atmosphere. The kitchen, accented with angles, has an abundance of cabinets for storage and is enhanced by a tiled work island. A sliding glass door leads from the Great room areas to a unique triangular-shaped covered deck. The master bedroom has an ample sized wardrobe, a large covered private deck, and personal bath with double vanity and tub bench. A non-handicapped master bath plan is also available. There are two secondary bedrooms that share a full bath.

Main living area — 1,345 sq. ft.
Width — 47'-8"
Depth — 56'-0"

Total living area: 1,345 sq. ft.

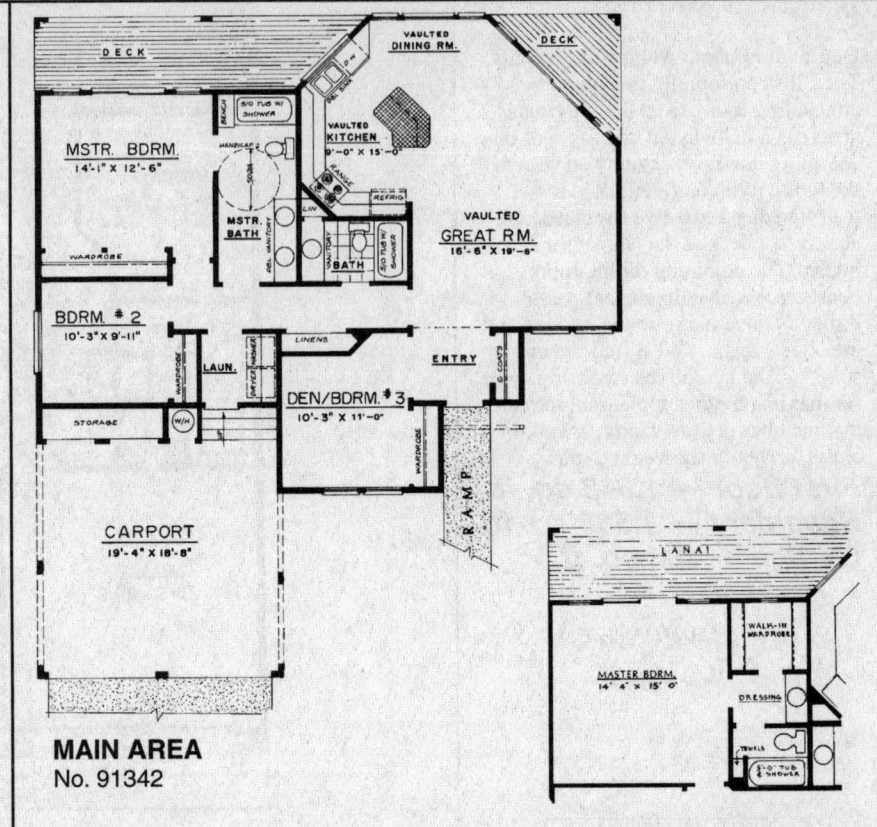

MAIN AREA No. 91342

ALTERNATE BATH

Refer to **Pricing Schedule A** on the order form for pricing information

CONVENIENT ONE LEVEL

Design 93059

Traditional in character, this efficiently designed one-story comes with all the amenities. Ten foot ceilings in all major living areas give the plan a big home feeling. The kitchen, breakfast room, and keeping room are adjacent and open to one another, perfect for family gatherings. The kitchen features a large walk-in pantry, a built-in desk and a forty-two inch high breakfast bar. The formal dining room directly accesses the kitchen for ease in serving. The bedrooms are situated to insure privacy to the master suite. Two walk-in closets and a lavish bath highlight the suite. Two additional bedrooms share a full hall bath. The study includes a walk-in closet and could be used for a home office or a nursery. This plan is available with a slab or crawl space foundation. Please specify when ordering. No materials list is available for this plan.

Main area— 2,559 sq. ft.
Garage — 544 sq. ft.

Total living area: 2,559 sq. ft.

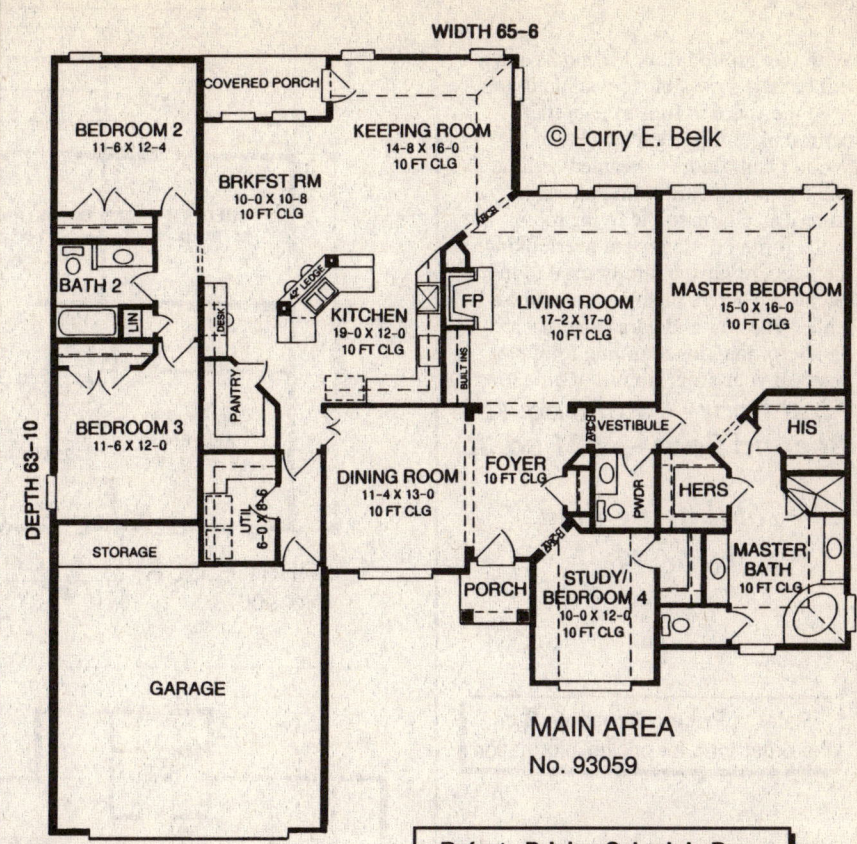

Refer to **Pricing Schedule D** on the order form for pricing information

COMPACT CLASSIC

Design 90671

With two ground floor bedrooms and a full bath, it's possible to wait until you need the space to finish the upstairs bedrooms of this compact classic. Wood plank floors, a beamed-ceiling, and a roaring hearth bring an early American charm to the living room. Eat in the formal dining room overlooking the patio, or have a family meal in the kitchen. There's plenty of room for a table. The rear and garage entries are handy for the kids returning from play, or when your arms are full of groceries.

First floor — 1,056 sq. ft.
Second floor — 531 sq. ft.

Total living area:
1,587 sq. ft.

Refer to **Pricing Schedule B** on the order form for pricing information

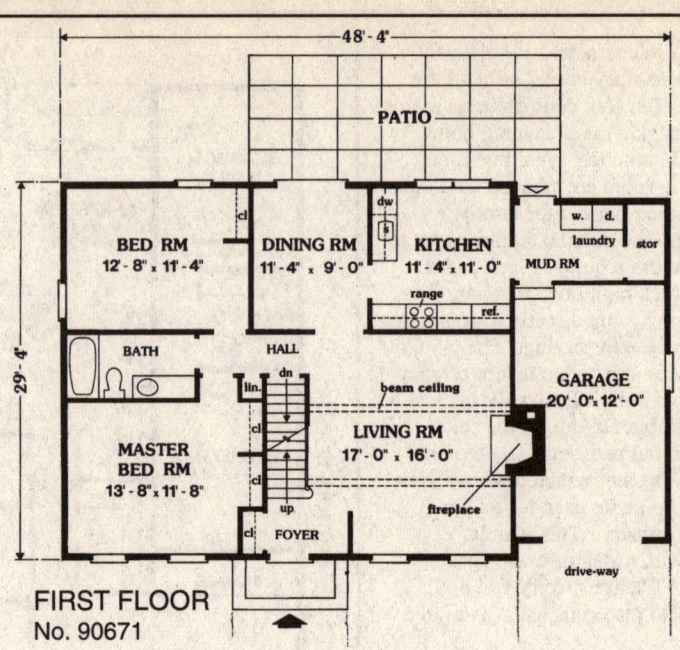

FIRST FLOOR
No. 90671

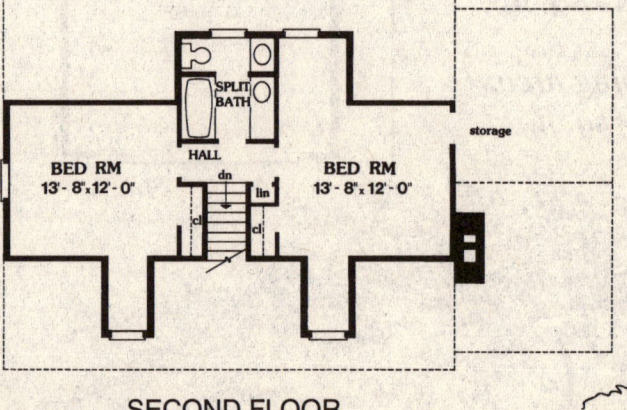

SECOND FLOOR

ORDER TODAY! 1-800-235-5700

COVERED FRONT AND REAR PORCHES

Design 92560

If you are looking for traditional country styling, this is the home for you. The dining room is to the right of the foyer and includes direct access to the kitchen and built-in cabinets. The kitchen is made more efficient by the peninsula counter/eating bar extending counter space and provides a perfect place for meals on the go. The den is enhanced by a vaulted ceiling and a lovely fireplace. The master suite is tucked into a private corner and pampered by a five-piece master bath. The two additional bedrooms are on the opposite side of the home and share the full bath located in the hall. This plan is available with a crawl space or slab foundation. Please specify when ordering.

Main floor — 1,660 sq. ft.
Garage — 544 sq. ft.

Total living area: 1,660 sq. ft.

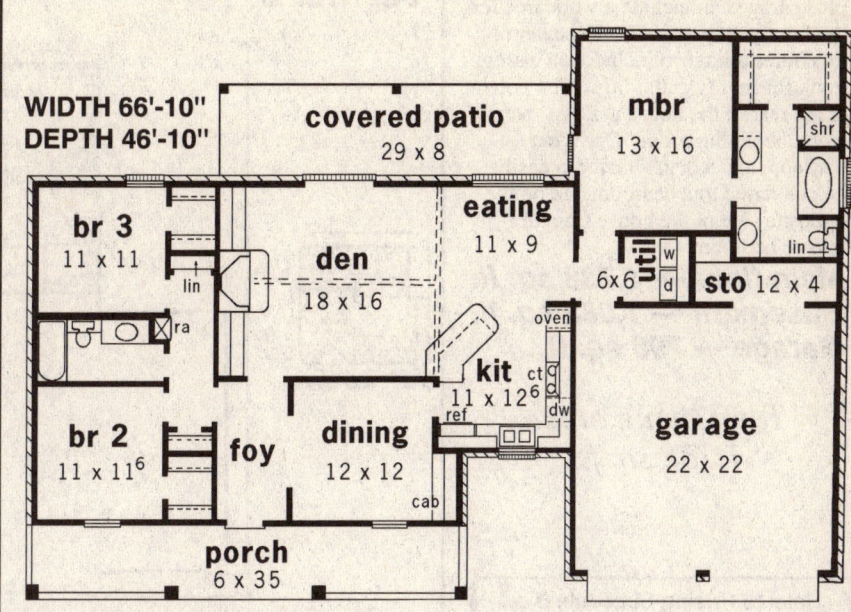

MAIN FLOOR
No. 92560

Refer to **Pricing Schedule C** on the order form for pricing information

PERFECT COMPACT RANCH

Design 10839

This Ranch home features a large sunken Great room, centralized with a cozy fireplace. The master bedroom has an unforgettable bathroom with a super skylight. The huge three-car plus garage can include a work area for the family carpenter. In the center of this home a kitchen includes an eating nook for family gatherings. The porch at the rear of the house has easy access from the dining room. One other bedroom and a den, which can easily be converted to a bedroom, are on the opposite side of the house from the master bedroom.

Main floor — 1,738 sq. ft.
Basement — 1,083 sq. ft.
Garage — 796 sq. ft.

Total living area: 1,738 sq. ft.

Refer to **Pricing Schedule B** on the order form for pricing information

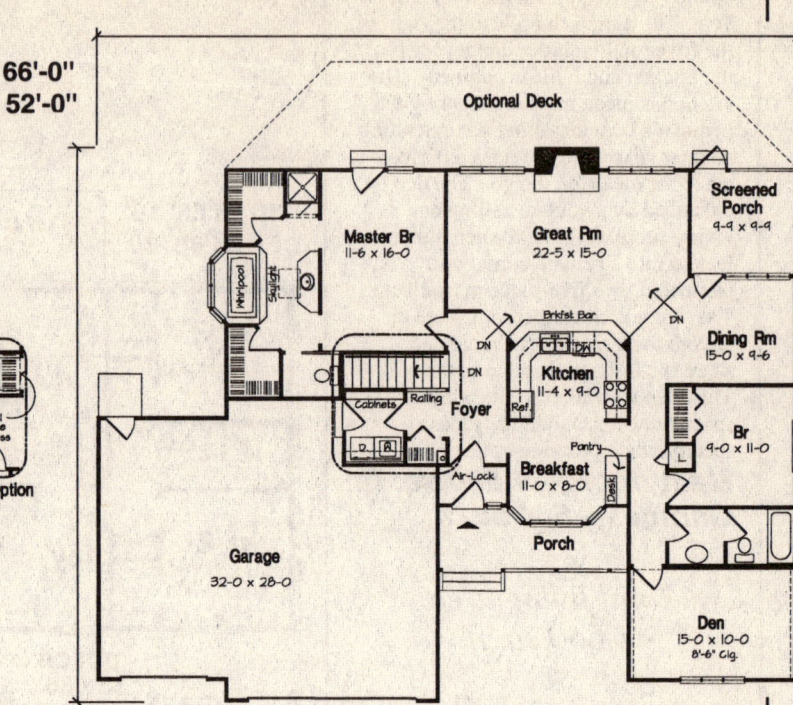

WIDTH 66'-0"
DEPTH 52'-0"

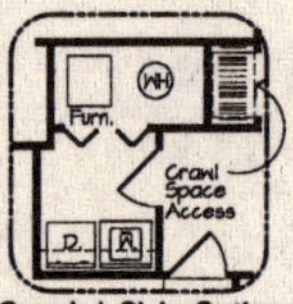

MAIN FLOOR
No. 10839

ARCHITECTURAL IMPACT

IMPRESSIVE TWO-STORY FOYER

Design 24594

Natural light streams into the two story foyer of this home from the huge window above. Windows continue to highlight living space in both the dining and living room, both accented by a bay window. The island kitchen and breakfast area are adjoined. The sunken family room is spacious and cozy with a grand fireplace. The future sun room will be accessed through French doors at either side of the fireplace. Four bedrooms and a study are located on the second floor. The master suite includes a whirlpool bath and the three additional bedrooms have easy access to the double vanity bath in the hall. The study may easily become a guest room with ample closet space.

First floor — 1,497 sq. ft.
Second floor — 1,460 sq. ft.
Basement — 1,456 sq. ft.

An **EXCLUSIVE DESIGN**
By Britt J. Willis

Future sunroom — 210 sq. ft.
Garage — 680 sq. ft.

Total living area:
2,957 sq. ft.

Refer to **Pricing Schedule E** on the order form for pricing information

We are highlighting Plan Number 24594 for it's architectural impact. This home features an impressive two-story foyer enhanced by streaming natural light from the huge window above. Windows highlight the first floor living space with the use of bay windows and culminating in the rear sun room. The cozy sunken family room is warmed by a fireplace. This home's impressive layout along with it's eye-catching appeal is sure to be an outstanding presence in your neighborhood.

ARCHITECTURAL IMPACT

ORDER TODAY!   1 - 800 - 235 - 5700

Design 20143

Stunning Split-Entry

An **Exclusive Design** *By Karl Kreeger*

This spacious split-entry home with a contemporary flavor is the perfect answer to the needs of your growing family. Imagine the convenience of a rec room with a built-in bar, powder room, and storage space on the garage level. Picture the luxury of your own, private master suite tucked off the foyer, featuring a walk-in closet, double-vanitied bath, and decorative ceilings. Active areas a few steps up include an expansive, fireplaced living room overlooking the foyer, an adjoining dining room graced with decorative ceilings and columns, and a skylit kitchen and breakfast room loaded with built-in amenities. Two bedrooms over the garage are just steps away from either the hall bath or the powder room, helping to prevent any bathroom tie-ups.

Upper floor — 1,599 sq. ft.
Lower floor — 346 sq. ft.
Garage — 520 sq. ft.

Total living area: 1,945 sq. ft.

Refer to **Pricing Schedule C** on the order form for pricing information

Family Home with Bedroom Tower

Design 34049

An EXCLUSIVE DESIGN *By Karl Kreeger*

Sloping ceilings and open spaces characterize this four-bedroom home. The dining room off the foyer adjoins the breakfast room and the convenient island kitchen. The beamed living room is crowned by a balcony overlook that links the upstairs bedrooms. The vaulted first-floor master suite features a private deck, a walk-in closet and a full bath with a double vanity.

First floor — 1,496 sq. ft.
Second floor — 520 sq. ft.
Basement — 1,487 sq. ft.
Garage — 424 sq. ft.

Total living area: 2,016 sq. ft.

Refer to **Pricing Schedule C** on the order form for pricing information

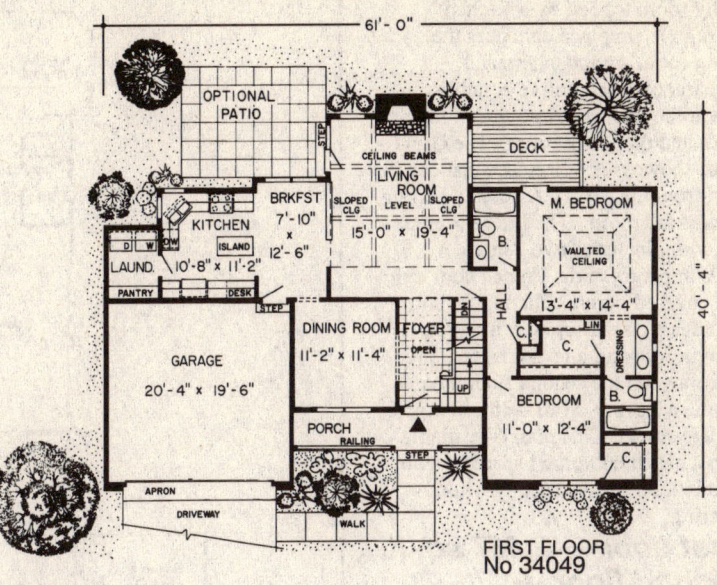

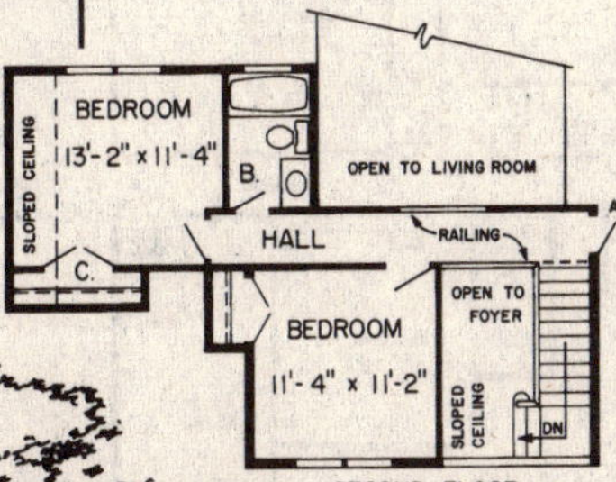

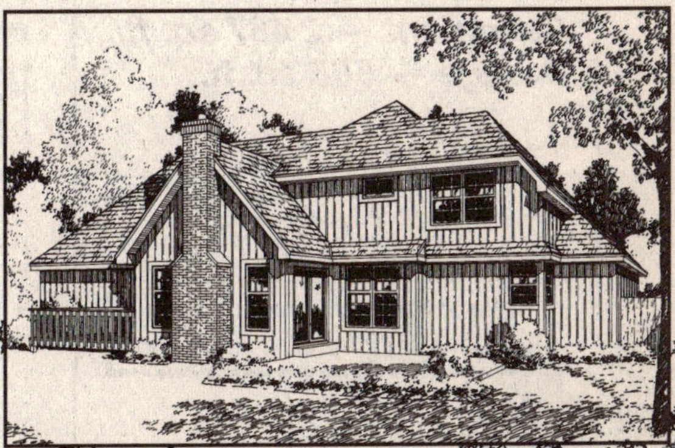

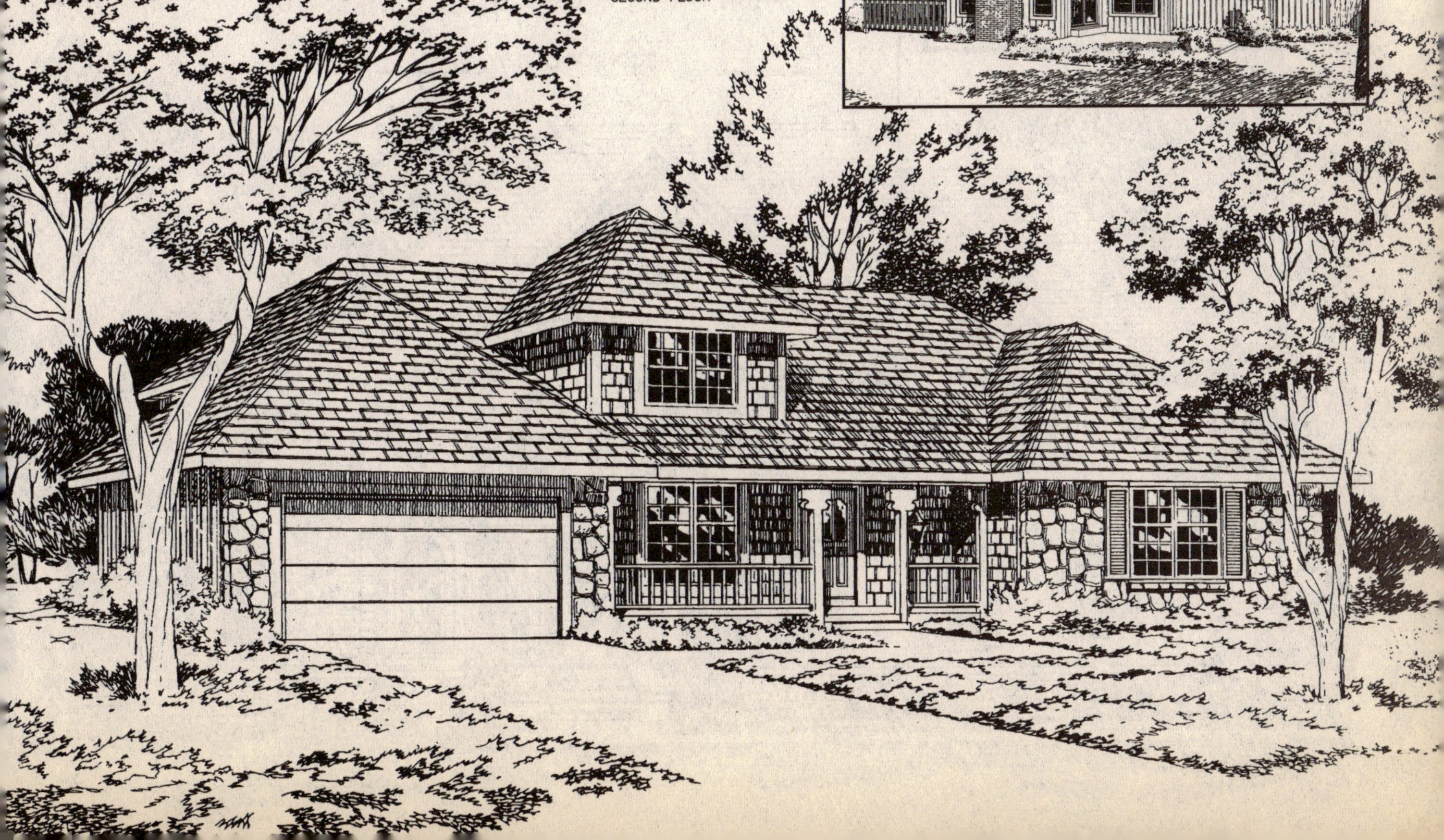

ORDER TODAY! 1 - 800 - 235 - 5700

Design 98403

LUXURIOUS AND COZY ALL IN ONE

The covered porch of this home offers a warm welcome to all who enter. The two-story foyer gives access to the living room topped by a vaulted ceiling. A fireplace enhances the living room's atmosphere and appearance. Decorative columns accent the openings into the dining room and the Great room. The Great room showcases a fireplace that can be seen from the foyer. A vaulted ceiling crowns the room. The kitchen/breakfast room includes two islands, a walk-in pantry and a French door exit to a covered porch. The master suite includes a cozy fireplace, a private sitting room and a lavish bath. Three bedrooms on the second floor have private access to a full bath and ample storage space. This plan is available with a basement, crawl space or slab foundation. Please specify when ordering.

First floor — 2,467 sq. ft.
Second floor — 928 sq. ft.
Basement — 2,467 sq. ft.
Garage — 566 sq. ft.

Total living area: 3,395 sq. ft.

Refer to **Pricing Schedule F** on the order form for pricing information

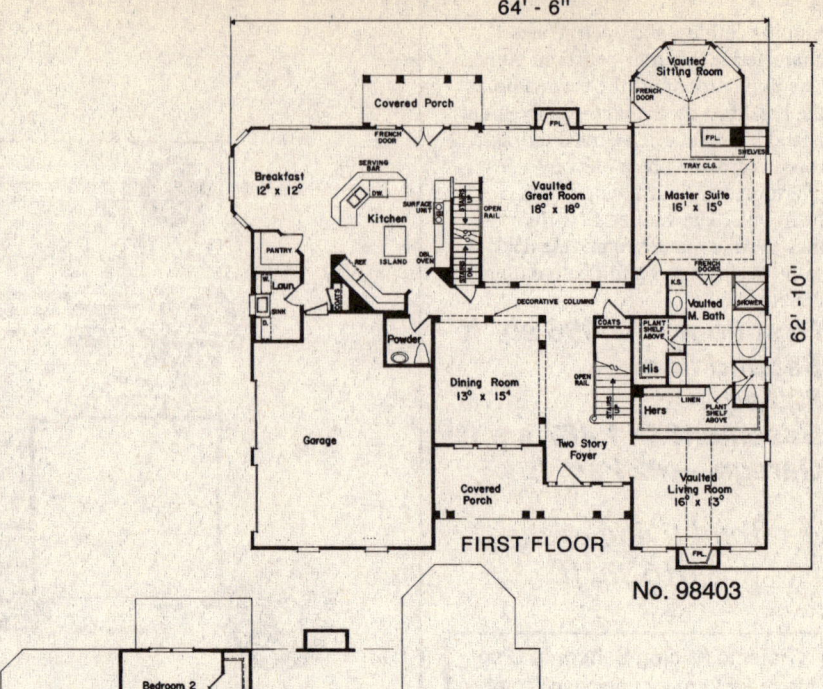

ORDER TODAY! 1 - 800 - 235 - 5700

UNIQUE AND SPECIAL HOME

Design 98528

Quality abounds in this unique and special home with its arched covered entry and arched windows, to its spacious and elegant floor plan for four bedrooms. A media/study room, and two living and dining areas are also featured. Retire to the master suite with it's own fireplace, or cook a fabulous meal in the amazing kitchen with brick arched opening over the range and breakfast area open to the cozy family room. No materials list is available for this plan.

Main floor — 2,748 sq. ft.
Garage — 660 sq. ft.

Total living area: 2,748 sq. ft.

WIDTH 75'-0"
DEPTH 64'-5"

MAIN FLOOR
No. 98528

Refer to **Pricing Schedule E** on the order form for pricing information

ORDER TODAY! 1-800-235-5700

Delightful Detailing

Design 98426

The exterior of this home projects a polished look created by the attention paid to details. The corner quoins, keystones, arches and shutters are eye-catching. The foyer boasts a vaulted ceiling and flows into both the living room and the dining room. The kitchen is enhanced by a cooktop island/serving bar and a pass through into the family room. The breakfast area adjoins the kitchen and includes a built-in desk. The family room is highlighted by a vaulted ceiling and a focal point fireplace. The master suite is outstanding. A tray ceiling tops the bedroom while the highly windowed sitting room has a two-sided fireplace that can be seen from the bedroom. The master bath is luxurious with a huge walk-in closet providing an abundance of storage space. Two additional bedrooms have private access to a full bath. This plan is available with a basement or crawl space foundation. Please specify when ordering.

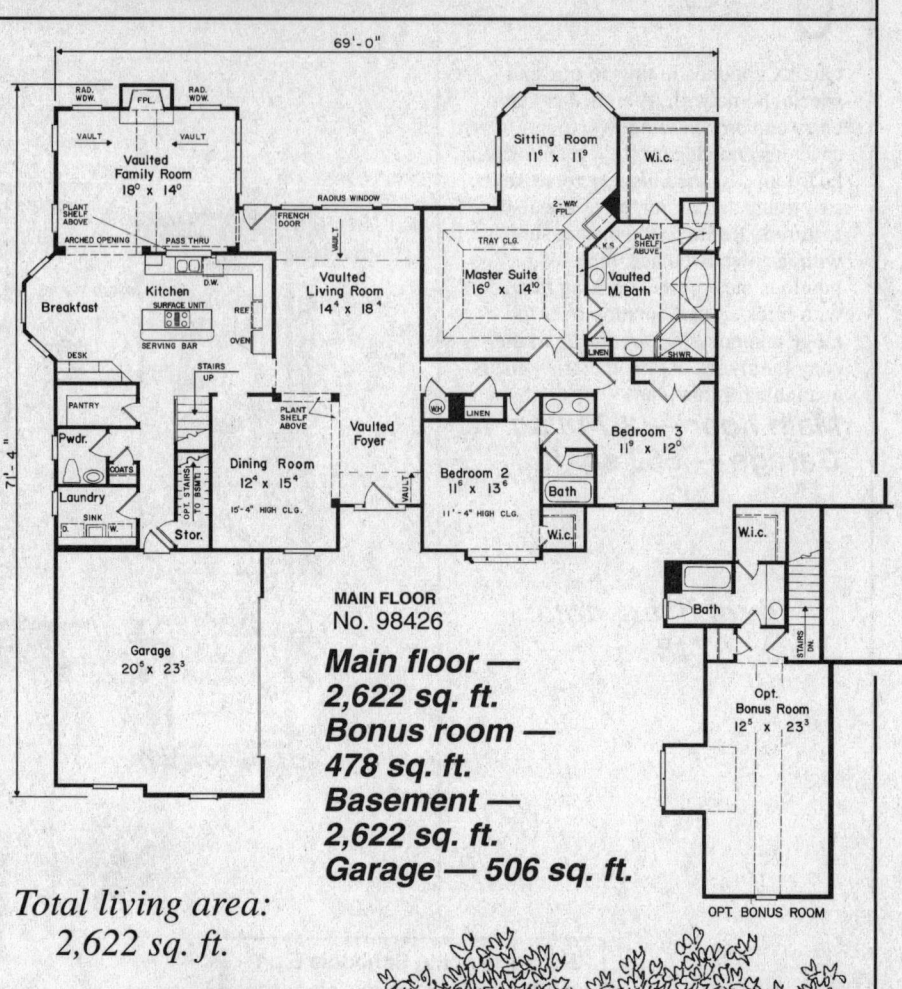

MAIN FLOOR
No. 98426

Main floor — 2,622 sq. ft.
Bonus room — 478 sq. ft.
Basement — 2,622 sq. ft.
Garage — 506 sq. ft.

Total living area: 2,622 sq. ft.

Refer to **Pricing Schedule E** on the order form for pricing information

Design 90925

OPEN, SPACIOUS FEELING

Looking for just the right plan for that hillside lot? Here's a design that will fit a smaller lot with a front-to-back or a side-to-side slope. Vaulted ceilings and lots of glass brighten the living areas, arranged to afford a view to the street. The large kitchen and breakfast nook overlook a cozy family room, which opens out onto an attractive patio. Up a short flight of stairs are three roomy bedrooms and family bath. The master suite has its own bathroom, a wall of mirrored closets for dressing and a beautiful vaulted ceiling with clerestory windows overhead.

Main floor — 1,118 sq. ft.
Upper floor — 688 sq. ft.
Unfinished basement — 380 sq. ft.
Garage — 430 sq. ft.
Width — 40'-0"
Depth — 37'-0"

Total living area:
1,806 sq. ft.

Refer to **Pricing Schedule C** on the order form for pricing information

An EXCLUSIVE DESIGN By Westhome Planners, Ltd.

FLOOR PLAN
No. 90925

UPPER FLOOR PLAN

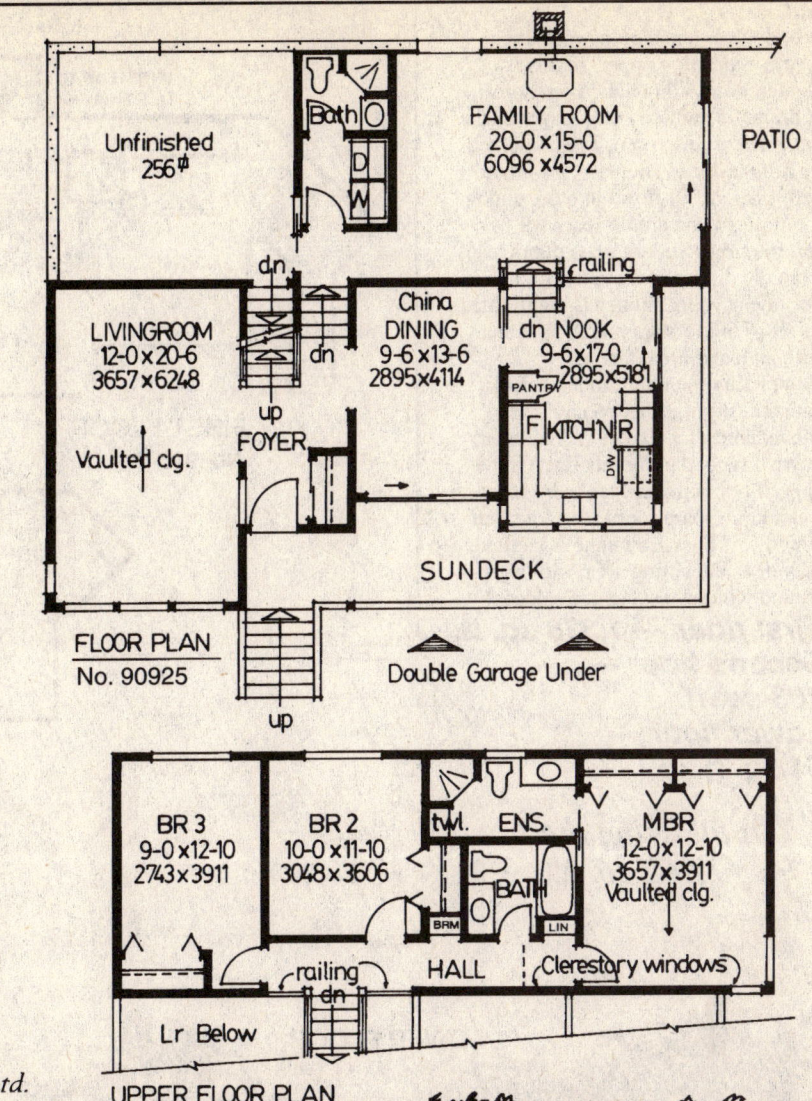

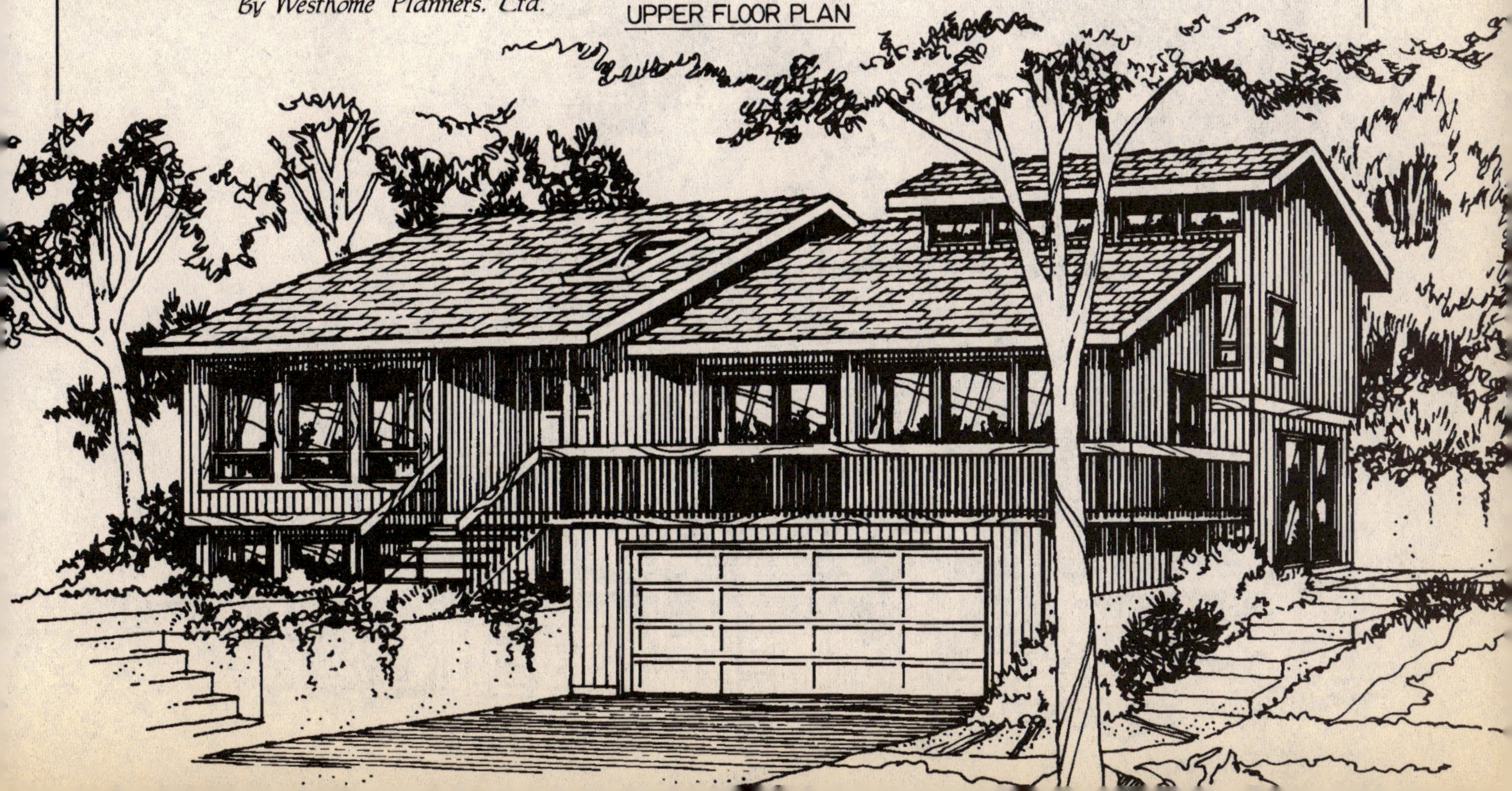

Customized for a Sloping Lot

Design 91343

Wood, glass and sloping roof lines create interesting appeal in this Contemporary three bedroom home. A dramatic vaulted entry serves as the hub. The living room, complimented by a stone-faced fireplace, is vaulted and spacious. It flows into the dining room providing ample space for entertaining. Sliding glass doors lead from the dining room to the adjacent front deck. The kitchen is highlighted by an island food-preparation center with sink and breakfast bar. Completing the main floor is a full bath and skylit utility room conveniently located in the hall near the two secondary bedrooms. On the upper floor is the master bedroom suite and a large spare room with a garden window. The master suite is vaulted, as well as the sitting area, with wrap-around window seat and fireplace.

First floor — 1,338 sq. ft.
Second floor — 763 sq. ft.
Lower floor — 61 sq. ft.

Total living area: 2,162 sq. ft.

Refer to **Pricing Schedule C** on the order form for pricing information

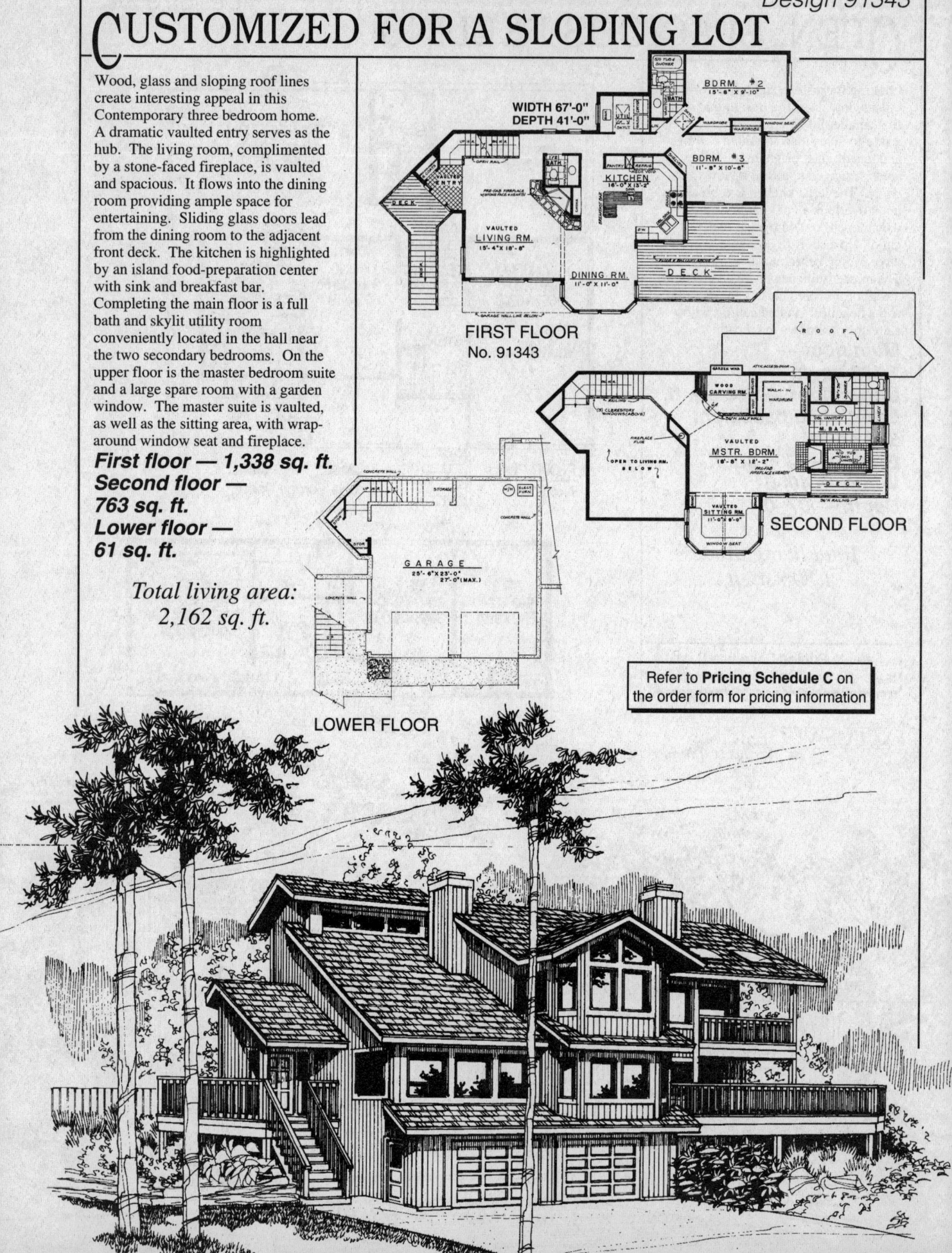

BREEZEWAY LEADS TO ANGLED GARAGE

Design 90011

A pleasing treatment of home design is presented by this large, farm-type residence. The garage is turned about 20 degrees, which allows the house to be located at various angles on the property or to take advantage of an irregular lot shape. The driveway may sweep across the lawn past the front entrance with this arrangement. The interior is full of pleasant surprises including a sunken living room, private master bath with dressing area and access to a porch, a glazed hot house for the plant enthusiast, and a private den off the breezeway.

Main area — 1,867 sq. ft.
Basement — 1,020 sq. ft.
Garage — 485 sq. ft.

Total living area:
1,867 sq. ft.

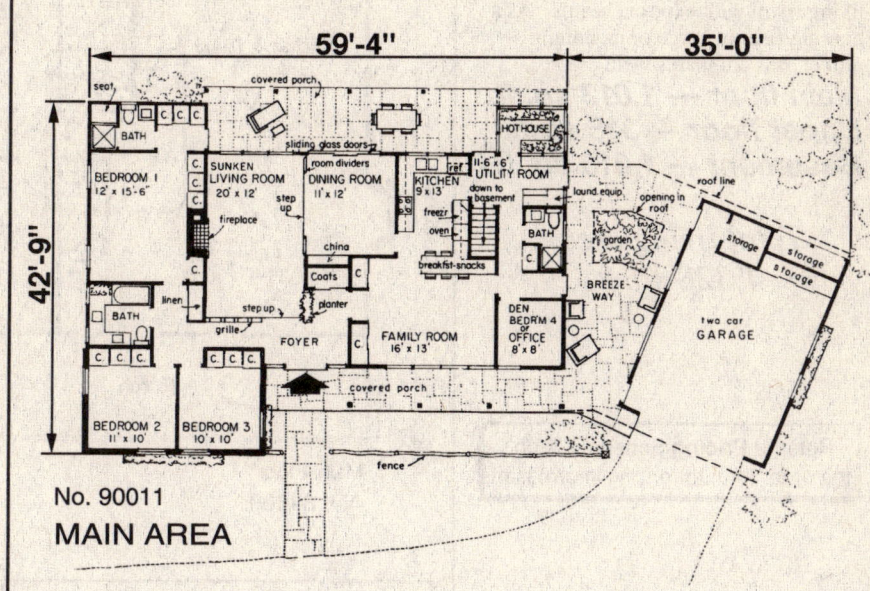

Refer to **Pricing Schedule C** on the order form for pricing information

Design 34600

Rustic Exterior; Complete Home

Although rustic in appearance, the interior of this cabin is quiet, modern and comfortable. Small in overall size, it still contains three bedrooms and two baths in addition to a large, two-story living room with exposed beams. As a hunting/fishing lodge or mountain retreat, this compares well.

Main floor — 1,013 sq. ft.
Upper floor — 315 sq. ft.
Basement — 1,013 sq. ft.

Total living area:
1,328 sq. ft.

Refer to **Pricing Schedule A** on the order form for pricing information

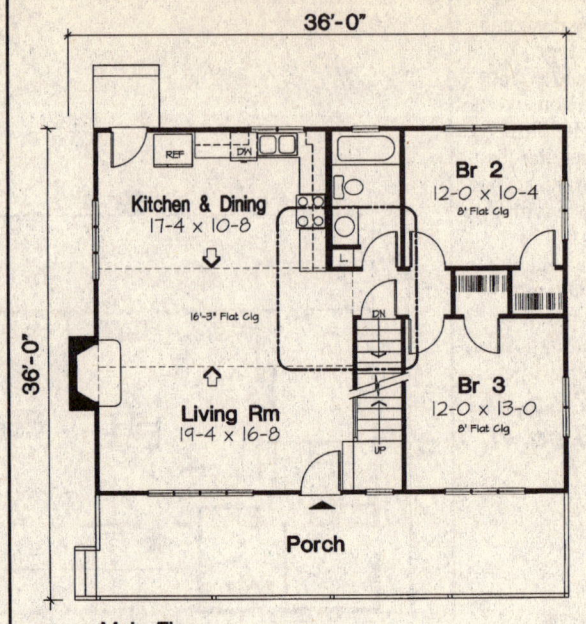

Main Floor
No. 34600

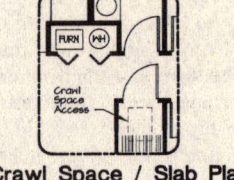

Crawl Space / Slab Plan

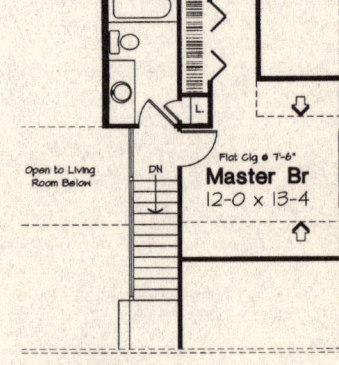

Upper Floor

WARM AND INVITING

Design 92647

The stone and siding exterior with a covered porch and a boxed window combine to create a warm and an inviting home. Family activities will center around the sunken Great room, a wood-burning fireplace and an entertainment center, and can be easily expanded to the outdoors. Across the rear wall of the Great room is a series of double hung windows which are repeated in the breakfast area, providing a bright and cheery place for everyday living. A pass through is featured at the kitchen sink and an expanded counter space, handy for serving quick meals. Steps away is the dining room which adds formality to those special occasions. Split stairs trimmed with wood rails lead to the second floor. A master suite, featuring an ultra bath and a sloped ceiling and two additional bedrooms are included on the second floor. No materials list is available for this plan.

First floor — 1,065 sq. ft.
Second floor — 833 sq. ft.
Bonus area — 255 sq. ft.
Basement — 995 sq. ft.
Garage — 652 sq. ft.

Total living area: 1,898 sq. ft.

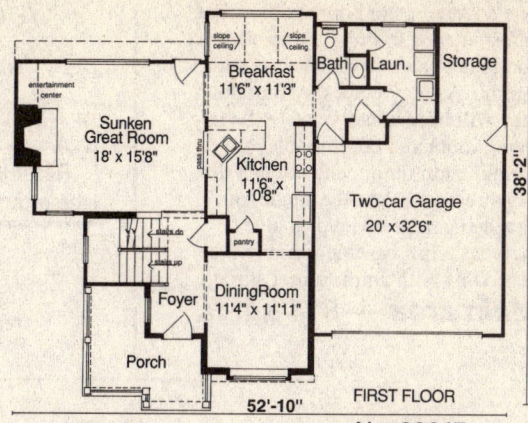

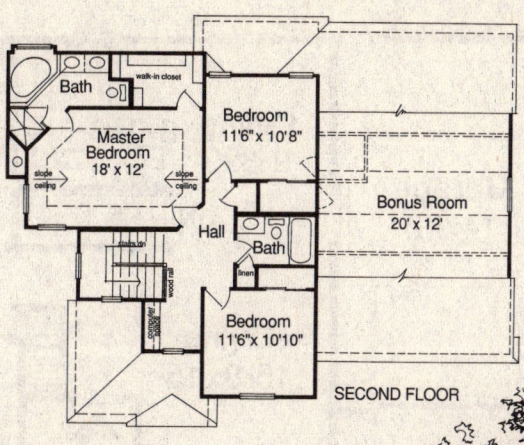

Refer to **Pricing Schedule C** on the order form for pricing information

COMFORTABLE LIVING ZONES

Design 92026

The covered front porch with railing and shuttered front windows all combine to say "Welcome" to your guests. As they enter the front door, they will immediately notice the large living room and comfortable combination dining and kitchen that has direct access to the single-car attached garage. The plan also includes a full basement and two bedrooms with ample closet storage.

Main area — 863 sq. ft.

Total living area: 863 sq. ft.

Refer to **Pricing Schedule A** on the order form for pricing information

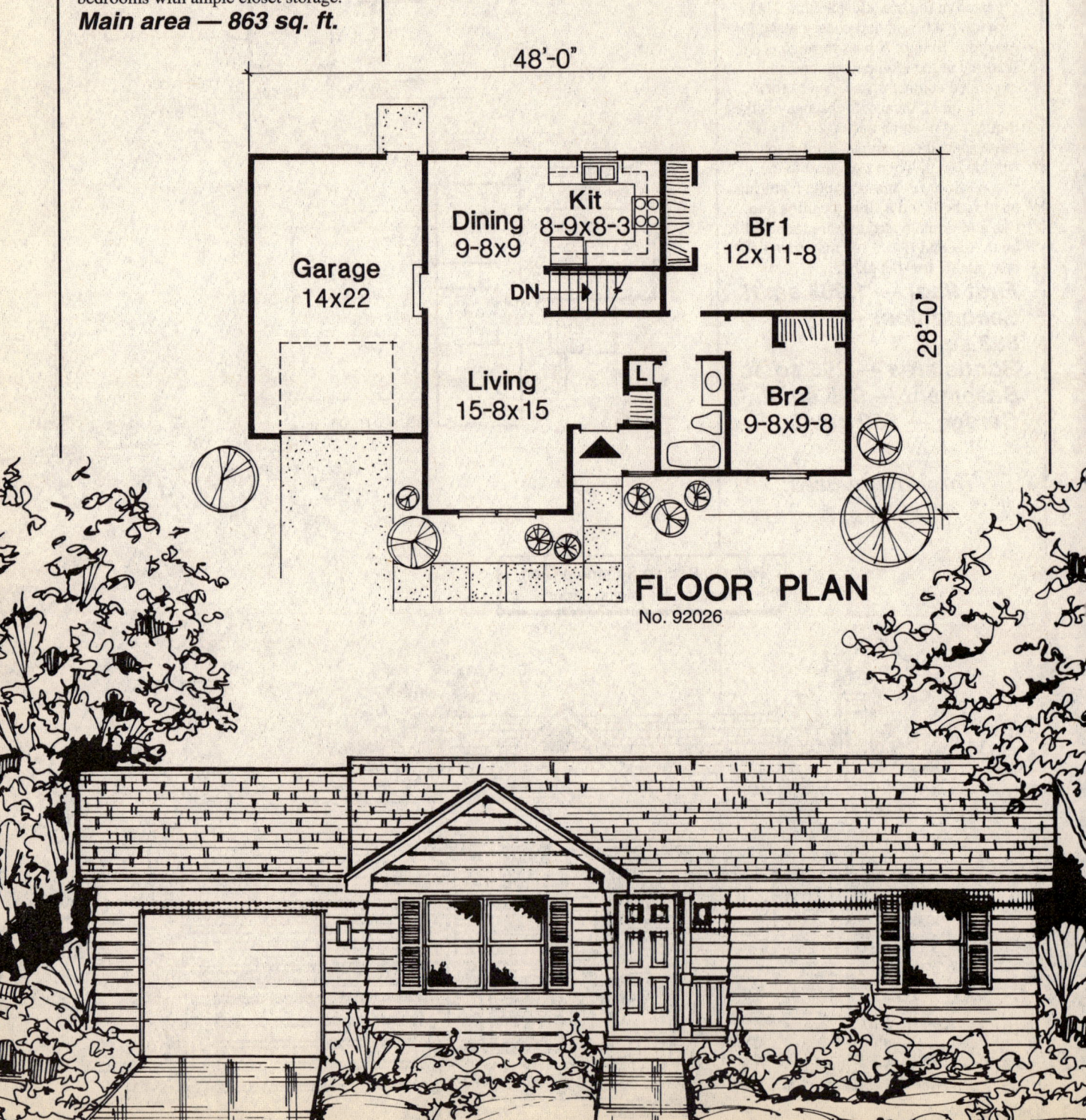

FLOOR PLAN
No. 92026

HAPPY HILL HOUSE

Design 91026

Built into a hill, this vacation house takes advantage of your wonderful view. It features a Great room that opens out on a deck and brings earth and sky into the home through sweeping panels of glass. The open plan draws the kitchen into the celebration of the outdoors and shares the warmth of the sturdy wood stove. Two bedrooms on the main floorw share a bath. Two large, upstairs lofts, one overlooking the Great room, have a full bath all to themselves. This house feels as airy and delightful as a tree house.

Main floor — 988 sq. ft.
Upper floor — 366 sq. ft.
Basement — 742 sq. ft.

Total living area: 1,354 sq. ft.

Refer to **Pricing Schedule A** on the order form for pricing information

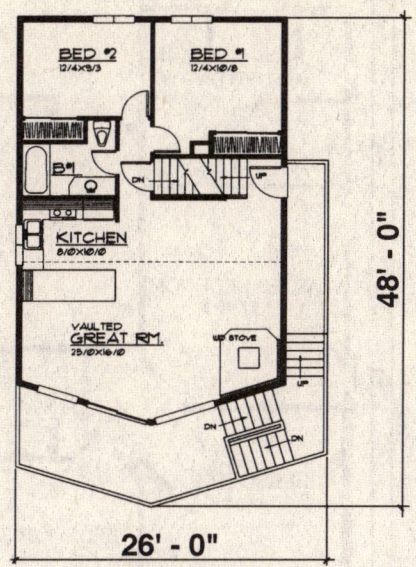

MAIN FLOOR PLAN
No. 91026

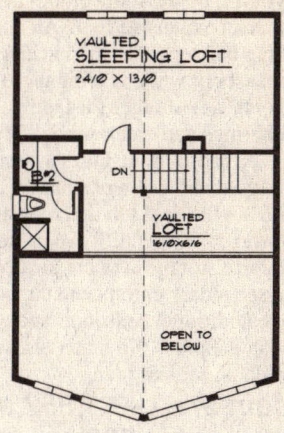

UPPER FLOOR PLAN

Cozy Traditional

Design 93000

This homey Traditional plan has all the amenities of a larger plan in a compact layout. The ten foot ceilings give this home an expansive feel. An angled eating bar separates the kitchen and the Great room while leaving these areas open to one another for family gatherings and entertaining. The master bedroom includes a huge walk-in closet and a superior master bath with a whirlpool tub and a separate shower. A large utility room and an oversize storage area are located near the secondary entrance to the home. Two additional bedrooms and a bath finish the plan. No materials list is available for this plan.

Main area — 1,862 sq. ft.
Garage — 520 sq. ft.

Total living area: 1,862 sq. ft.

Refer to **Pricing Schedule C** on the order form for pricing information

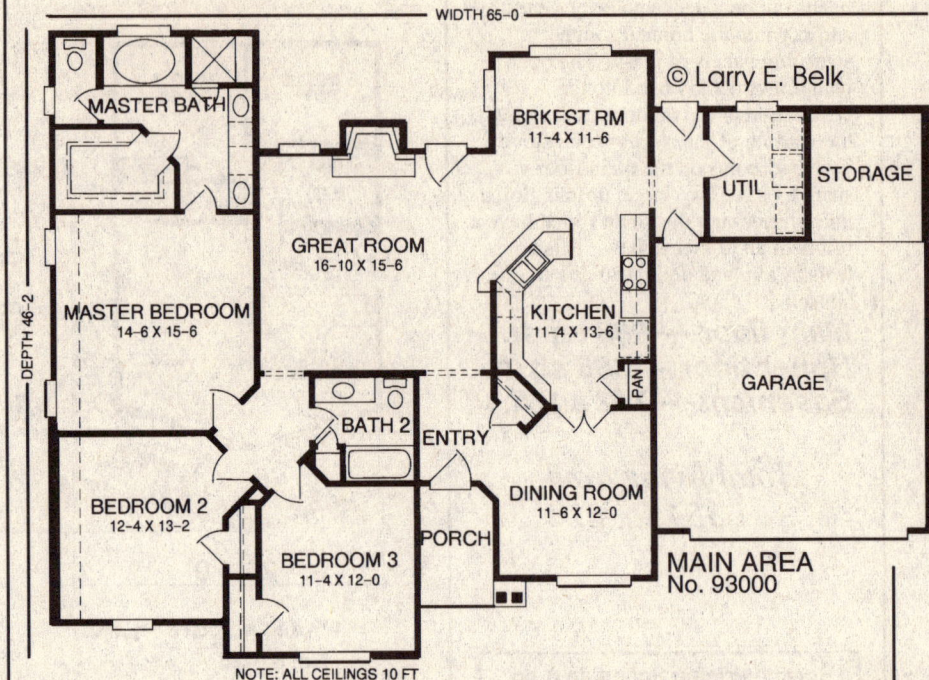

ONE-STORY COUNTRY HOME

Design 99639

The entrance to the house is sheltered by the front porch that leads into the living room with its imposing high ceiling that slopes down to a normal height of eight feet focusing on the decorative heat-circulating fireplace at the rear wall. Widely open to the living room is the dining room. Its front wall is windowed from side to side. The adjoining fully equipped kitchen is also a feature of the house.

The convenient dinette can comfortably seat six people and leads to the rear terrace through six foot sliding glass doors. The master suite is arranged with a large dressing area that has a walk-in closet plus two linear closets and space for a vanity. The main part of the bedroom contains a media wall designed for TV viewing with shelving and cabinets for a VCR, radio, speakers, records and CD player.

Main area — 1,367 sq. ft.
Garage — 431 sq. ft.
Basement — 1,267 sq. ft.

Total living area: 1,367 sq. ft.

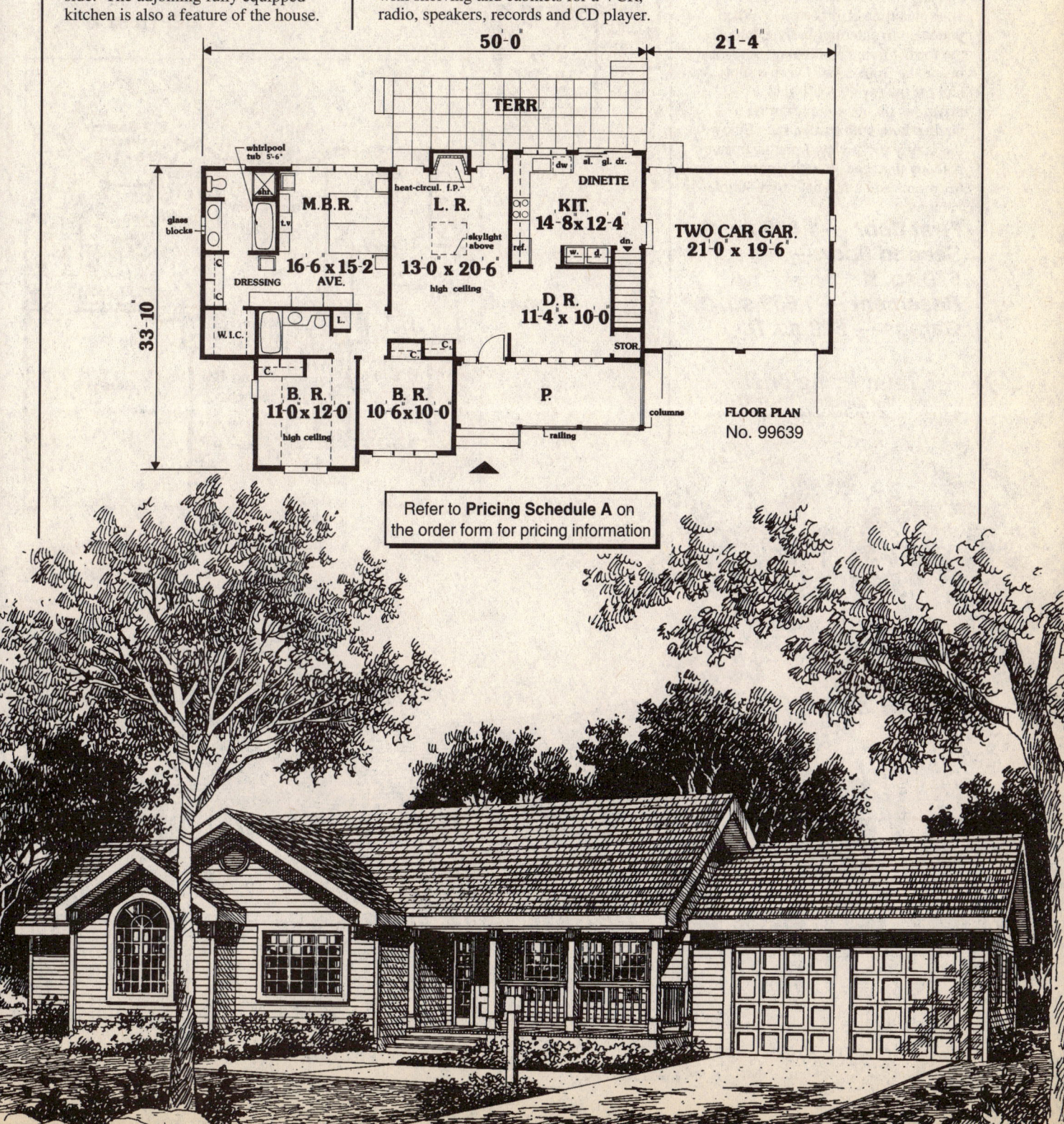

Refer to **Pricing Schedule A** on the order form for pricing information

ELEGANT SETTING PROVIDES COMFORT

Design 20363

Transom windows, skylights, and an open plan combine to make this sturdy brick classic a sun-filled retreat you'll love coming home to. The soaring ceilings of the foyer are mirrored in the fireplaced family room, a perfect place for informal gatherings. Its proximity to the island kitchen with built-in bar and adjoining breakfast room makes your mealtime efforts easier. When you want to entertain in style, choose the formal living and dining rooms just inside the front door. Down a short hall off the foyer, you'll find a luxurious master suite featuring a vaulted bath with garden spa. Enjoy the family room view from the upstairs balcony that leads to two more bedrooms and a full bath with double vanities.

First floor — 1,859 sq. ft.
Second floor — 579 sq. ft.
Basement — 1,859 sq. ft.
Garage — 622 sq. ft.

Total living area: 2,438 sq. ft.

Refer to **Pricing Schedule D** on the order form for pricing information

WIDTH 62'-0"
DEPTH 62'-0"

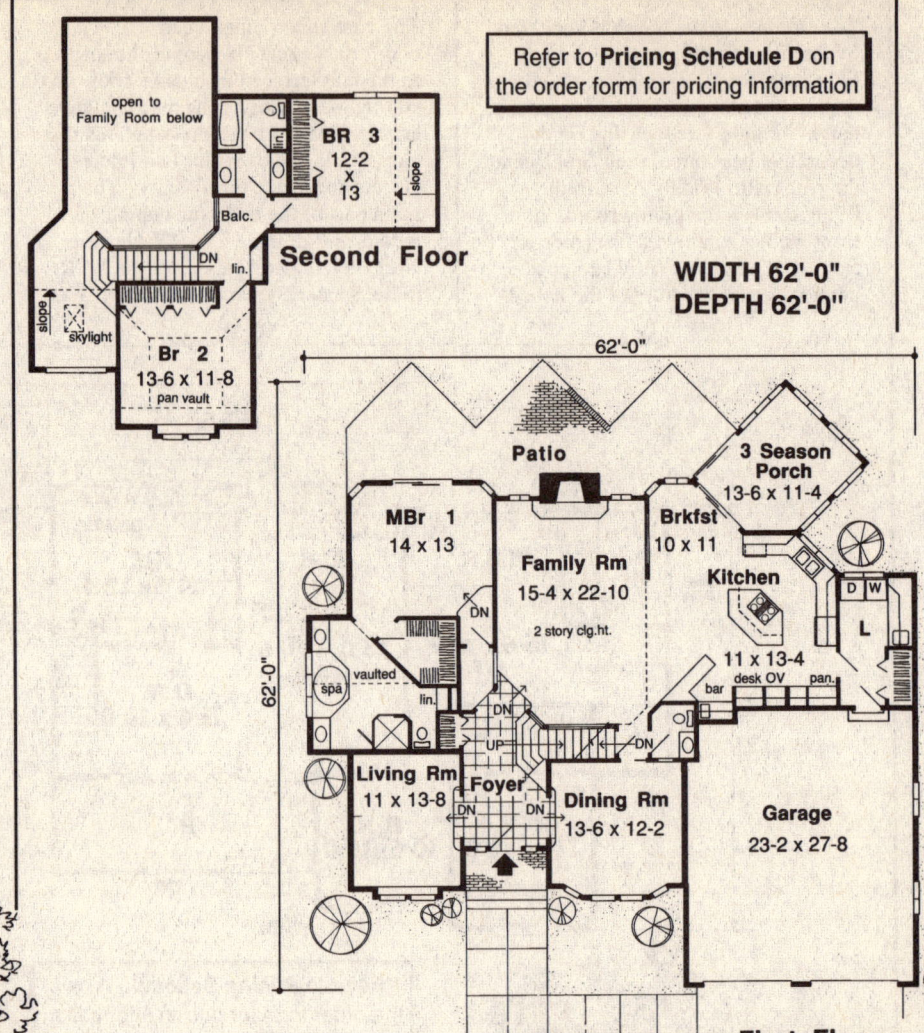

ORDER TODAY! 1-800-235-5700

CHARMING APPEAL

Design 98536

One can't help but fall in love with this absolutely charming Victorian home. A massive covered porch provides a relaxing spot to watch sunsets, or enjoy a loved one's company. Once inside, entertain your guests in the large living, or formal dining room. For the cozy moments, a large angled family room, and huge breakfast area awaits your enjoyment. A spacious kitchen with all the amenities, makes preparing those family meals a snap. The bedroom wing of the home provides a quiet solitude from the entertainment area of the home and contains a master suite with a luxurious bath and walk-in closet and three other bedrooms plus a utility room. The upstairs boasts a huge bonus room with a raised loft area and an arched window. This plan is available with a crawl space or slab foundation. Please specify when ordering. No materials list is available for this plan.

Main floor — 2,787 sq. ft.
Upper floor — 636 sq. ft.
Garage — 832 sq. ft.

Total living area: 3,423 sq. ft.

Refer to **Pricing Schedule F** on the order form for pricing information

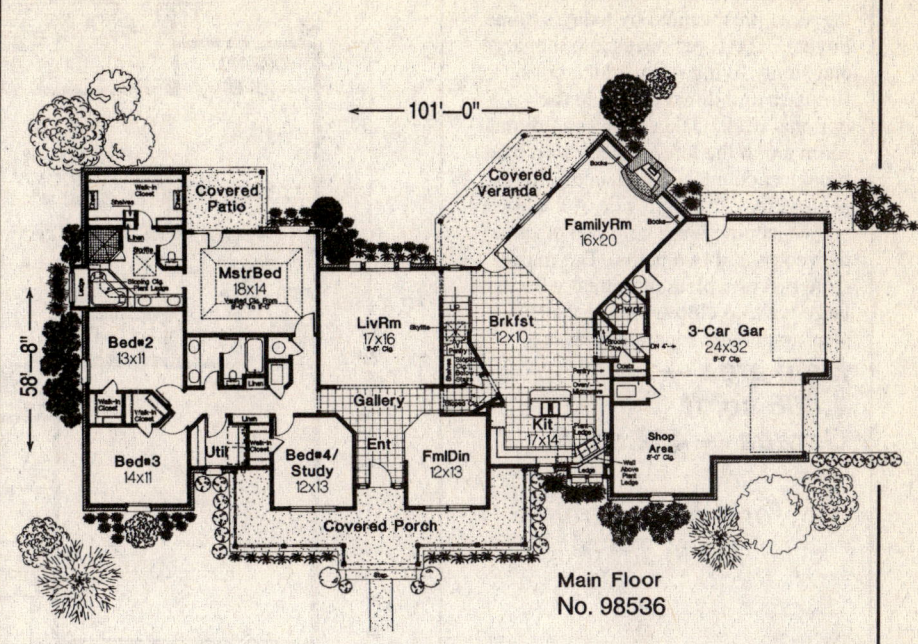

Main Floor No. 98536

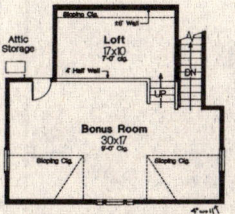

Upper Floor

ORDER TODAY! 1-800-235-5700

Design 34154

MASTER RETREAT WELCOMES YOU

This great Ranch design features all the amenities wanted by today's home buyers. The foyer opens into the large and sunny living room which boasts a fireplace and direct access to the optional deck. The kitchen and dining room are to the left and separated by a breakfast counter. The laundry room is close by. The right side of the house is the sleeping wing with two or three bedrooms and two baths. The master suite makes a pleasant retreat with its large walk-in closet, double vanity, step-up tub and separate shower.

**Main area —
1,486 sq. ft.
Garage — 462 sq. ft.**

*Total living area:
1,486 sq. ft.*

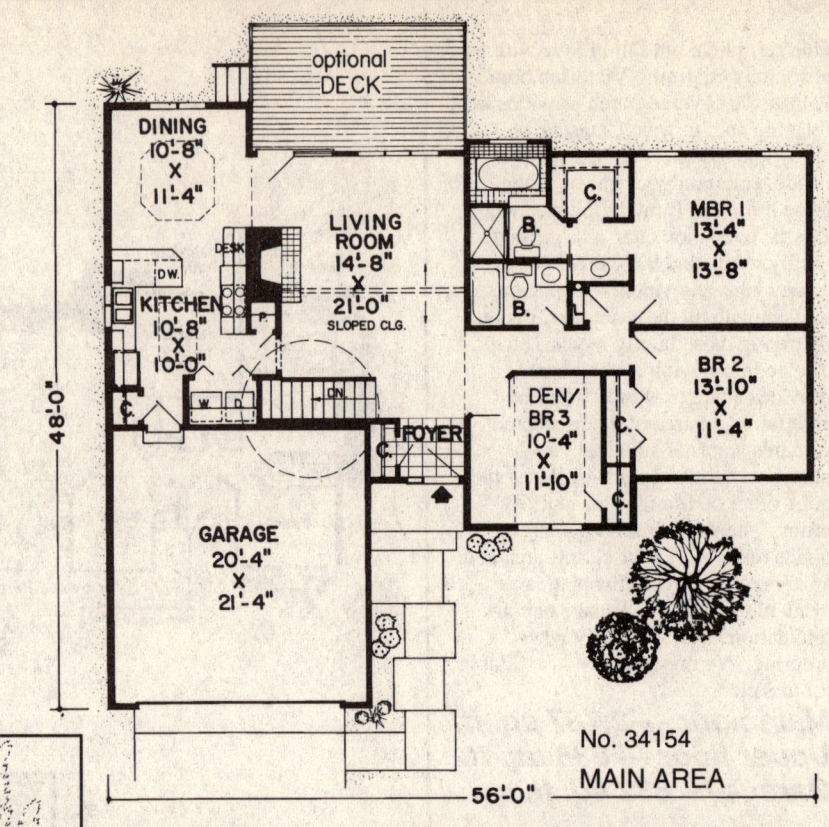

No. 34154
MAIN AREA

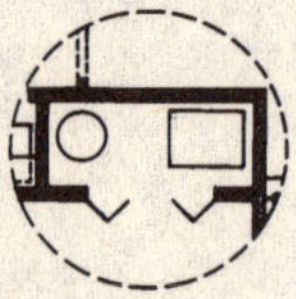

Slab/Crawlspace Option

Refer to **Pricing Schedule A** on the order form for pricing information

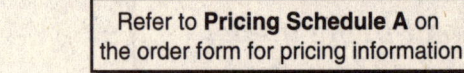

ORDER TODAY! 1 - 800 - 235 - 5700

Design 90001

MOAT AND BRIDGE GREET GUESTS

Impressive in length and form, this rustic, sprawling western ranch is not as huge as it looks, thanks to the clever design that makes the most out of its modest size. Its angled walls, exposed beams, planters, timber posts, split-rail fence, two chimneys, and cupola all blend together to make this a charming residence. Inside the double front entrance doors, the angled plan creates the striking, octagonal shape of the large living room. The entrance to the room is dramatically designed with a moat and bridge. A large log-burning, stone fireplace centers in the entrance on the opposite wall.

Main area — 2,177 sq. ft.
Garage — 2-car

Total living area: 2,177 sq. ft.

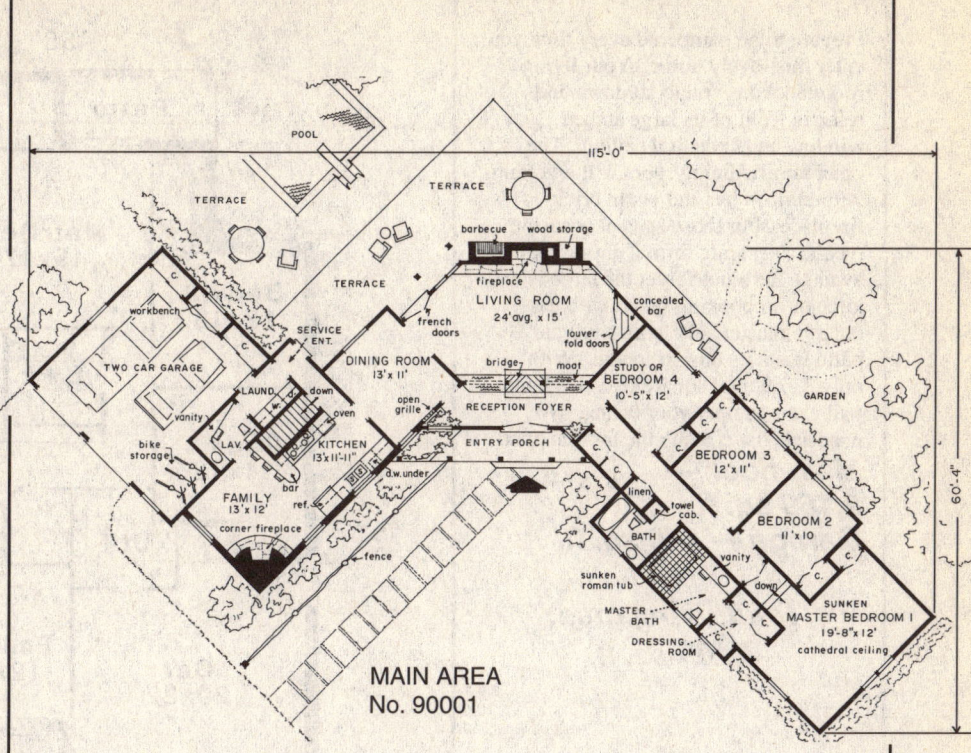

Refer to **Pricing Schedule C** on the order form for pricing information

PREPARE TO BE PAMPERED

Design 98500

Prepare to be pampered every time you enter this lovely home. Your living room beckons you to sit down and relax in front of its large arched window and cathedral ceiling. The open family/dining room will entertain with built-in bar and warm brick fireplace. For those special occasion meals, a separate formal dining room awaits. Let's not forget the large island kitchen for cooking meals with ease. A large master suite with a private patio waits its turn to soothe. With only 2,169 total square feet, this home will even pamper your wallet. No materials list is available for this plan.

**Main floor —
2,169 sq. ft.
Garage — 440 sq. ft.**

Total living area:
2,169 sq. ft.

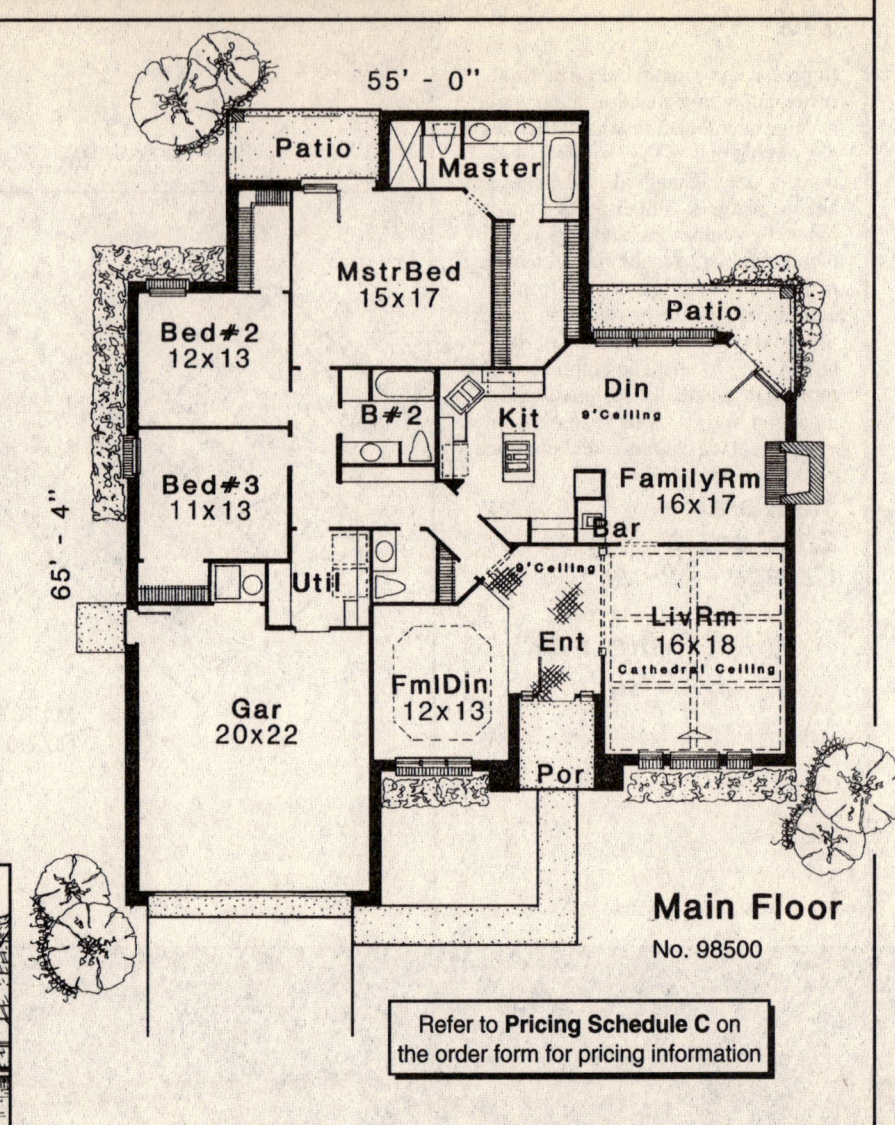

Main Floor
No. 98500

Refer to **Pricing Schedule C** on the order form for pricing information

Features of a Much Larger Plan

Design 90441

This rustic Ranch design has only 1,811 square feet, yet it offers many amenities found in much larger homes. The large Great room has a vaulted ceiling and a stone fireplace with book shelves on either side. The kitchen is spacious with a lot of cabinet space, and is located between the large dining room with a bay on one side, and the screened porch on the other. The master suite has a large bath with a garden tub and two vanities. The large walk-in closet offers plenty of space. Two other large bedrooms, each with a walk-in closet, share another full bath. The utility room is located conveniently off of the main hall. The large wood deck in the rear of the house offers a space for outdoor living. This plan is available with a basement, slab or crawl space foundation. Please specify when ordering.

Main area — 1,811 sq. ft.

Total living area: 1,811 sq. ft.

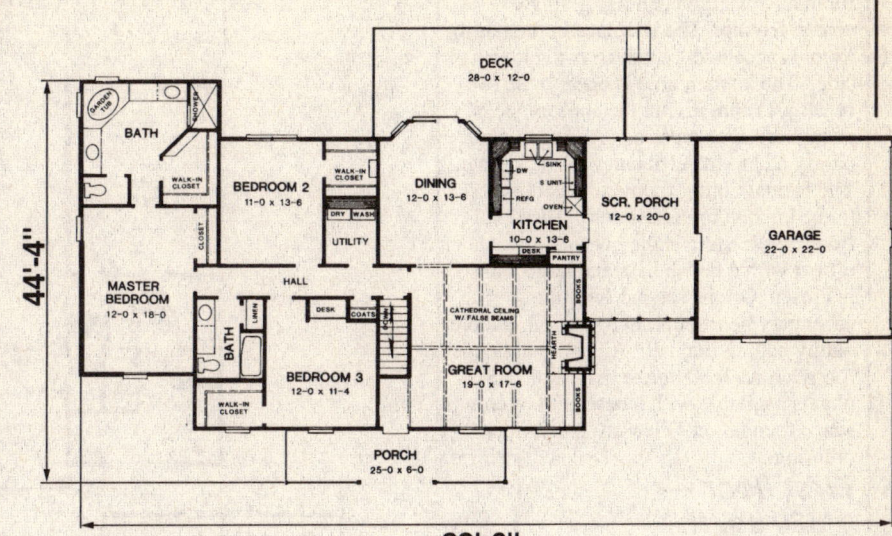

MAIN AREA
No. 90441

Refer to **Pricing Schedule C** on the order form for pricing information

FAMILY SIZE ACCOMMODATIONS

ORDER TODAY! 1 - 800 - 235 - 5700

Design 98454

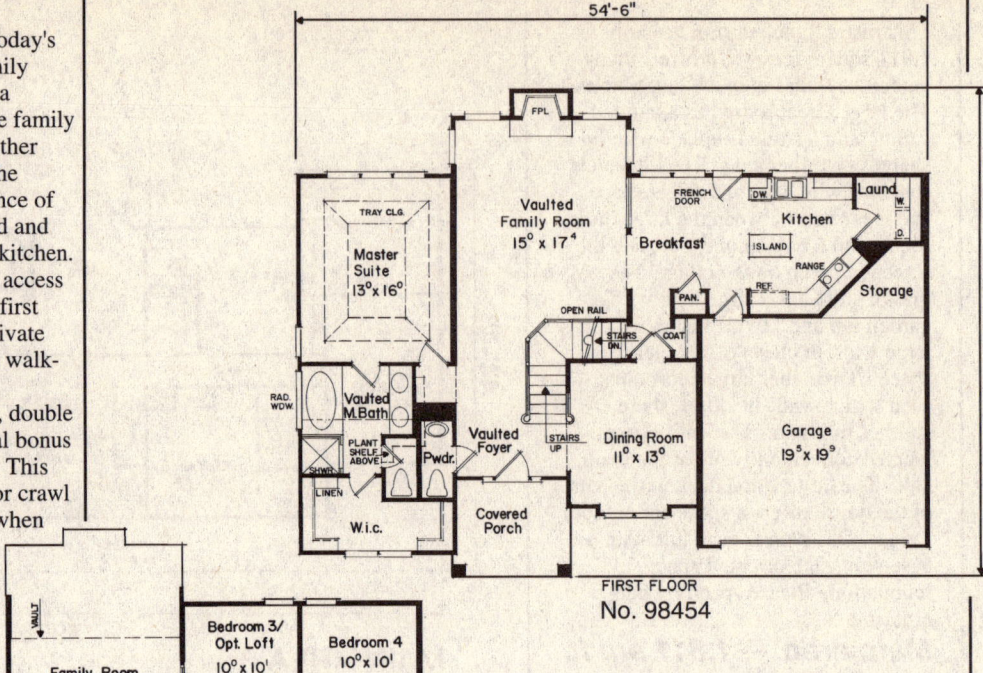

This home has been designed for today's hectic lifestyle. The foyer and family room have vaulted ceilings giving a spatial feeling. The fireplace in the family room is accented by windows to either side. The kitchen area is open to the breakfast room giving the appearance of even more spaciousness. An island and pantry add to the efficiency of the kitchen. The formal dining room has direct access to the kitchen/breakfast area. The first floor master suite is the owner's private retreat with a lavish bath and large walk-in closet. On the second floor the secondary bedrooms share the full, double vanity bath in the hall. An optional bonus room allows for future expansion. This plan is available with a basement or crawl space foundation. Please specify when ordering.

**First floor —
1,320 sq. ft.
Second floor —
554 sq. ft.
Basement —
1,320 sq. ft.
Bonus — 155 sq. ft.
Garage — 406 sq. ft.**

*Total living area:
1,874 sq. ft.*

Refer to **Pricing Schedule C** on the order form for pricing information

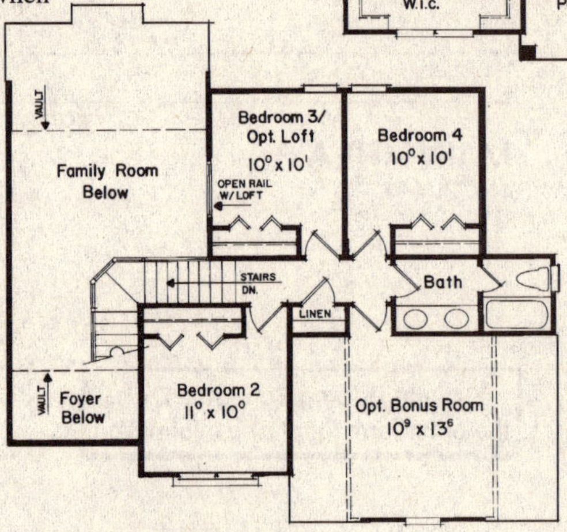

COMPACT WITH A SPACIOUS FEEL

Design 93015

This compact plan features a roomy breakfast room and kitchen combination. The use of 10' ceilings in the Great room gives the home a spacious feel. Twin arches off the entry add architectural interest to this efficient layout. A bay window in the master bedroom provides a cozy sitting area with beautiful light for the homeowner. The master bath is highlighted by a dual vanity and huge walk-in closet. Bedrooms two and three are located on one side the house away from the master bedroom. No materials list is available for this plan.

Main area — 1,087 sq. ft.
Porch — 20 sq. ft.

Total living area: 1,087 sq. ft.

Refer to **Pricing Schedule A** on the order form for pricing information

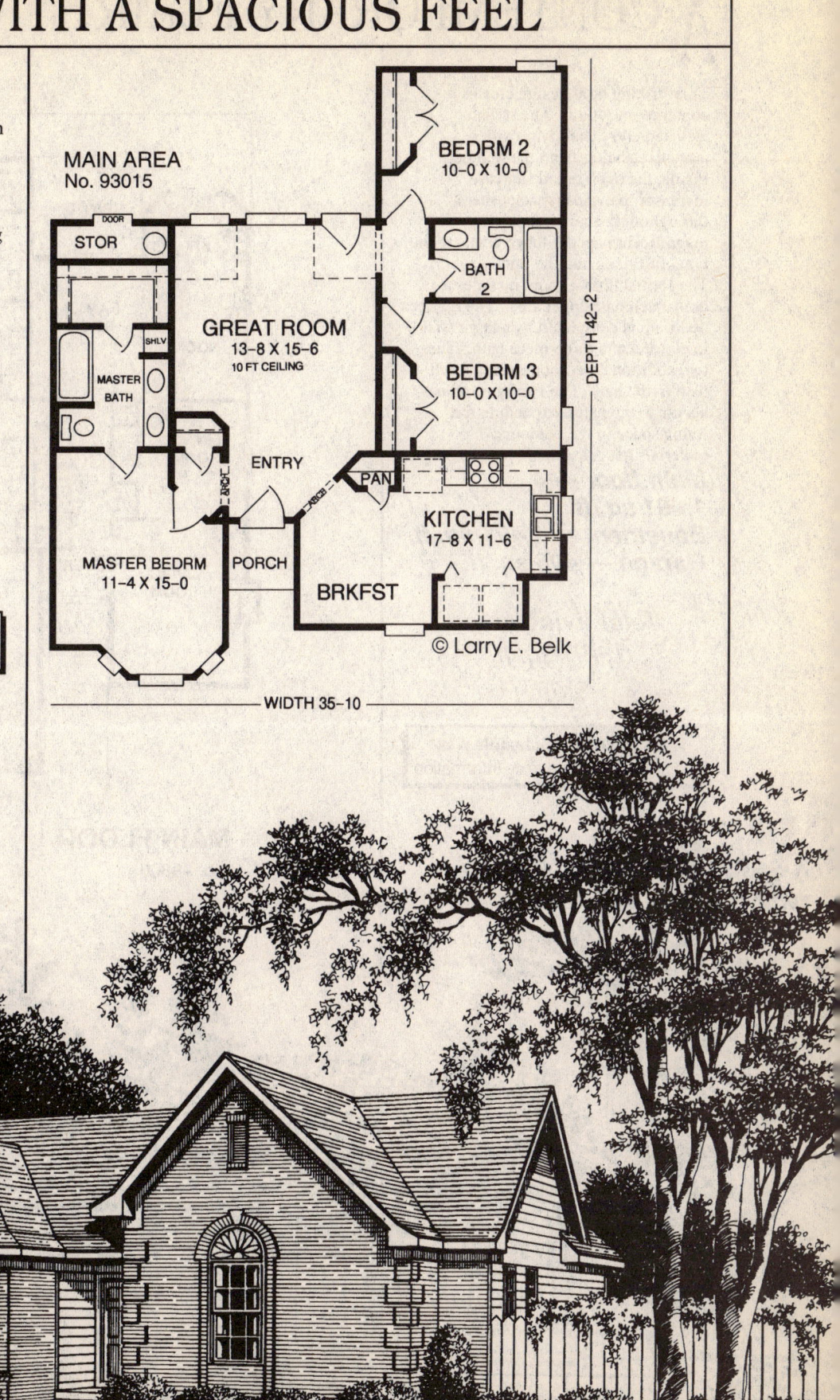

ORDER TODAY! 1 - 800 - 235 - 5700

Design 98806

A CONTEMPORARY FLAIR

This striking bold design creates a contemporary flair. The stylish elevated entry canopy provides attractive shelter from the weather. Inside, the open railed staircase increases the visual spaciousness throughout the center hall. The magnificent bayed kitchen opens to the breakfast nook and the family room. The formal dining room includes a built-in china cabinet area. The master bedroom is completed by a large walk-in closet and a three-piece bath. The two additional bedrooms share a full bath in the hall. The family room has access to the patio, expanding the living space to the outdoors. No materials list is available for this plan.

Main floor — 1,491 sq. ft.
Basement — 1,491 sq. ft.
Garage — 408 sq. ft.

Total living area: 1,491 sq. ft.

Refer to **Pricing Schedule A** on the order form for pricing information

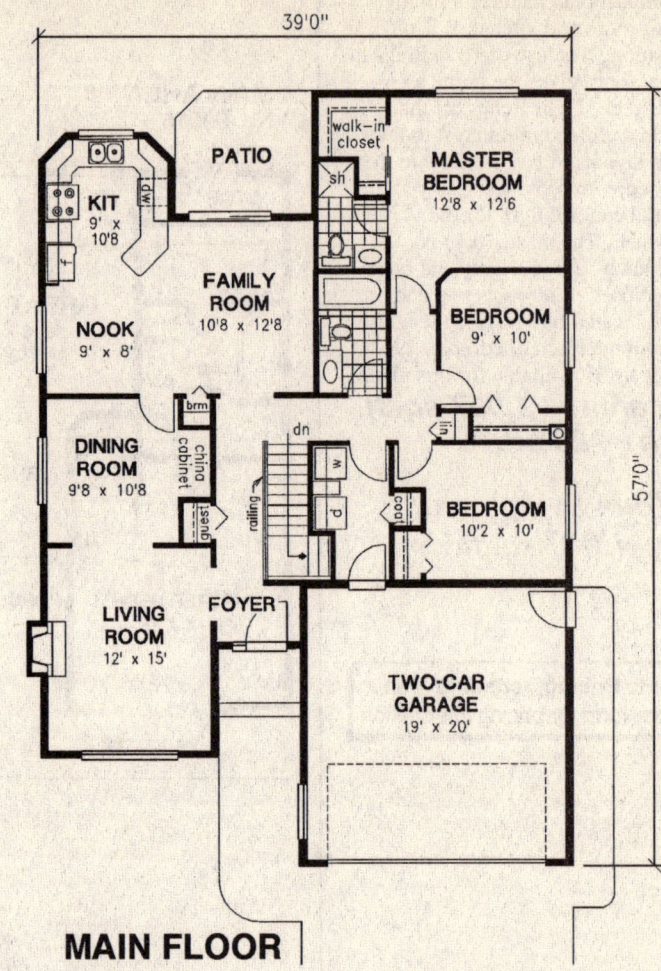

MAIN FLOOR
No. 98806

HIGH IMPACT FAMILY HOME

Design 20111

The Traditional facade of this four bedroom home doesn't even hint at the exciting interior behind the front door. A balcony linking the upstairs bedrooms and skylit bath divides a dramatic two-story foyer and soaring living room. All active areas benefit from the warmth of the massive fireplace and the added living space afforded by the outdoor deck. You'll love the well-situated kitchen, handy to both the formal dining room and sunny breakfast room. And you'll wonder how you lived without the convenience of a private, first floor master suite with a garden tub, step-in shower, double vanities and walk-in closet.

First floor — 1,701 sq. ft.
Second floor — 665 sq. ft.
Basement — 1,045 sq. ft.
Garage — 633 sq. ft.
Porch — 80 sq. ft.

Total living area: 2,366 sq. ft.

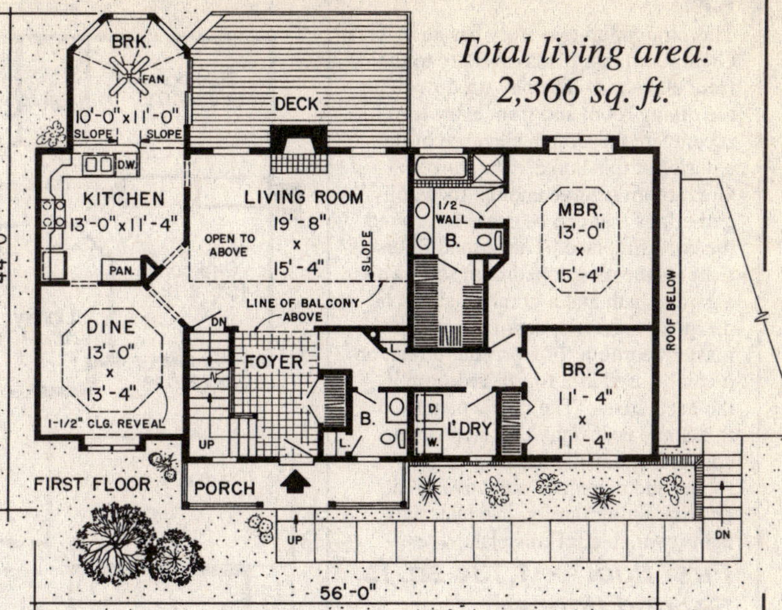

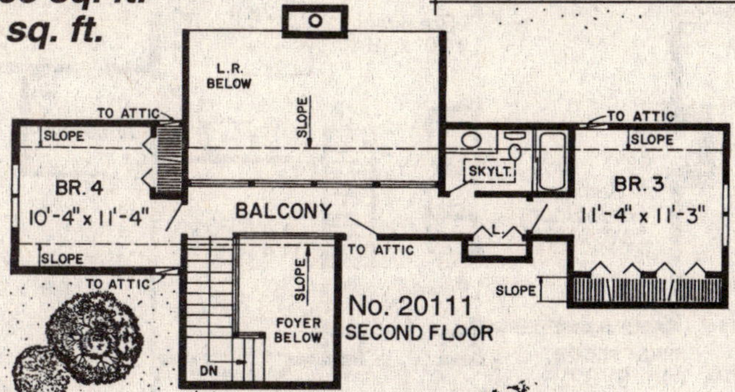

An EXCLUSIVE DESIGN By Karl Kreeger

Refer to **Pricing Schedule D** on the order form for pricing information

ORDER TODAY! 1-800-235-5700

SIMPLE ELEGANCE

Design 92622

This straight up two-story has an offset Great room that lends diversity to the front elevation. The bay window in the dining room and front entry trim accentuate the simple elegance of the exterior of this home. The sunken Great room is large enough for family gatherings that can be centered around the cozy fireplace. The second floor features the master bedroom suite with a garden bath and a library that can be designed to have access from the master bedroom for a private retreat, or it can be used as a fourth bedroom if the need arises. The traffic pattern of this home is designed for step saving convenience while offering large rooms and amenities attractive to the discriminating family. No materials list is available for this plan.

First floor — 1,134 sq. ft.
Second floor — 1,083 sq. ft.

Total living area: 2,217 sq. ft.

Refer to **Pricing Schedule D** on the order form for pricing information

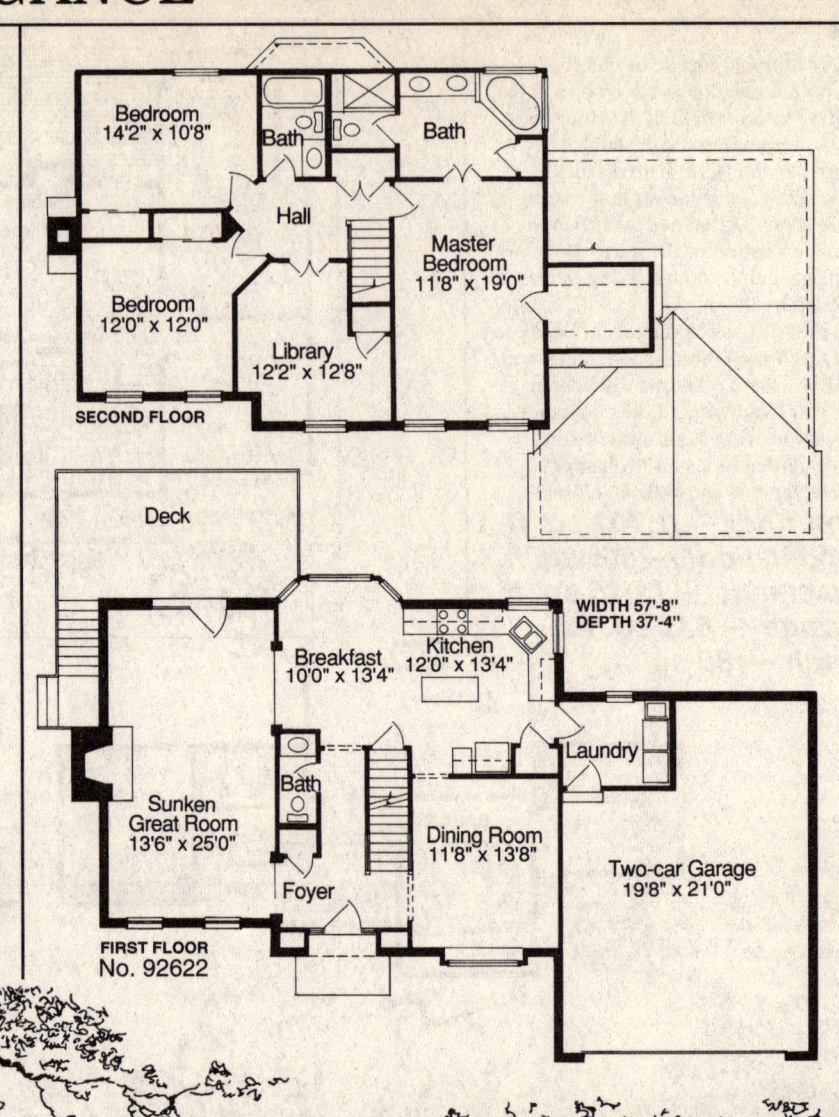

ORDER TODAY! 1-800-235-5700

Design 34005

DECORATIVE DETAILING ADDS CHARM

The covered entrance of this classy home adds a touch of charm and elegance. The living room features a cozy fireplace set between two windows and a sloped ceiling. Off the living room is the kitchen equipped with a plant shelf, perfect for growing a fresh herb garden. A patio is accessible through sliding glass doors, providing a quiet escape from everyday life confusion. The dining room features a beautifully designed ceiling enhancing formal occassions. Up a few stairs, past an octagonal window, is the sleeping wing. The master bedroom, also featuring a decorative ceiling, has a private bath and linen closet. A second bath is equipped with washer and dryer, located across the hall from the other two bedrooms.

Main floor — 1,441 sq. ft.
Basement — 769 sq. ft.
Garage — 672 sq. ft.

Total living area: 1,441 sq. ft.

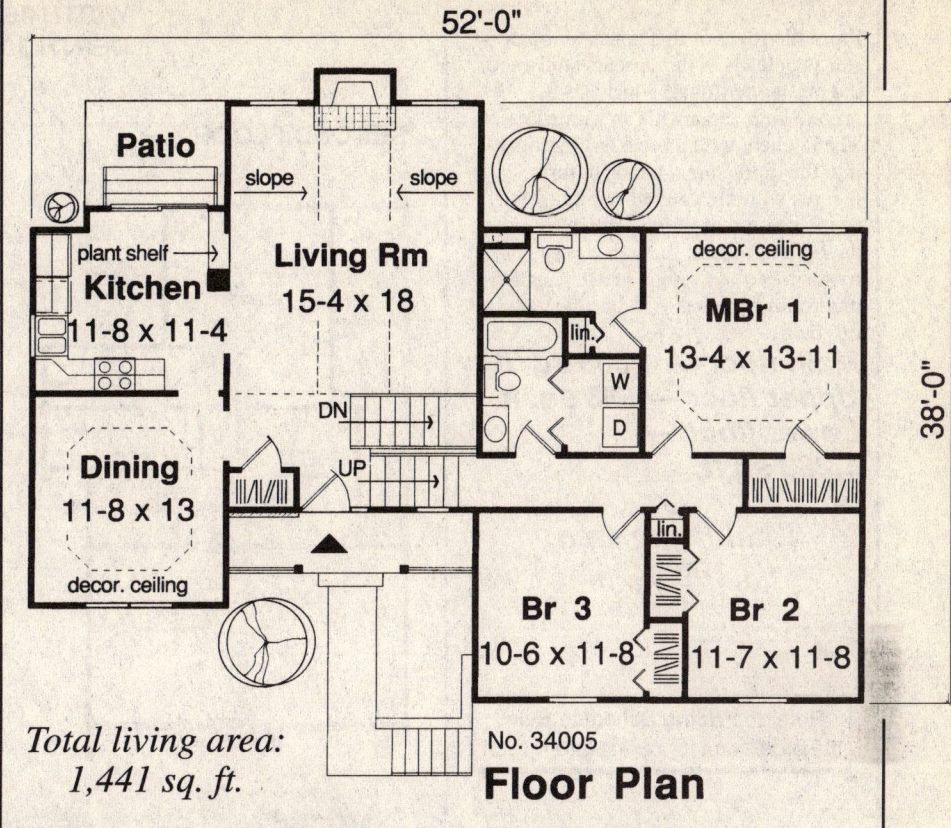

No. 34005
Floor Plan

Refer to **Pricing Schedule A** on the order form for pricing information

An EXCLUSIVE DESIGN *By Karl Kreeger*

All Seasons

Design 91319

From the foyer of this home, an open stairway leads to the upstairs study and the master bedroom, which has a private bath and a walk-in wardrobe. The kitchen, with a breakfast bar opens into the dining area, which in turn merges with the vaulted ceiling, stone-fireplaced living room. The full, daylight basement features a variety of rooms to serve storage, laundry, and mudroom purposes with an adjacent full bath.

Main floor — 1,306 sq. ft.
Upper floor — 598 sq. ft.
Lower floor — 1,288 sq. ft.

Total living area: 3,192 sq. ft.

Refer to **Pricing Schedule E** on the order form for pricing information

WIDTH 46'-0"
DEPTH 30'-0"

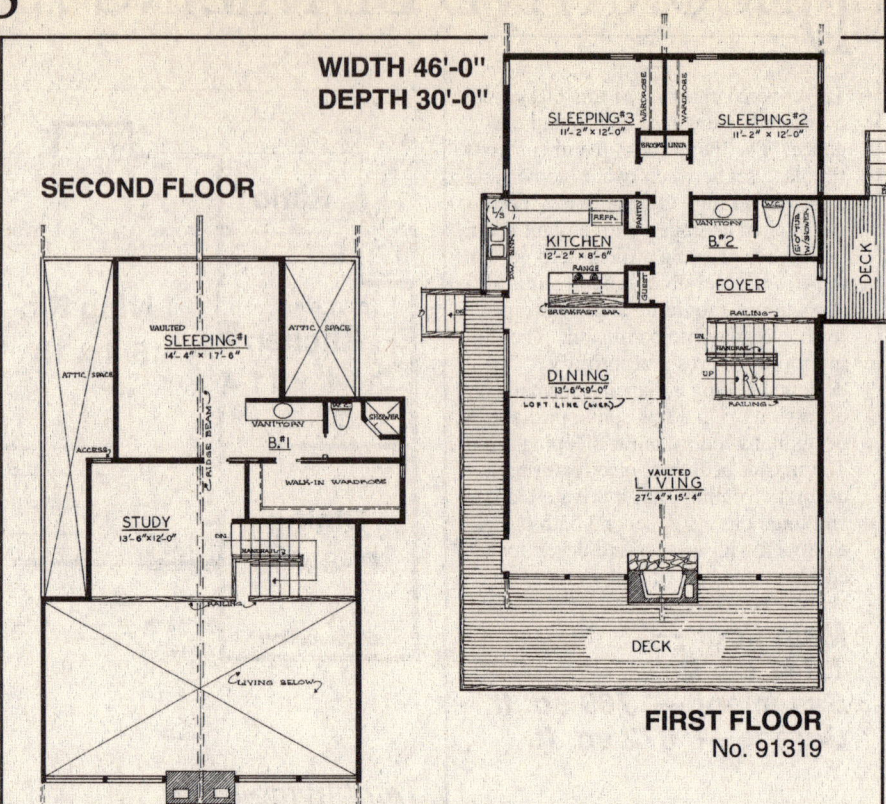

SECOND FLOOR

FIRST FLOOR
No. 91319

A-FRAME UPDATE

Design 90844

Here's a superb home that truly defines the term "open space". You'll feel the spectacular spaciousness of this updated A-frame the moment you walk past the foyer and peek through the galley kitchen. Savor the view through the two-story glass walls in the fireplaced living/dining room surrounded by an outdoor deck. Look up at the towering ceilings crowned by an open loft. Even the bedrooms are exceptionally large. The master suite, including a private powder room, and a second bedroom lie at the rear of the first floor, as well as an adjoining full bath. The loft overlooking active areas shares the second floor with an expansive bedroom with its own private deck and full bath.

First floor — 1,086 sq. ft.
Second floor — 466 sq. ft.
Basement — 1,080 sq. ft.

Total living area: 1,552 sq. ft.

Refer to **Pricing Schedule B** on the order form for pricing information

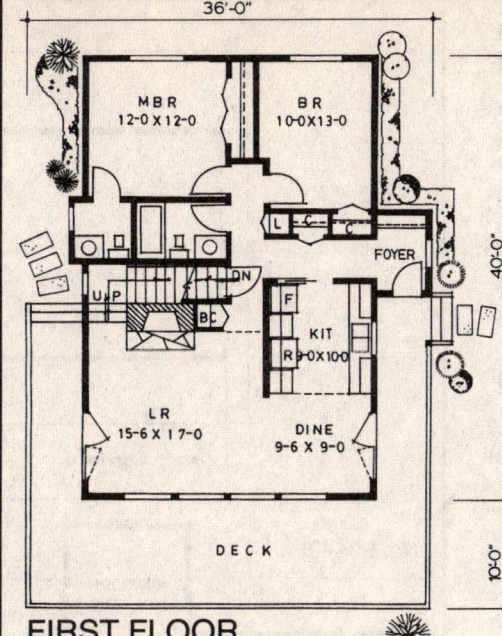

FIRST FLOOR
No. 90844

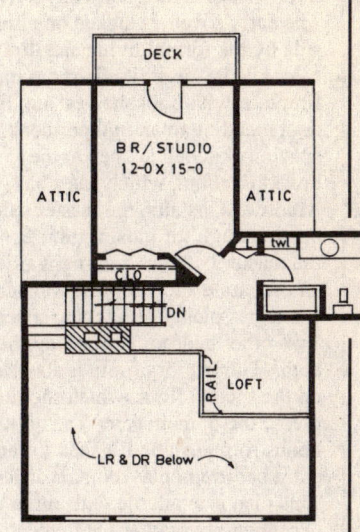

SECOND FLOOR

An EXCLUSIVE DESIGN *By Westhome Planners, Ltd.*

Classic Colonial with Ammenities

ORDER TODAY! 1-800-235-5700

Design 90449

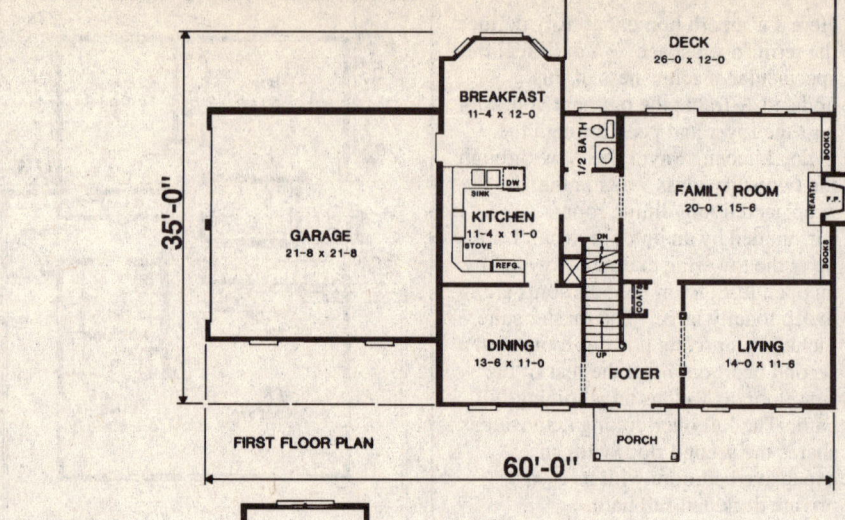

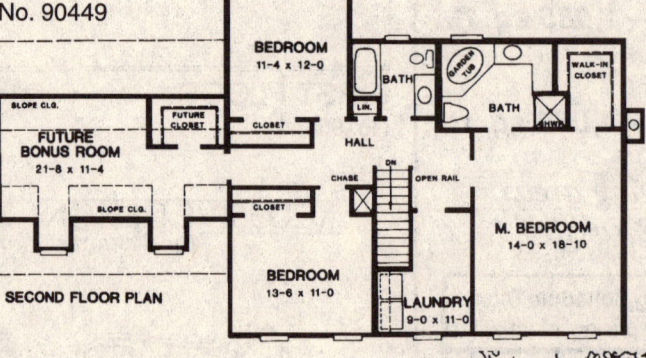

This Colonial two-story home has the exterior features of long ago, but the interior is designed for today's living. The entry foyer is flanked on either side by the formal living and dining rooms. The large family room has a fireplace with bookshelves, and French doors leading to an outdoor deck. The spacious kitchen is open to the breakfast room, which has a bay window. Upstairs, the master suite is large enough for most furniture, and the master bath has a corner garden tub and separate shower. The walk-in closet has plenty of hanging space. Two other bedrooms share another full bath. The laundry room is also located on the second floor, which should please the homemaker. The optional bonus room can be finished for an extra bedroom, playroom or office. This plan is available with either a basement or crawl space foundation. Please specify when ordering.

First floor — 1,138 sq. ft.
Second floor — 1,124 sq. ft.
Optional bonus — 284 sq. ft.
Basement — 1,124 sq. ft.
Garage — 484 sq. ft.

Total living area: 2,262 sq. ft.

Refer to **Pricing Schedule D** on the order form for pricing information

Cozy Country Trimmings

Design 34602

A wrap-around porch and dormer windows lend an old-fashioned country feeling to this home. Yet inside, a floor plan designed for today's lifestyle unfolds. A Great room enhanced by a large hearth fireplace and a vaulted ceiling gives a cozy welcome to guests. It is separated by the breakfast bar from the kitchen/dining area. An island extends the work space in this efficiently laid out area. The dining area has direct access to the rear yard. The first floor master suite also includes a vaulted ceiling and is highlighted by a private, double vanity bath. Two additional bedrooms on the second floor share a full double vanity bath in the hall.

First floor — 1,061 sq. ft.
Second floor — 499 sq. ft.
Basement — 1,061 sq. ft.

Total living area: 1,560 sq. ft.

Refer to **Pricing Schedule B** on the order form for pricing information

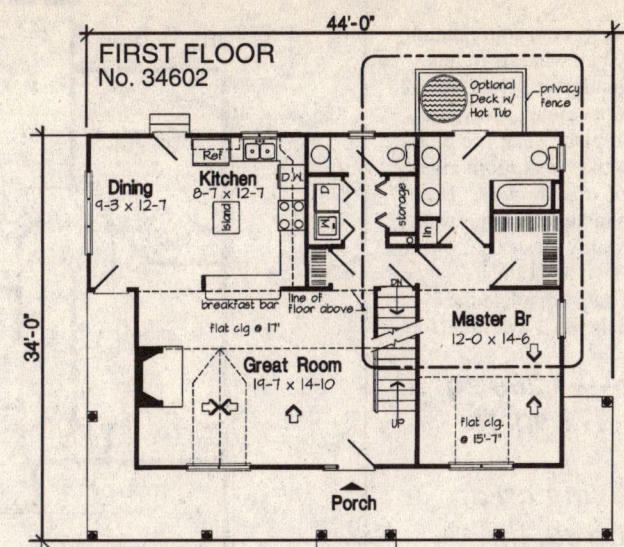

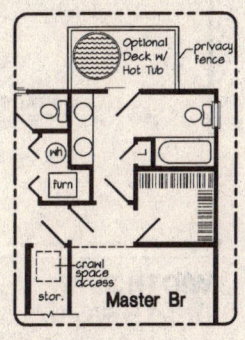

Alternate Foundation Plan

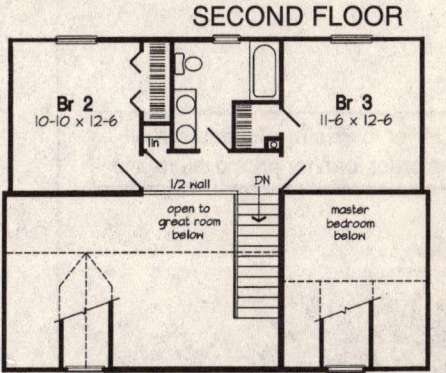

Accented with a Lovely Bay Window

Design 93024

A kitchen/breakfast room combination features a lovely bay window in this efficiently designed plan. The Great room with ten foot ceiling, showcases a flush hearth fireplace. The use of a higher ceiling in the Great room gives the impression of spaciousness. The master bedroom includes a large walk-in closet and a roomy master bath with double vanity. Two additional bedrooms and a bath complete the plan. No materials list is available for this plan.

Main floor — 1,268 sq. ft.
Garage — 471 sq. ft.

Total living area: 1,268 sq. ft.

Refer to **Pricing Schedule A** on the order form for pricing information

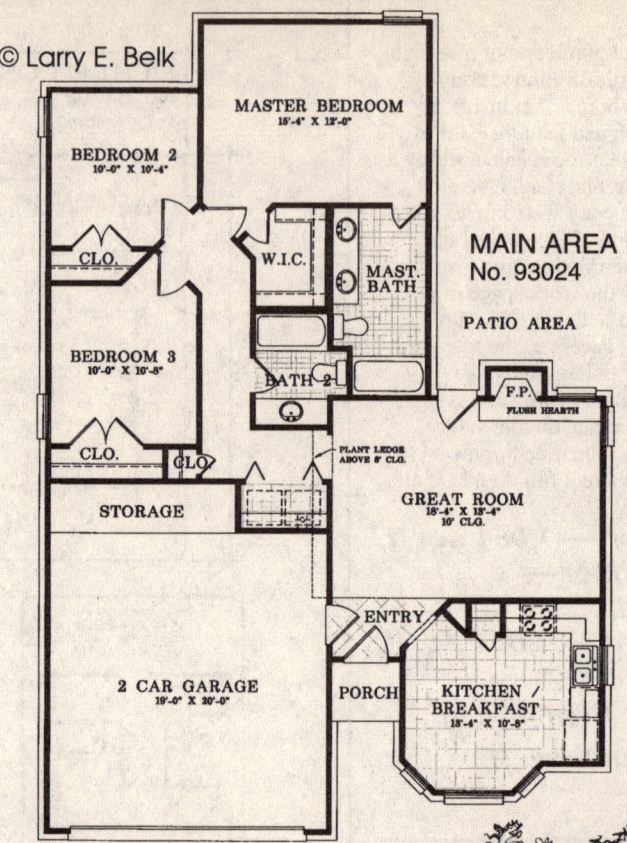

MAIN AREA
No. 93024

WIDTH 39'-2"
DEPTH 55'-10"

ORDER TODAY! 1-800-235-5700

UNUSUAL AND DRAMATIC

Design 92048

Unusual and dramatic would describe this 3,500 square foot two-story. When you step into the entry you are surrounded by arched doorways leading to the den on one side, the living/dining room on the other and the sunken family room straight ahead. The master bedroom is on the first floor and has two large walk-in closets and a master bath with a large sunken tub and double vanity. The kitchen area features an island with raised counter and lots of built-ins. Adjacent to the kitchen is an octagonal shaped breakfast room looking out over the deck. A first floor laundry and triple garage round out the main features of the first floor. A double curved stairway takes you upstairs to a balcony looking down over the family room, three more bedrooms and two full baths.

First floor — 2,646 sq. ft.
Second floor — 854 sq. ft.
Basement — 2,656 sq. ft.

Total living area: 3,500 sq. ft.

Refer to **Pricing Schedule F** on the order form for pricing information

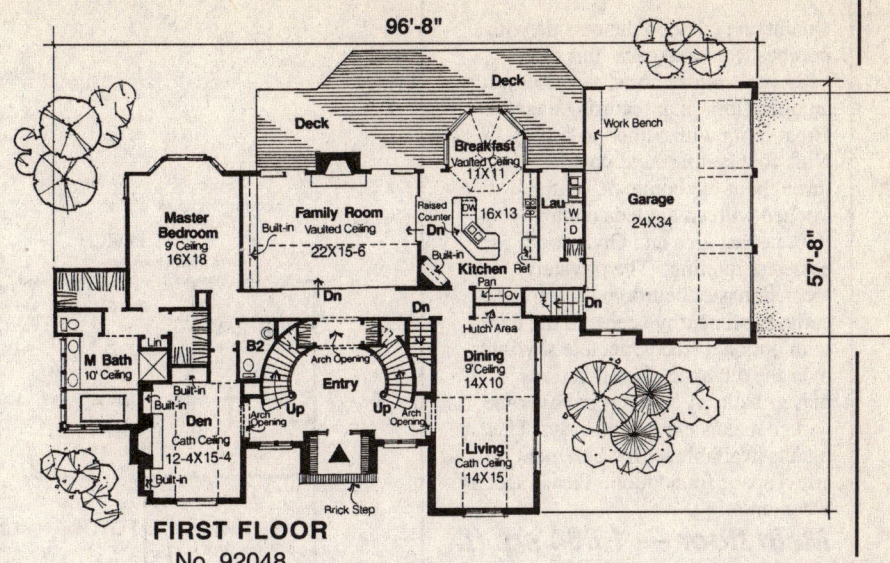

FIRST FLOOR
No. 92048

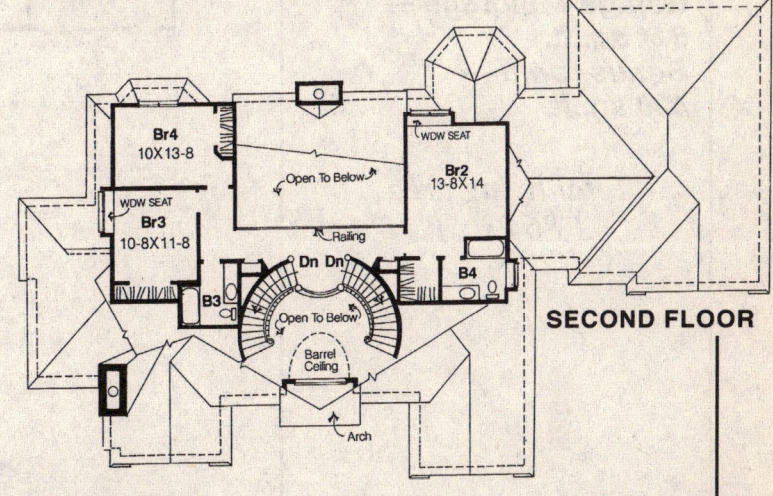

SECOND FLOOR

Quaint and Cozy

Design 99878

Quaint and cozy on the outside with porches front and back, this three-bedroom country home surprises with an open floor plan featuring a large Great room with cathedral ceiling. Nine foot ceilings add volume throughout the home. A central kitchen with an angled counter opens to breakfast area and Great room for easy entertaining. The privately located master bedroom has cathedral ceiling and nearby access to the deck with optional spa. Operable skylights over the tub accent the luxurious master bath. A bonus room over the garage makes expanding easy. This plan is available with a basement or crawl space foundation. Please specify when ordering.

Main floor — 1,864 sq. ft.
Garage & storage — 614 sq. ft.
Bonus room — 420 sq. ft.

Total living area:
1,864 sq. ft.

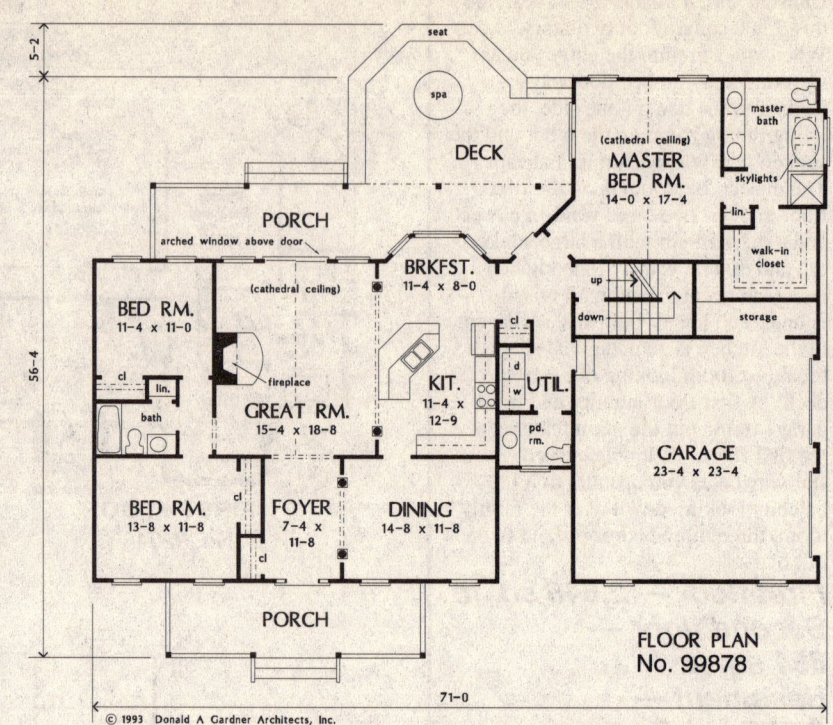

Refer to **Pricing Schedule C** on the order form for pricing information

© 1993 Donald A. Gardner Architects, Inc.

TRADITIONAL RANCH

Design 20220

This traditional ranch home adds a bit of drama to the convenience of a single level. The large front palladium window gives great curb appeal as well as a view of the front yard from the living room. The vaulted ceiling in the living room adds to the architectural interest and to the spacious feel of the room. The dining room adjoins the living room and has sliders to the wood deck. A built-in pantry, double sink and breakfast bar highlight the efficient kitchen. The private master suite is located at the opposite end of the house from the other bedrooms. A large walk-in closet and a private bath with a double vanity add to the convenience of the suite. The two additional bedrooms share the full hall bath.

Main area — 1,568 sq. ft.
Basement — 1,568 sq. ft.
Garage — 509 sq. ft.

Total living area: 1,568 sq. ft.

Refer to **Pricing Schedule B** on the order form for pricing information

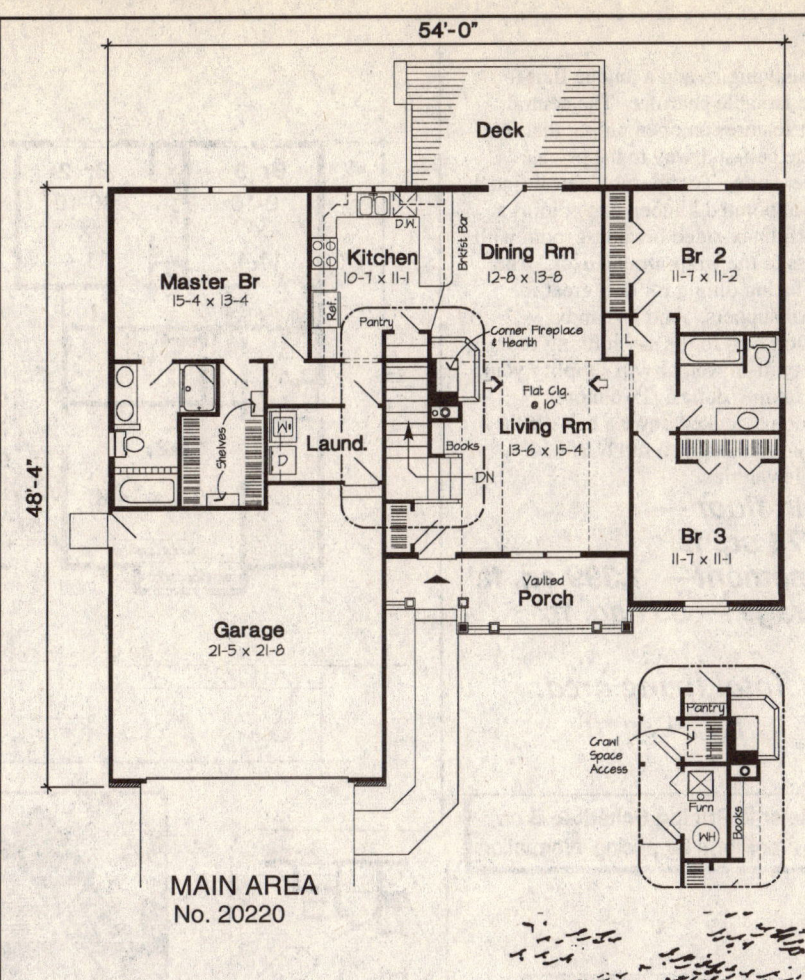

MAIN AREA
No. 20220

An EXCLUSIVE DESIGN *By Karl Kreeger*

ORDER TODAY! 1 - 800 - 235 - 5700

Design 20148

HILLSIDE HAVEN

Unusual angles add a unique flair to this adaptable charmer. The central foyer features an open railing that sets off the half-stairway to the private master suite. To the right, you'll find a well-appointed kitchen that adjoins a cheerful, six-sided breakfast room with access to the wrap-around deck. The rear-facing dining room is great for formal suppers. And its handy location next to the skylit living room with built-in wetbar will simplify your entertaining duties. Two more bedrooms, tucked down a hall off the living room, share a full bath with double vanities.

Main floor — 1,774 sq. ft.
Basement — 1,399 sq. ft.
Garage — 551 sq. ft.

Total living area: 1,774 sq. ft.

Refer to **Pricing Schedule B** on the order form for pricing information

An **EXCLUSIVE DESIGN** *By Karl Kreeger*

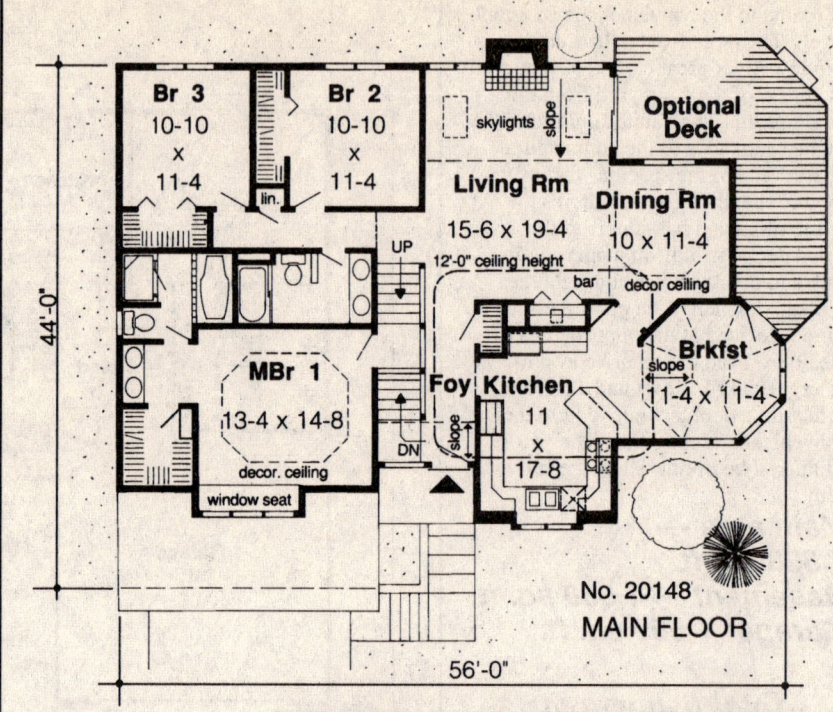

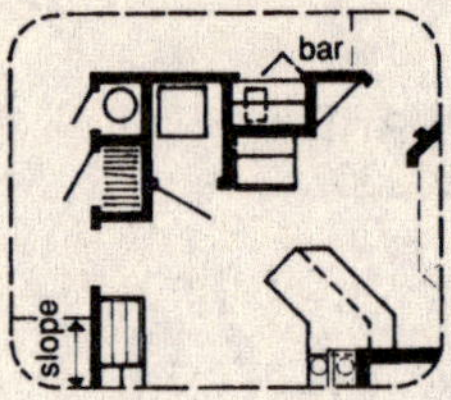

ORDER TODAY! 1 - 800 - 235 - 5700

An Executive Estate

Design 98539

A stately two-story covered entry, brick dormer window, and bay window with copper roofing, along with brick quoin corners and massive front chimney, provide a bold statement of success to all. Quality continues inside as well. A curved staircase flanked by a large living room with fireplace and adjacent to the formal dining room is sure to impress. A huge island kitchen and impressive master suite with bay window sitting area, and a luxurious bath with gigantic walk-in closet are included in this spectacular home. There other bedrooms, play room and a study are upstairs. This plan is available with a basement or slab foundation. Please specify when ordering. No materials list is available of this plan.

Main floor — 2,751 sq. ft.
Upper floor — 1,185 sq. ft.
Bonus room — 343 sq. ft.
Garage — 790 sq. ft.

Total living area: 3,936 sq. ft.

Refer to **Pricing Schedule F** on the order form for pricing information

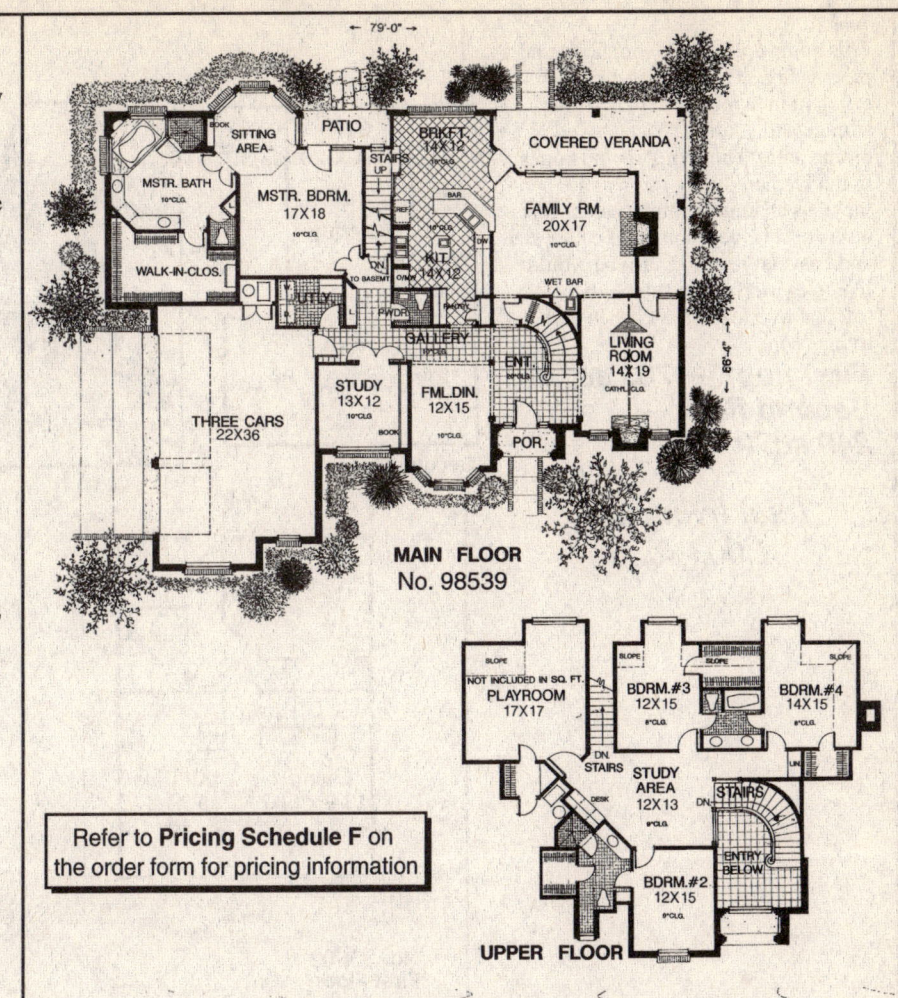

ORDER TODAY! 1-800-235-5700

Design 35009

SIMPLE AND PRACTICAL

This home epitomizes simplicity and practicality. The U-shaped kitchen is efficient in layout. There is ample storage and counter space as well as a dining area. The living room is open to the kitchen/dining room and includes an entertainment center that is built-in. The bedroom is of a nice size and has a large closet. If you would like to expand in the future, there is a loft that overlooks the kitchen and living room.

First floor — 763 sq. ft.
Second floor — 240 sq. ft.

Total living area: 1,003 sq. ft.

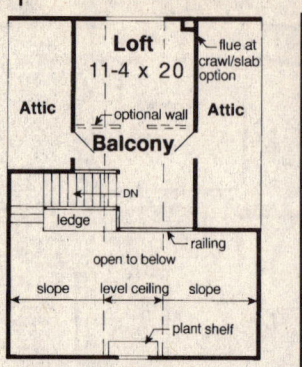

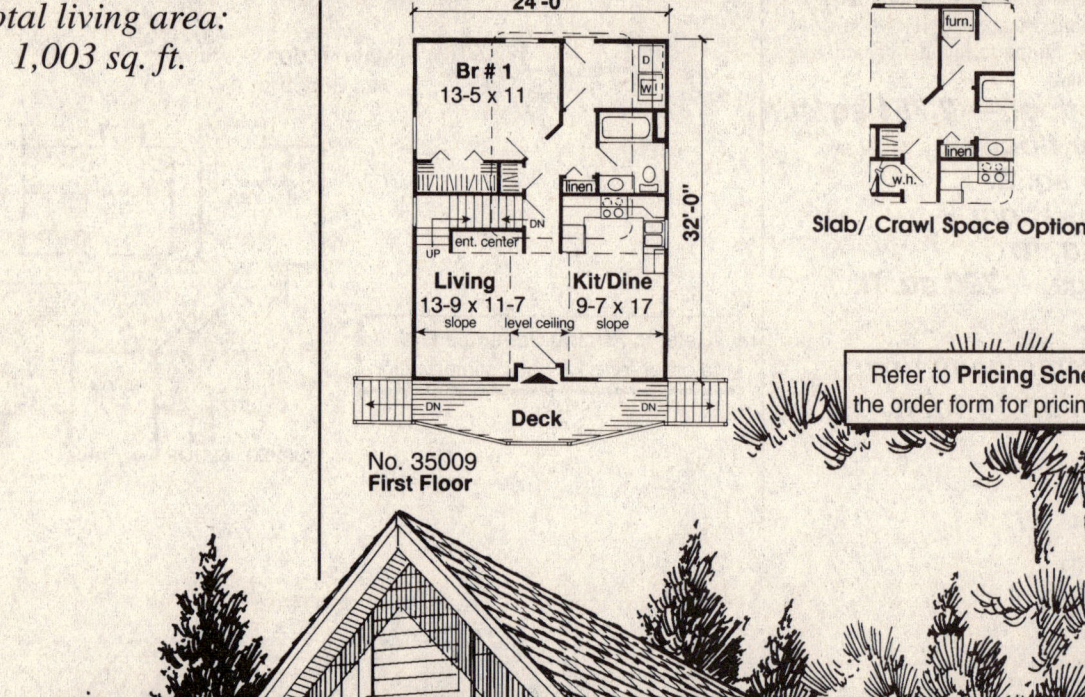

Refer to **Pricing Schedule A** on the order form for pricing information

ORDER TODAY! 1-800-235-5700

AN EXECUTIVE ESTATE

Design 98539

A stately two-story covered entry, brick dormer window, and bay window with copper roofing, along with brick quoin corners and massive front chimney, provide a bold statement of success to all. Quality continues inside as well. A curved staircase flanked by a large living room with fireplace and adjacent to the formal dining room is sure to impress. A huge island kitchen and impressive master suite with bay window sitting area, and a luxurious bath with gigantic walk-in closet are included in this spectacular home. There other bedrooms, play room and a study are upstairs. This plan is available with a basement or slab foundation. Please specify when ordering. No materials list is available of this plan.

Main floor — 2,751 sq. ft.
Upper floor — 1,185 sq. ft.
Bonus room — 343 sq. ft.
Garage — 790 sq. ft.

Total living area: 3,936 sq. ft.

Refer to **Pricing Schedule F** on the order form for pricing information

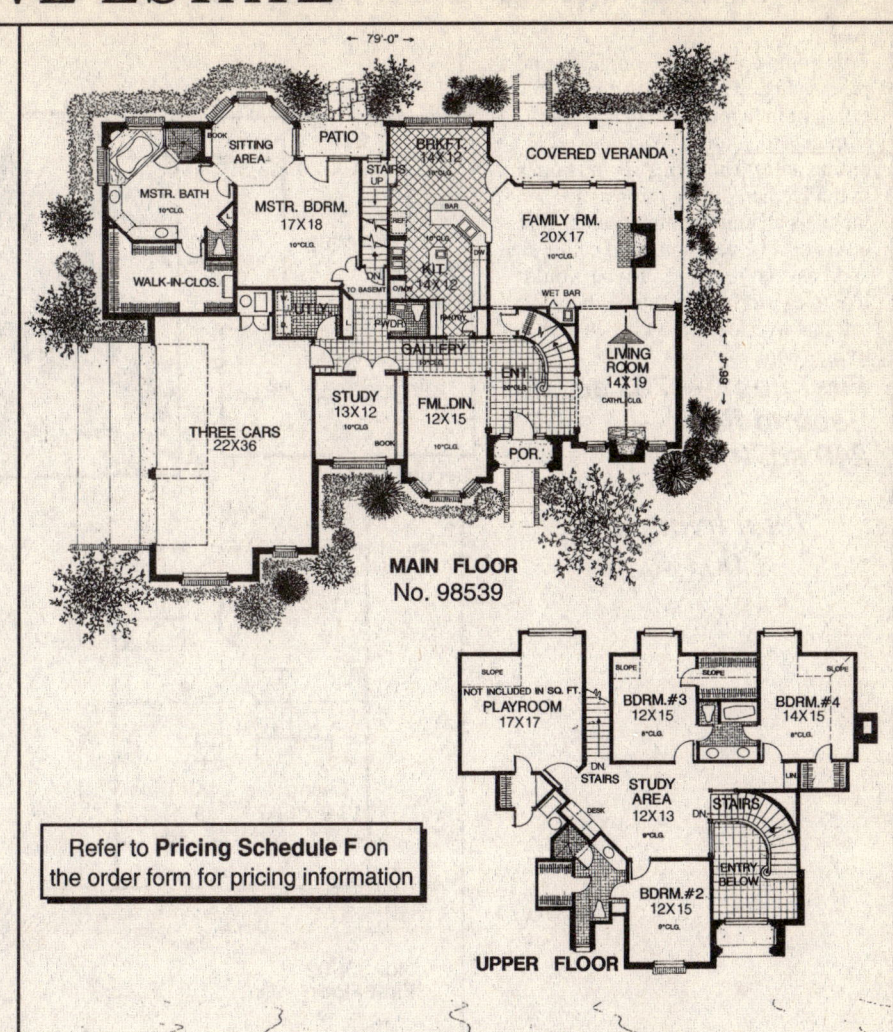

ORDER TODAY! 1-800-235-5700

Simple and Practical

Design 35009

This home epitomizes simplicity and practicality. The U-shaped kitchen is efficient in layout. There is ample storage and counter space as well as a dining area. The living room is open to the kitchen/dining room and includes an entertainment center that is built-in. The bedroom is of a nice size and has a large closet. If you would like to expand in the future, there is a loft that overlooks the kitchen and living room.

First floor — 763 sq. ft.
Second floor — 240 sq. ft.

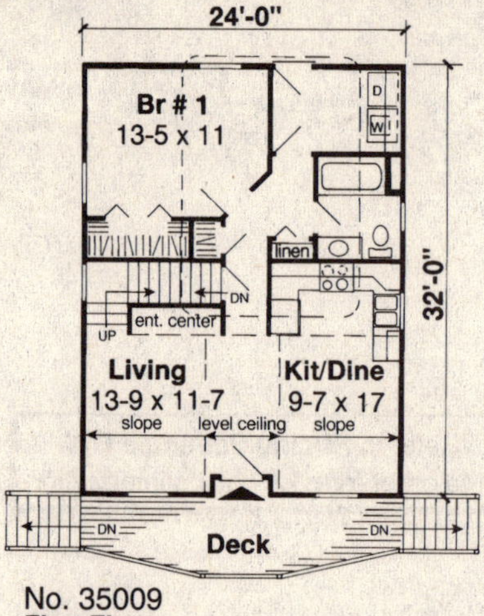

Total living area: 1,003 sq. ft.

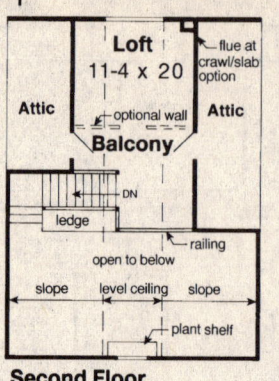

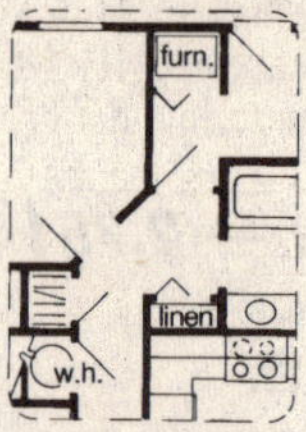

Refer to **Pricing Schedule A** on the order form for pricing information

Design 90941

GRADE-LEVEL ENTRY HOME

Looking for a grade-level-entry house that is a little different? Here is a multi-featured design with many desirable items. Entry from the double carport is through an attractive grade-level foyer, up an open staircase to the main floor. Once on the main floor, you will notice the attractive corner fireplace and high-vaulted ceiling of the living room. The entire living area is accessible to the large covered deck which provides for an excellent relationship between indoor-outdoor living spaces.

Main floor — 1,464 sq. ft.
Basement floor — 1,187 sq.ft.
Garage — 418 sq.ft.

Total living area:
2,651 sq. ft.

MAIN FLOOR PLAN

No. 90941

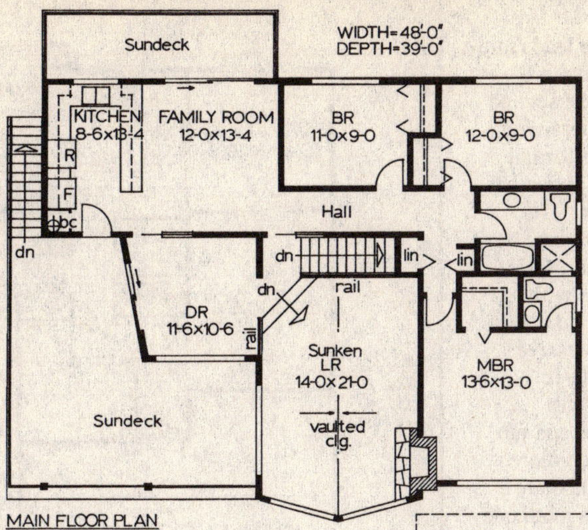

An EXCLUSIVE DESIGN *By Westhome Planners, Ltd.*

Refer to **Pricing Schedule E** on the order form for pricing information

BASEMENT FLOOR PLAN

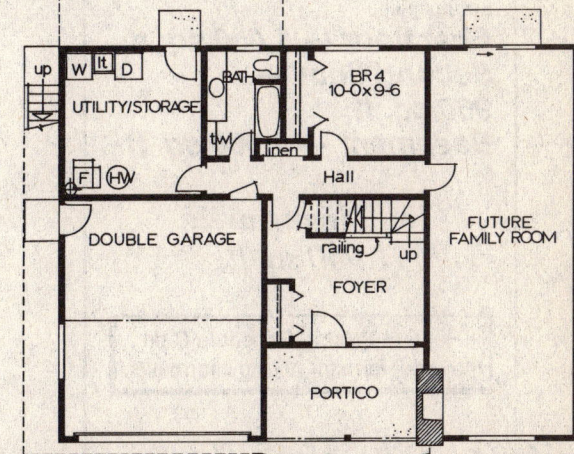

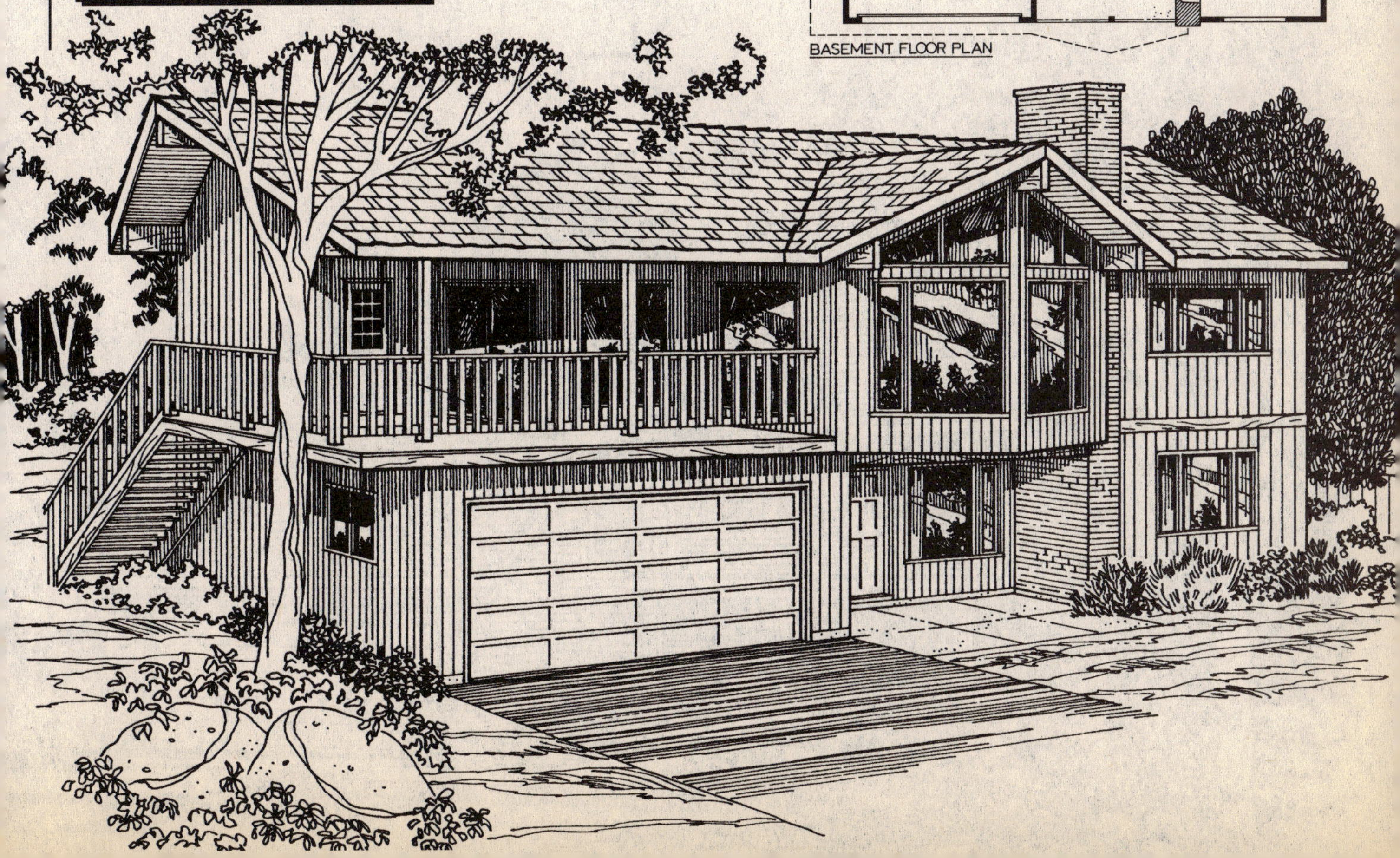

ORDER TODAY! 1 - 800 - 235 - 5700

Design 99129

ROOM FOR A LARGE FAMILY

The front porch of this home leads into the two-story foyer with an open L-shaped staircase leading to the second floor. To the left is a gracious living room with an archway to the formal dining room. The modern kitchen has a pantry and a planning desk. The large family room with a fireplace is perfect for large family gatherings. The first floor is rounded out with a guest bath and a convenient first floor laundry. Upstairs, is an impressive master suite with a large walk-in closet, and a private master bath featuring a sit-down vanity, a spa tub and a shower. There are three more bedrooms on this floor which share a full bath. No materials list is available for this plan.

First floor — 1,000 sq. ft.
Second floor — 960 sq. ft.
Basement — 1,000 sq. ft.

Total living area: 1,960 sq. ft.

Refer to **Pricing Schedule C** on the order form for pricing information

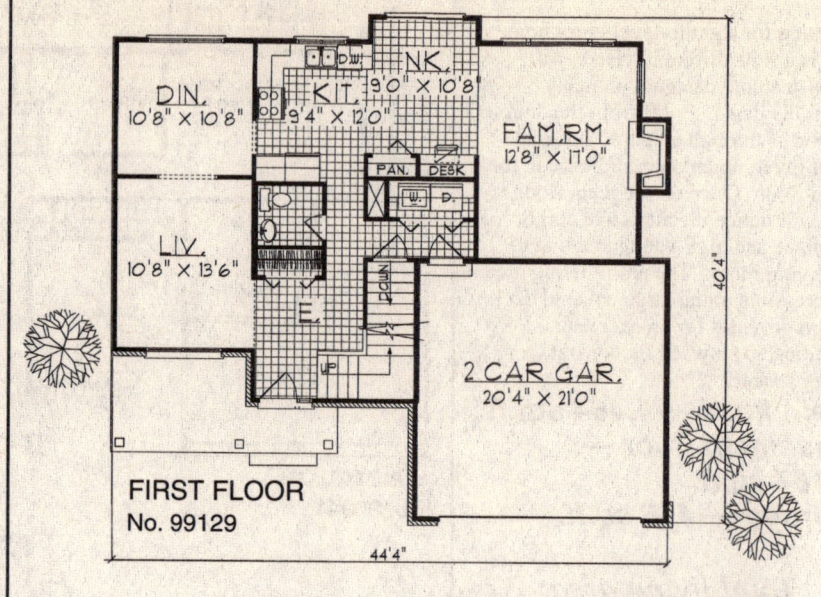

FIRST FLOOR
No. 99129

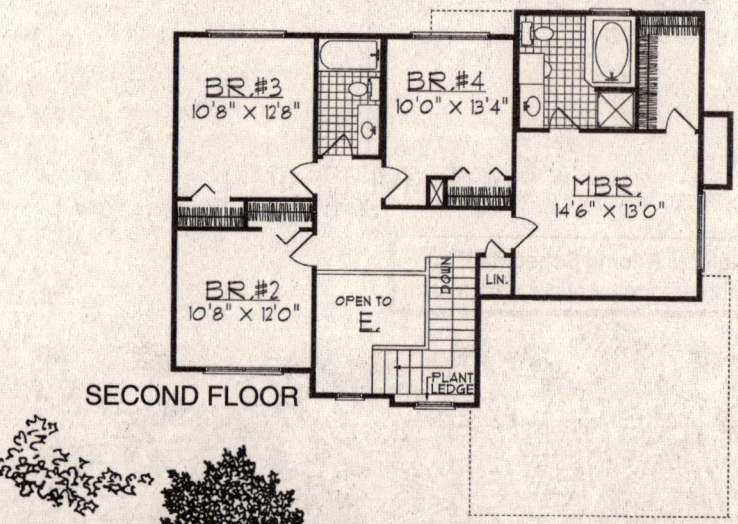

SECOND FLOOR

ORDER TODAY!   1 - 800 - 235 - 5700

Dine on the Deck

Design 10679

Here's a sunshine special with a character all its own. The covered porch opens to a spacious foyer dominated by a U-shaped staircase. Step to the right, past the powder room, and you'll enter a rear-facing master suite with his-and-her walk-in closets and a luxurious bath overlooking the deck. It's hard to miss the sunken living room to the left, with its expansive stacked windows and sloping ceiling, pierced by skylights. A rangetop island separates the efficient kitchen from the dining bay with windows on three sides. The window ledge over the sink is an ideal spot for an indoor herb garden. Upstairs, you'll find a full bath and two bedrooms, each with a walk-in closet.

First floor — 1,445 sq. ft.
Second floor — 739 sq. ft.
Basement — 1,229 sq. ft.
Garage — 724 sq. ft.

Total living area: 2,184 sq. ft.

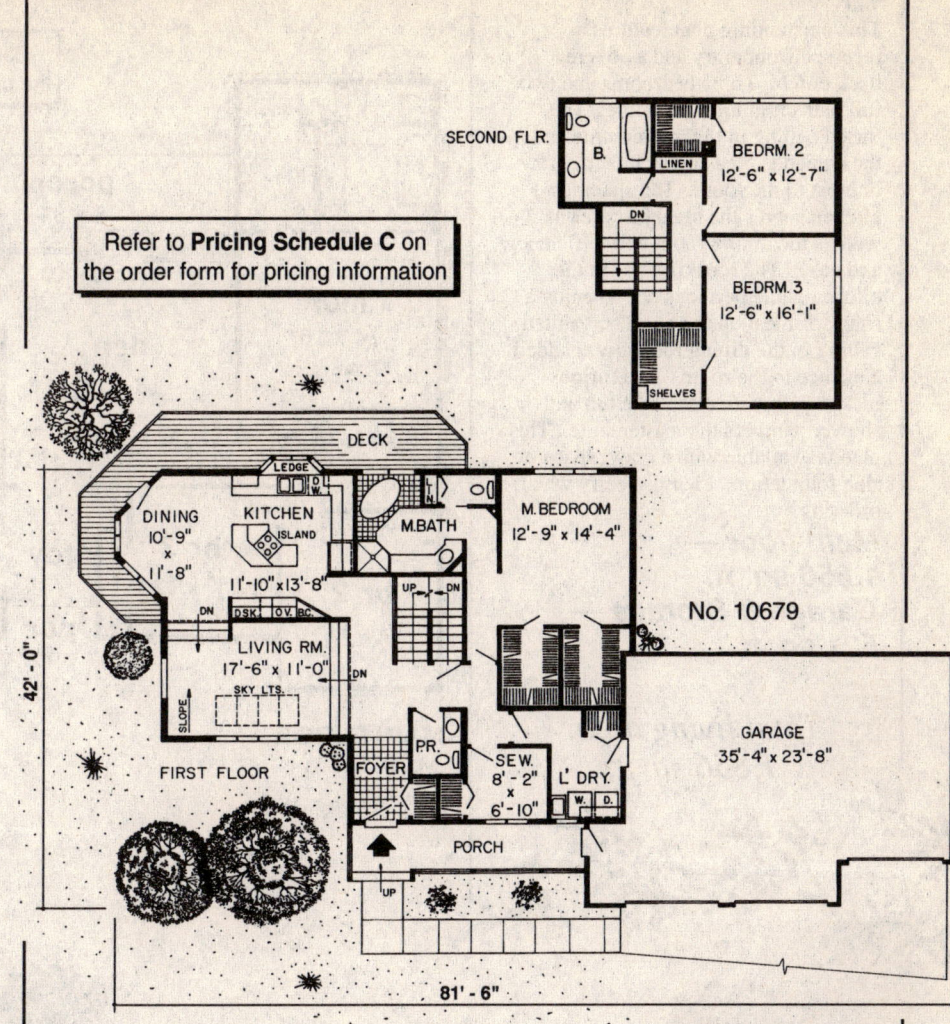

ORDER TODAY! 1 - 800 - 235 - 5700

Sophisticated European Stucco

Design 92562

This outstanding plan features a recessed front entry and a covered back porch. Three bedrooms and two full baths highlight the home. The raised ceiling in the master suite and in the den adds pleasing architectural interest to the room. The spacious kitchen serves the breakfast area as well as the dining room with efficiency and ease. The breakfast bar in the kitchen is the perfect place to enjoy a snack or meal on the go. The vaulted ceiling in the dining room gives added elegance to the room. A luxurious master bath with a separate tub and shower pampers the master suite. This plan is available with a crawl space or slab foundation. Please specify when ordering.

**Main floor —
1,856 sq. ft.
Garage & Storage —
521 sq. ft.**

*Total living area:
1,856 sq. ft.*

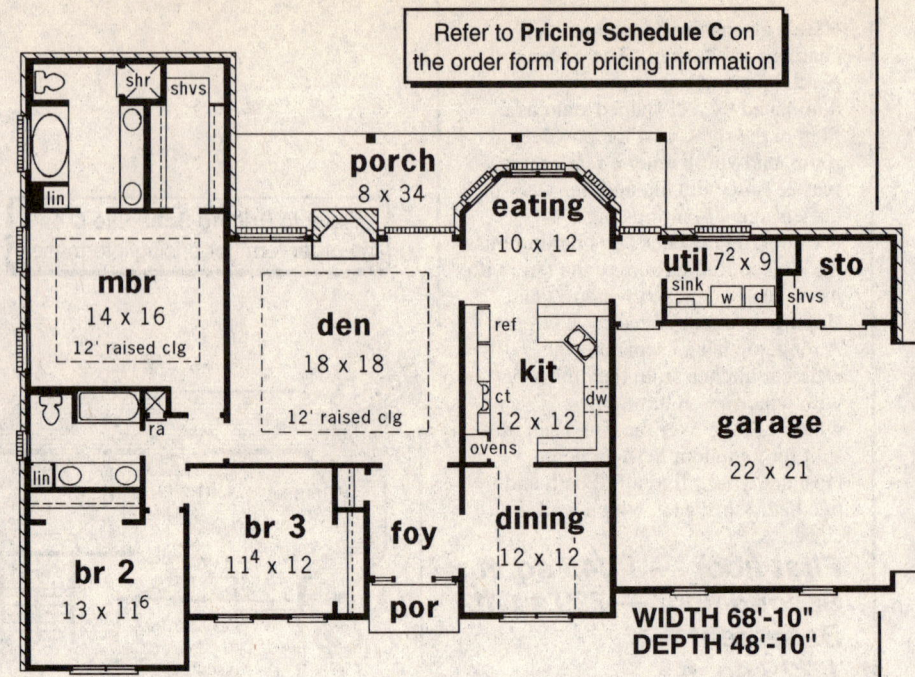

Refer to **Pricing Schedule C** on the order form for pricing information

MAIN FLOOR
No. 92562

WIDTH 68'-10"
DEPTH 48'-10"

ORDER TODAY! 1 - 800 - 235 - 5700

LOTS OF SPACE AND DRAMA

Design 90288

Here's a one-level home with an airy feeling accentuated by oversized windows and well-placed skylights. You'll love the attractive garden court that adds privacy to the front facing bedroom, the sheltered porch that opens to a central foyer, and the wide-open active areas. Two bedrooms, tucked down a hall off the foyer, include the sunny master suite with its sloping ceilings, private terrace entry, and luxurious garden bath with adjoining dressing room. The gathering room, study, and formal dining room flow together along the rear of the house, sharing the warmth of the gathering room fireplace, and a magnificent view of the terrace. Convenient pass-throughs add to the efficiency of the galley kitchen and adjoining breakfast room.

Main area — 1,387 sq. ft.
Garage — 440 sq. ft.

Total living area:
1,387 sq. ft.

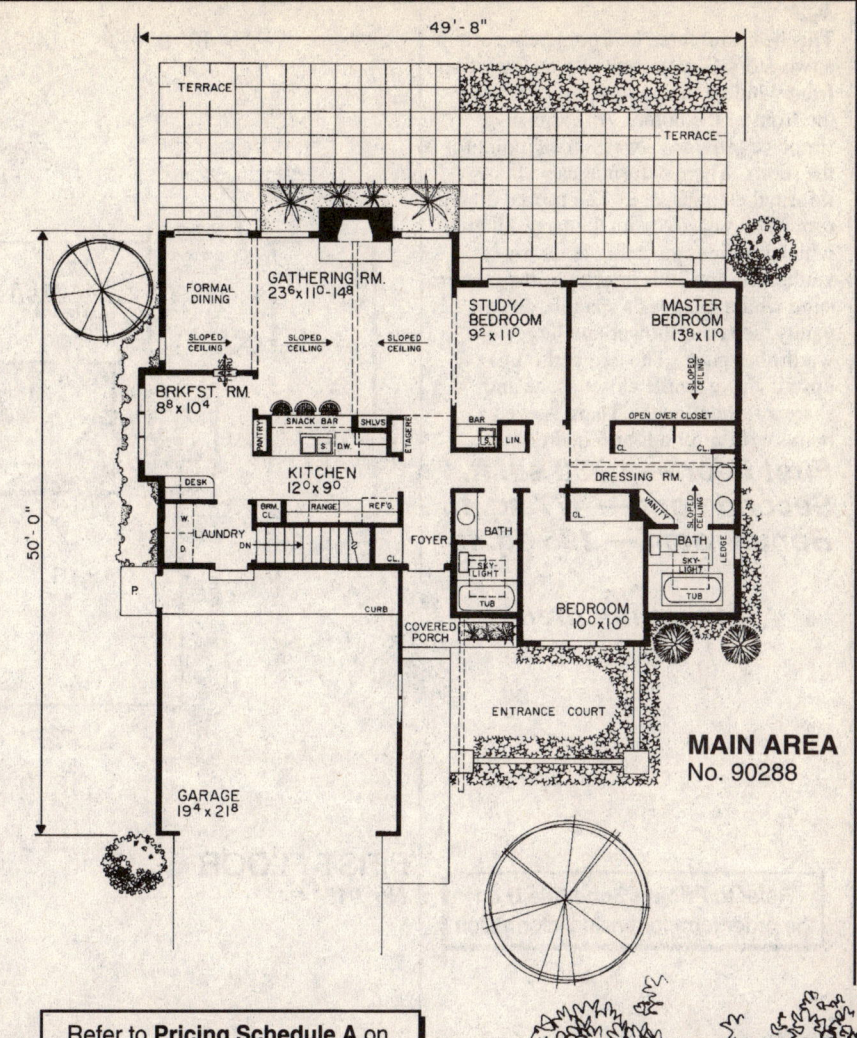

Refer to **Pricing Schedule A** on the order form for pricing information

STREAMING WITH NATURAL LIGHT

Design 91514

This beautiful three bedroom home offers a two-story Great room with an attractive front window that almost wraps around the front of the home. An exquisite fireplace provides a warm focal point for the room. There is formal as well as informal eating space. The formal dining room flows easily from the large kitchen which provides an eating nook. A vaulted ceiling adds interest to the master suite which includes a spa tub, double vanity, separate shower and large wardrobe space. The two bedrooms upstairs have ample closet space and share a full hall bath. There is even a bonus option for a fourth bedroom.

First floor — 1,230 sq. ft.
Second floor — 477 sq. ft.
Bonus room — 195 sq. ft.

Total living area: 1,707 sq. ft.

Refer to **Pricing Schedule B** on the order form for pricing information

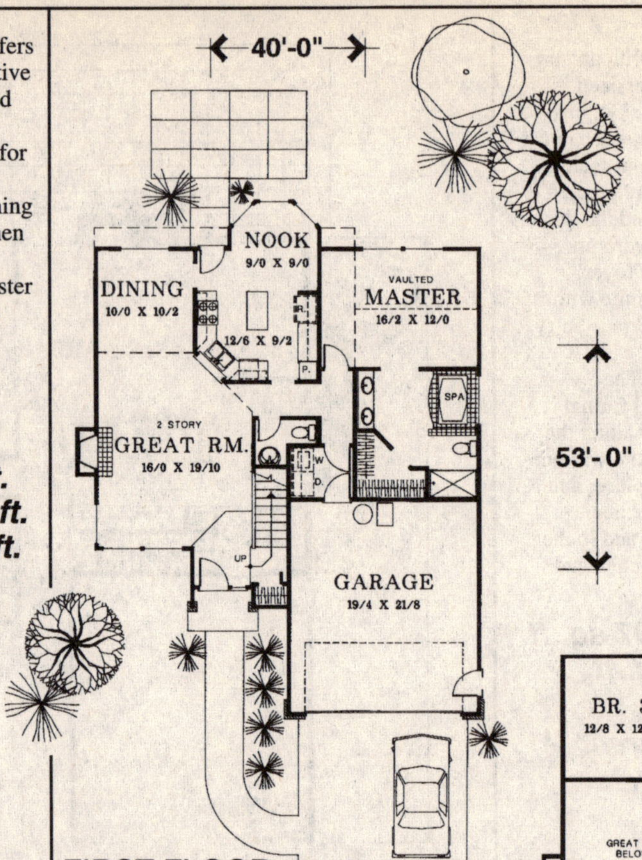

FIRST FLOOR
No. 91514

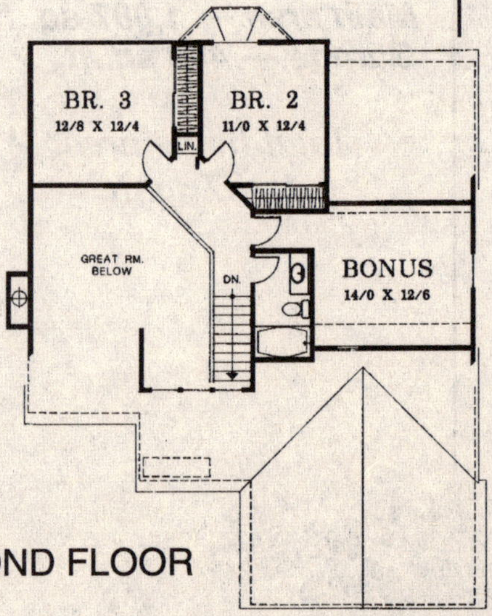

SECOND FLOOR

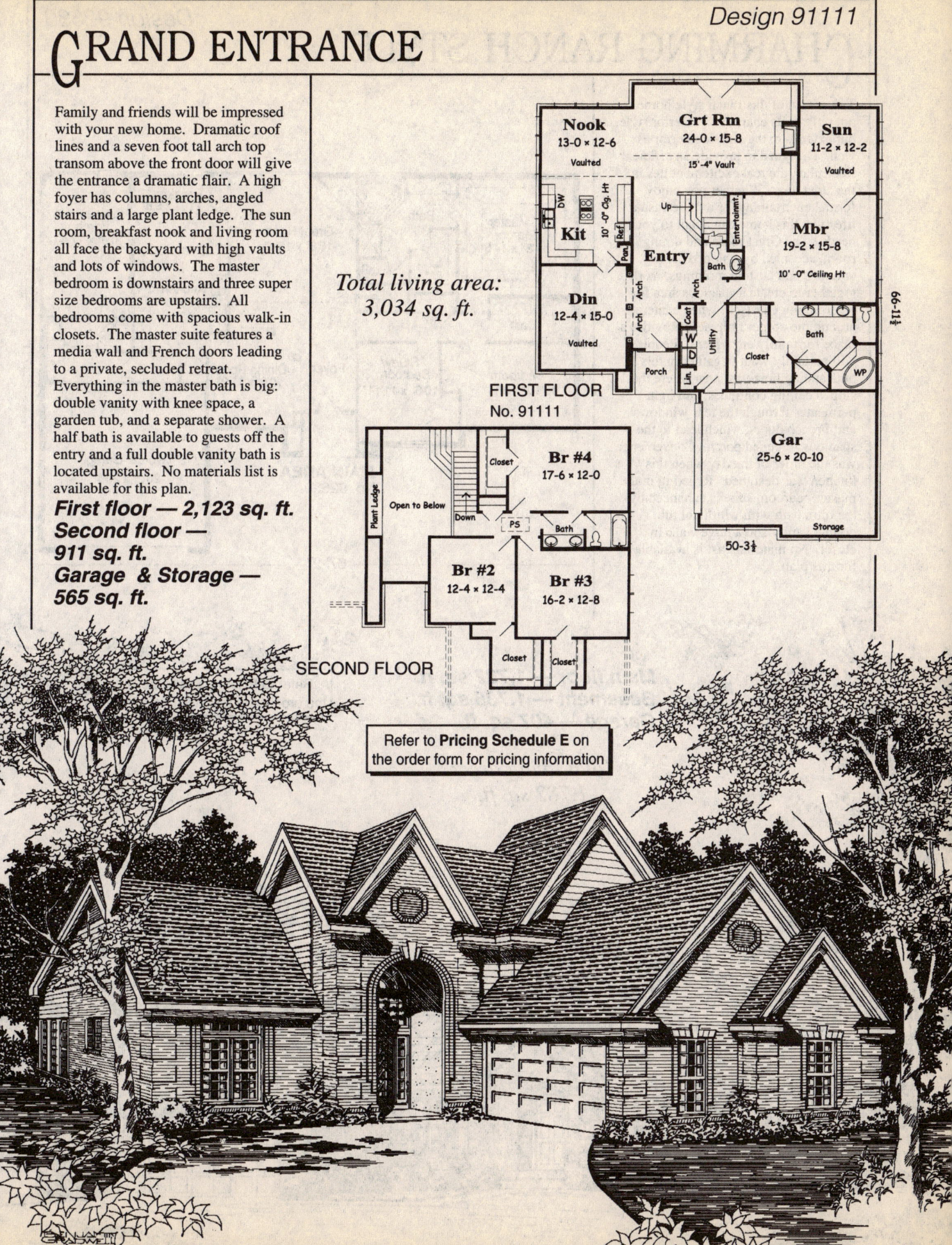

ORDER TODAY! 1-800-235-5700

Design 91111

GRAND ENTRANCE

Family and friends will be impressed with your new home. Dramatic roof lines and a seven foot tall arch top transom above the front door will give the entrance a dramatic flair. A high foyer has columns, arches, angled stairs and a large plant ledge. The sun room, breakfast nook and living room all face the backyard with high vaults and lots of windows. The master bedroom is downstairs and three super size bedrooms are upstairs. All bedrooms come with spacious walk-in closets. The master suite features a media wall and French doors leading to a private, secluded retreat. Everything in the master bath is big: double vanity with knee space, a garden tub, and a separate shower. A half bath is available to guests off the entry and a full double vanity bath is located upstairs. No materials list is available for this plan.

First floor — 2,123 sq. ft.
Second floor — 911 sq. ft.
Garage & Storage — 565 sq. ft.

Total living area: 3,034 sq. ft.

FIRST FLOOR No. 91111

SECOND FLOOR

Refer to **Pricing Schedule E** on the order form for pricing information

CHARMING RANCH STYLE

Design 92630

The appeal of this ranch style home is not only in its charm and exterior style, but extends to the classic interior as well. Designed to provide an efficient floor plan, the real excitement lies in the amenities. Whether you enjoy formal entertaining, or a more casual lifestyle, this home can adapt to your needs. The Great room and dining room, accented by a sloped ceiling, columns and custom moldings, work together to create a spacious area for entertaining guests, or when centered around the corner fireplace, provides a place for family enjoyment. People will naturally want to gather in this outstanding breakfast area where the sloped ceiling continues, and light permeates through the rear windows and French doors, which lead to the spacious screened porch. Convenience was the order of the day when this kitchen was designed. Relaxing in the master bedroom suite is enhanced by the ultra bath with whirlpool tub, double vanity and a large walk-in closet. No materials list is available for this plan.

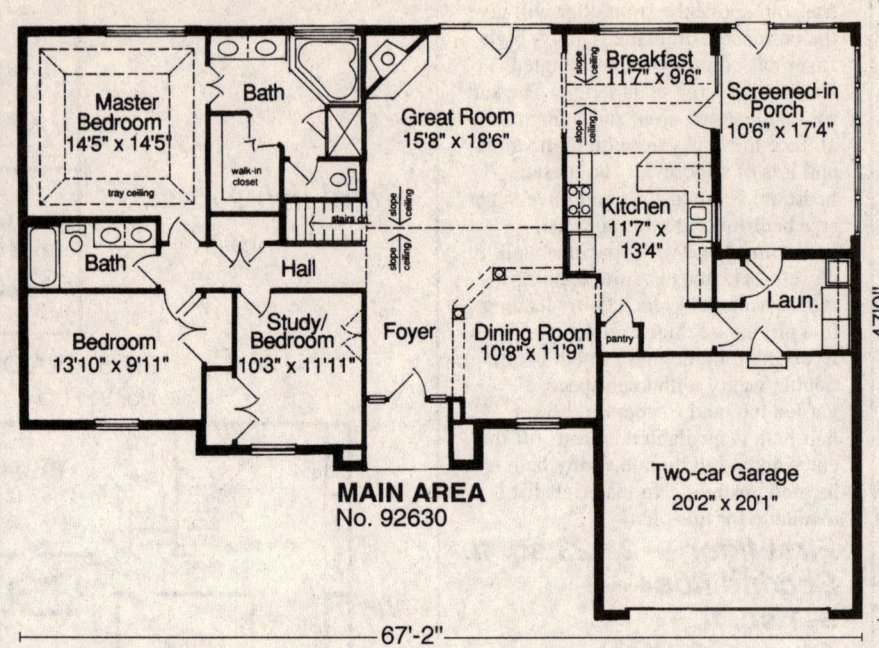

Main floor — 1,782 sq. ft.
Basement — 1,735 sq. ft.
Garage — 407 sq. ft.

Total living area:
1,782 sq. ft.

Refer to **Pricing Schedule B** on the order form for pricing information

INTERESTING ANGLES ADD STYLE

Design 92804

This home has a style all its own with the use of angles and windows. The wood deck provides the entrance area. Once inside the home, the living room is sunny and spacious with windows to the second floor. There is also a fireplace, providing warmth and atmosphere to the room. The kitchen/dining area also enjoys the use of angles in its shape. Efficiently layed out, the kitchen provides the cook of your family the room, cabinet space and appliances that allow less time preparing and more time relaxing and enjoying. There are two bedrooms on the first floor and a gorgeous master suite upstairs. The master suite includes a spa area and a private master bath. There is a balcony overlooking the living room. This plan is available with a basement, pole, slab or crawl space foundation. Please specify when ordering.

First floor — 1,051 sq. ft.
Second floor — 635 sq. ft.

Total living area: 1,686 sq. ft.

Refer to **Pricing Schedule B** on the order form for pricing information

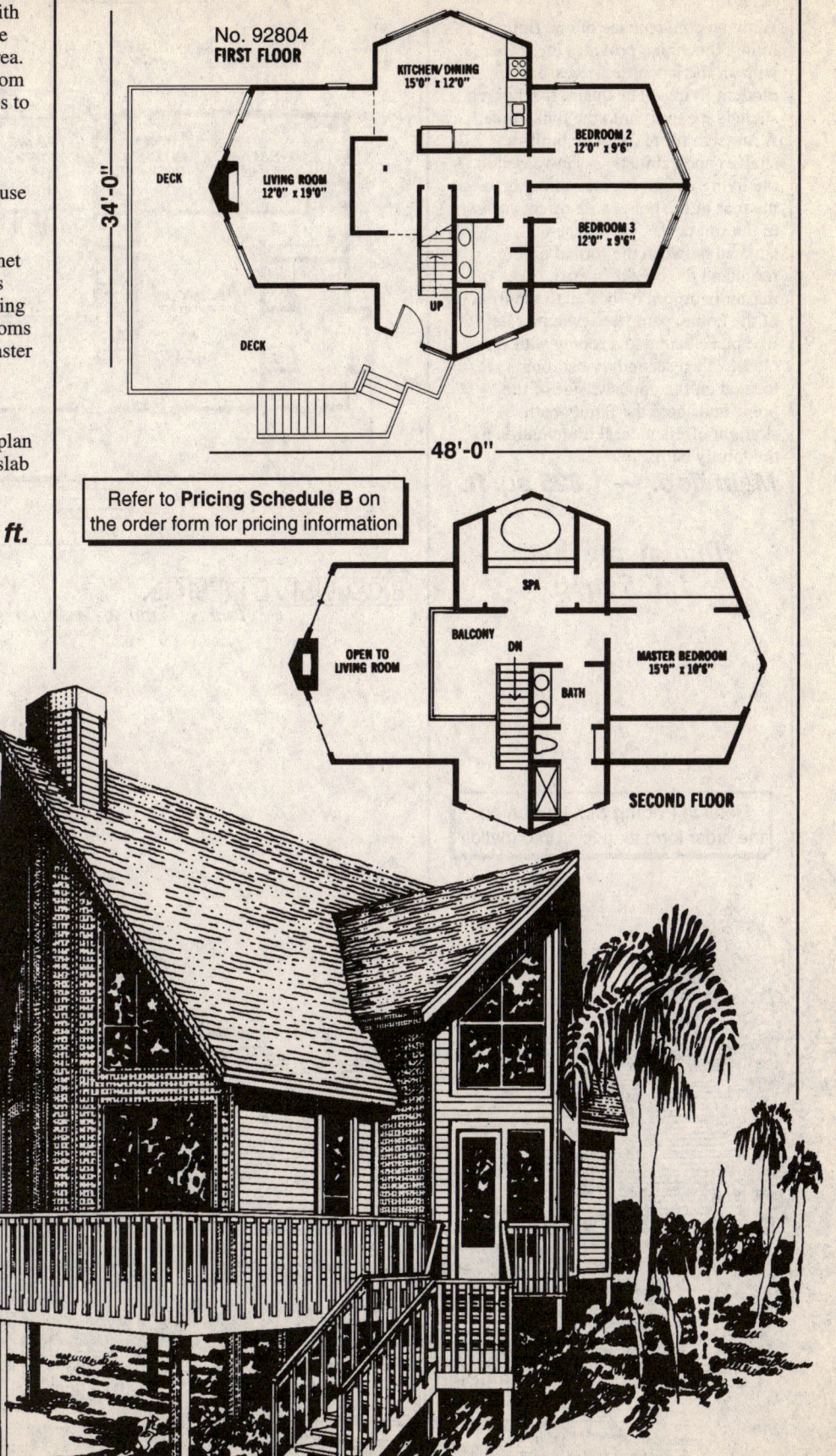

ORDER TODAY! 1-800-235-5700

Design 98912

SIMPLY COZY

With the convenience of one floor living, this home provides the owner with all the amenities necessary for modern living. The quaint front porch shelters the entry into the living area. A massive fireplace, with built-in shelves and cabinets, is showcased in the living room. Formal dining is to the rear of the home with direct access to the sun deck. The kitchen is situated between the formal dining room and the breakfast area. The master bedroom is located to the front of the home, pampered by a private five piece bath and a roomy walk-in closet. Two secondary bedrooms are located on the opposite side of the home and share the family bath. A skylight offers natural illumination to the family bath.

Main floor — 1,325 sq. ft.

Total living area: 1,325 sq. ft.

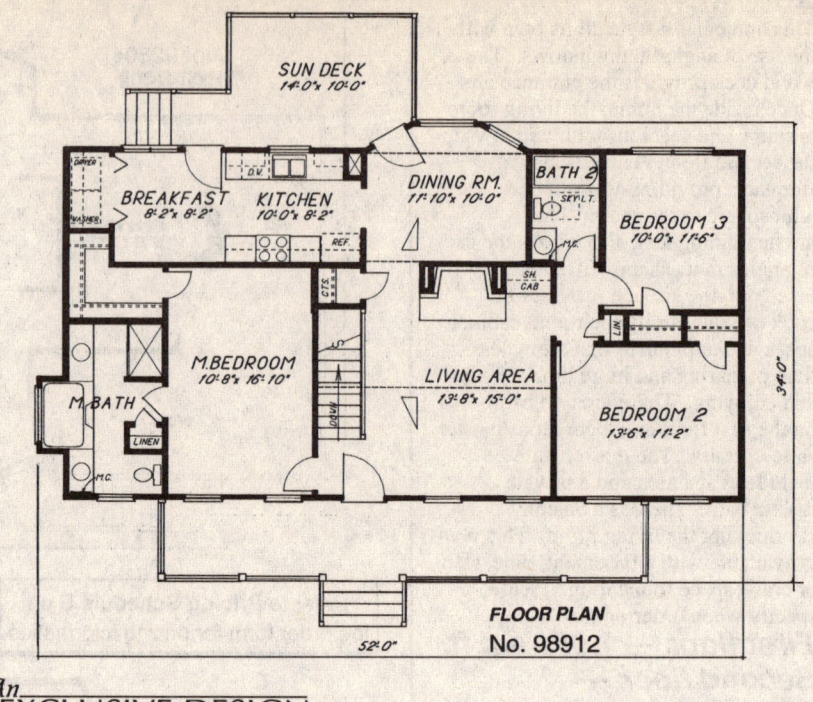

An **EXCLUSIVE DESIGN** *By Jannis Vann & Associates, Inc.*

Refer to **Pricing Schedule A** on the order form for pricing information

Traditional Splendor

Design 91339

A gourmet kitchen with an elegant eating bar that will comfortably seat seven people and open to the family room is a popular feature of this home. A large deck, conveniently located off the kitchen/family room is ideally suited for those summer barbecues. Note, also, the close proximity of the formal dining room to the kitchen. With 6 bedrooms and 4 1/2 bathrooms this home accommodates easily a large or extended family. The bayed sitting area in the master bedroom is an ideal quiet spot for the avid reader. The first floor (daylight basement to the rear) was designed for two guest rooms, a party room and a multipurpose area and full bath. No materials list is available for this plan.

First floor— 2,498 sq. ft.
Second floor— 1,190 sq. ft.

Total living area: 3,688 sq. ft.

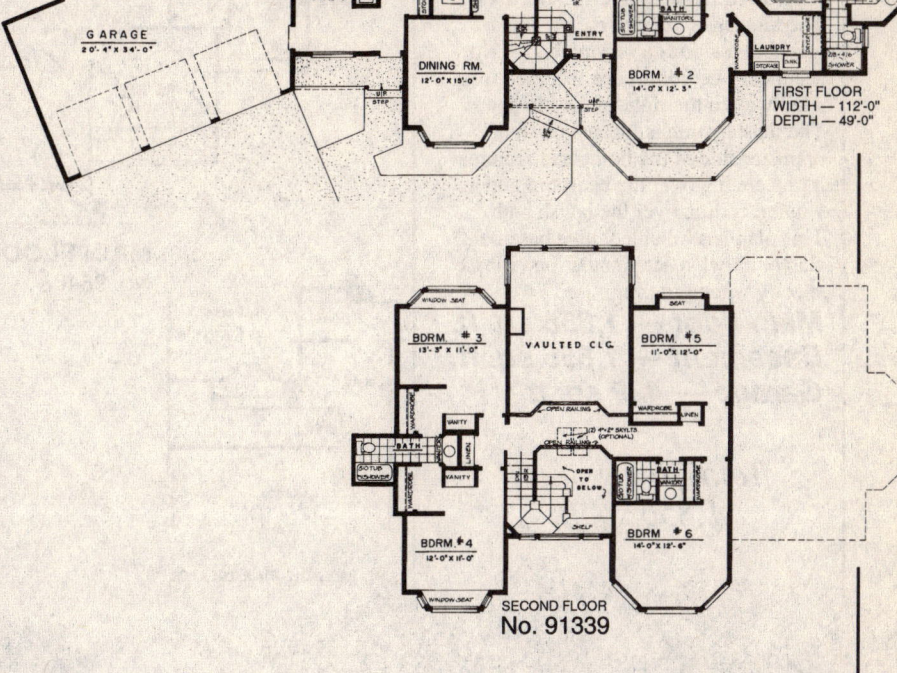

Refer to **Pricing Schedule F** on the order form for pricing information

ORDER TODAY! 1-800-235-5700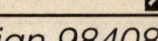

Design 98408

SOUTHERN STYLE

Columns and detailing dress this home with elegance. The feeling of true southern hospitality emanates from the covered porch. Inside, that homey feeling continues. From the foyer, through a decorative columned, arched opening, the visitor can see the glowing embers in the focal point fireplace of the family room. For formal entertaining the living room and dining room are located off the foyer to the right and left respectively. The kitchen is open to the breakfast area and includes a serving bar. Two secondary bedrooms are accessed from a hallway to the right of the kitchen. The master suite is located on the opposite side of the home and features a tray ceiling over the bedroom and a vaulted ceiling over the lavish bath. This plan is available with a basement, slab or crawl space foundation. Please specify when ordering.

Main floor — 1,856 sq. ft.
Basement — 1,856 sq. ft.
Garage — 429 sq. ft.

Total living area: 1,856 sq. ft.

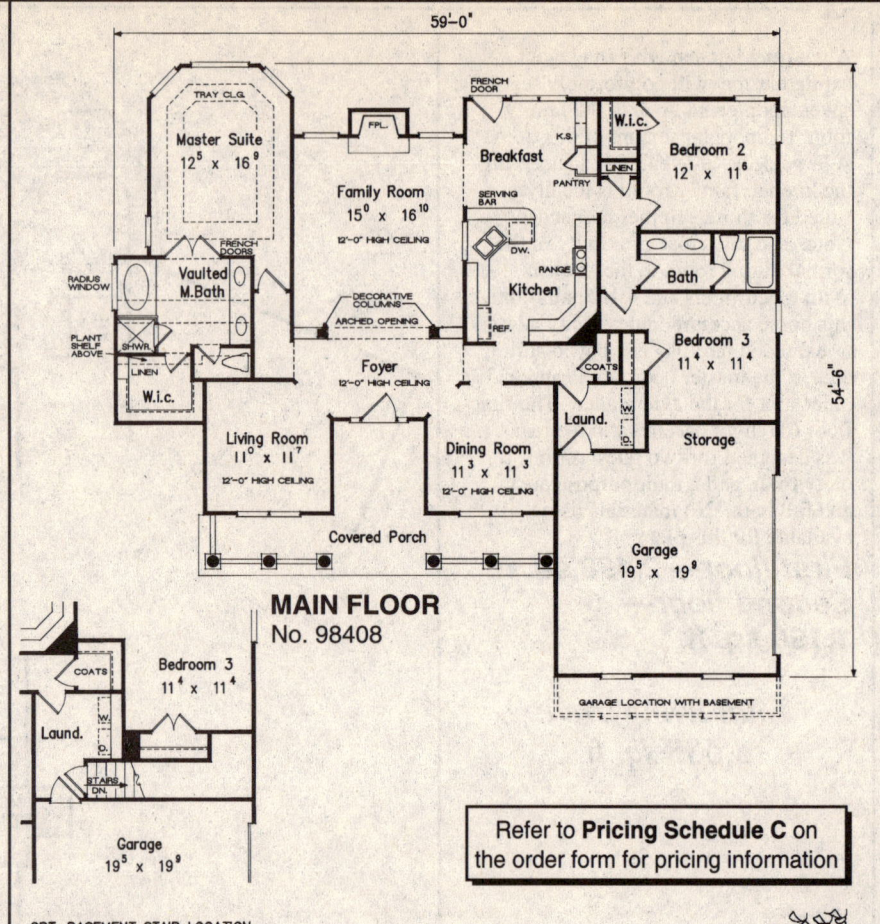

Refer to **Pricing Schedule C** on the order form for pricing information

PLENTY OF ROOM FOR YOUR BOAT

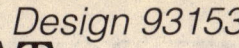
Design 93153

This three bedroom ranch has a unique three-car garage with access to the large main floor laundry room. The kitchen has plenty of counter and cupboard space, including room for a breakfast bar or sunny nook. The living and dining area both have high ceilings. The living room includes a fireplace flanked by built-in cabinetry. The dining area has french doors which lead to the screened in porch, with an optional deck looking over the back yard. Down the hall is the majestic master bedroom with large windows, an extra deep walk-in closet and a private bath featuring a double vanity, a linen cabinet, a free standing shower and a whirlpool tub. There are two more ample bedrooms which share a full bath. No materials list is available for this plan.

Main floor — 2,049 sq. ft.
Basement — 2,049 sq. ft.

Total living area:
2,049 sq. ft.

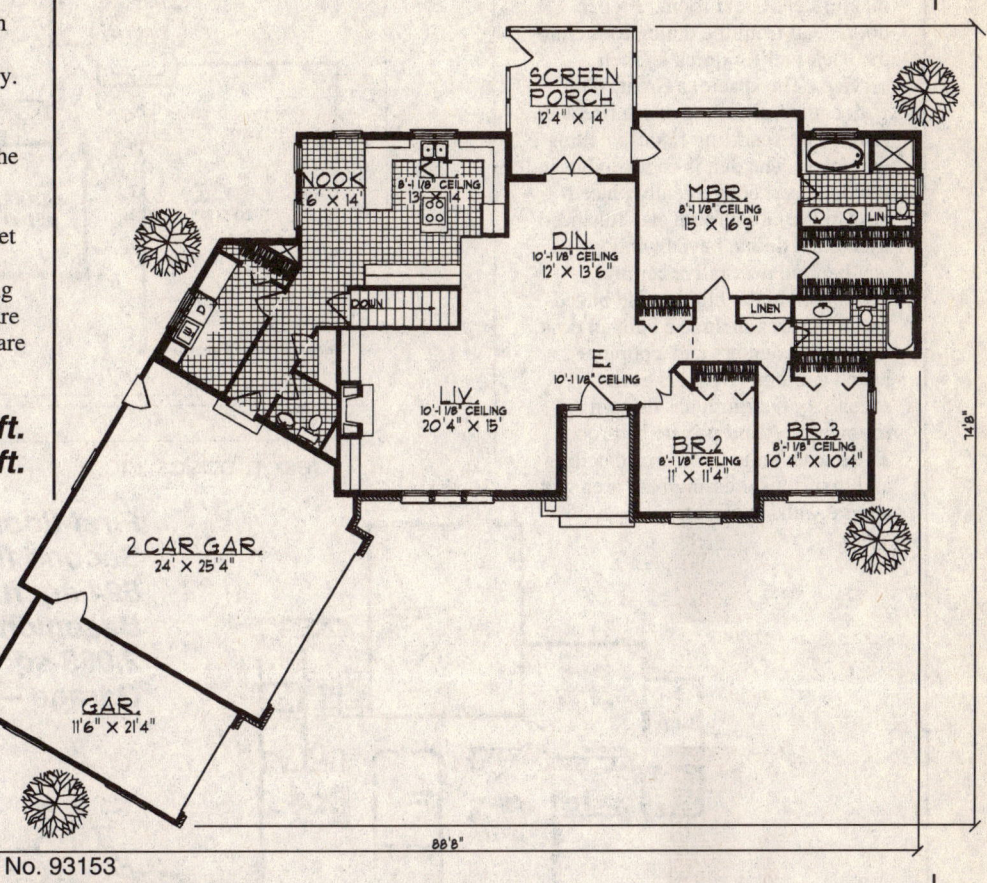

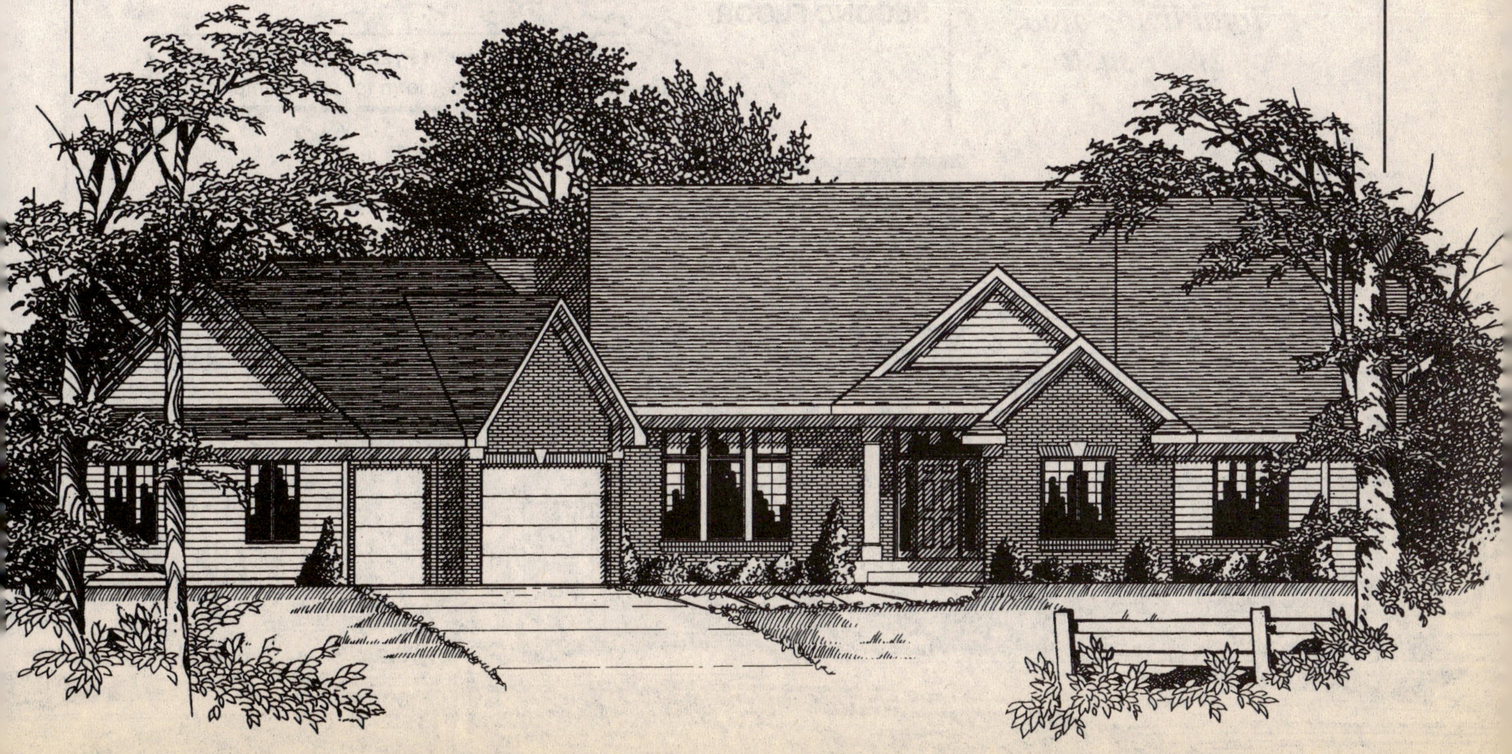

ELEGANT BRICK ELEVATION

Design 94994

This elegant brick elevation and rows of shuttered windows lend timeless beauty to this colonial design. A two-story entry hall surveys the formal dining and living room and views the magnificent Great room. French doors lead from the dining room into the back hall for quick kitchen service. The spacious Great room, with cathedral ceiling, has a fireplace flanked by sparkling floor to ceiling windows. The den is comfortable and secluded, yet conveniently placed next to the Great room and enhanced by French doors, bayed windows, a wet bar and decorative ceiling. Amenities in the kitchen and bayed breakfast area include a built-in desk, wrapping counters and a popular island counter. Upstairs each secondary bedroom has its own roomy closet and private bathroom. The master suite has a boxed ceiling and luxurious dressing/bath area with a large walk-in closet.

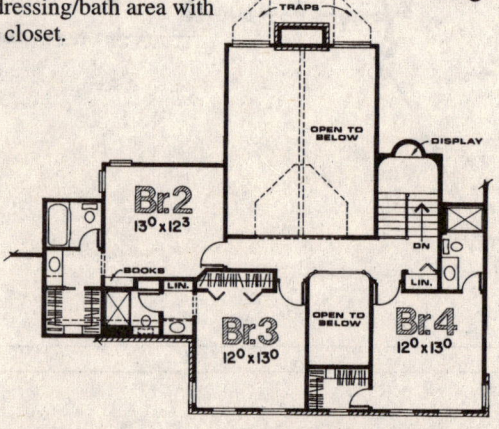

FIRST FLOOR
No. 94994

© design basics, inc.

SECOND FLOOR

Total living area: 2,957 sq. ft.

First floor — 2,063 sq. ft.
Second floor — 894 sq. ft.
Basement — 2,063 sq. ft.
Garage — 666 sq. ft.

Refer to **Pricing Schedule E** on the order form for pricing information

Classic Exterior, Modern Plan

Design 93118

This two-story brick home features the classic look of turn-of-the-century homes mixed with a contemporary floor plan. The bright two-story foyer is framed by an elegant dining room to the left and a den, for after hours work, on the right. The generous, island kitchen opens into a breakfast area surrounded by glass — perfect for reading the morning paper. The enticing master suite features a sitting area that makes the perfect getaway. Upstairs you'll enjoy a dramatic view of both the foyer and the family room below as you cross the bridge to any of the three additional bedrooms, all with walk-in closets and one with a private bath. No materials list is available for this plan.

Main floor — 2,385 sq. ft.
Second floor — 1,012 sq. ft.
Basement — 2,385 sq. ft.
Garage — 846 sq. ft.

Total living area: 3,397 sq. ft.

This plan is not to be built within a 75 mile radius of Cedar Rapids, IA

Refer to **Pricing Schedule F** on the order form for pricing information

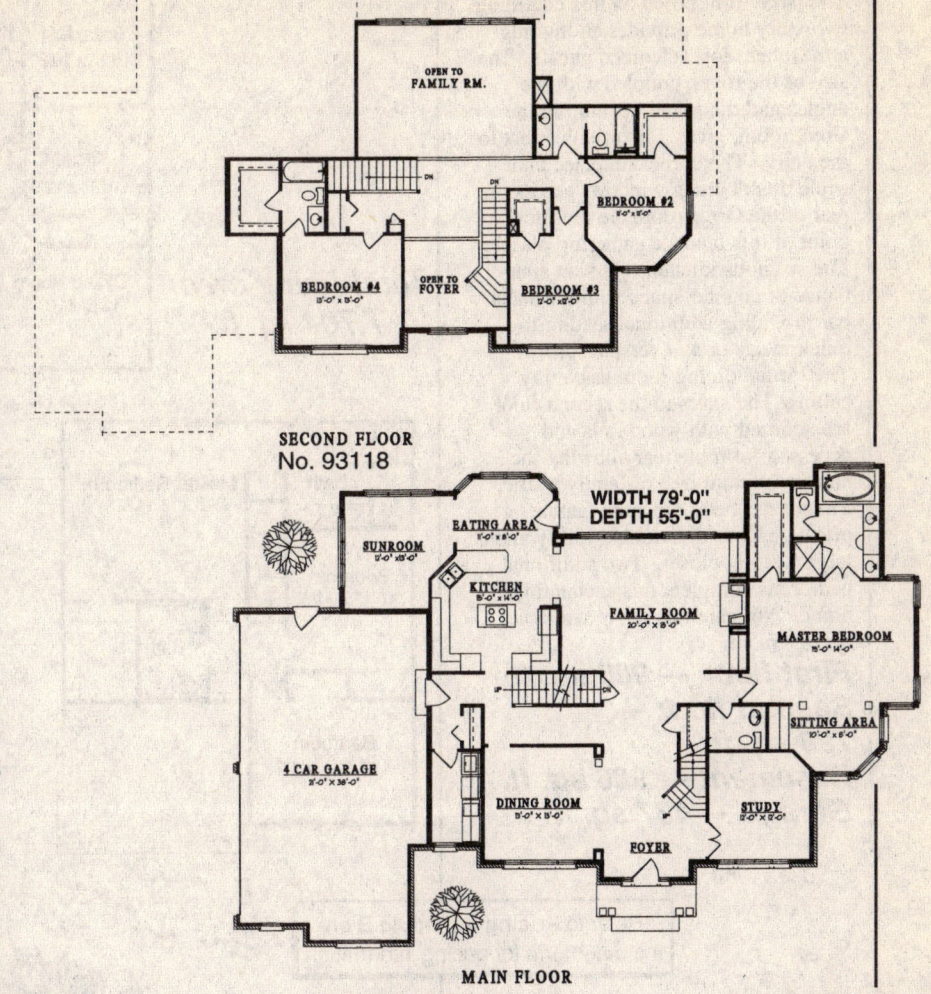

ENCHANTING HOME WITH ATMOSPHERE

Design 92695

The large front porch on this charming two-story home provides an inviting atmosphere for welcomed guests. The size of the foyer, coupled with the angles and the grand opening to the Great room, gives a luxurious effect to the entry. The corner fireplace and triple double hung windows across the rear of the Great room are the focal point of this favorite gathering place. The spacious kitchen offers an abundance of counter space with the snack bar providing additional seating for quick meals or an oversized crowd. The formal dining room has a tray ceiling. The stairs to the second floor are adorned with wood rails and accessed from the rear allowing the entry to remain free of family traffic. The master bedroom suite features a private bath with a double vanity and a large walk-in closet. Two additional bedrooms complete this enchanting home. No materials list is available for this plan.

First floor — 906 sq. ft.
Second floor — 798 sq. ft.
Basement — 906 sq. ft.
Garage — 437 sq. ft.

Total living area: 1,704 sq. ft.

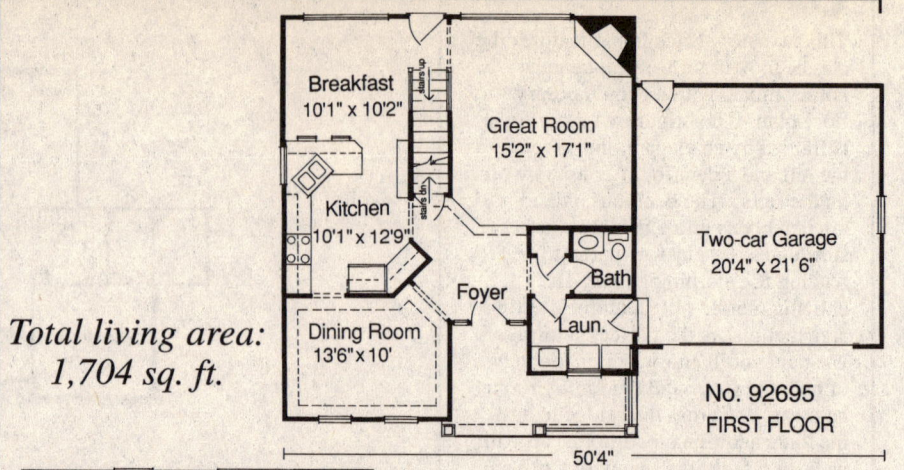

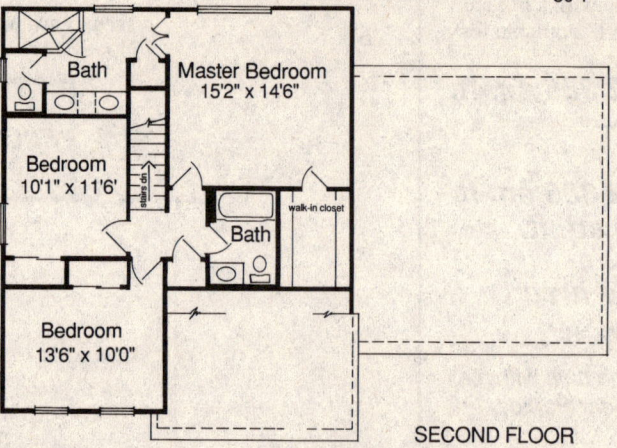

Refer to **Pricing Schedule B** on the order form for pricing information

STATELY RANCH

Design 93165

This brick and siding ranch has much to offer. The foyer leads into the Great room with cathedral ceilings and direct vent corner gas fireplace. There are arched pass-throughs to the kitchen. The kitchen has all of the amenities including plenty of cupboard and counter space. The adjoining dining area has large windows and a glass door leading to the back yard, and a screen porch. The private master suite has a large walk-in closet and full bath with corner whirlpool tub and free standing shower. Two more bedrooms can be found off the Great room. Both have large closets, and share a full bath. From the two car garage, you will enter into the main floor laundry with a large closet for storage. This plan is not to be built within a 20 mile radius of Iowa city, Iowa.

Main floor — 1,472 sq. ft.
Basement — 1,472 sq. ft.

Total living area: 1,472 sq. ft.

No materials list available

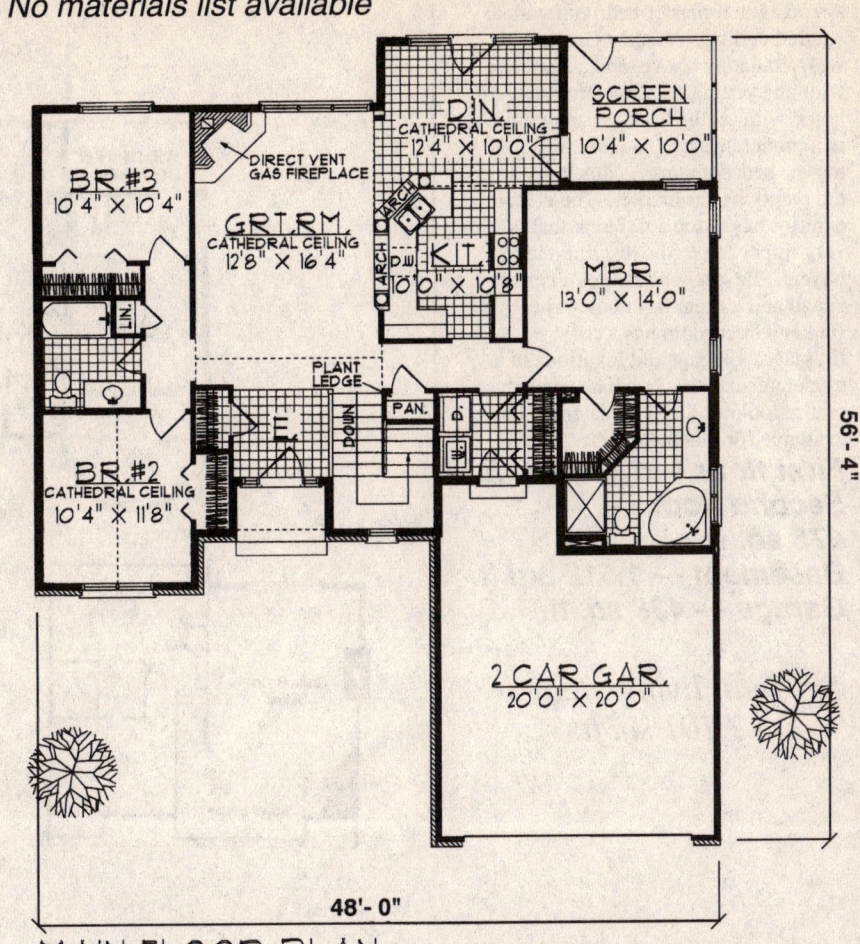

MAIN FLOOR PLAN
No. 93165

Refer to **Pricing Schedule A** on the order form for pricing information

LUXURIOUS IN A MODERATE SIZE

Design 92610

An octagonal master bedroom with a vaulted ceiling, a sunken Great room with a balcony above, and an exterior with an exciting roof line provide this home with all the luxurious amenities in a moderate size. The first floor master bedroom targets this home to the empty nester market. The elegant exterior has a rich solid look that is very important to the discriminating buyer. The kitchen features a center island and a breakfast nook. The sunken Great room has a cozy fireplace. Elegant and luxurious in a moderate size, this home has what you're looking for. No materials list is available for this plan.

First floor — 1,626 sq. ft.
Second floor — 475 sq. ft.
Basement — 1,512 sq. ft.
Garage — 438 sq. ft.

Total living area: 2,101 sq. ft.

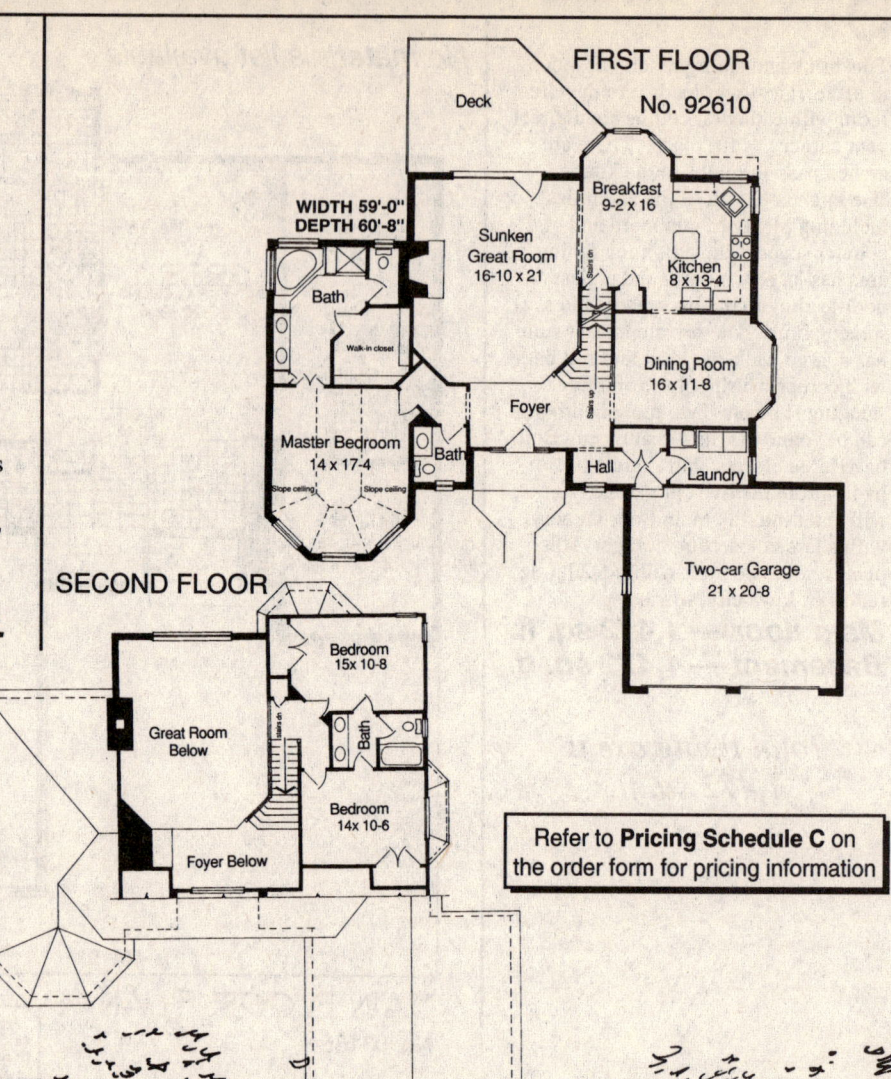

Refer to **Pricing Schedule C** on the order form for pricing information

ORDER TODAY! 1 - 800 - 235 - 5700

Design 96505

PRIVATE MASTER SUITE

This family home features a secluded master bedroom suite. The suite is the perfect place to relax after a stressful day. Tucked into the left rear corner of the home, privacy is assured and luxury is the theme of the suite. The two additional bedrooms are at the opposite side of the home, sharing use of the full hall bath. The expansive living room features a corner fireplace and access to the rear porch. The kitchen is sandwiched between the bright, bayed nook and the formal dining room. This convenient layout allows for ease in serving, whether for a formal dinner party or a family meal. An angled extended counter doubles as a snack bar.

Main floor — 2,069 sq. ft.
Garage — 481 sq. ft.

Total living area:
2,069 sq. ft.

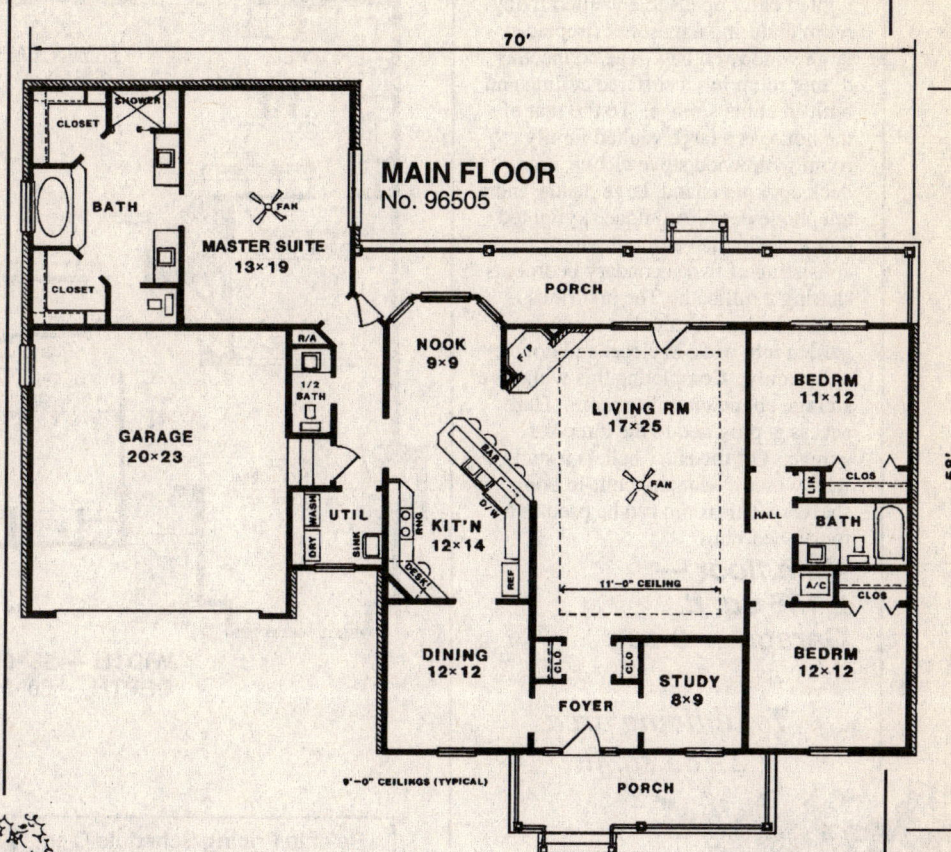

Refer to **Pricing Schedule D** on the order form for pricing information

FOUR BEDROOM CHARMER

Design 91346

Abounding with amenities, this single level ranch home has an attractive street appearance with brick accents on cedar siding. A vaulted naturally lighted entry opens to a vaulted living room featuring a masonry fireplace, large windowed bay. The connecting dining room has a coffered ceiling and built-in china storage. To the rear of the house is a large vaulted family room with wood stove alcove, rear deck cooking island, large pantry and a telephone desk. A unique skylighted hall leads to the bedroom wing, consisting of two secondary bedrooms sharing a full bath. The luxurious master bedroom suite has a whirlpool garden tub, walk-in closet and double sink vanity. Completing this wing, is a storage abundant utility room. Hall access is provided to the three-car garage. Off the entry hall, is a study with window seat and built-in book shelves. This room can be used as a fourth bedroom.

**Main floor —
2,185 sq. ft.
Garage — 3-car**

*Total living area:
2,185 sq. ft.*

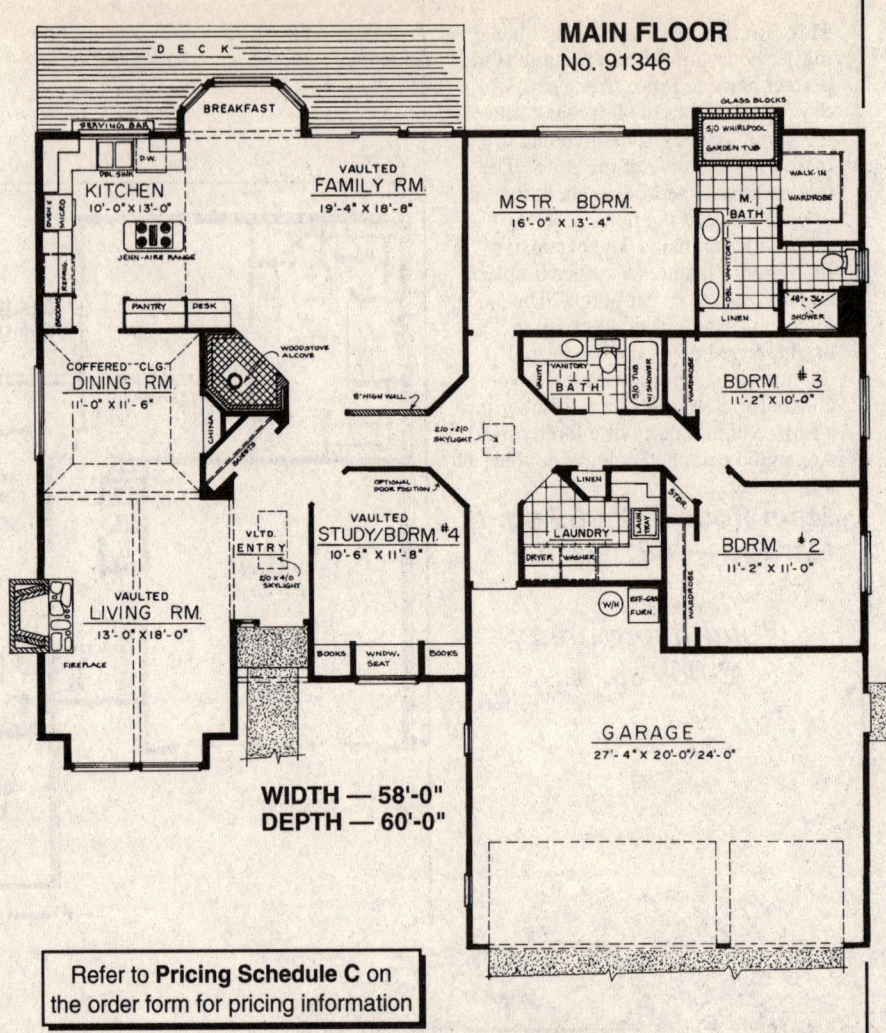

Refer to **Pricing Schedule C** on the order form for pricing information

WINDOWS ADD DISTINCTION

Design 93213

The windows of this home give it character and distinction. The formal areas are located at the front of the home. The living room and the dining room enjoy the natural light from the bayed windows. The expansive family room is enhanced by a fireplace and view of the rear yard. A U-shaped kitchen efficiently serves the dining room and the breakfast bay. Both the breakfast bay the the family room have access to the patio. The master suite is elegantly crowned by a decorative ceiling. The private master bath offers a garden tub and a step-in shower. Two large additional bedrooms share a full hall bath. There is a convenient second floor laundry center. This plan is avaialble with a basement or slab foundation. Please specify when ordering. No materials list is available for this plan.

First floor — 1,126 sq. ft.
Second floor — 959 sq. ft.
Basement — 458 sq. ft.
Garage — 627 sq. ft.

Total living area: 2,085 sq. ft.

Refer to **Pricing Schedule C** on the order form for pricing information

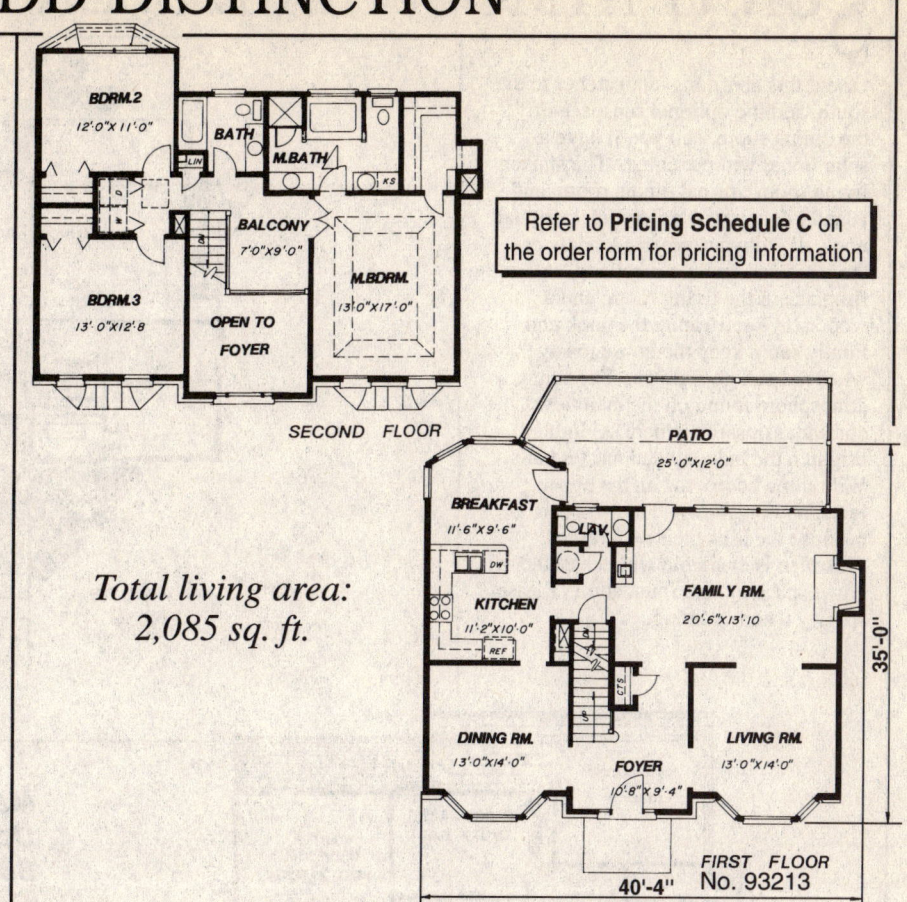

An **EXCLUSIVE DESIGN** *By Jannis Vann & Associates, Inc.*

Sunny Atmosphere Pleases All

Design 91411

Orient this charming sun-catcher to the south, add the optional sunspace off the dining room, and you'll have a solar home without equal. The sunken living room, formal dining room, and island kitchen with adjoining, informal nook all enjoy an expansive view of the patio and backyard beyond. A fireplace in the living room, and a wood stove separating the nook and family room keep the house toasty when the sun goes down. The sunny atmosphere found on the main level continues upstairs, where skylights brighten the balcony and master bath. With three bedrooms on the upper level, and one downstairs, you can promise the kids their own rooms. This plan is available with a basement, crawl space or slab foundation. Please specify when ordering.

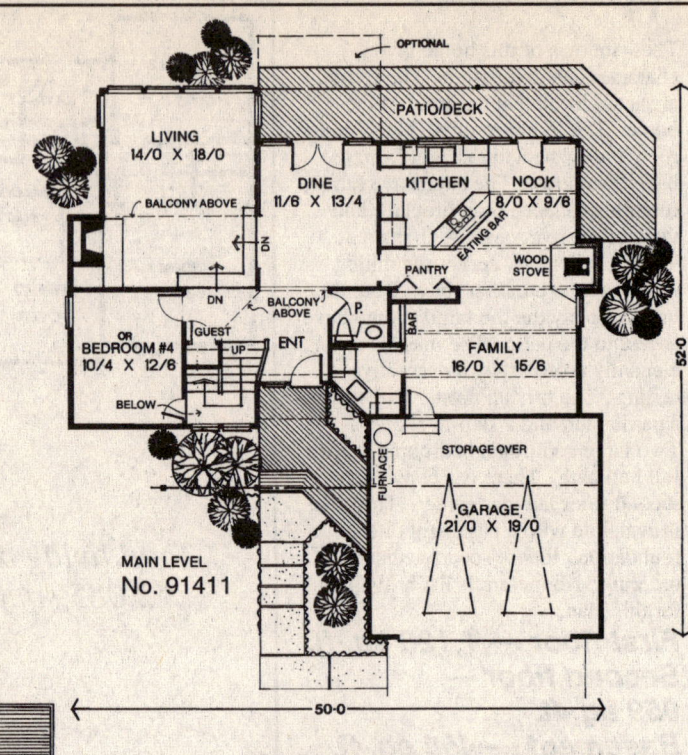

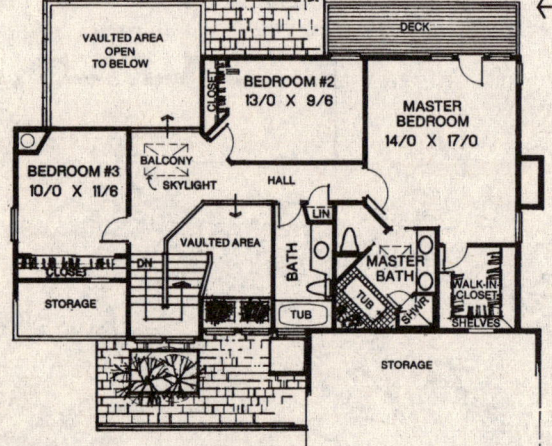

Main level — 1,249 sq. ft.
Upper level — 890 sq. ft.
Garage — 462 sq. ft.

Total living area: 2,139 sq. ft.

Refer to **Pricing Schedule C** on the order form for pricing information

ORDER TODAY! 1-800-235-5700

Graceful Stucco & Brick Home

Design 93056

A graceful stucco arch supported by columns sets this elevation apart at the curb. Stucco quoins are used to accent the traditional brick finish. Upon entering, an angled foyer steps down into the living room and directs the eye to a duplicate of the exterior arch with columns. Built-in display shelving on either side gives plenty of room for collectibles or books. Another step down leads to the formal dining room. The kitchen features a breakfast room with a bay window and a coffered ceiling treatment. The family room and kitchen are conveniently grouped with the breakfast room to provide a large area for family and informal entertaining. The master suite is entered through angled double doors. The eye is drawn to the master bath visible through French doors. Columns mounted on pedestals flank the entry. Inside, a luxury bath awaits with a whirlpool tub as a centerpiece. On the opposite side of the home are two additional bedrooms with large walk-in closets and a roomy bath. This plan is available with a crawl space or slab foundation. Please specify when ordering.

Main floor — 2,517 sq. ft.
Garage — 443 sq. ft.

Total living area:
2,517 sq. ft.

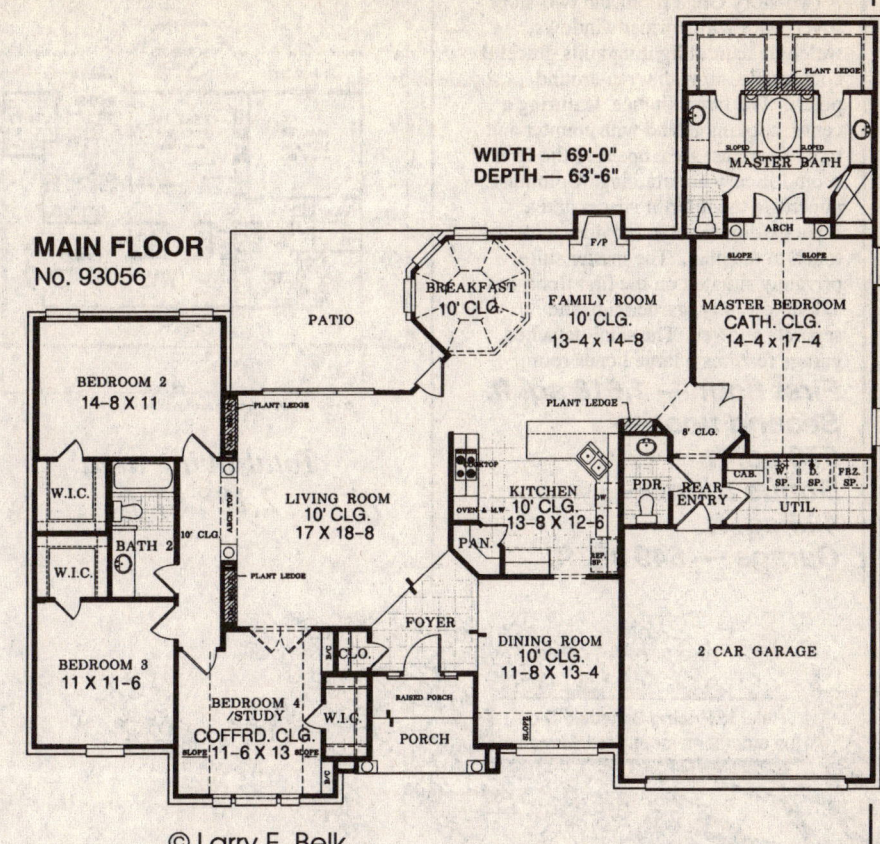

© Larry E. Belk

Refer to **Pricing Schedule D** on the order form for pricing information

TWO-STORY GREAT ROOM

Design 99801

HOME PLAN OF THE YEAR

A two-story Great room and two-story foyer, both with dormer windows, welcome natural light into this graceful country classic with wrap-around porch. The large kitchen, featuring a center cooking island with counter and large breakfast area, opens to the Great room for easy entertaining. Columns punctuate the interior spaces and a separate dining room provides a formal touch to the plan. The master suite, privately situated on the first floor, has a double vanity, garden tub, and separate shower. The semi-detached garage features a large bonus room.

**First floor — 1,618 sq. ft.
Second floor — 570 sq. ft.
Bonus room — 495 sq. ft.
Garage — 649 sq. ft.**

Total living area: 2,188 sq. ft.

Refer to **Pricing Schedule D** on the order form for pricing information

© 1997 Donald A Gardner Architects, Inc.

Our Home Plan of the Year, Plan Number 99801, has a country feel with contemporary features. The wrap-around porch makes the 2,188 square foot house appear larger and gives the home its graceful, classic, country appearance. The efficient, island kitchen opens into the great room creating the perfect family living space. Spiced by the past but seasoned for a modern lifestyle, this is a home for your family to grow in and to create a lifetime of new memories.

HOME PLAN OF THE YEAR

COUNTRY STYLE

Design 91335

A feature not often found in a duplex is the covered-railed sitting porch. A touch of cedar shingles in the gable ends of this eye-appealing unit, as well as wood shutters and planter boxes, give it a truly "Country" look. The large upstairs bedrooms are perfectly suited for twin beds. Maximum privacy for the bedroom areas is assured by the roof separating the two units. A computer area for today's busy lifestyle can be located in the study/third bedroom, ideally placed near the kitchen for easy access.

**Main floor — 700 sq. ft.
Upper floor — 588 sq. ft.**

Total living area per unit: 1,288 sq.ft.

Refer to **Pricing Schedule G** on the order form for pricing information

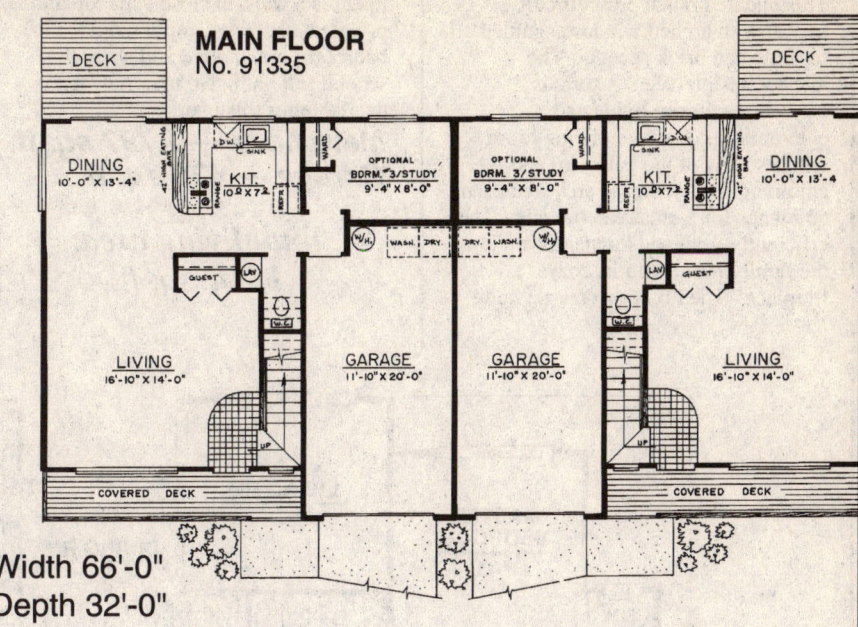

Width 66'-0"
Depth 32'-0"

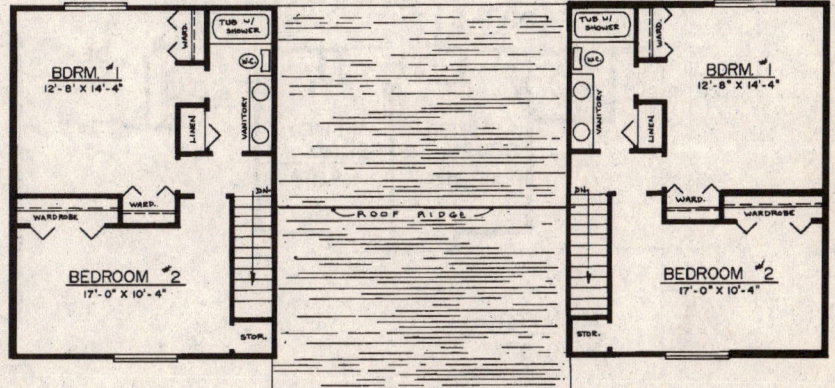

UPPER FLOOR

An Updated Ranch

Design 91077

This updated ranch presents curb appeal with arched windows, gabled roofline and brick accents. The interior design offers luxurious, convenient family living and entertaining. A sunken living room with its view of the backyard and adjoining formal dining area creates an ambiance for formal entertaining. The efficiently designed kitchen flows into the family room with its cozy fireplace. The luxurious master suite features a walk-in closet, spa tub and a private bath. Two ample sized bedrooms are vaulted and share the second full bath. No materials list is available for this plan.

Main floor — 1,797 sq. ft.
Garage — 473 sq. ft.

Total living area: 1,797 sq. ft.

Refer to **Pricing Schedule B** on the order form for pricing information

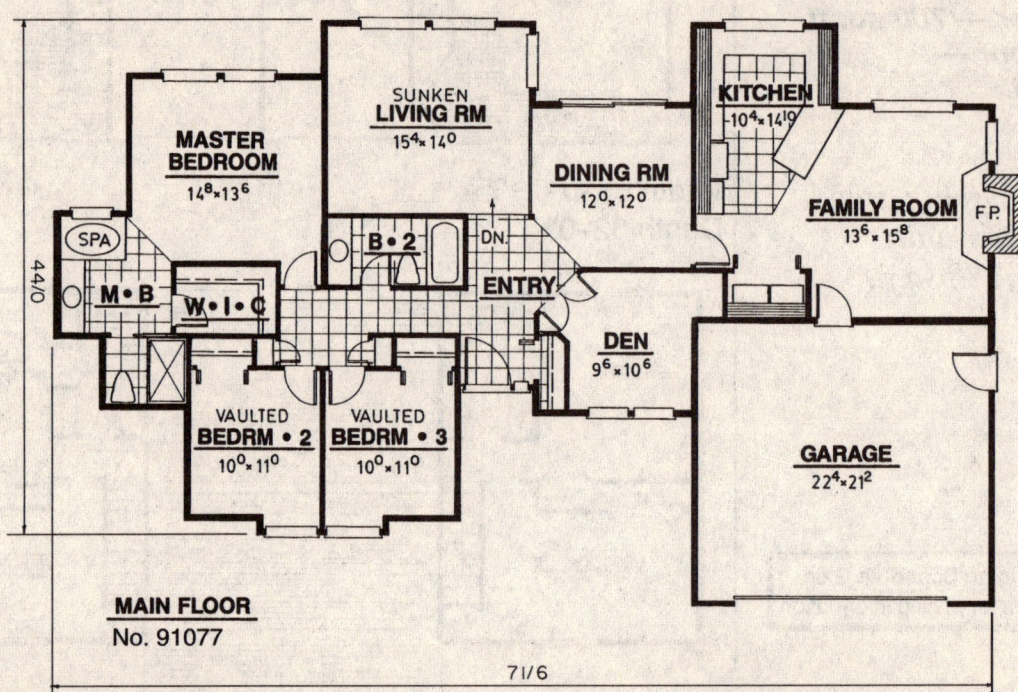

Design 98714

EFFICIENT VACATION LIVING

This home offers efficient vacation living with the amenities of a full sized house. Identical bedroom suites flank the central living area. Each room has its own private bath, vanity and walk-in closet, as well as access and a view onto the large front deck. Dominating the central area is the living room with a vaulted ceiling which looks out onto the front deck through tall windows and glass doors. The living room floor is sunken one step below the rest of the main floor, further accentuating the impression of space. Besides the bedroom suites and living room, the main floor includes a kitchen with eating bar, a dining area, and a half bath. An open staircase leads up to a loft that overlooks the living room directly opposite the arch front widow. It has its own full bath, walk-in closet, and outside deck above the carport.

First floor — 1,704 sq. ft.
Second floor — 313 sq. ft.
Width — 58'-0"
Depth — 48'-0"

Total living area: 2,017 sq. ft.

FIRST FLOOR
No. 98714

SECOND FLOOR

Refer to **Pricing Schedule C** on the order form for pricing information

ORDER TODAY! 1 - 800 - 235 - 5700

Design 94130

EFFICIENT USE OF SPACE

In only 1,006 square feet, this floor plan offers three great bedrooms. The living room, dining room and kitchen are laid out in an efficient L-shape. The living and dining rooms flow into each other as do the kitchen and dining room giving an illusion of more space. The master bedroom has private access to the full bath in the hall. If you are looking for a modern floor plan that offers a lot of living in a small amount of space, this plan is for you. No materials list available for this plan.

Main floor — 1,006 sq. ft.
Basement — 1,006 sq. ft.
Garage — 433 sq. ft.

Total living area: 1,006 sq. ft.

Refer to **Pricing Schedule C** on the order form for pricing information

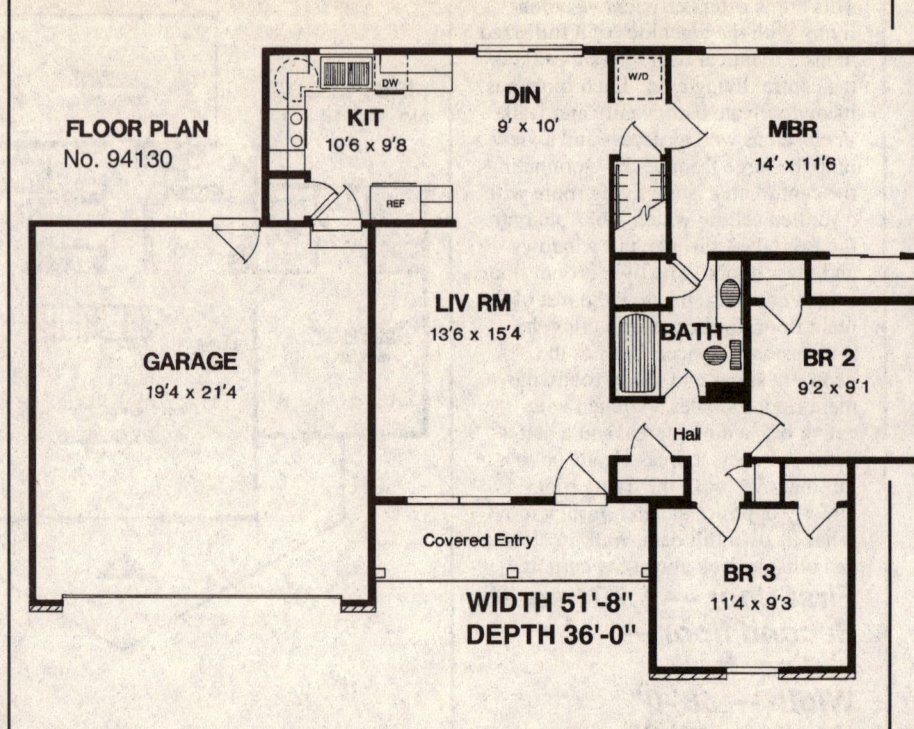

COMPACT COMFORT

Design 10787

With its abundant windows and open plan, this sunny home will be warm and bright even on a chilly day. Soaring ceilings and a wall of stacked windows add dramatic volume to the spacious living room off the large central foyer. A step down, past the open railing, the dining room completes the formal area of the house so perfect for entertaining. For informal gatherings, walk into the kitchen-family room combination, separated by a handy breakfast bar. A cozy fireplace with wood storage and a built-in entertainment center combine with the efficient kitchen layout for a comfortable, convenient family area. Upstairs, you'll find three bedrooms and two full baths, including the luxury bath in the master suite.

First floor — 1,088 sq. ft.
Second floor — 750 sq. ft.
Basement — 750 sq. ft.
Garage — 548 sq. ft.

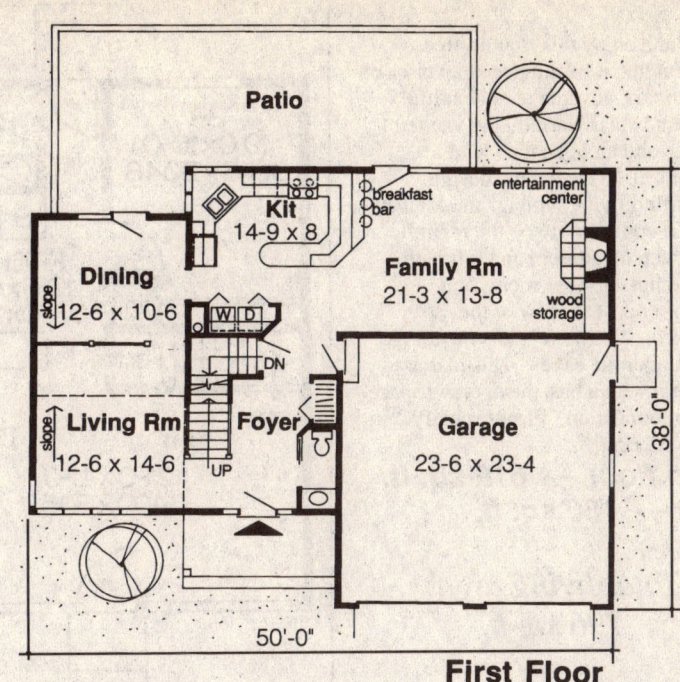

First Floor
No. 10787

Total living area: 1,838 sq. ft.

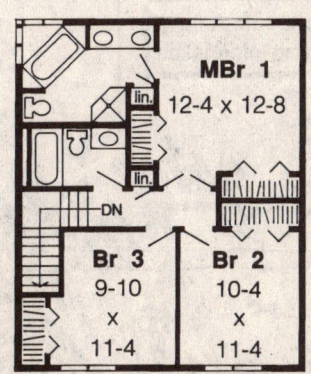

Second Floor

Refer to **Pricing Schedule C** on the order form for pricing information

A PLEASURE TO OWN

Design 90821

Relax and enjoy this trouble-free vacation home. With huge expanses of glass to take advantage of beautiful vistas and solar warmth, the vaulted ceilings and an open plan lend a spacious air to a compact design. You'll find living, dining, and kitchen areas fit comfortably on the main floor along with a bedroom and full bath. Tucked upstairs, the roomy loft bedroom boasts a view of the backyard. Plus there's lots of storage space under the eaves. This plan is available with a basement, crawl space or slab foundation. Please specify when ordering.

Main floor — 616 sq. ft.
Loft — 180 sq. ft.

Total living area: 796 sq. ft.

Refer to **Pricing Schedule A** on the order form for pricing information

An EXCLUSIVE DESIGN *By Westhome Planners, Ltd.*

WIDTH 22'-0"
DEPTH 28'-0"

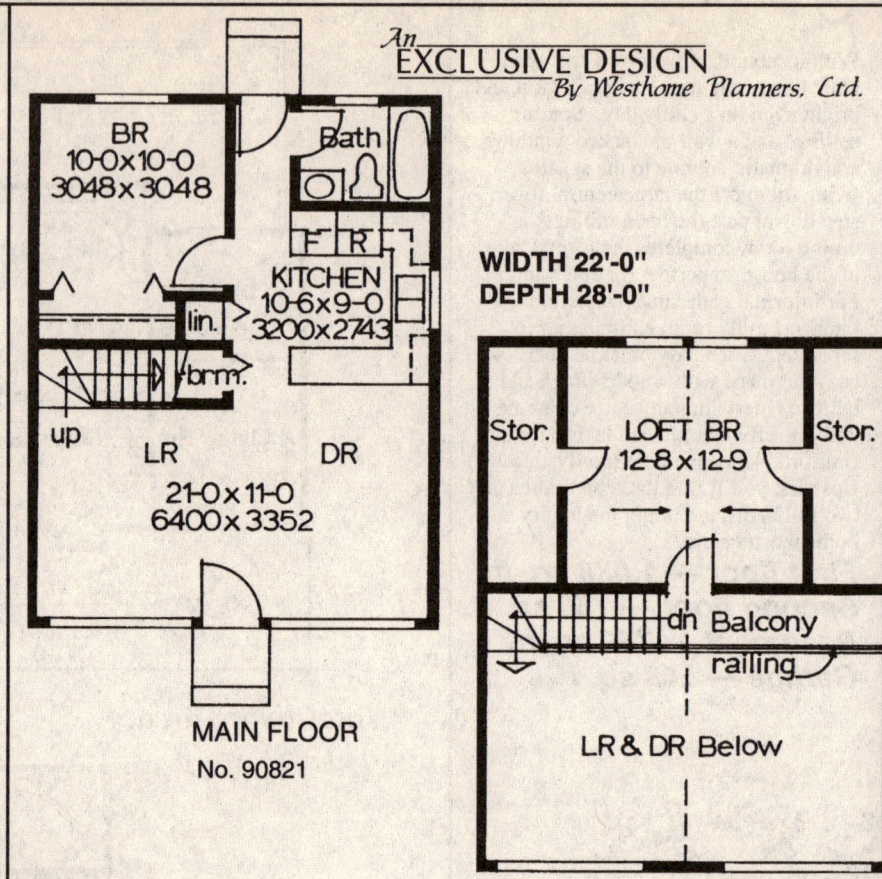

MAIN FLOOR No. 90821

LOFT

ORDER TODAY! 1-800-235-5700

ORDER TODAY! 1 - 800 - 235 - 5700

Design 98514

STATELY MANOR LEAVES IMPRESSION

Are you looking for a home that says that you've made it? Then take a look at this two-story gem. Upon entering this stately manor, guests can't help being impressed with the curved staircase, as well as the formal living room with its own brick fireplace and arched windows. Just a few steps away, a study beckons you through double doors. The large family room with a balcony above is sure to get a second glance. The gourmet kitchen will please the chef of the family where an abundance of workspace and ample storage space are featured. The downstairs master suite has two large walk-in closets, four more bedrooms and an optional bonus room which occupy the upstairs. Please specify slab or crawl space foundation when ordering. No materials list is available for this plan.

Main floor — 2,208 sq. ft.
Upper floor — 1,173 sq. ft.
Bonus — 224 sq. ft.
Garage — 520 sq. ft.

Total living area: 3,381 sq. ft.

Refer to **Pricing Schedule F** on the order form for pricing information

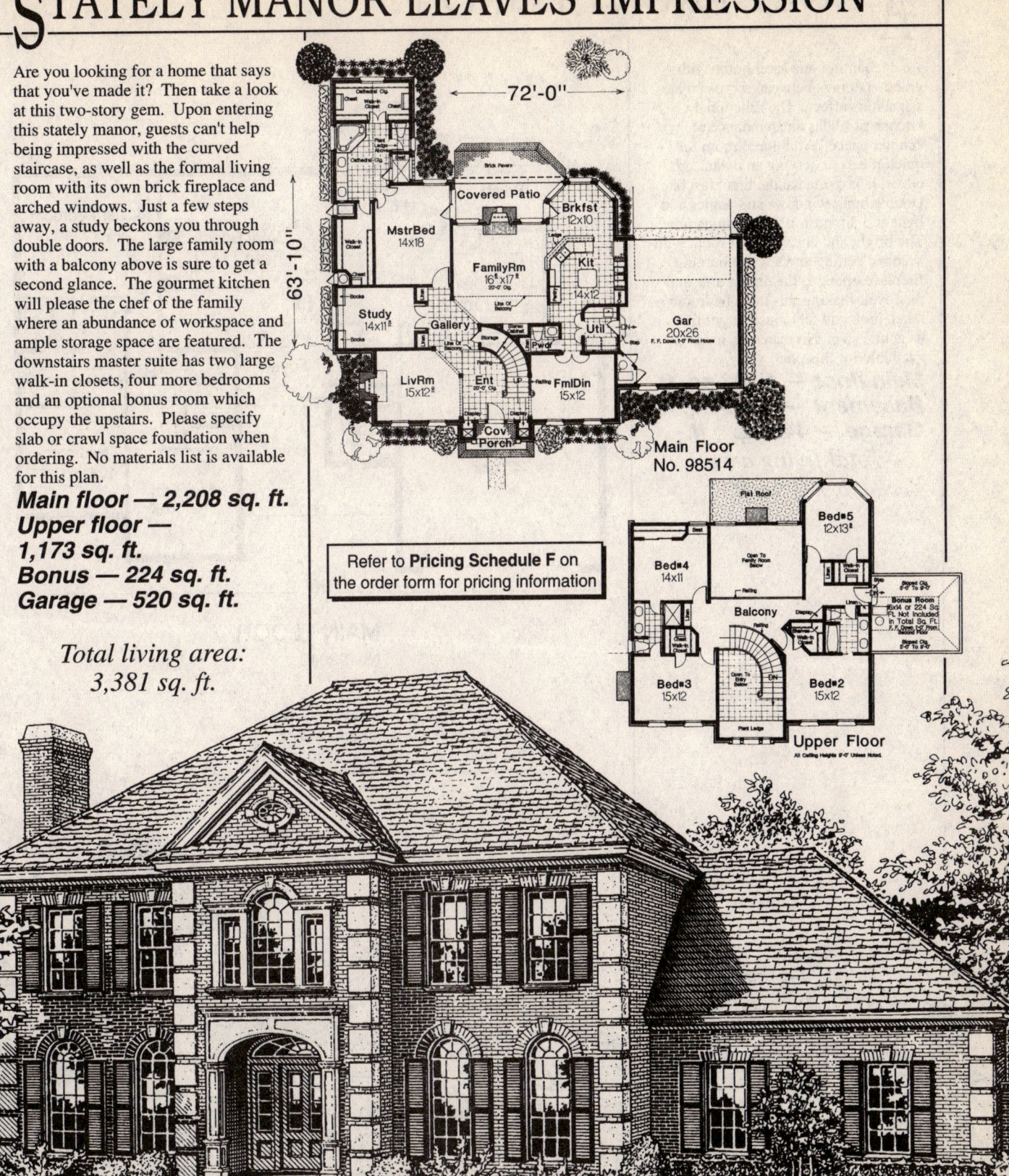

A COZY FRONT PORCH

Design 92649

An enchanting one level home with grand openings between rooms creates a spacious effect. The functional kitchen provides an abundance of counter space. Additional room for quick meals or serving an oversized crowd is provided at the breakfast bar. Double hung windows and angles add light and dimension to the dining area. The bright and cheery Great room with a sloped ceiling and a wood burning fireplace opens to the dining area and the foyer, making this three bedroom ranch look and feel much larger than its actual size. No materials list is available for this plan.

Main floor — 1,508 sq. ft.
Basement — 1,429 sq. ft.
Garage — 440 sq. ft.

Total living area: 1,508 sq. ft.

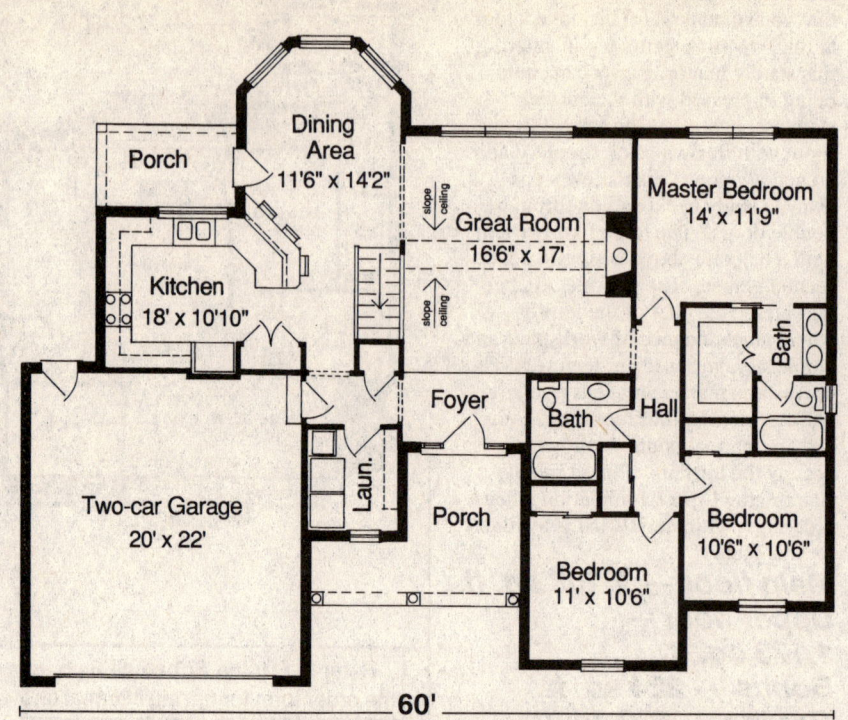

MAIN FLOOR
No. 92649

Refer to **Pricing Schedule B** on the order form for pricing information

Charming One-Level

Design 92660

A frame and stone facade embellish the exterior of this charming one-level home. From the foyer a wide open view to the Great room is presented where a fireplace, framed with built-in units, graces one wall and triple French doors adorn the rear wall. Varied ceiling heights throughout the house add interest and excitement. An extra large window in the breakfast area provides an infusion of daylight, and a view to the outdoors for the spacious kitchen. The master bedroom suite located to the rear of the home offers a whirlpool tub, separate vanities and a shower stall to pamper the senior members of the family. The easy flow floor plan is designed for step saving convenience while providing a friendly, comfortable atmosphere for relaxing with family and friends. No materials list is available for this plan.

Main floor — 1,964 sq. ft.
Basement — 1,809 sq. ft.
Garage — 447 sq. ft.

Total living area:
1,964 sq. ft

Refer to **Pricing Schedule C** on the order form for pricing information

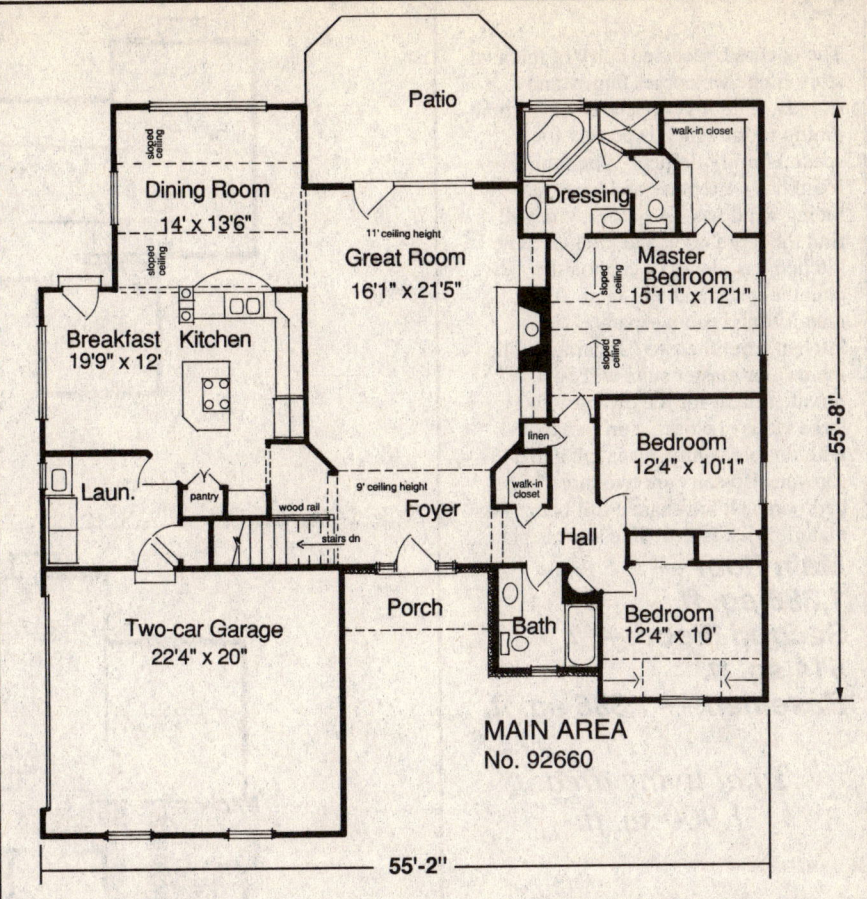

ORDER TODAY! 1-800-235-5700

COLUMNED ENTRY

Design 99132

The covered, recessed entry of this two story home welcomes family and friends. The foyer opens to the formal dining room which is perfect for special family dinners. The family room has a fireplace and large rear facing windows. Adjacent, you will find the large nook and kitchen. The kitchen has plenty of cupboards, counter space and an island. The laundry/mud room separates the kitchen from the two car garage. The main floor master suite will be a private retreat for the owner with a large walk-in closet, a private bath with double vanity, a spa tub and a shower. Upstairs are two more large bedrooms which share a full bath. No materials list is available for this plan.

**Main floor — 1,386 sq. ft.
Second Floor — 514 sq. ft.
Basement — 1,386 sq. ft.**

Total living area: 1,900 sq. ft.

Refer to **Pricing Schedule C** on the order form for pricing information

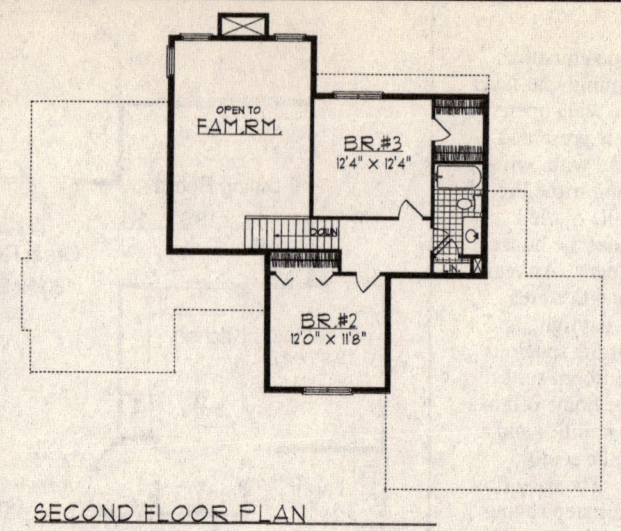

SECOND FLOOR PLAN

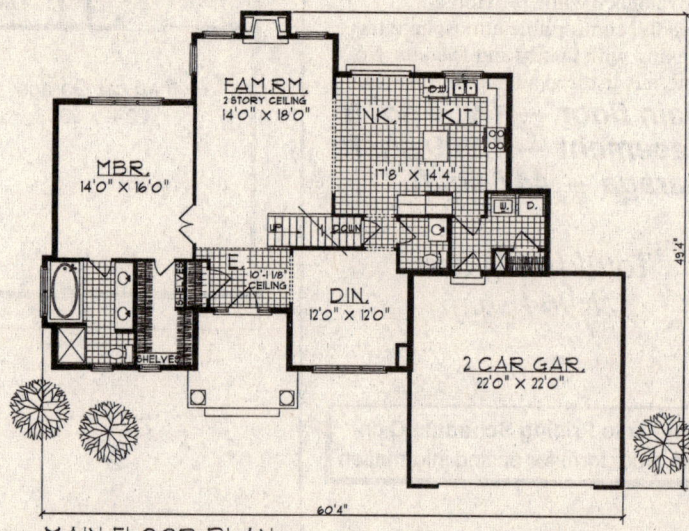

MAIN FLOOR PLAN
No. 99132

DESIGNED FOR UP-SLOPING LOTS

Design 91517

This home features multi-paned windows and high ceilings, giving a feeling of spaciousness to what may be considered a smaller home. Upon entering the home, you step up to enter the dining room which is separated from the kitchen by only a peninsula counter, again adding to the spaciousness. The elegant living room makes quite an impression; the tall, multi-paned window seems to climb to the roof, since the room is two stories in height. A fireplace completes the picture and adds to the ambience of the room. Informal family gatherings will be comfortably accommodated in the large family room. There is a convenient half bath located to the rear of the family room. Sleeping quarters are located on the second floor. The master suite has a vaulted ceiling and French doors. There is a walk-in closet and a full lead to a small private deck.

The two additional bedrooms have ample closet space and easy access to a full bath.

**First floor — 1,022 sq. ft.
Second floor — 813 sq. ft.**

Total living area: 1,835 sq. ft.

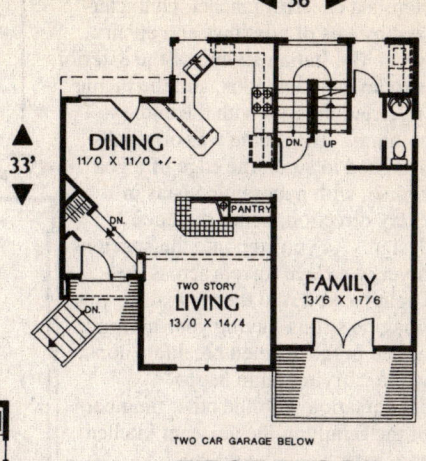

FIRST FLOOR
No. 91517

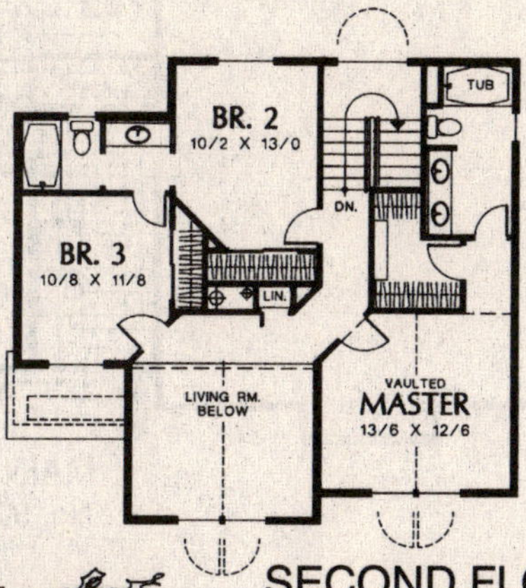

SECOND FLOOR

Refer to **Pricing Schedule C** on the order form for pricing information

Surrounded with Sunshine

Design 90986

Here's a cheerful rancher, characterized by lots of windows and an airy plan. The Italian styling of the exterior is today's hottest look, and the theme is carried indoors with tile and columns. This home was originally designed to sit on the edge of a golf course, with panoramic vistas in every direction, hence the open design. As you step into the spacious foyer, your eye travels across the Great room out to the view at the rear. Imagine sitting having your morning coffee in the turreted breakfast nook, while carrying on in happy conversation with the other members of the family in the adjacent kitchen.

This plan is available with a basement or crawl space foundation. Please specify when ordering.

Main area — 1,731 sq. ft.
Basement — 1,715 sq. ft.
Garage — 888 sq. ft.

Total living area: 1,731 sq. ft.

Refer to **Pricing Schedule B** on the order form for pricing information

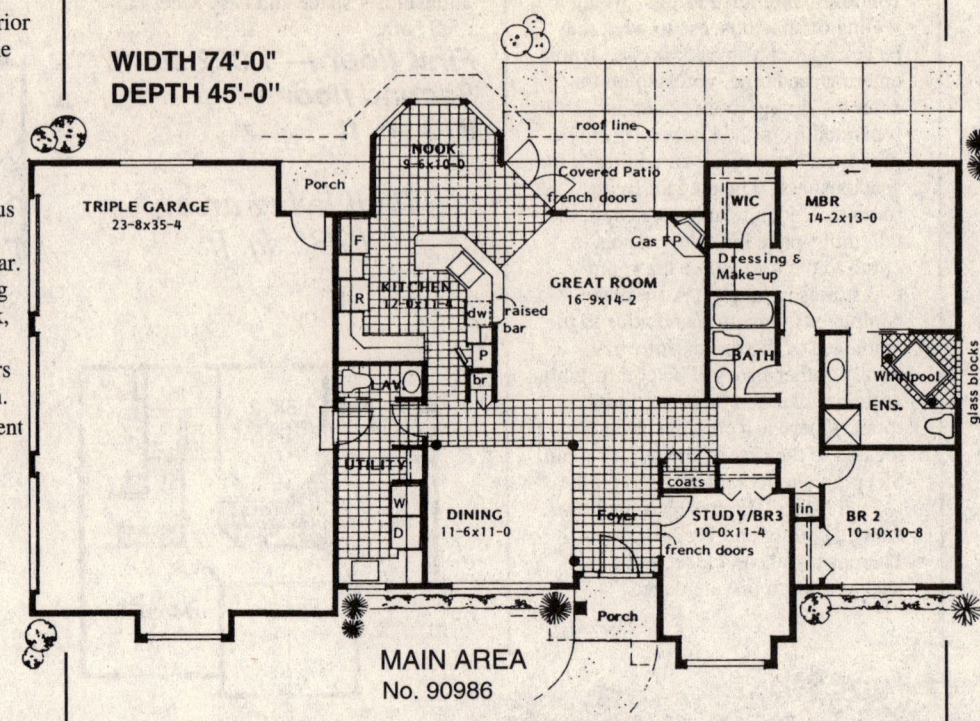

MAIN AREA No. 90986

An EXCLUSIVE DESIGN *By Westhome Planners, Ltd.*

A SPLIT BEDROOM PLAN

Design 93030

This split bedroom plan features a traditional elevation coupled with an up-to-date, efficiently designed floor plan. Upon entering, an angled foyer opens the home to a large Great room with a fireplace. A formal dining room is defined with a series of columns that give the home an elegant feel. The master suite is entered through double doors and is privately located away from the other bedrooms. The master bath features all the luxuries with an angled whirlpool tub, separate shower and double vanity. An enormous walk-in closet complete the arrangement. The kitchen features a pantry and has plenty of cabinet and counter space. A coffered ceiling treatment adds character to the breakfast room located on the rear of the home. Bedrooms two and three are arranged nearby with convenient access to the second bath. No materials list is available for this plan.

Main floor — 1,955 sq. ft.
Garage — 561 sq. ft.

Total living area:
1,955 sq. ft.

Refer to **Pricing Schedule C** on the order form for pricing information

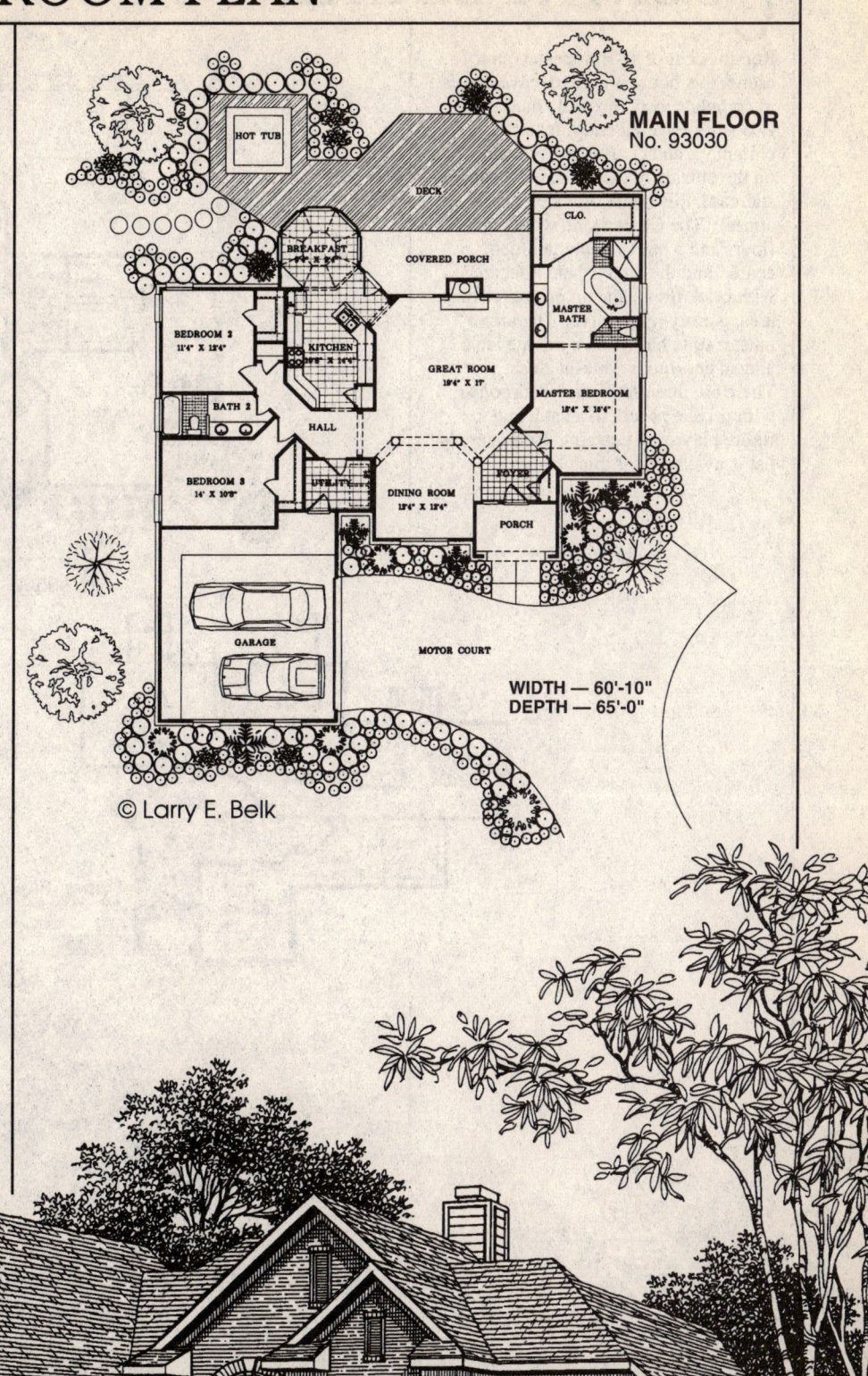

MAIN FLOOR
No. 93030

WIDTH — 60'-10"
DEPTH — 65'-0"

© Larry E. Belk

ORDER TODAY! 1 - 800 - 235 - 5700

COUNTRY ESTATE

Design 98508

Reminiscent of an European country estate, this home is sure to leave guests in complete awe. From its massive two-story covered entry, majestic chimneys, and charming bay window on the outside to the impressive curved staircase, this home offers plenty of appeal. The Great room, with wood floors and a built-in entertainment center, and the huge island kitchen, with brick floors and an open breakfast area, is truly impressive. The large master suite has its own private lanai and an enormous walk-in closet. There are three secondary bedrooms, with private access to a bath, and a future playroom upstairs. No materials list is available for this plan.

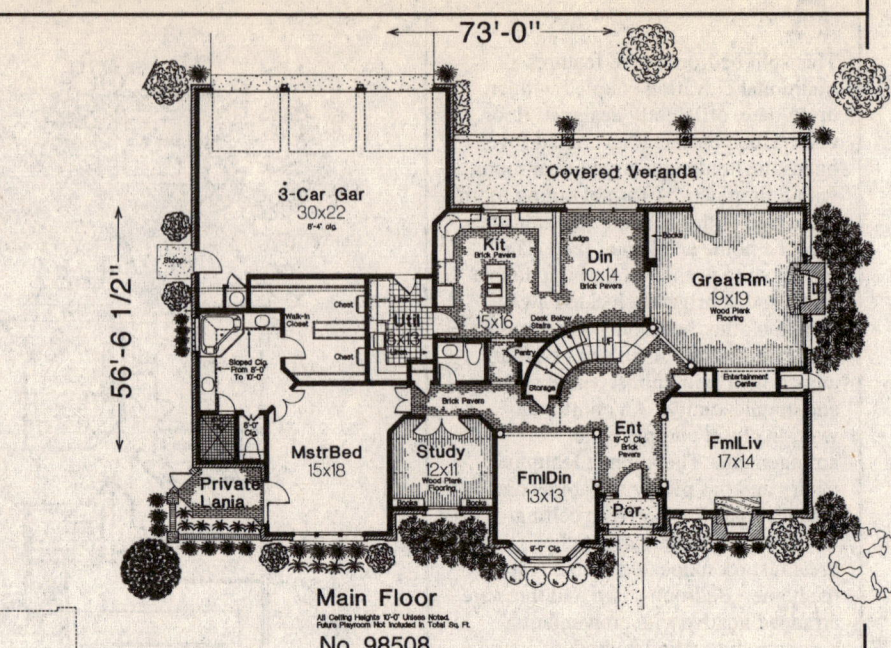

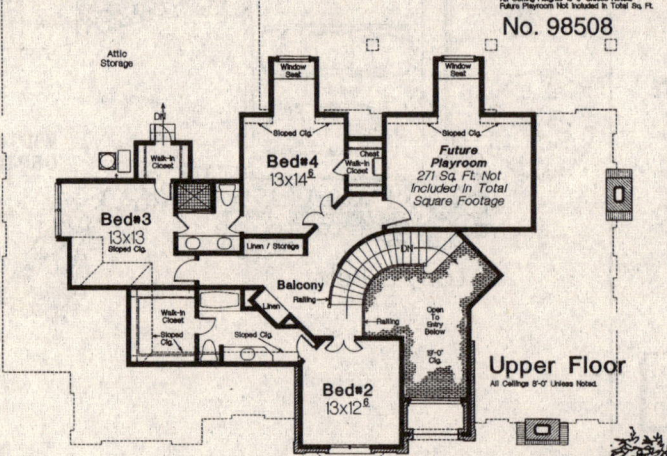

Main floor —
2,441 sq. ft.
Second floor —
1,039 sq. ft.
Garage —
660 sq. ft.
Bonus — 271 sq. ft.

Total living area:
3,480 sq. ft.

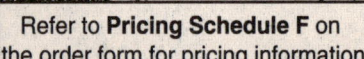

Refer to **Pricing Schedule F** on the order form for pricing information

ORDER TODAY!   1 - 800 - 235 - 5700

Easy One-Floor Living

Design 98423

The center piece of this home is the spacious family room topped by a vaulted ceiling. A large fireplace and a French door to the rear yard highlights the room. The kitchen is located between the breakfast room and the formal dining room. A serving bar open to the family room and dining room, a pantry and a peninsula counter between the kitchen and breakfast room are just a few of the amenities outfitting the kitchen. The master suite is crowned in a tray ceiling and contains a vaulted ceiling over the master bath and sitting area and a large walk-in closet. The two additional bedrooms are roomy in size and share the full bath in the hall. This plan is available with a basement, crawl space or slab foundation. Please specify when ordering.

Main floor — 1,671 sq. ft.
Basement — 1,685 sq. ft.
Garage — 400 sq. ft.

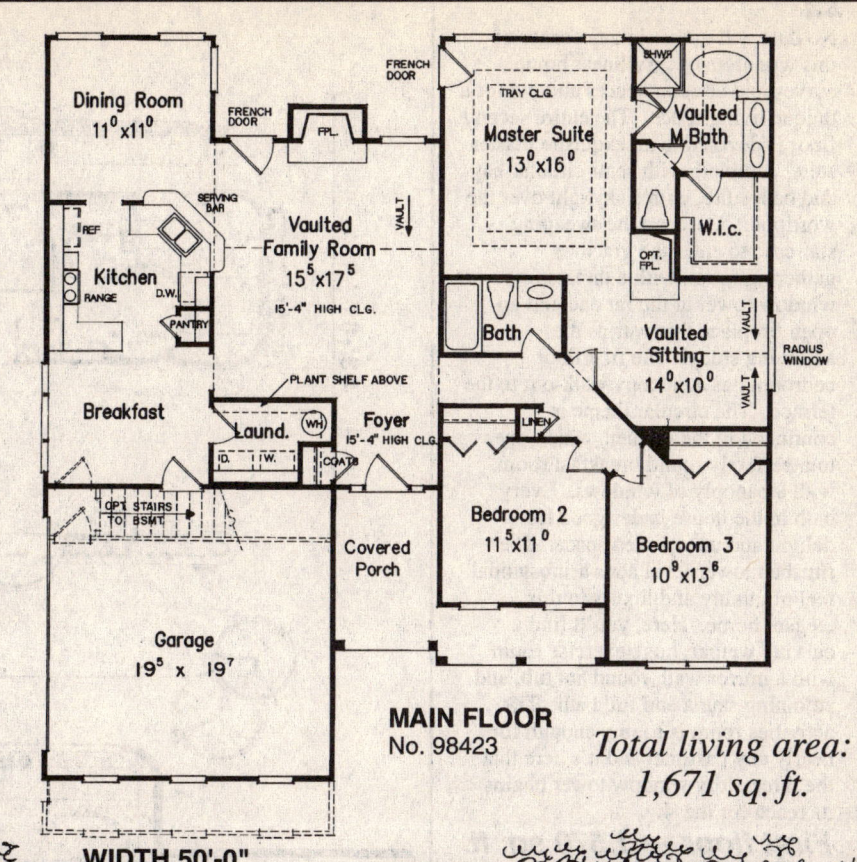

MAIN FLOOR
No. 98423

Total living area: 1,671 sq. ft.

WIDTH 50'-0"
DEPTH 51'-0"

Refer to **Pricing Schedule B** on the order form for pricing information

LIFE IN THE ROUND

Design 99230

No dust will gather in any corner of this wondrously curvilinear home; curves and circular spaces abound for a unique living space. The entire second floor is devoted to an exquisite master suite, complete with semi-circular bay and bath suite, with a skylight over the whirlpool. Descend the sweeping staircase to enter the gracious gathering room, with a three-story window tower at the far end and an open fireplace that warms the adjoining study. The first floor bedroom has a balcony walk-out to the terrace. The circular theme is continued in the kitchen, which opens to a perfectly round breakfast room, with a panoply of windows. Every bath in the house is designed for delight and unexpected space. The finished lower level adds a substantial feel of quality and luxury to this elegant home. Here, you'll find a curving wetbar, huge exercise room with a mirror wall, round hot tub, and adjoining sauna and full bath. The activities room is roomy enough for nearly any pastime, and it's here that the three-story window tower begins its reach for the sky.

First floor — 1,570 sq. ft.
Second floor — 598 sq. ft.
Lower floor — 1,080 sq. ft.
Garage — 462 sq. ft. & storage

Total living area: 3,248 sq. ft.

Refer to **Pricing Schedule F** on the order form for pricing information

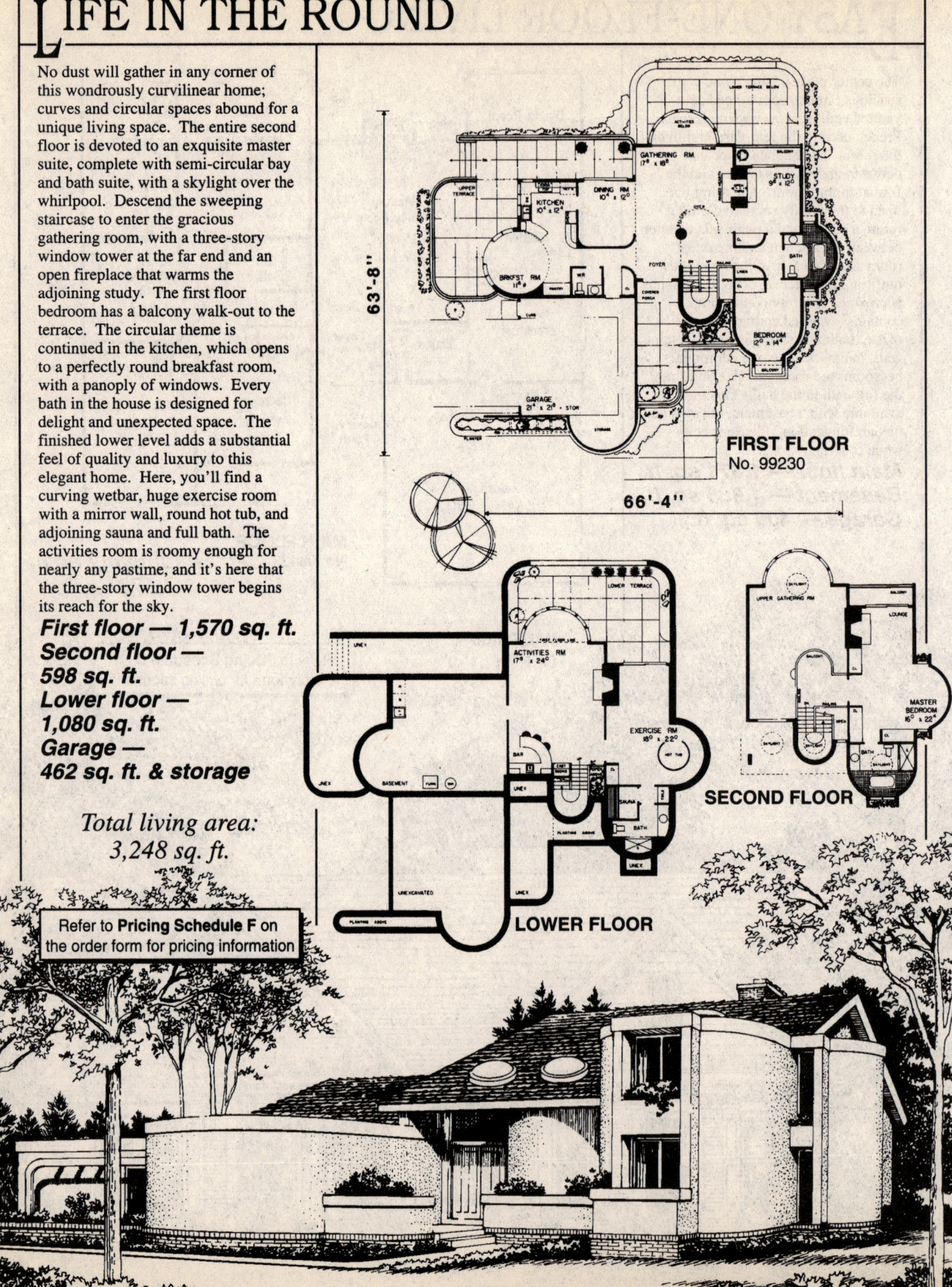

Design 20128

COOK'S DREAM

Enjoy family activities while you cook in the kitchen of this well-conceived, three-bedroom home. The range peninsula separates the kitchen from the skylit breakfast nook without walls, affording a view into the living room, dining room, and out to the adjoining deck. Built-ins add convenience throughout the house, from the pantry and plant shelf, to the planning desk, to the walk-in closets and double vanity upstairs. And, tall bay windows let the sun shine into the fireplaced living room, which adjoins the formal dining room. The master suite directly overhead, featuring a private bath and his-n-hers walk-in closets, mirrors the living room's intruguing, angular shape.

First floor — 942 sq. ft.
Second floor — 895 sq. ft.
Basement — 942 sq. ft.
Garage — 484 sq. ft.

An EXCLUSIVE DESIGN *By Karl Kreeger*

Total living area: 1,837 sq. ft.

First Floor
No. 20128

Second Floor

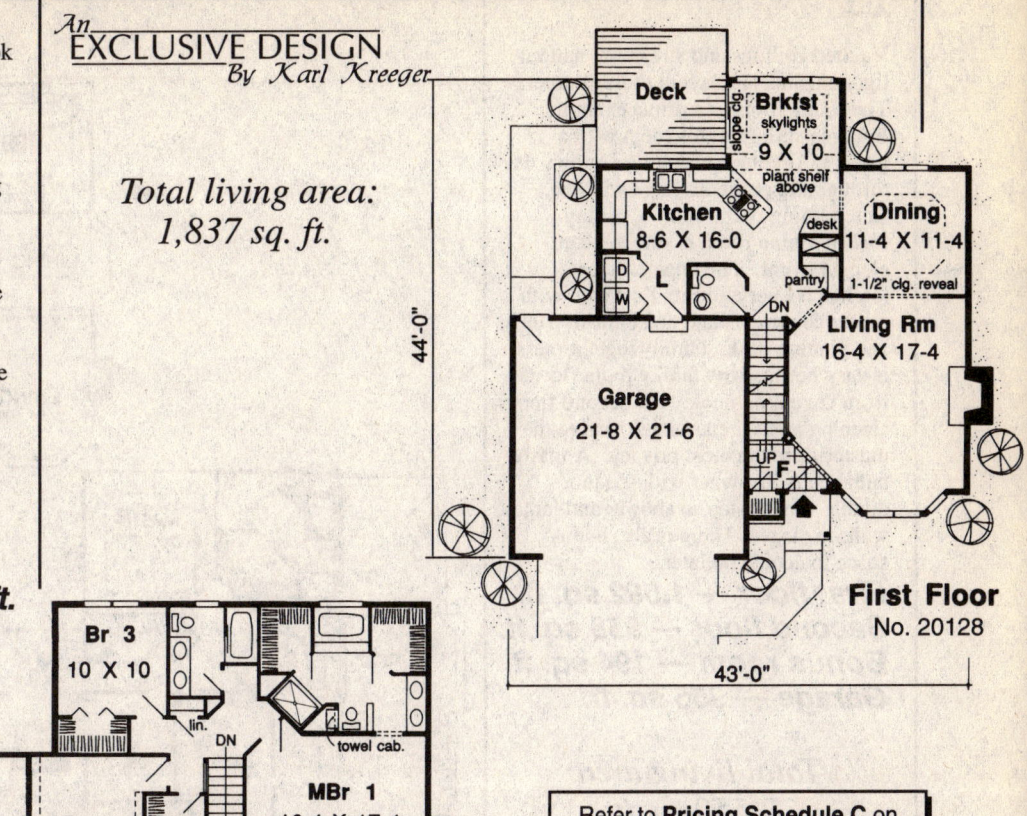

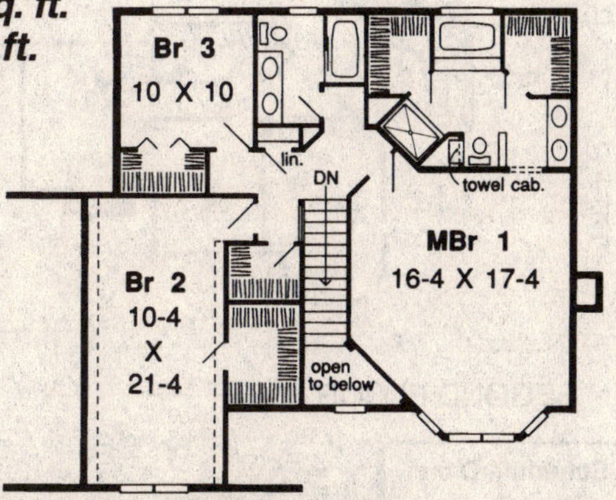

Refer to **Pricing Schedule C** on the order form for pricing information

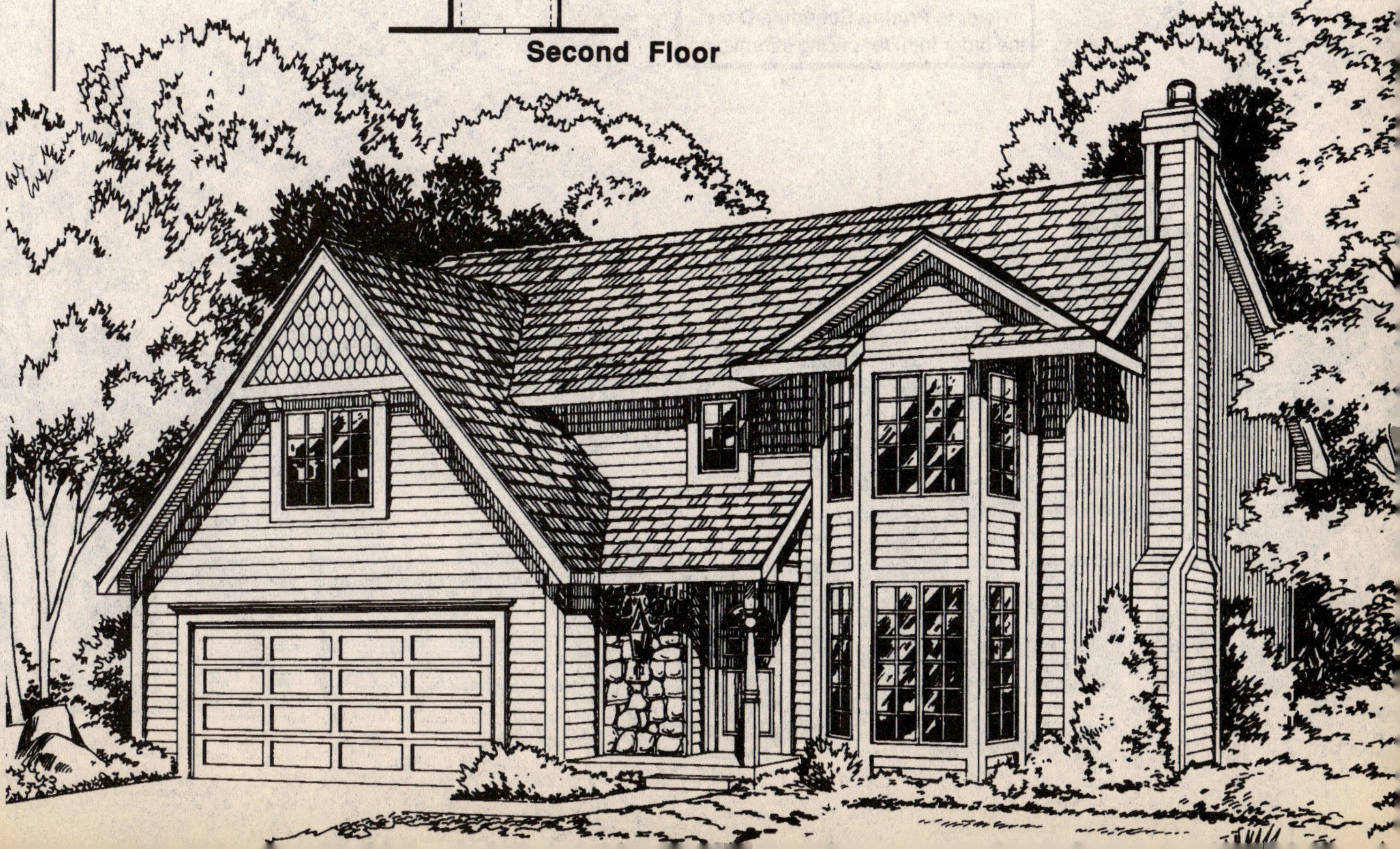

Design 91518

ATTRACTIVE USE OF WINDOWS

Vaulted ceilings and streaming natural light enhance the layout of this home. The living room is a prime example. Imagine sitting in this room with a glowing fireplace watching a snowy day through the gorgeous front window. Entertaining in the vaulted ceiling formal dining room is sure to be an elegant event. The huge efficient kitchen is every gourmet's dream with a center cooktop island and built-in pantry and planing desk. Family togetherness is easy because the family room flows from the eating nook. The second floor sleeping areas are arranged to give the master suite the most privacy. A master bath spoils its owner with spa tub, double vanity, step-in shower and large walk-in closet. There is also bonus space to decide on later.

First floor — 1,592 sq. ft.
Second floor — 958 sq. ft.
Bonus room — 194 sq. ft.
Garage — 956 sq. ft.

Total living area:
2,550 sq. ft.

FIRST FLOOR
No. 91518

SECOND FLOOR

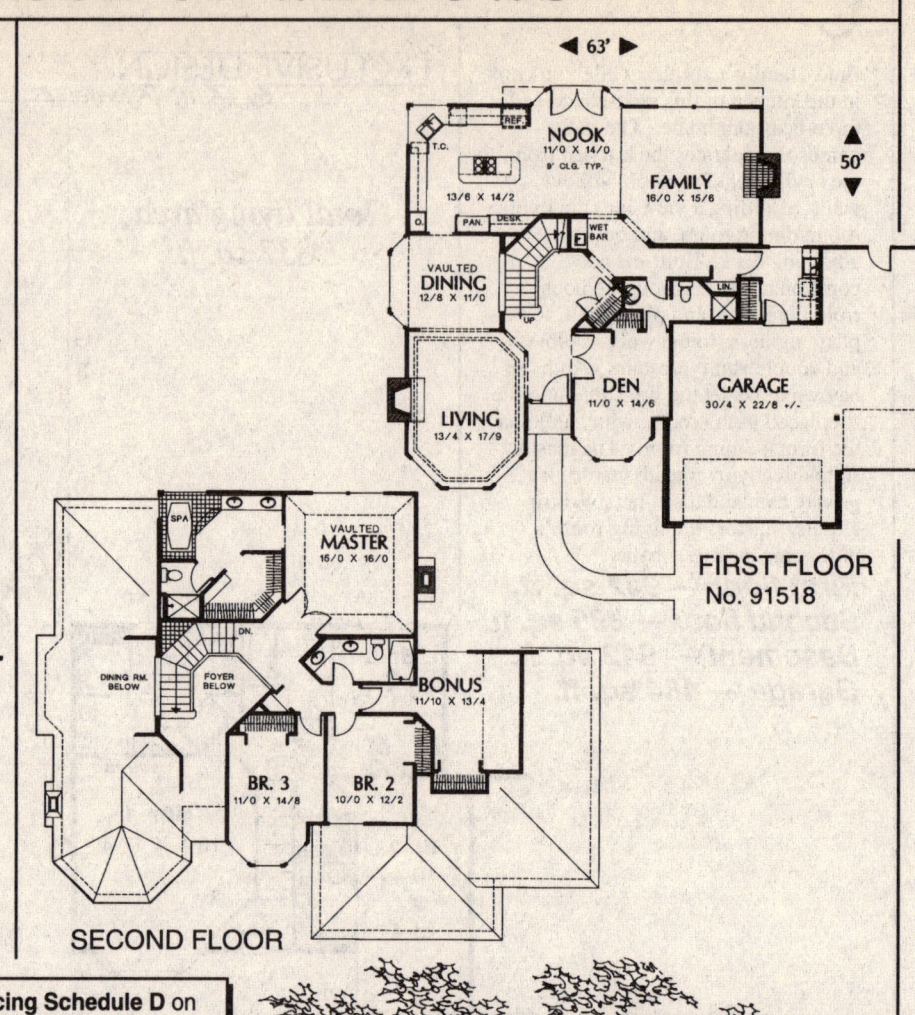

Refer to **Pricing Schedule D** on the order form for pricing information

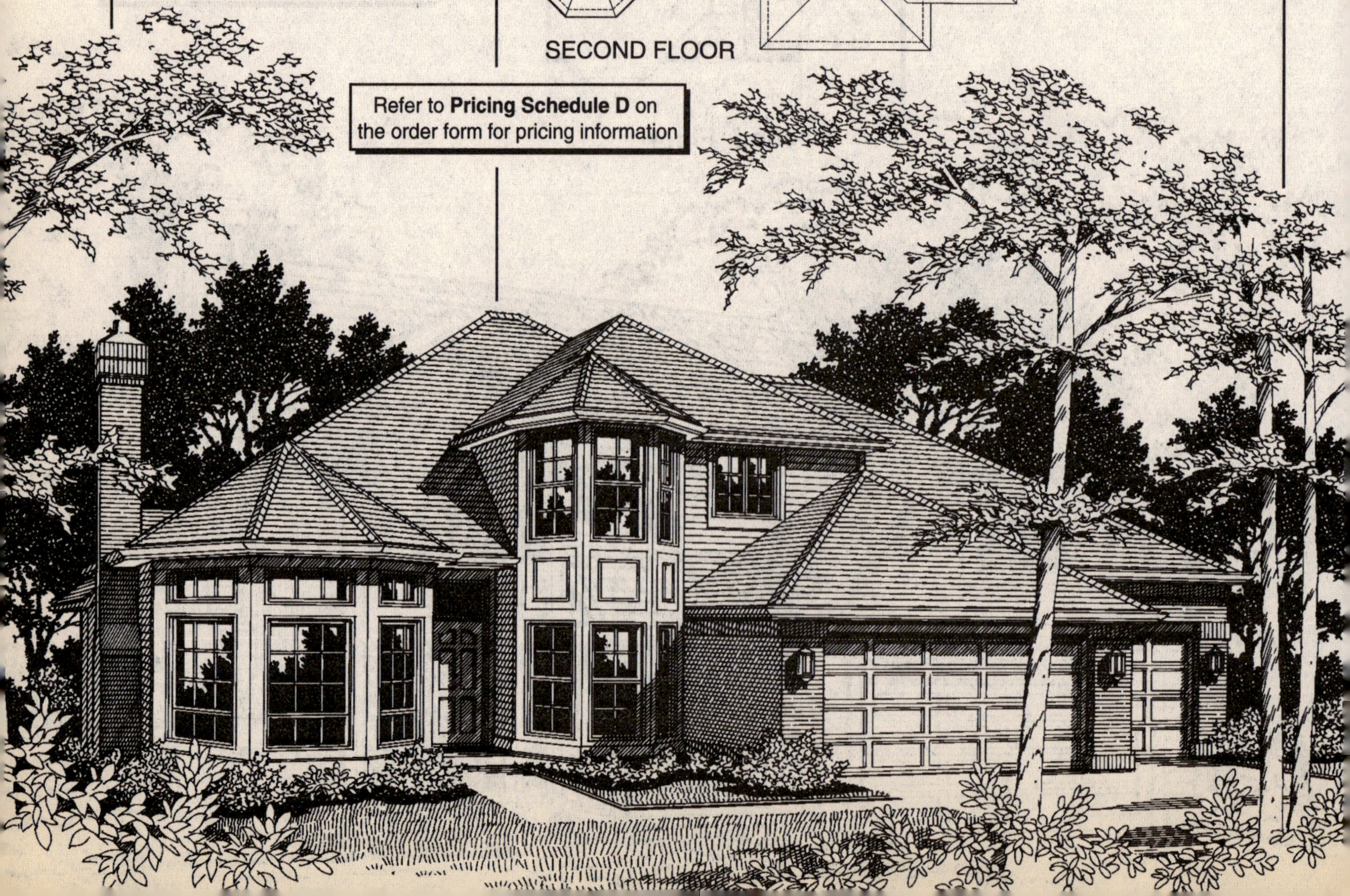

ORDER TODAY! 1-800-235-5700

Design 98501

STUNNING FAMILY PLAN

Absolutely stunning is the only way to describe this exciting home plan with its gorgeous front elevation with bay window, huge arch window, and brick gables, to the angled family room with elegant brick fireplace and cathedral ceiling. A large angled island kitchen with bright and airy breakfast area adds to the uniqueness of this plan. A large separate master suite and bath, formal living room and dining room, and three other bedrooms complete this masterpiece of design. With its well thought out floor plan and wonderful amenities, you're sure to enjoy this home for many years to come. No materials list is available for this plan.

Main floor — 2,194 sq. ft.
Garage — 462 sq. ft.

Total living area: 2,194 sq. ft.

Refer to **Pricing Schedule C** on the order form for pricing information

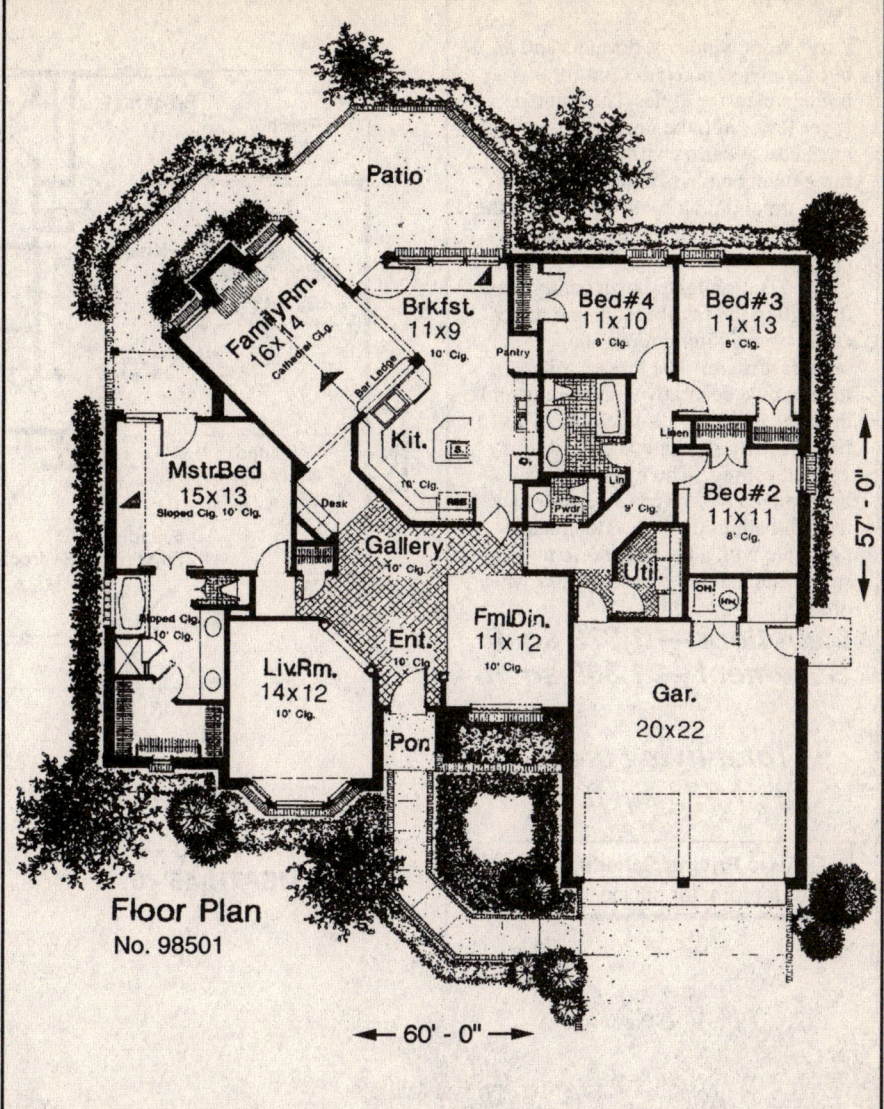

STYLE AND CONVENIENCE

Design 98411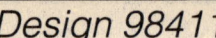

Large front windows, dormers and an old-fashioned porch account for this home's pleasing style. The vaulted foyer flows into the family room which emanates a warm charm as one views the glowing embers in the fireplace. The formal dining room flows from the family room and also includes an elegant vaulted ceiling. The efficient kitchen is highlighted by a pantry, pass through to the family room and direct access to the dining room and breakfast room. The master suite is topped by a decorative tray ceiling and includes a large walk-in closet. The five piece master bath is topped by a vaulted ceiling. The two additional bedrooms are roomy in size and share the full bath in the hall. This plan is available with a basement or crawl space foundation. Please specify when ordering.

Main floor — 1,373 sq. ft.
Basement — 1,386 sq. ft.

Total living area: 1,373 sq. ft.

Refer to **Pricing Schedule A** on the order form for pricing information

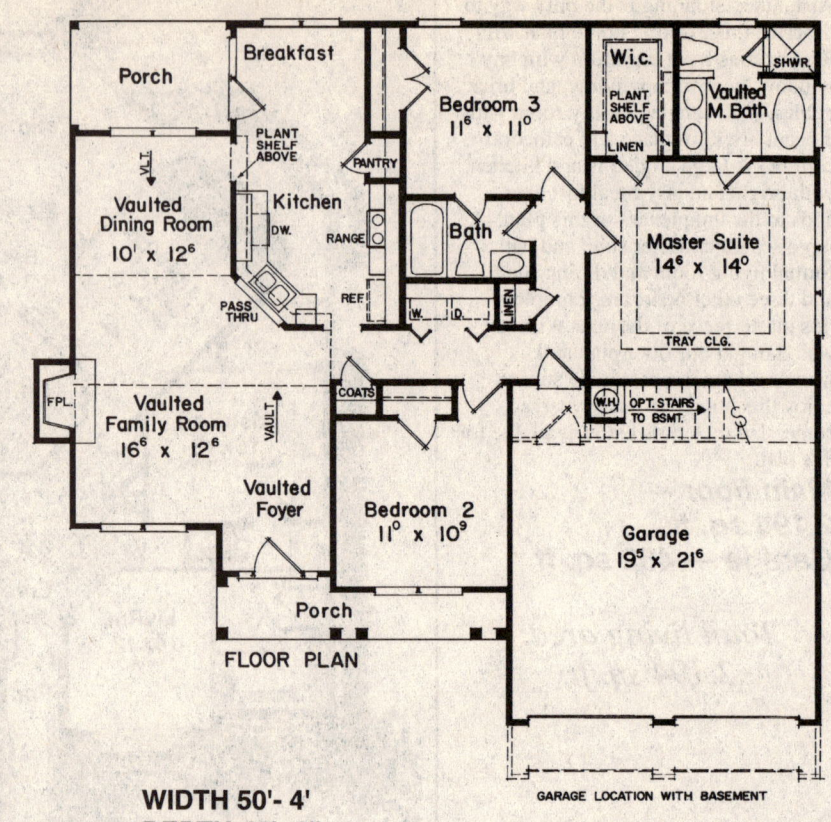

WIDTH 50'- 4'
DEPTH-45'- 0"

ORDER TODAY! 1 - 800 - 235 - 5700

Design 20179

Classic Style

The classic clapboard exterior of this home, graced with artful detailing, brings back memories of long ago. But its wide-open interior spaces takes it right into the future. A staircase to the four bedrooms on the second floor dominates the central foyer. Walk up to see the spacious, sunny sleeping rooms, cedar closet, two-part hall bath and master suite with every amenity. Back on the main floor, you'll find a huge living room that flows into the formal dining room in an open arrangement. A hallway past the powder room leads to family areas overlooking the rear deck, which include a gourmet kitchen with rangetop island, a bay breakfast nook, and just over the railing, a sunken fireplaced hearth room lined with bookcases.

First floor — 1,086 sq. ft.
Second floor — 1,057 sq. ft.
Basement — 881 sq. ft.
Garage — 484 sq. ft.

Refer to **Pricing Schedule C** on the order form for pricing information

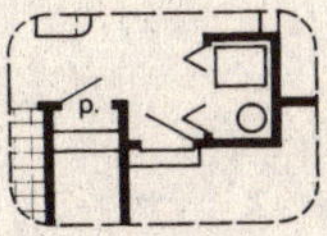

Total living area: 2,143 sq. ft.

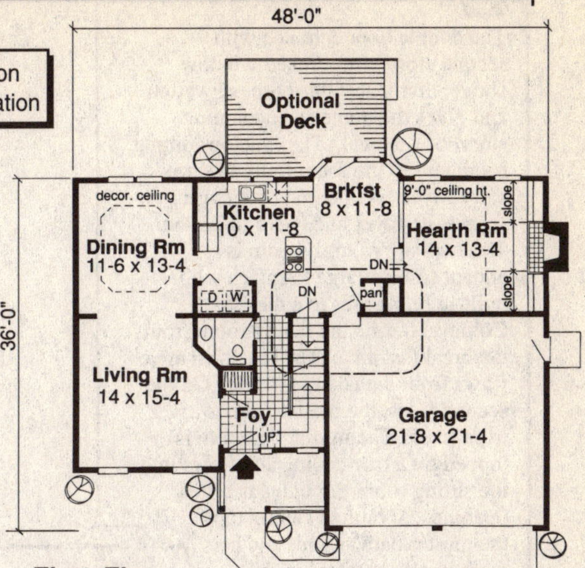

Slab/Crawl Space Option

First Floor No. 20179

48'-0"

Optional Deck

Kitchen 10 x 11-8
Brkfst 8 x 11-8
Dining Rm 11-6 x 13-4
Hearth Rm 14 x 13-4
9'-0" ceiling ht.
decor. ceiling
Living Rm 14 x 15-4
Foy UP
Garage 21-8 x 21-4

36'-0"

Second Floor

Br 2 10 x 10-6
Br 3 10-6 x 11
MBr 1 14x 15-4 decor. ceiling
Br 4 10-10 x 11
open to below

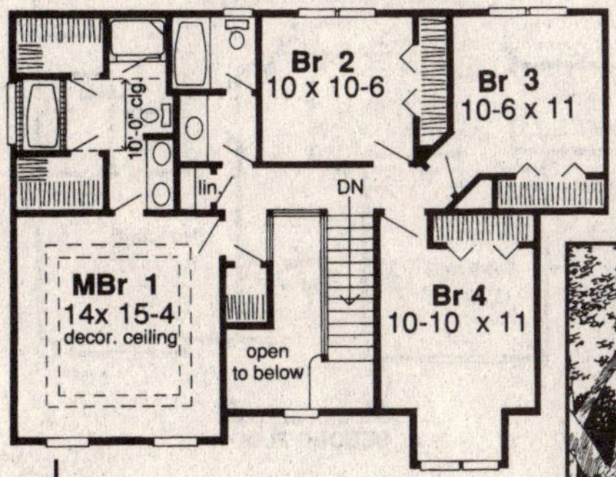

An **EXCLUSIVE DESIGN** *By Karl Kreeger*

ORDER TODAY! 1-800-235-5700

ENCHANTING STORYBOOK ENTRANCE

Design 98438

The double door entrance with a second story large arched window above, dominates this home elevation and gives the home an enchanting storybook appeal. The spacious dining room and living room flank the two-story foyer. A charming staircase graces the foyer and the dining room. The two-story family room is enhanced by a large fireplace with built-in bookcases to either side. Columns define the family room from the breakfast area. The breakfast area flows from the island kitchen. On the second floor, the master suite is expansive. The master bedroom is topped by a tray ceiling and flows into the sitting room through an arched opening. A vaulted ceiling tops the master bath and his and her walk-in closets provide an abundance of closet space. The three additional second floor bedrooms have private access to a full bath and ample closet space. This plan is available with a basement or crawl space foundation. Please specify when ordering.

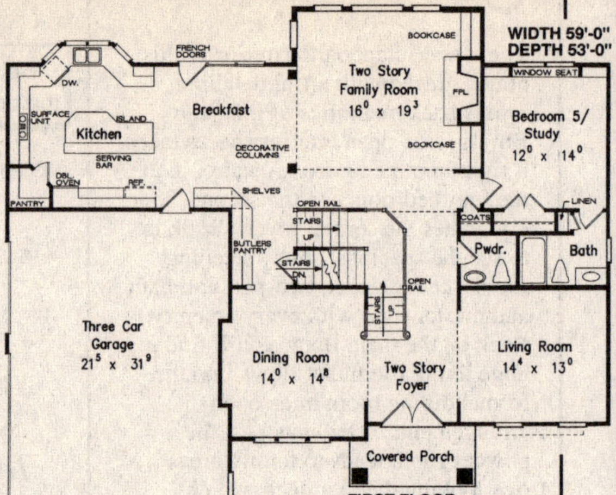

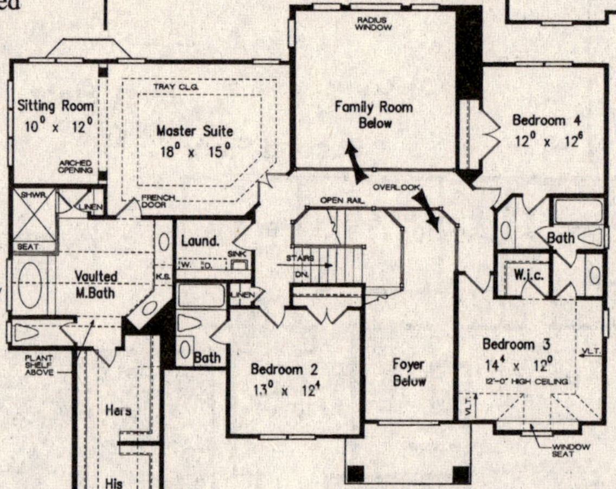

First floor —
1,786 sq. ft.
Second floor —
1,739 sq. ft.
Basement —
1,786 sq. ft.
Garage — 704 sq. ft.

Total living area:
3,525 sq. ft.

Refer to **Pricing Schedule F** on the order form for pricing information

Design 91900

TRADITIONAL ELEMENTS HIGHLIGHTED

Traditional elements like roof dormers, shutters and tumbled brick belie the spacious, contemporary floor plan awaiting inside. Angled entry walls hold French doors that lead into the bayed den. Columns, capped by plant shelves, define dining areas from living areas. The large Great room is made visually larger with the addition of liberal expanses of windows and a see-thru fireplace. The roomy kitchen features step-in pantry, separate ovens, built-in desk and sit-down snack counter. This kitchen in conjunction with the gazebo breakfast area will definitely be the gathering point for informal entertaining. Don't overlook the very private master suite containing a full amenity bath and large walk-in closet. Follow the dramatic skylit staircase up past the custom planter, to the two bedrooms and additional bath upstairs, ideally suited for teenage children or frequent guests. No materials list is available for this plan.

First floor — 1,855 sq. ft.
Upper floor — 530 sq. ft.

Total living area:
2,385 sq. ft.

FIRST FLOOR
No. 91900

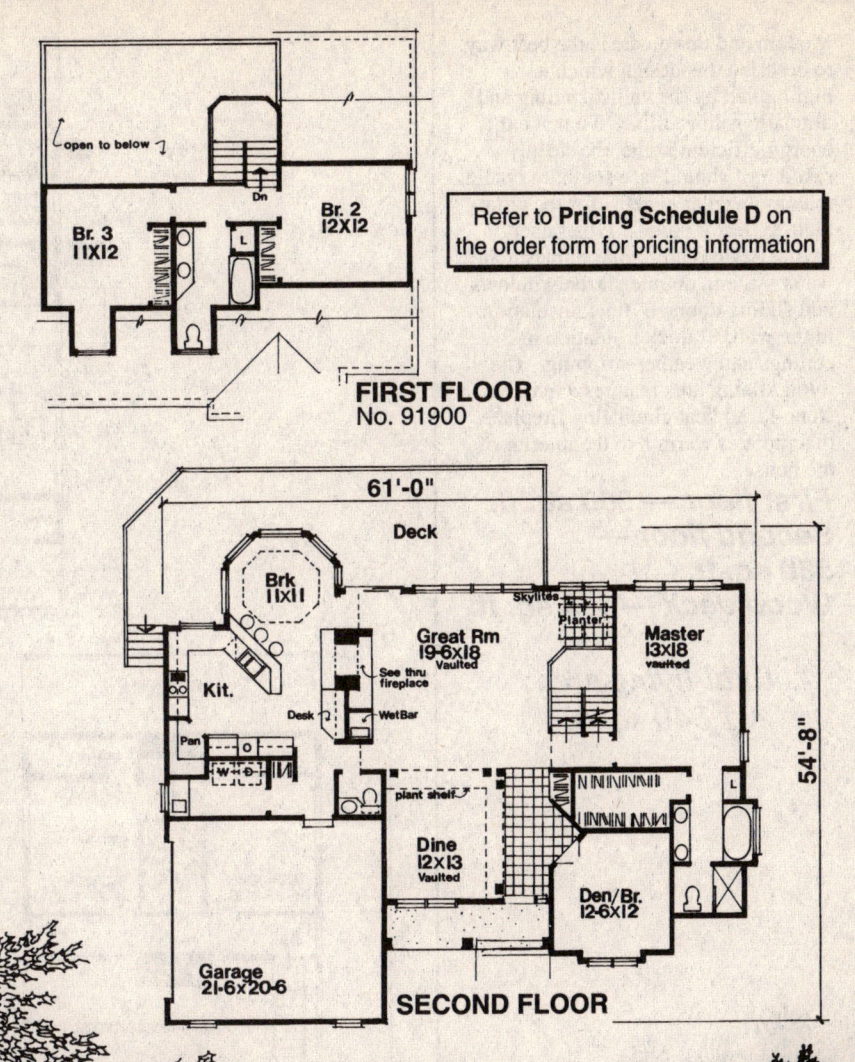

Refer to **Pricing Schedule D** on the order form for pricing information

SECOND FLOOR

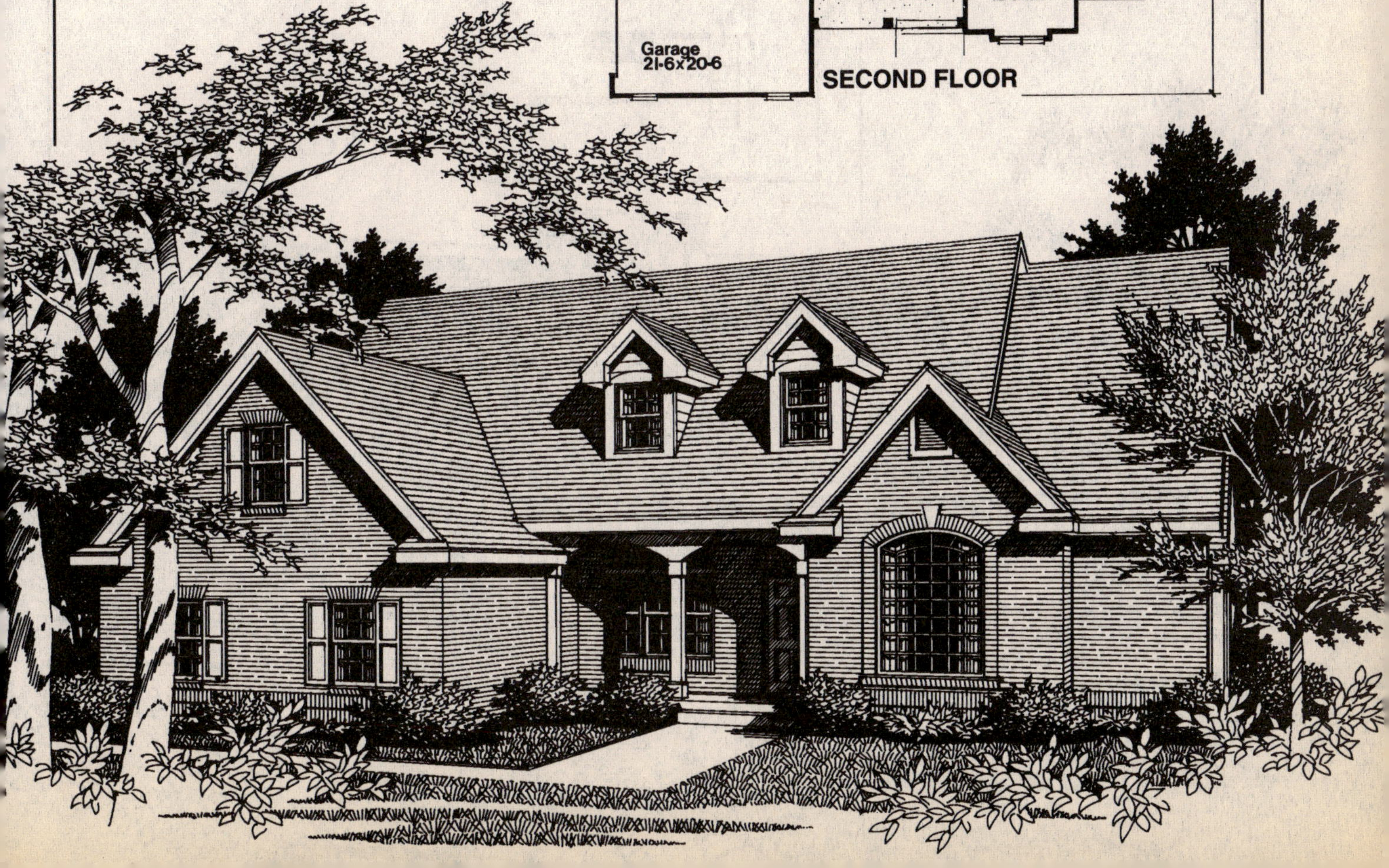

DESIGN HIGHLIGHTS SPLIT ROOFLINE

Design 90028

Modern and up-to-date is the best way to describe this design which is highlighted by the vertical siding and dramatic split roofline. To make this energy-efficient home, the steeply raked roof should face south, to obtain maximum solar benefits for the wflat-plate collector panels. Other energy saving devices are: solar domestic hot water system, double glazed windows and sliding doors, 6" thick insulation in the wall, 9" thick insulation in ceilings and weather-stripping. The living/dining area features a massive stone-faced heat circulating fireplace that radiates warmth to the interior of the house.

First floor — 960 sq. ft.
Second floor — 580 sq. ft.
Wood deck — 460 sq. ft.

Total living area: 1,540 sq. ft.

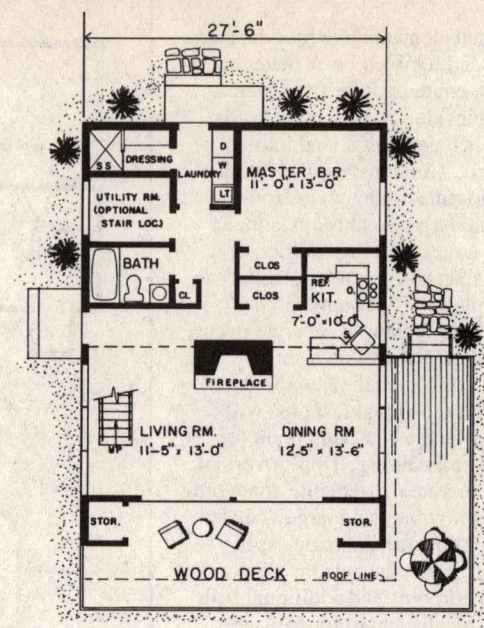

FIRST FLOOR
No. 90028

SECOND FLOOR

Refer to **Pricing Schedule B** on the order form for pricing information

FAMILY ROOM WITH A FIREPLACE

Design 93319

This beautiful family home includes all the amenities you have been looking for. The island kitchen includes a built-in pantry, double sink and dinette area. The dinette area flows into the family room. A cozy fireplace enhances the family room and can be seen from the formal living room. The formal dining room is easily accessible from the kitchen. All the bedrooms are located on the second floor. The master suite includes a walk-in closet, double vanity, separate shower and tub and compartmented toilet. The three additional bedrooms share a full hall bath. No materials list is available for this plan.

First floor — 1,228 sq. ft.
Second floor — 1,191 sq. ft.
Basement — 1,228 sq. ft.
Garage — 528 sq. ft.

Total living area: 2,419 sq. ft.

Refer to **Pricing Schedule D** on the order form for pricing information

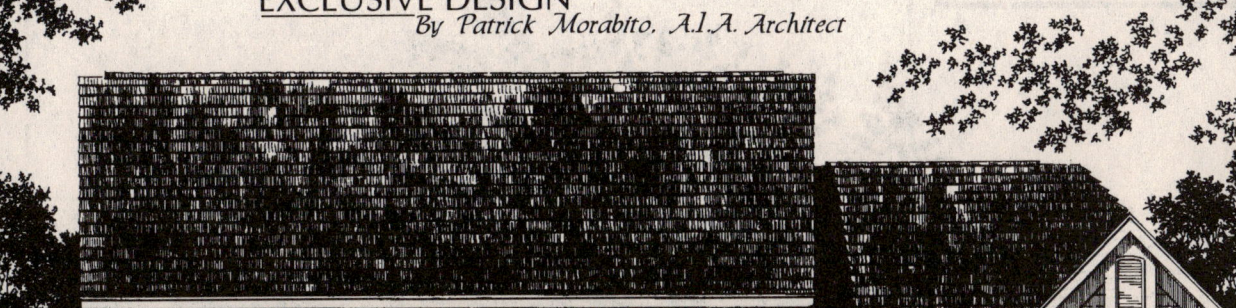

An EXCLUSIVE DESIGN
By Patrick Morabito, A.I.A. Architect

ENJOY A COUNTRY KITCHEN

Design 98810

The smell of a fresh apple pie, or chocolate chip cookies baking in the oven awaken happy childhood memories. Just imagine creating those same type of memories for your children in this large country kitchen. The work island gives ample elbow room for those family projects. The eating area opens onto the wrap-around porch or flows into the family room. A gas fireplace in the family room provides its own magic to a cold winter's evening. The formal areas are to the front of the home. On the second floor, four bedrooms provide the sleeping accommodations. The master suite offers needed privacy to the owner with a private bath and a walk-in closet. No materials list is available for this plan.

First floor — 1,163 sq. ft.
Second floor — 934 sq. ft.
Basement — 1,163 sq. ft.
Garage — 488 sq. ft.

Total living area: 2,097 sq. ft.

Refer to **Pricing Schedule C** on the order form for pricing information

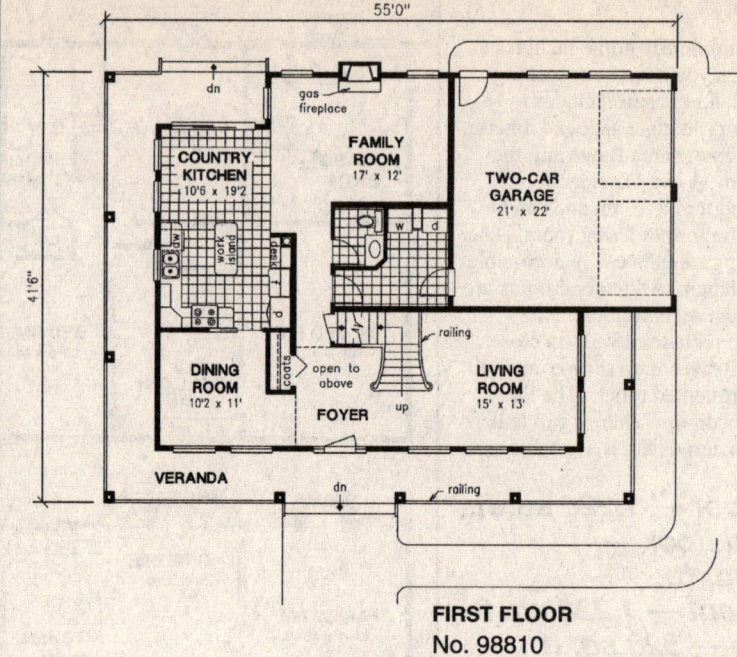

FIRST FLOOR
No. 98810

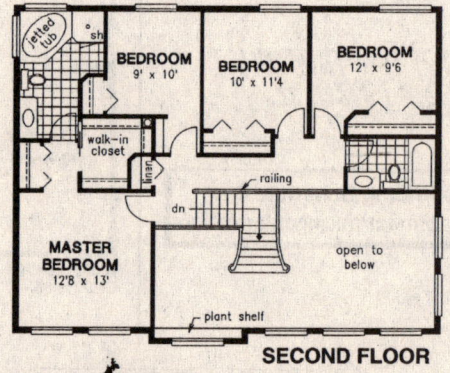

SECOND FLOOR

SKYLIGHTS BRIGHTEN TUDOR

Design 10673

Step from the arched fieldstone porch into the two-story foyer, and you can see that this traditional four bedroom home possesses a wealth of modern elements. Behind double doors lie the library and fireplaced living room, bathed in sunlight from two skylights in the sloping roof. Step out to the brick patio from the laundry room or bay-windowed breakfast room. For ultimate relaxation, the master bedroom suite contains a whirlpool tub. One bedroom boasts bay windows; another features a huge walk-in closet over the two car garage.

First floor — 1,265 sq. ft.
Second floor — 1,210 sq. ft.
Basement — 1,247 sq. ft.
Garage — 506 sq. ft.

An 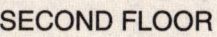 *By Karl Kreeger*

Total living area: 2,475 sq. ft.

FIRST FLOOR No. 10673

SECOND FLOOR

Refer to **Pricing Schedule D** on the order form for pricing information

ORDER TODAY! 1 - 800 - 235 - 5700

Design 98804

COMPACT DESIGN

This compact design captures views to the rear of the lot. A railed staircase increases the visual space in the combined living and dining rooms. The open kitchen design features a built-in pantry, built-in planning desk and a bright and cheery breakfast bay. The formal dining room has access to the covered deck. The thoughtfully planned master suite, with access to the sun deck, is complete with a double closet and a deluxe three-piece bath. The unfinished walk-out basement completes the home. No materials list is available for this plan.

**Main floor —
1,372 sq. ft.
Basement —
1,372 sq. ft.
Garage — 484 sq. ft..
Deck — 310 sq. ft.**

*Total living area:
1,372 sq. ft.*

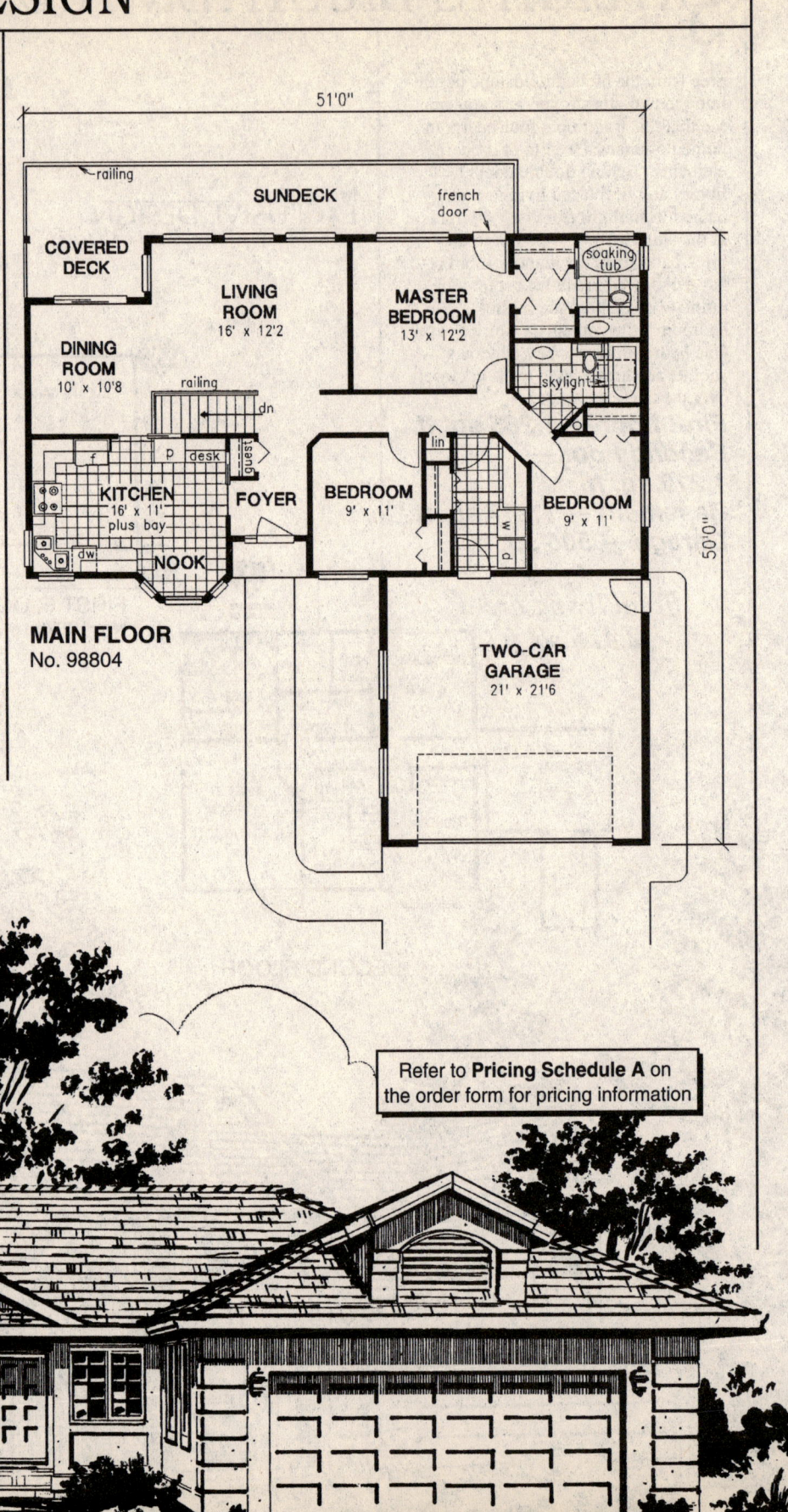

Refer to **Pricing Schedule A** on the order form for pricing information

COMFORT AND STYLE

Design 90990

This three-bedroom, two-bath home offers comfort and style. The master suite is complete with its own bath with a skylight. In the center of this design the kitchen includes an eating nook that takes full advantage of the view, and is just the right size for family gatherings. The large sundeck is easily accessible from the master suite, nook and living/dining area. A gas fireplace adds a cozy touch to the living room and the open staircase to the basement level ties both floors together very nicely. The unfinished daylight basement will provide plenty of space for family recreation, extra bedrooms and storage space. The front porch is a very practical feature and leads you into an attractive foyer complete with vaulted ceiling.

Main area — 1,423 sq. ft.
Basement — 1,423 sq. ft.
Garage — 399 sq. ft.
Width — 46' 0"
Depth — 52'- 0"

Total living area: 1,423 sq. ft.

Refer to **Pricing Schedule A** on the order form for pricing information

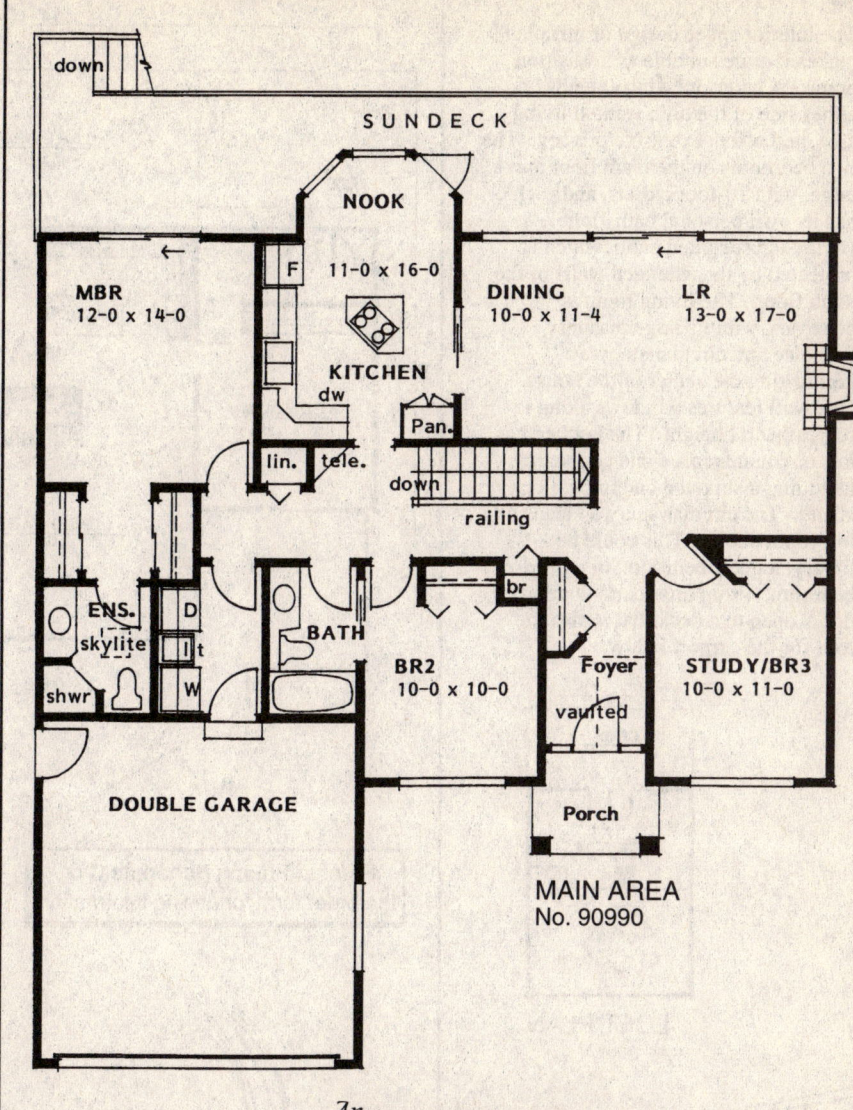

SECLUDED VACATION RETREAT

Design 91704

The interior space design of this plan makes it quite suitable as a vacation home. A bedroom wing extends on either side of the high vaulted living area, and offers extensive privacy. The two bedrooms on the main floor are large, with 10-foot closets, and each has its own personal bath, double vanity and secluded patio, which is protected by the extended walls of the main floor. The living room is generous, with its large masonry fireplace and circular stairway dominating the center of the house. One wall features windows along its full cathedral height. The kitchen has lots of counter space and cupboards, including a sink and chopping block island. The circular stairway leads to a loft room above. This could be a library, a guest bedroom, or a third bedroom. From this room, windowed doors open to a deck that is also the roof for the carport below.

MAIN FLOOR No. 91704

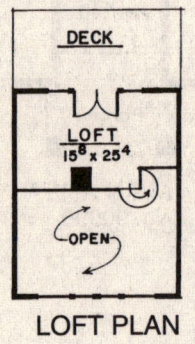

LOFT PLAN

Refer to **Pricing Schedule C** on the order form for pricing information

Main floor — 1,448 sq. ft.
Loft plan — 389 sq. ft.
Carport — 312 sq. ft.

Total living area: 1,837 sq. ft.

Economical Vacation Home

Design 99238

This simply-styled vacation cottage is economical to construct, a perfect match for a mountainside setting, and very easy to enjoy. The large rectilinear living room features a fireplace at one end and plenty of room for separate activities. The galley-style kitchen is big and spacious, and includes an adjoining dining area. Sleeping room for up to seven is easy with a downstairs bedroom and full bath, second floor master bedroom, and a children's dormitory across the hall. Greet the day as you walk out onto the second floor deck just outside the master suite.

First floor — 784 sq. ft.
Second floor — 504 sq. ft.

Total living area: 1,288 sq. ft.

Refer to **Pricing Schedule A** on the order form for pricing information

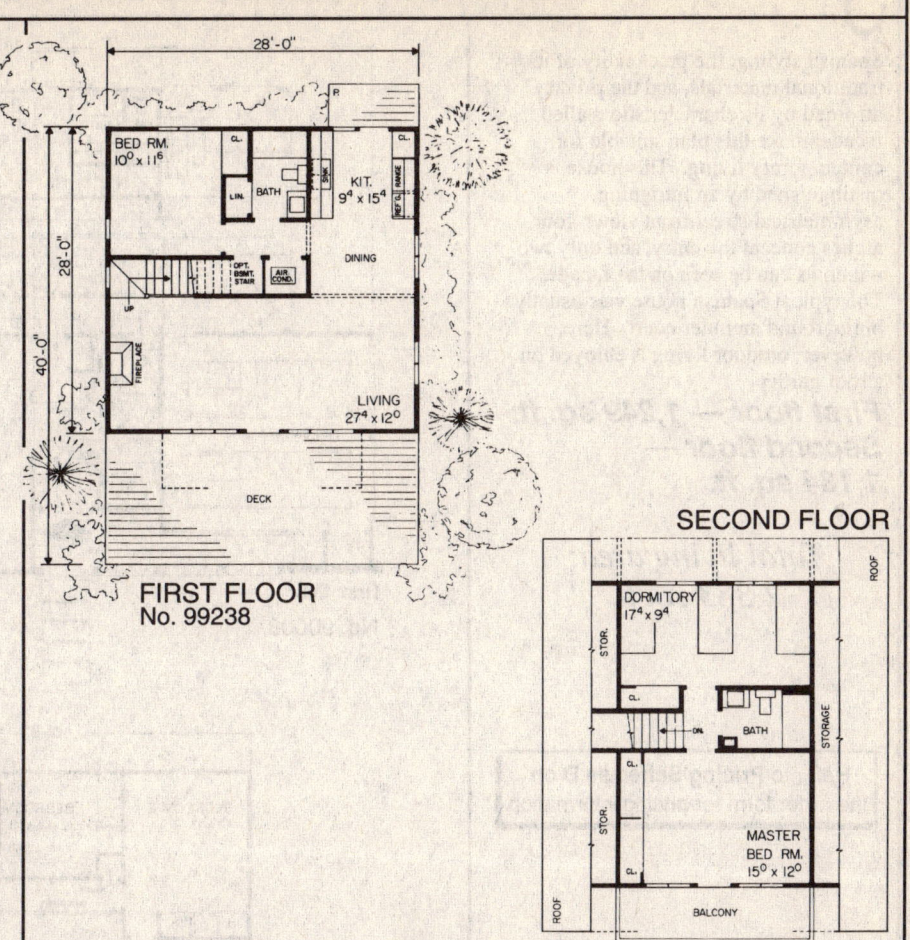

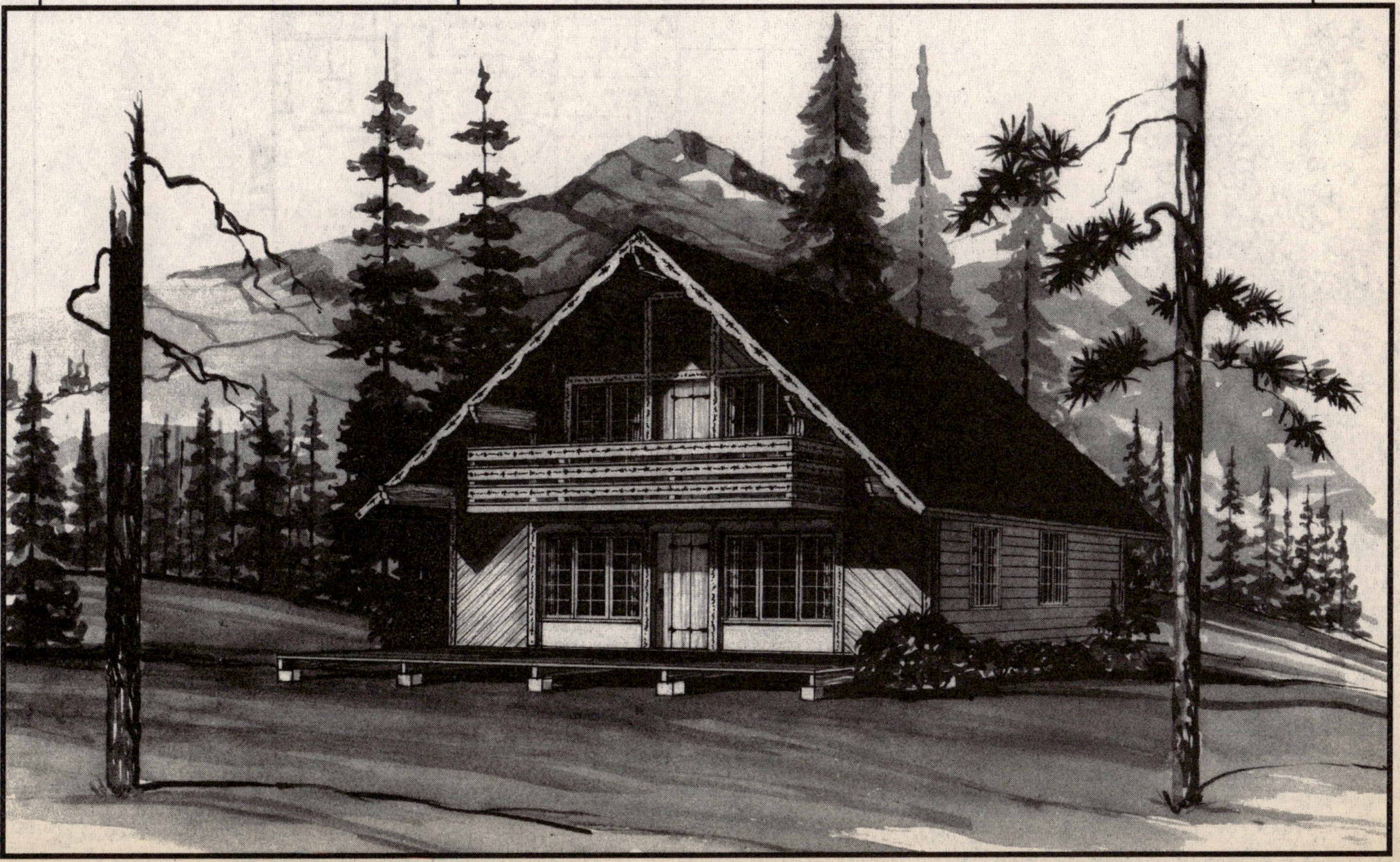

Design 90008

SPANISH TWO-STORY DESIGN

Spanish styling, the practicality of its traditional materials, and the privacy afforded by its characteristic walled facade, make this plan suitable for contemporary living. This house is distinguished by an intriguing, asymmetrical street front view: four arches conceal the entry, and only two windows can be seen on the facade. The typical Spanish house was usually built around an inner court. Here, however, outdoor living is enjoyed on a roof garden.

First floor — 1,249 sq. ft.
Second floor — 1,134 sq. ft.

Total living area:
2,383 sq. ft.

Refer to **Pricing Schedule D** on the order form for pricing information

first floor
No. 90008

second floor

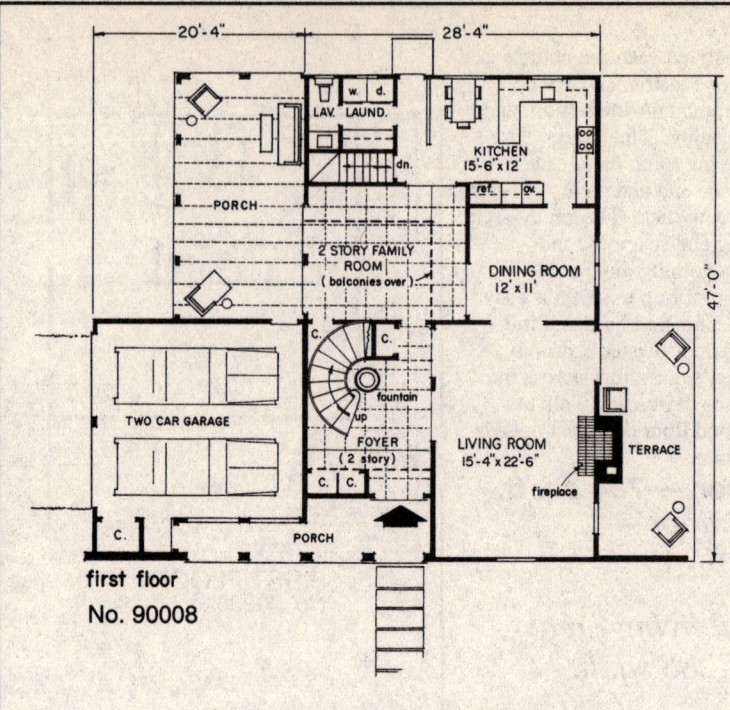

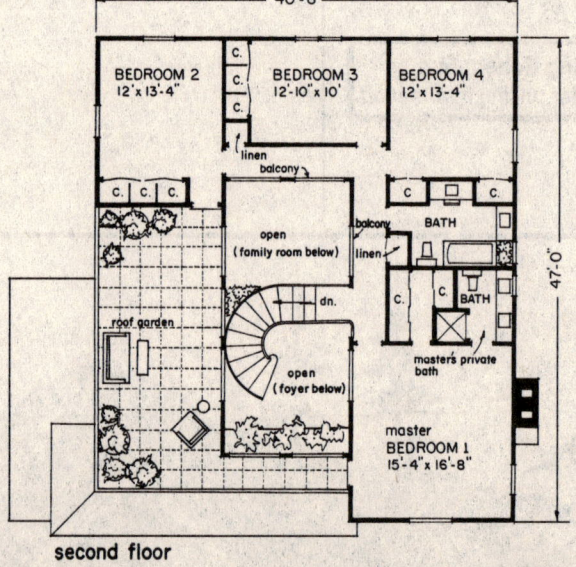

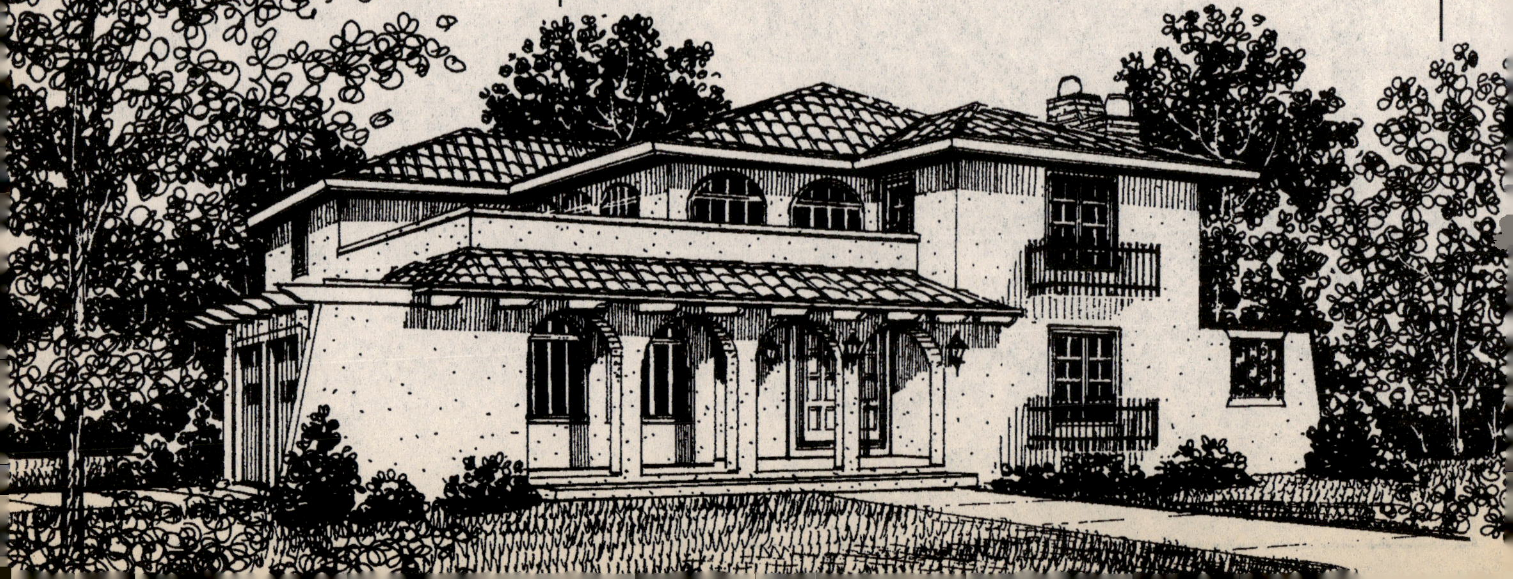

ORDER TODAY!   1 - 800 - 235 - 5700

Design 91082

Highlited by a Wrap-Around Porch

The traditional exterior of this home is highlighted by a wrap-around porch and Victorian trim. Great care and attention to detail is expressed throughout the comfortable family-oriented floor plan. Lots of windows, including a transom window on the second level, provide an abundance of light for the entry, living room and dining room. The efficient galley kitchen has a preparation island and a very large pantry. The nook is an enjoyable area with patio door access to the deck and an arched opening leading into the family room. Sliding glass doors open to the deck beyond and a second fireplace offers a warm environment for family gatherings. Bedroom four could be a guest room or den and shares the full bath on the main level. The stairway has a cozy window seat on the landing and leads to the master suite, two large secondary bedrooms and a full bath on the second level. The master suite is fully appointed with a vaulted ceiling, a large walk-in closet and large bath. No materials list available for this plan.

Refer to **Pricing Schedule E** on the order form for pricing information

First floor — 1,614 sq. ft.
Second floor — 1,024 sq. ft.
Garage — 672 sq. ft.

Total living area: 2,638 sq. ft.

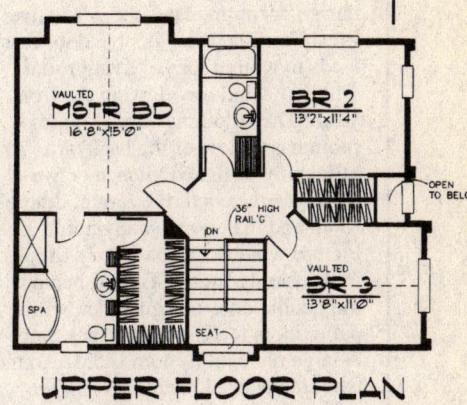

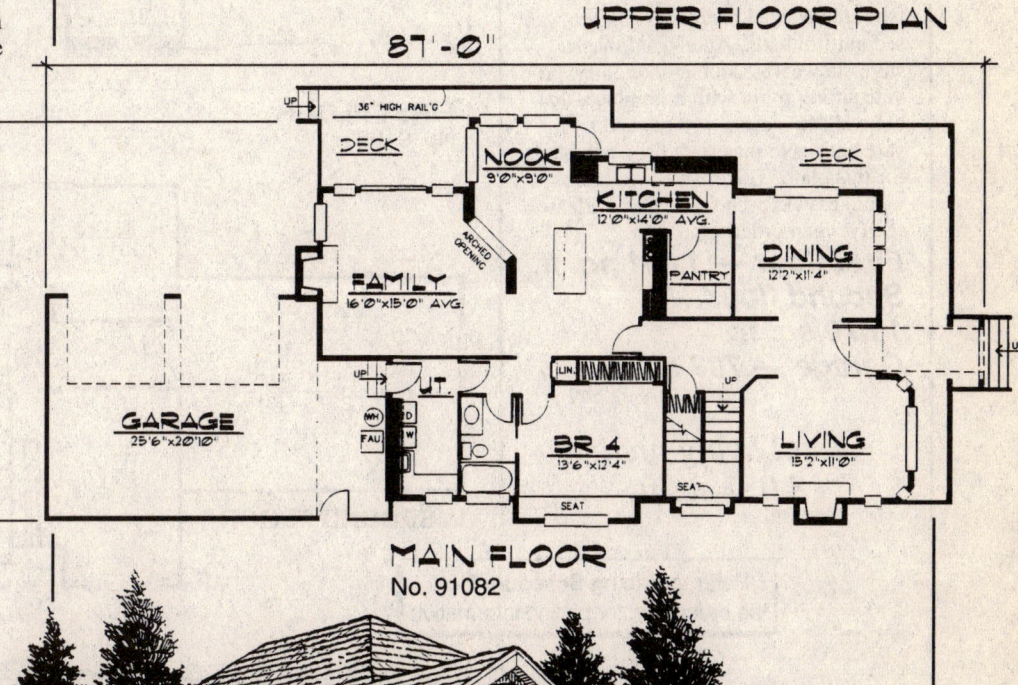

Suitable for Many Settings

Design 91083

ORDER TODAY! 1-800-235-5700

A covered porch and dormers enhance this traditional two-story home, making it suitable for either an urban or country setting. The modern interior design accommodates today's active lifestyle with ease. Double door entry leads to a large formal living room with bay windows viewing the front yard. The adjoining formal dining room has a view of the backyard. An efficiently designed kitchen conveniently serves both the formal dining room and the casual sunny nook. Picture windows flank a cozy fireplace in the family room. Tucked behind the double door is a quiet den with patio doors leading to the back yard. A large recreation room is close to the two ample sized bedrooms and the second full bath. An elegant master suite showcases double door entry, private sitting room with a fireplace, double walk-in closets, spa tub and a private bath. No materials list available for this plan. This plan is available with a crawl space foundation. Please secify when ordering.

First floor — 1,411 sq. ft.
Second floor — 1,670 sq. ft.
Garage — 703 sq. ft.

Total living area: 3,081 sq. ft.

Refer to **Pricing Schedule E** on the order form for pricing information

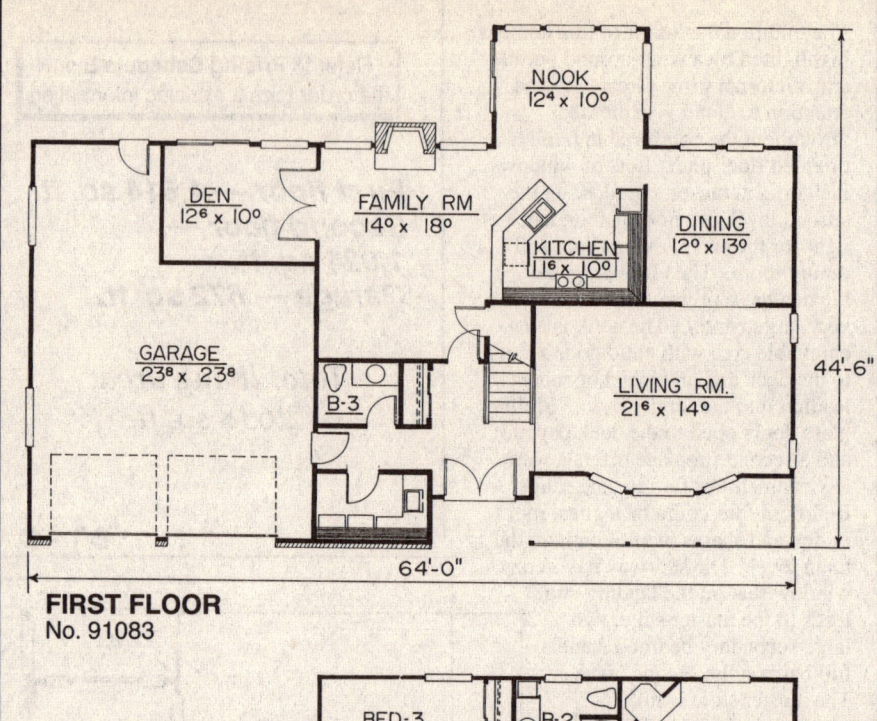

FIRST FLOOR
No. 91083

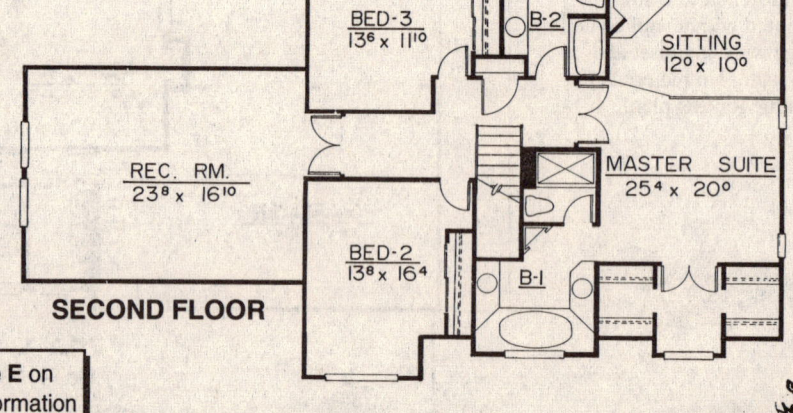

SECOND FLOOR

Modern Look — Colonial Style

Design 93287

An **EXCLUSIVE DESIGN** *By Jannis Vann & Associates, Inc.*

Brick detailing and keystones highlight this elevation. Inside the open two-story foyer provides volume and an illusion of more area. The formal living and dining rooms are located on either side of the foyer. The family room sports a fireplace with built-in shelving to either side. Relaxed family living is encouraged between the kitchen, breakfast bay and family room. The rooms are laid out in an open floor plan. The U-shaped kitchen includes a peninsula counter, a built-in pantry and double sinks. The breakfast bay is bright and cheery, the perfect atmosphere to start your day. There is direct access to the rear deck from the family room. A decorative ceiling adds a touch of elegance to the second floor master suite. A full bath with a dual vanity and a walk-in closet insure privacy and provide storage for the owner. Two additional bedrooms, located in close proximity to the full hall bath, are also on the second floor. A bonus room over the garage allows for future expansion.

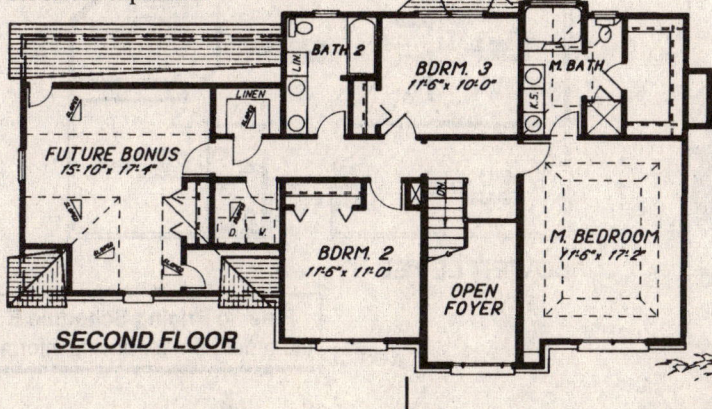

First floor — 987 sq. ft.
Second floor — 965 sq. ft.
Lower floor — 72 sq. ft.

Total living area: 2,024 sq. ft.

Refer to **Pricing Schedule C** on the order form for pricing information

ORDER TODAY! 1 - 800 - 235 - 5700

Design 91089

EXPANSIVE VIEWS

This daylight lower level home is ideal for a sloping lot and provides expansive views. Extensive decking allows outdoor enjoyment from barbecues to bird watching. Although centrally located, the fireplace is tucked into an unobtrusive niche in the living room. The master bedroom suite has a walk-in closet, dual vanity and a bumped out spa tub. Downstairs, the family room is centered between two bedrooms, another bath and two unfinished spaces, a bonus room and a mechanical room.

Main floor — 1,803 sq. ft.
Lower level — 982 sq. ft.
Unfinished space — 577 sq. ft.
Garage — 440 sq. ft.

Total living area: 2,785 sq. ft.

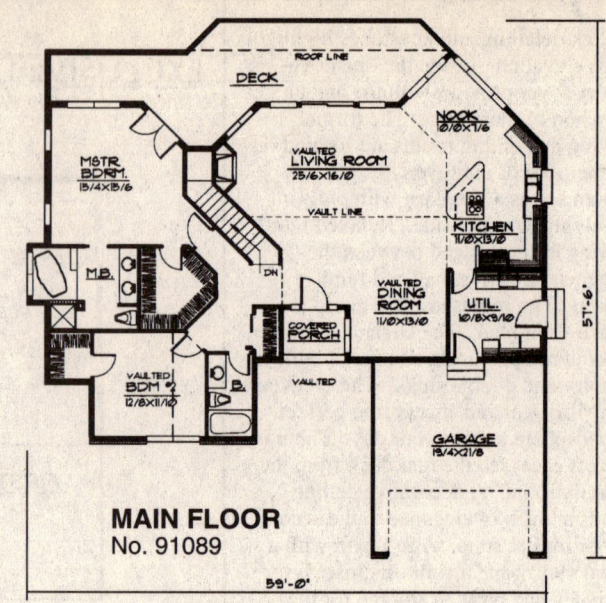

MAIN FLOOR
No. 91089

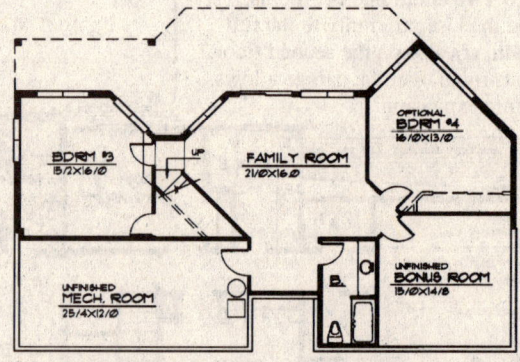

LOWER LEVEL

Refer to **Pricing Schedule E** on the order form for pricing information

FOR THE DISCRIMINATING BUYER

Design 92625

A classic design and spacious interior make this home attractive and exciting to the discriminating buyer. Brick and wood trim, multiple gables, and wing walls enhance the outside; while the interior offers features that are designed for entertaining guests or family enjoyment. Sloped ceilings, a corner fireplace, windows across the rear of the Great room and a boxed window in the dining room area are immediately visible as you enter the open foyer. The extra large kitchen provides an abundance of counter space, and a pantry. The breakfast area is surrounded by windows that flood the room with natural light. In the master bedroom suite there is an ultra bath with whirlpool tub, a double sink, a shower and a walk-in closet. This three bedroom Ranch can be expanded to twice its original size by accessing the full basement. No materials list is available for this plan.

Main area — 1,710 sq. ft.
Basement — 1,560 sq. ft.
Garage — 455 sq. ft.
Width — 65'-10"
Depth — 56'-0"

Total living area: 1,710 sq. ft.

Refer to **Pricing Schedule B** on the order form for pricing information

A LIBRARY IN EVERY ROOM

Design 10686

Spectacular is one word you could use to describe the remarkable quality of light and space in this four-bedroom family home. Well-placed skylights and abundant windows bathe every room in sunlight. The huge, two-story foyer features an angular, open staircase that leads to the bedrooms, and divides the space between the vaulted living and dining rooms. At the rear of the house, the wide-open family area includes the kitchen, dinette, and fireplaced family room complete with built-in bar and bookcases. Vaulted ceilings in the screened porch are mirrored upstairs in the master suite, which features two walk-in closets, double vanities, and a luxurious jacuzzi.

First floor — 1,786 sq. ft.
Second floor — 1,490 sq. ft.
Basement — 1,773 sq. ft.
Garage — 579 sq. ft.

Total living area: 3,276 sq. ft.

Refer to **Pricing Schedule F** on the order form for pricing information

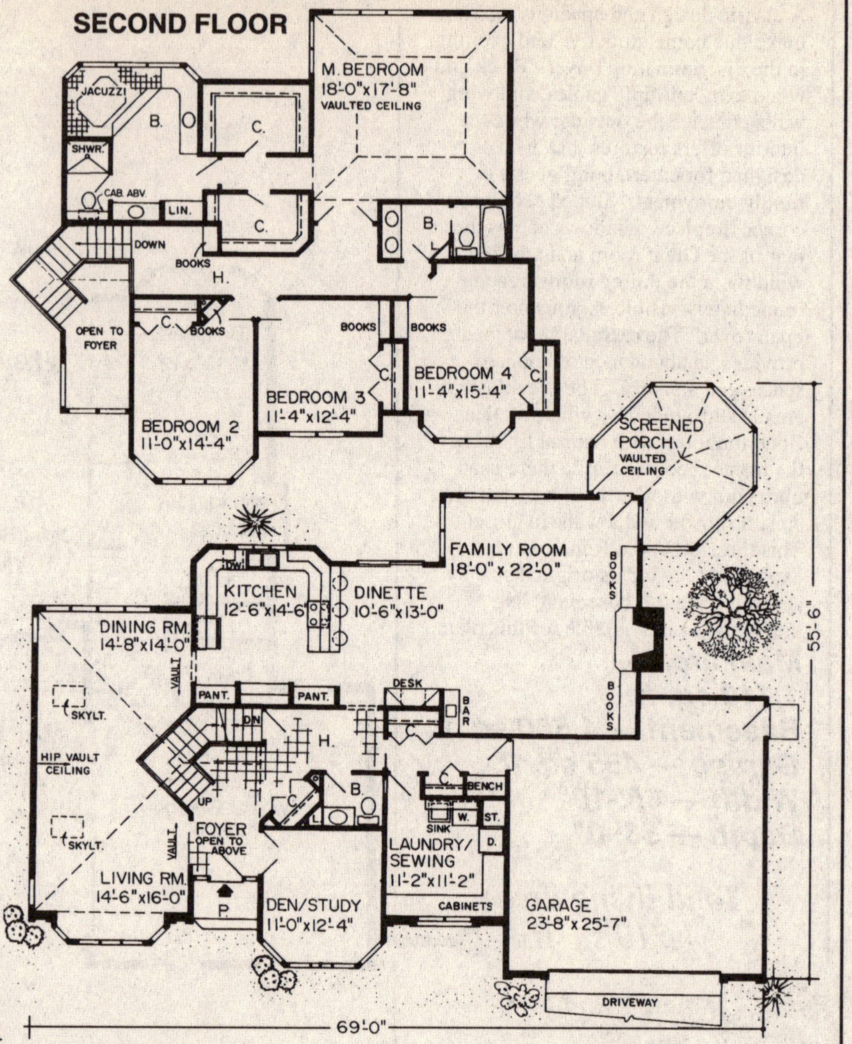

SECOND FLOOR

FIRST FLOOR
No. 10686

WINDOWS ADD LIGHT & SPACE

Design 20108

Shutters, round-cut shingles, and an attractive railed porch lend classic charm to this three-bedroom home. But this traditional exterior houses an open, updated interior designed for privacy and convenience. A central entry leads three ways: into the formal living room, past the open stairs to a huge, sunny family room crowned by a fireplace, and down an L-shaped hall to the bedroom wing, which includes two full baths. Notice the elegant ceiling treatment and room-sized walk-in closet in the master suite. The kitchen is a gourmet's dream, with its range-top island, bump-out window, perfect for an indoor herb garden, and strategic location between family and dining rooms.

Main living area — 2,120 sq. ft.
Basement — 2,120 sq. ft.
Garage — 576 sq. ft.

Total living area: 2,120 sq. ft.

Refer to **Pricing Schedule C** on the order form for pricing information

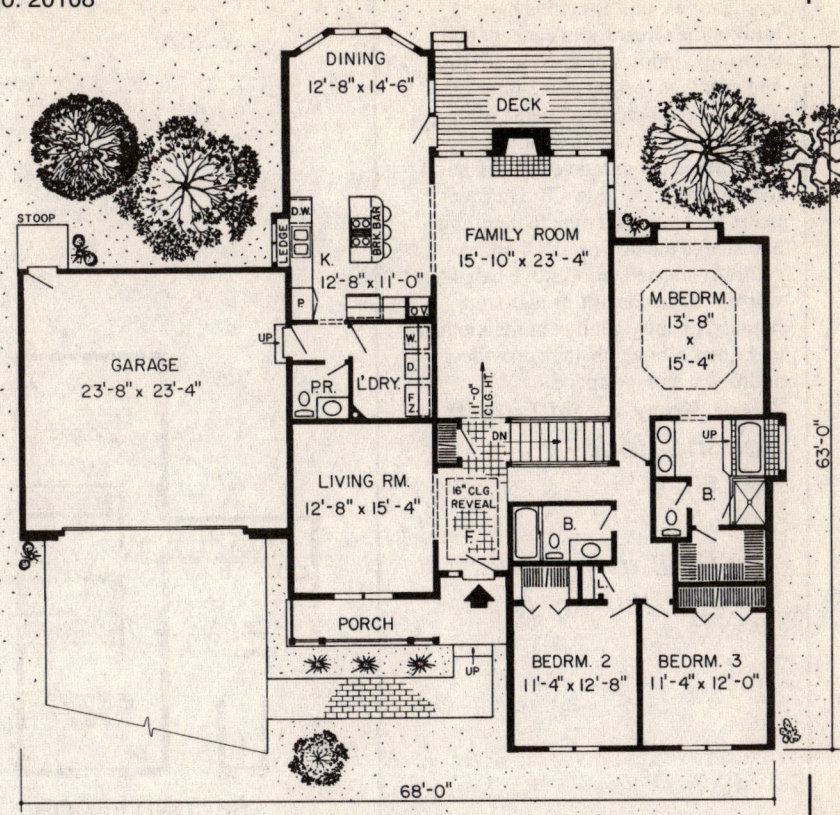

MAIN AREA
No. 20108

An EXCLUSIVE DESIGN *By Karl Kreeger*

ORDER TODAY! 1-800-235-5700

PERFECT FOR A NARROW LOT

Design 91091

Designed to accommodate narrow lot applications, this attractive home utilizes the Great room concept and transom windows to provide a light and spacious feeling to the interior. The covered porch and trellis offer a relaxing retreat any time of the day. The double car garage entry can be located from any side. The master bedroom features a nine foot ceiling and shares the downstairs bath. A centrally located wood stove helps to warm both levels of this two-story home. A pantry cabinet in the kitchen and linen cabinet upstairs provides additional storage space.

First floor — 842 sq. ft.
Second floor — 408 sq. ft.

Total living area: 1,250 sq. ft.

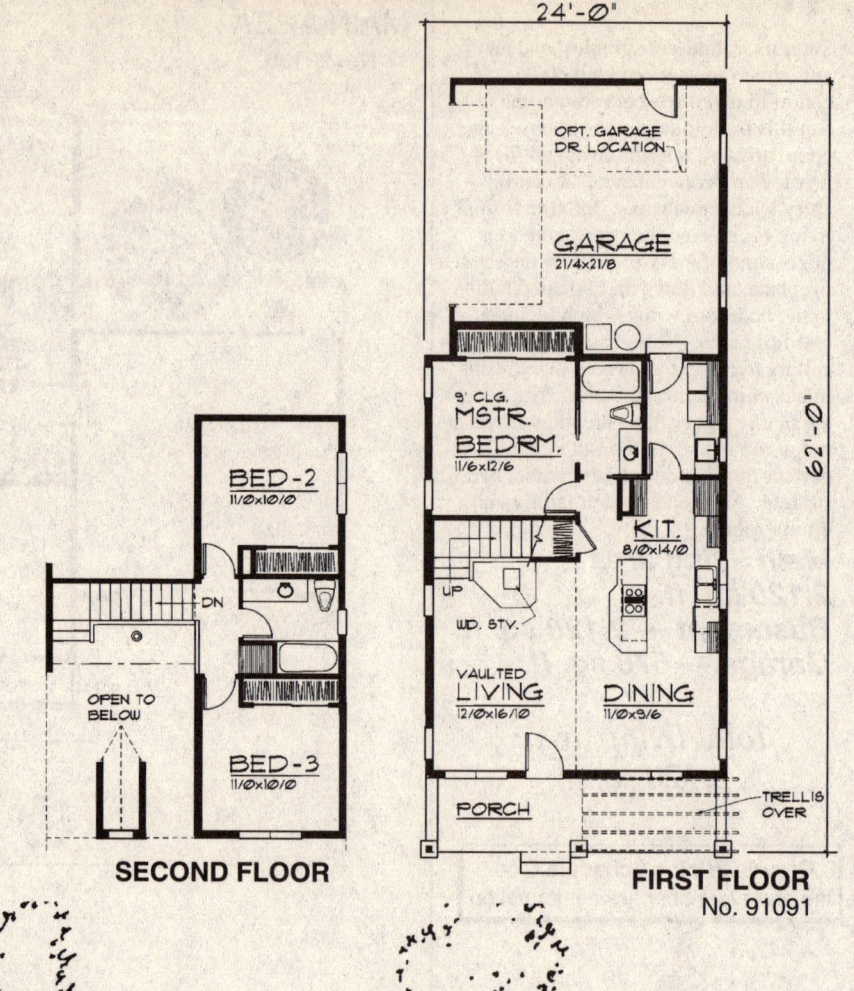

Refer to **Pricing Schedule A** on the order form for pricing information

Design 93401

GLORIOUS FRONT WINDOW

This home's many features accentuate your entertaining endeavors. The large front window enhances the curb appeal of this home, and illuminates the dining room. The expansive kitchen/breakfast room is close at hand. The cooktop island, double sinks and more than ample counter and cupboard space add to the room's efficiency. A private master suite, with a decorative ceiling, provides a personal getaway for the owner. The master bath and walk-in closet give convenience and privacy to the suite. Two additional bedrooms on the second floor, with walk-in closets, share a full hall bath with a dual vanity. No materials list available.

First floor — 1,901 sq. ft.
Second floor — 803 sq. ft.
Basement — 1,901 sq. ft.
Garage — 550 sq. ft.

Total living area: 2,704 sq. ft.

2nd FLOOR

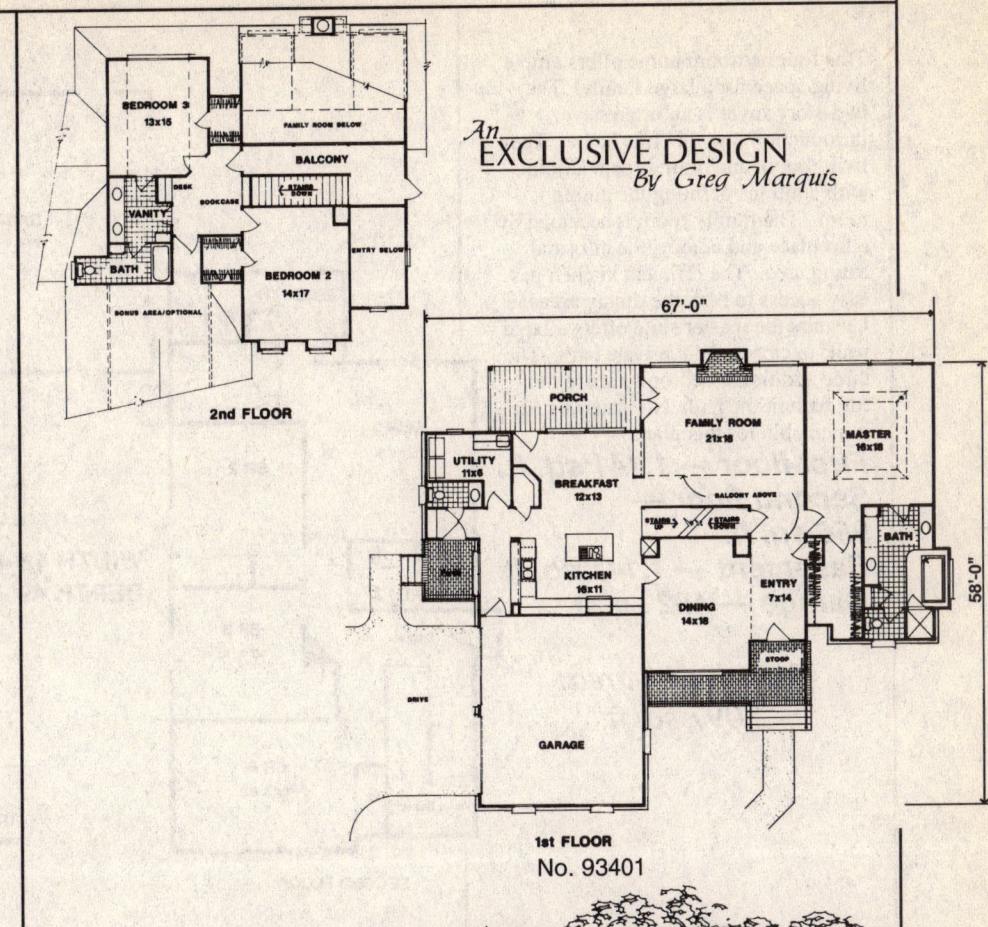

An EXCLUSIVE DESIGN
By Greg Marquis

1st FLOOR
No. 93401

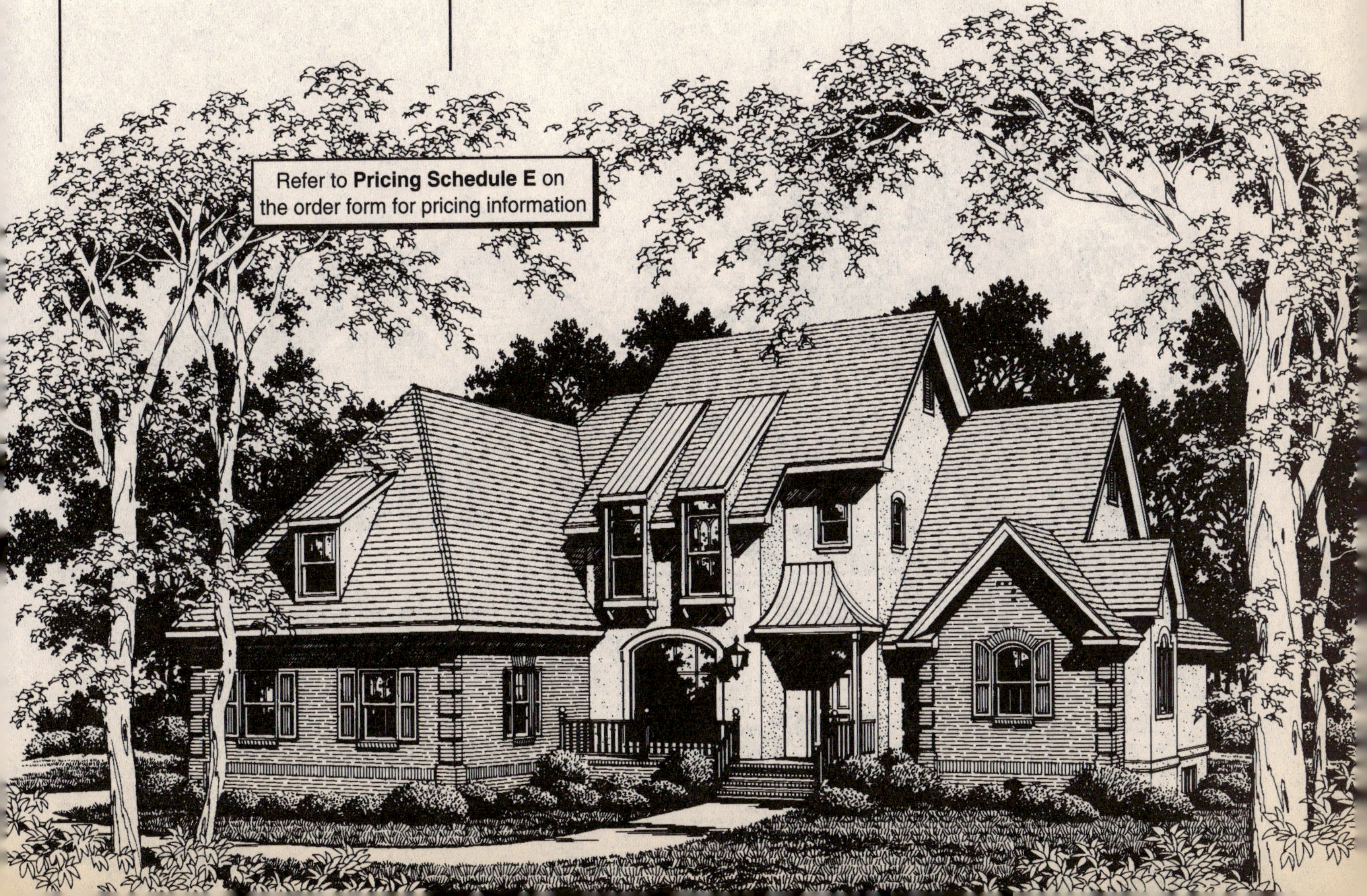

Refer to **Pricing Schedule E** on the order form for pricing information

FAMILY DWELLING

Design 94146

This four bedroom home offers ample living space for a large family. The two-story foyer is an impressive introduction into this fine home. The living room and dining room adjoin with columns defining the dining room. The family room is accented by a fireplace and adjoins the informal eating area. The efficient kitchen has easy access to both the dining areas. Upstairs the master suite offers a large walk-in closet and a private bath. The three additional bedrooms share the full bath in the hall. No materials list is available for this plan.

First floor — 1,141 sq. ft.
Second floor — 956 sq. ft.
Basement — 1,141 sq. ft.
Garage — 482 sq. ft.

Total living area: 2,097 sq. ft.

WIDTH 48'-0"
DEPTH 49'-0"

Refer to **Pricing Schedule D** on the order form for pricing information

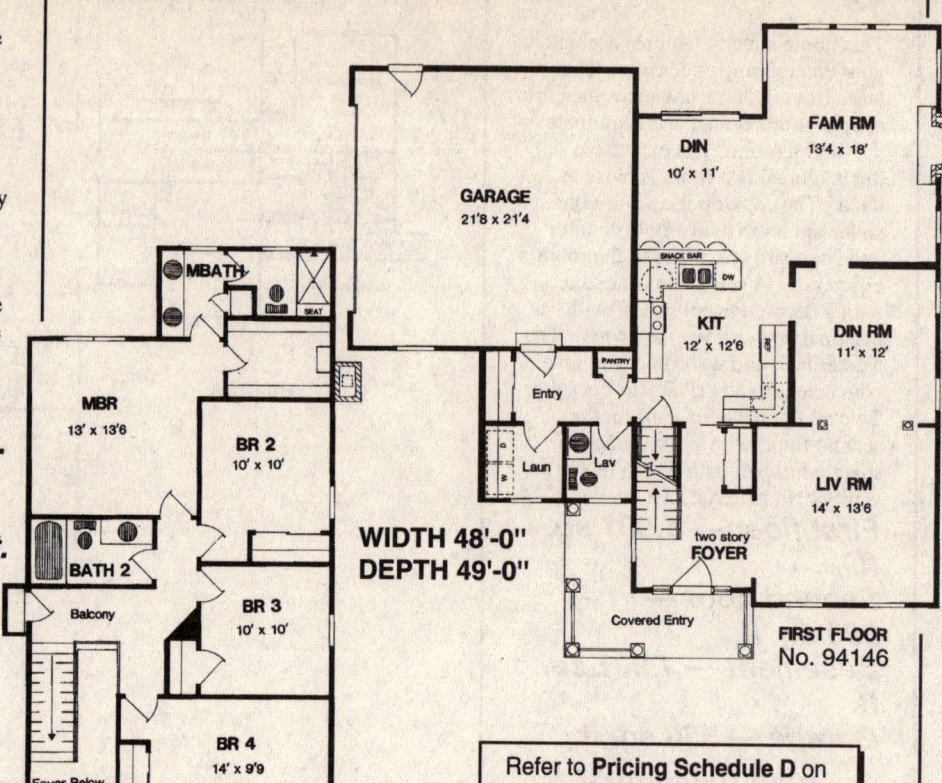

ORDER TODAY! 1 - 800 - 235 - 5700

Design 20368

Spacious Stucco

If open space suits your taste, here's a sturdy stucco classic that fits the bill with style. The vaulted foyer is flanked by a soaring living room with a huge palladium window and a formal dining room. Step up the stairs to the loft for a great view of the family room, separated from the huge kitchen-dinette arrangement by a two-way fireplace. And while you're upstairs, be sure to notice the two bedrooms with walk-in closets and adjoining bath. You'll find the master suite, with its garden spa, private deck access, and walk-in closet on the first floor, just off the foyer.

First floor — 1,752 sq. ft.
Second floor — 620 sq. ft.
Basement — 1,726 sq. ft.
Garage — 714 sq. ft.

Total living area: 2,372 sq. ft.

Refer to **Pricing Schedule D** on the order form for pricing information

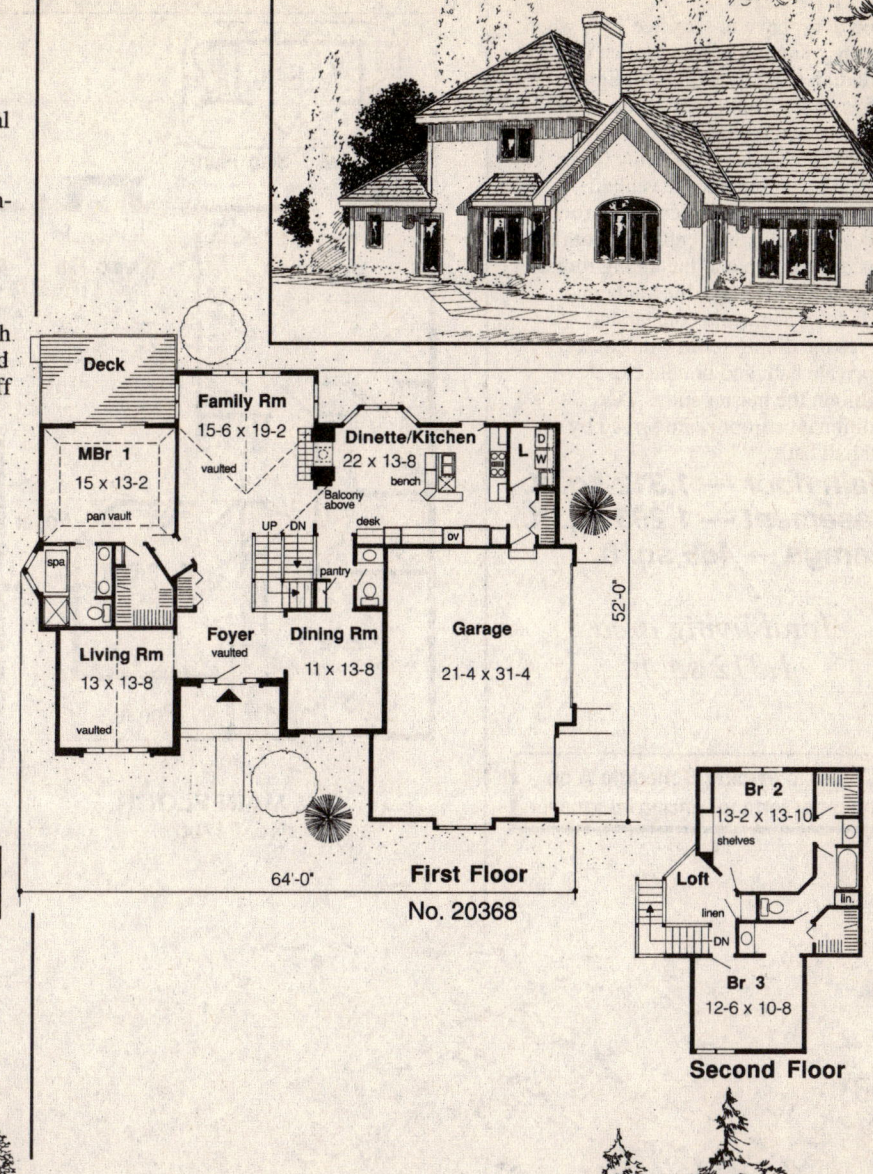

EXTRA TOUCHES OF STYLE

Design 24700

You don't have to sacrifice style when buying a smaller home. Notice the palladian window with a fan light above at the front of the home. The entrance porch includes a turned post entry. Once inside, the living room is topped by an impressive vaulted ceiling. A fireplace accents the room. A decorative ceiling enhances both the master bedroom and the dining room. Efficiently designed, the kitchen includes a peninsula counter and serves the dining room with ease. A private bath and double closet highlight the master suite. Two additional bedrooms are served by a full hall bath.

Main floor — 1,312 sq. ft.
Basement — 1,293 sq. ft.
Garage — 459 sq. ft.

Total living area: 1,312 sq. ft.

Refer to **Pricing Schedule A** on the order form for pricing information

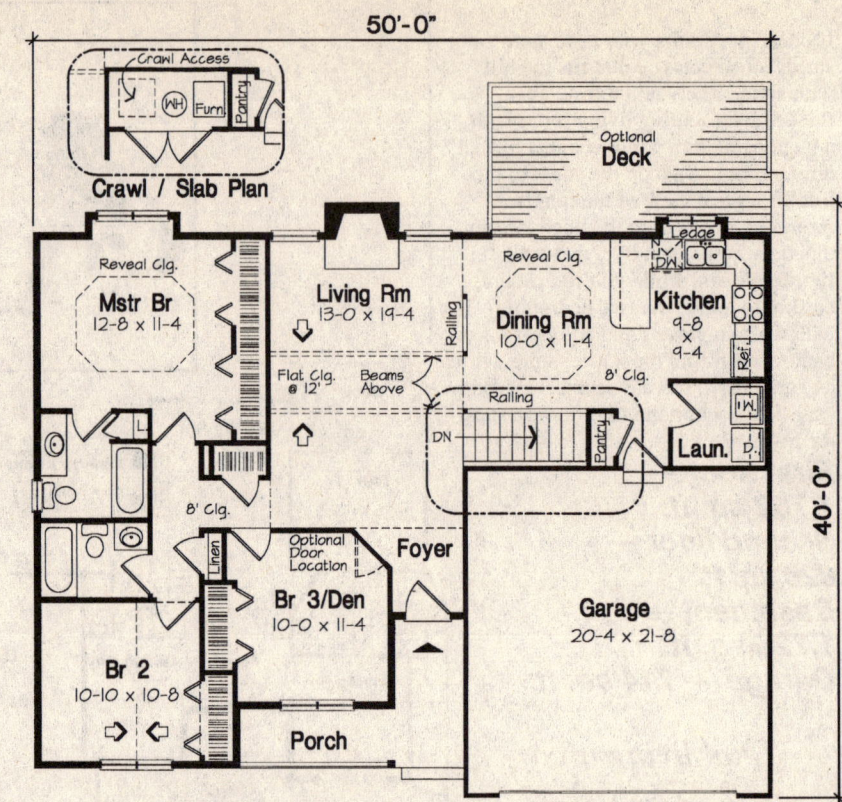

MAIN FLOOR
No. 24700

Opulent Luxury

Design 92237

A magnificent columned entry leads to a tiled entrance foyer graced by a staircase. The formal living and dining rooms are located in the traditional positions, to either side of the foyer. Built-in shelves and a stone hearth fireplace further enhance the living room. A spacious island kitchen and a breakfast area access the covered veranda which is accented by skylights. The family room flows from the breakfast room. A cathedral ceiling crowns this room while a fireplace adds warmth. Full oak paneling enhances the study. The lavish master suite includes decorative ceiling treatments, two walk-in closets, a huge bath and a sitting area. Three additional bedrooms, each with private access to a full bath and a walk-in closet, are located on the upper level. No materials list is available for this plan.

Lower level — 2,804 sq. ft.
Upper level — 979 sq. ft.
Basement — 2,804 sq. ft.
Garage — 802 sq. ft.

Total living area: 3,783 sq. ft.

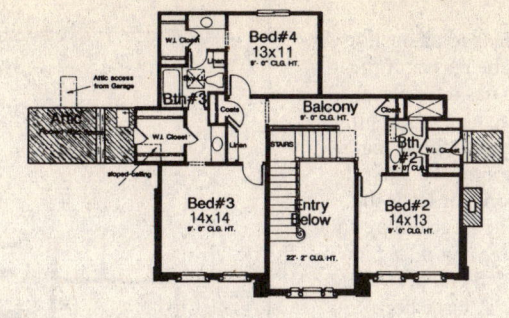

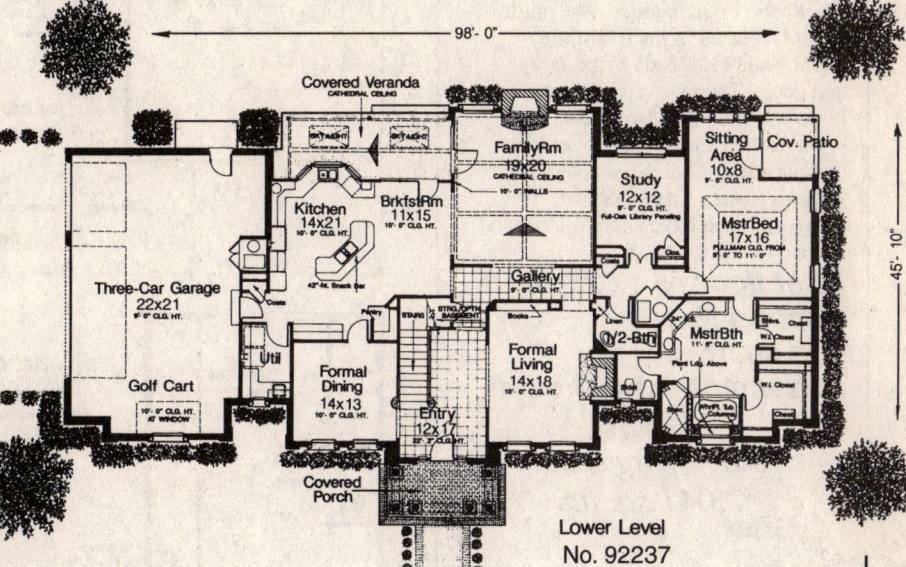

Refer to **Pricing Schedule F** on the order form for pricing information

ORDER TODAY! 1 - 800 - 235 - 5700

RHYTHMICALLY COLUMNED PORCH

Design 99666

The front porch leads to an open foyer and coat closet at the corner of the Great room which has a fireplace flanked by shelving as its focal point. Stairs to the left lead to the second floor all purpose room. To the right center, a central corridor feeds the bedroom wing. The large dining room blends with the Great room and leads left to the kitchen which opens to a grand dinette bay. A large deck extends across one-half the rear and is accessed from the dining room and dinette via French doors. The mud room is located to the left of the kitchen and also leads to the garage and deck. The master suite contains a luxurious bath with two sinks, a separate stall shower and toilet compartment. It also has a very large walk-in closet. The other two bedrooms each have a large closet and share a hall bath.

First floor — 1,623 sq. ft.
Second floor — 418 sq. ft.
Basement — 1,623 sq. ft.

Total living area: 2,041 sq. ft.

Refer to **Pricing Schedule C** on the order form for pricing information

ORDER TODAY! 1 - 800 - 235 - 5700

Executive Home

Design 99803

With a traditional, elegant exterior and lively interior spaces, this three bedroom executive home makes both everyday life and entertaining a breeze. A palladian window floods the foyer with light for a dramatic entrance alluding to a surprising, open floor plan. Whip up a gourmet meal in the well-planned kitchen while chatting with family and friends in the large Great room with cathedral ceiling, fireplace, and built-in cabinets. The screened porch, breakfast area, and master suite access the deck with optional spa. The large master suite, located in the rear for privacy, features a luxurious skylit bath with separate shower, corner whirlpool tub, and separate vanities. A skylit bonus room above the garage adds space when needed. This plan is available with a basement or crawl space foundation. Please specify when ordering.

Main floor — 1,977 sq. ft.
Bonus room — 430 sq. ft.
Garage — 610 sq. ft.

Total living area: 1,977 sq. ft.

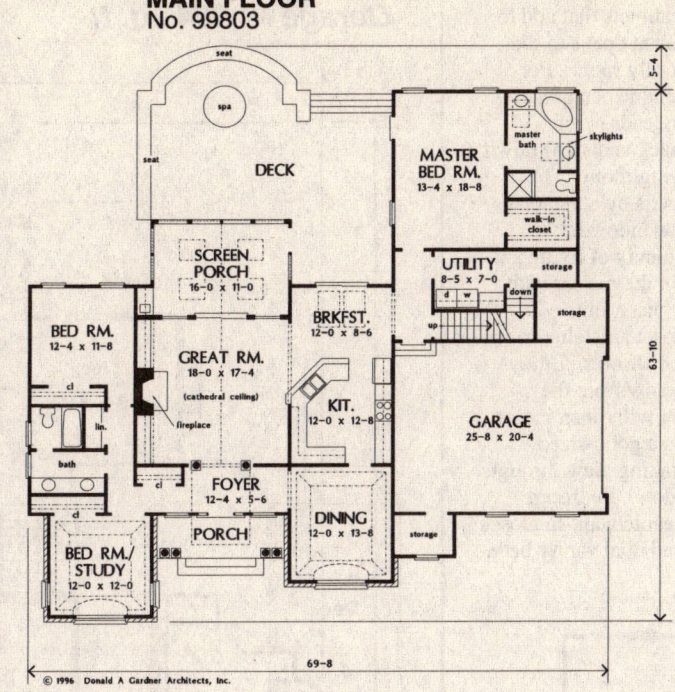

Refer to **Pricing Schedule C** on the order form for pricing information

© 1996 Donald A Gardner Architects, Inc.

ORDER TODAY! 1-800-235-5700

SURROUNDED BY MULTI-LEVEL DECKS

Design 92106

Enter your home through the utility room with its built-in counter and ample closet space from your stuccoed 3-car garage. The kitchen features extra lighting and cabinets that add to the island. The kitchen opens to the bright and sunny family room. For formal dining the unique octagonally shaped dining room leads to an immense covered deck and steps down to the fireplaced living room. The master bedroom has its own personal deck and features a window in the walk-in closet and plenty of living and decorating space. In the master bath you will find his 'n' her vanities, a convenient linen closet and a luxurious circular glass-walled shower. Enjoy view of the foyer below from the second floor landing with linen closet. Bedroom two offers a good-sized closet and a breathtaking view through the extra-large window. Bedroom three includes a sizeable walk-in closet and opens to a shared dual vanity bath.

First floor — 2,358 sq. ft.
Second floor — 700 sq. ft.
Garage — 954 sq. ft.

Total living area: 3,058 sq. ft.

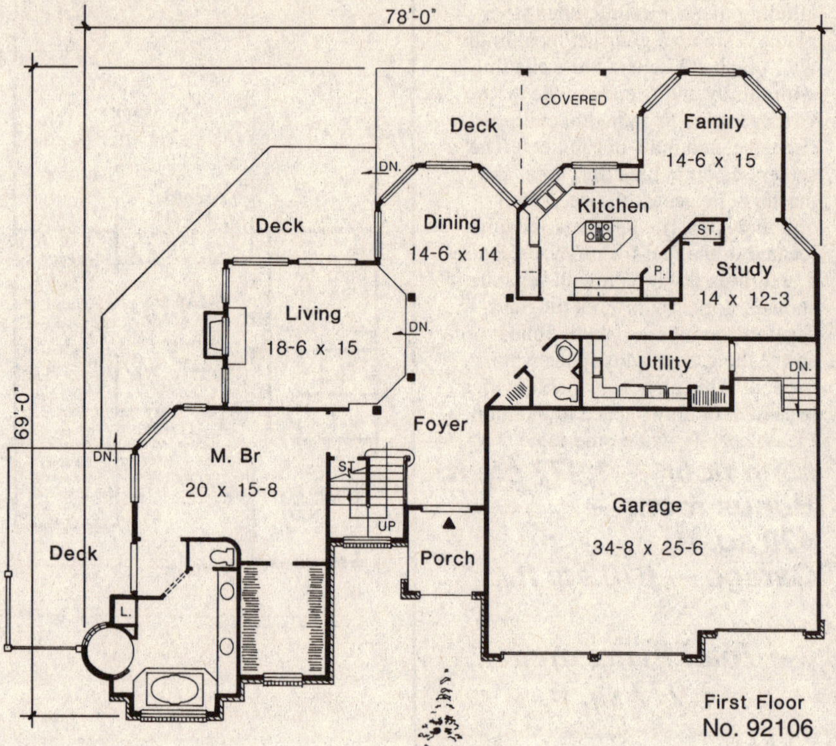

First Floor No. 92106

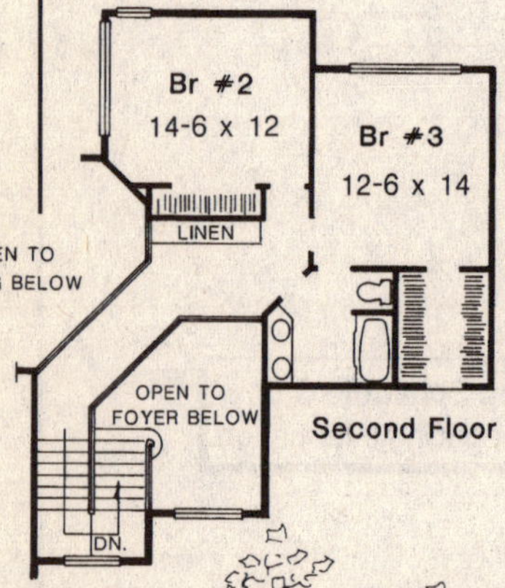

Second Floor

Refer to Pricing Schedule E on the order form for pricing information

ORDER TODAY!   1 - 800 - 235 - 5700

Rhythmically Columned Porch

Design 99666

The front porch leads to an open foyer and coat closet at the corner of the Great room which has a fireplace flanked by shelving as its focal point. Stairs to the left lead to the second floor all purpose room. To the right center, a central corridor feeds the bedroom wing. The large dining room blends with the Great room and leads left to the kitchen which opens to a grand dinette bay. A large deck extends across one-half the rear and is accessed from the dining room and dinette via French doors. The mud room is located to the left of the kitchen and also leads to the garage and deck. The master suite contains a luxurious bath with two sinks, a separate stall shower and toilet compartment. It also has a very large walk-in closet. The other two bedrooms each have a large closet and share a hall bath.

First floor — 1,623 sq. ft.
Second floor — 418 sq. ft.
Basement — 1,623 sq. ft.

Total living area: 2,041 sq. ft.

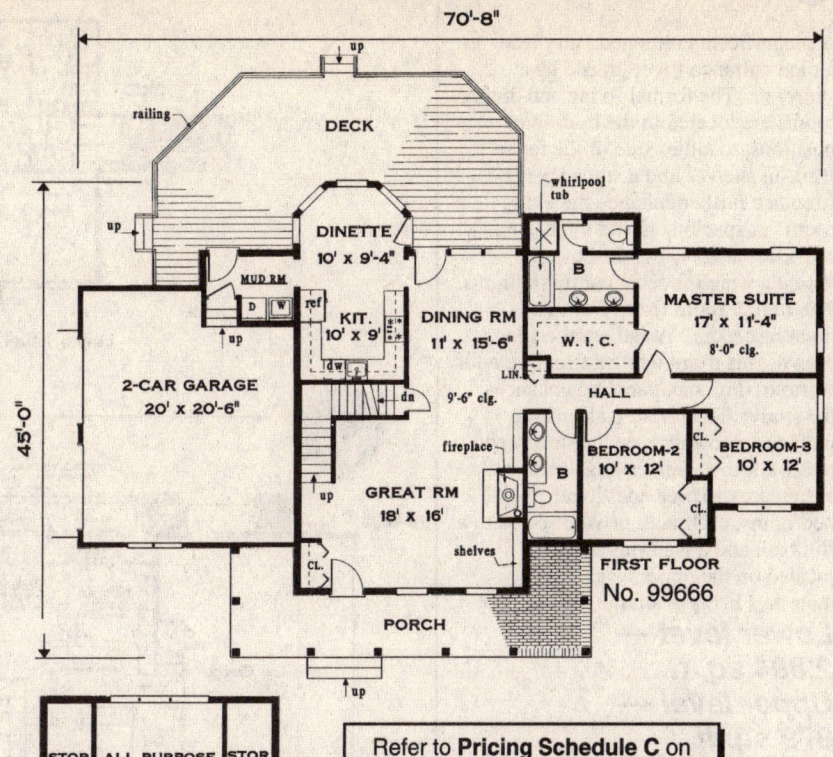

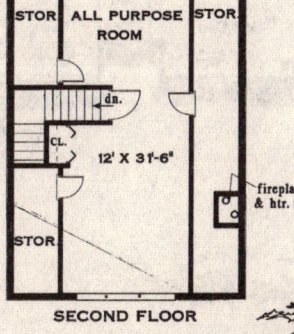

Refer to **Pricing Schedule C** on the order form for pricing information

Opulent Luxury

Design 92237

A magnificent columned entry leads to a tiled entrance foyer graced by a staircase. The formal living and dining rooms are located in the traditional positions, to either side of the foyer. Built-in shelves and a stone hearth fireplace further enhance the living room. A spacious island kitchen and a breakfast area access the covered veranda which is accented by skylights. The family room flows from the breakfast room. A cathedral ceiling crowns this room while a fireplace adds warmth. Full oak paneling enhances the study. The lavish master suite includes decorative ceiling treatments, two walk-in closets, a huge bath and a sitting area. Three additional bedrooms, each with private access to a full bath and a walk-in closet, are located on the upper level. No materials list is available for this plan.

Lower level — 2,804 sq. ft.
Upper level — 979 sq. ft.
Basement — 2,804 sq. ft.
Garage — 802 sq. ft.

Total living area: 3,783 sq. ft.

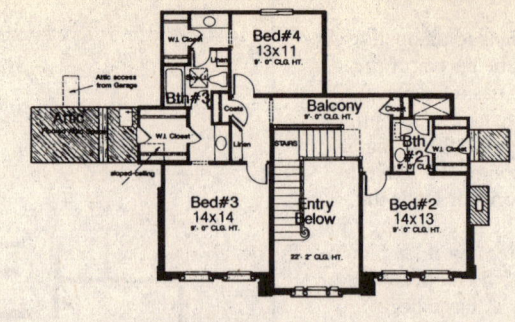
Upper Level

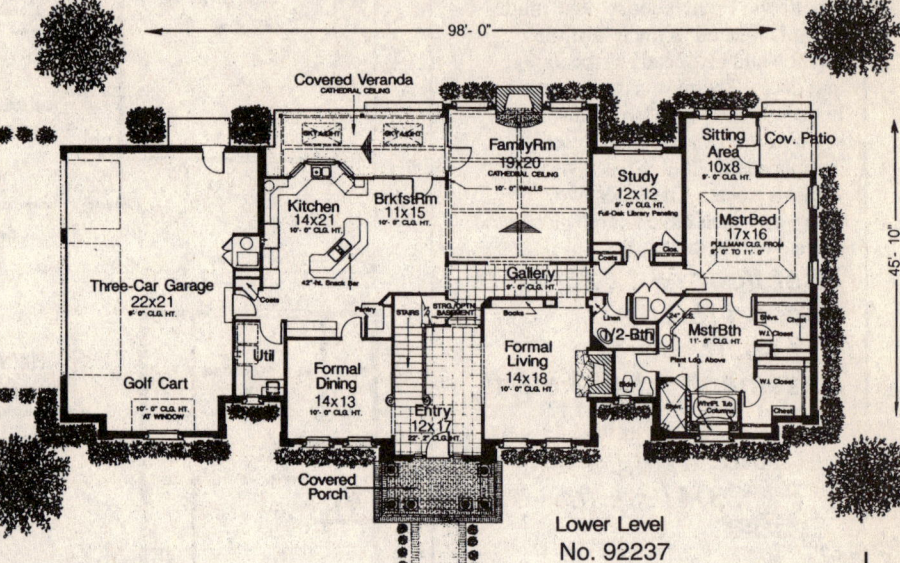
Lower Level
No. 92237

Refer to **Pricing Schedule F** on the order form for pricing information

Design 99315

LATTICE TRIM ADDS NOSTALGIC CHARM

Thanks to vaulted ceilings and an ingenious plan, this wood and fieldstone classic feels much larger than its compact size. The entry, dominated by a skylit staircase to the bedroom floor, opens to the vaulted living room with a balcony view and floor-to-ceiling corner window treatment. Eat in the spacious, formal dining room, in the sunny breakfast nook off the kitchen, or, when the weathers nice, out on the adjoining deck. Pass-through convenience makes meal service easy wherever you choose to dine. A full bath at the top of the stairs serves the kids' bedrooms off the balcony hall. The master suite boasts its own, private bath, along with a private dressing area.

First floor — 668 sq. ft.
Second floor — 691 sq. ft.
Garage — 459 sq. ft.

Total living area: 1,359 sq. ft.

Refer to **Pricing Schedule A** on the order form for pricing information

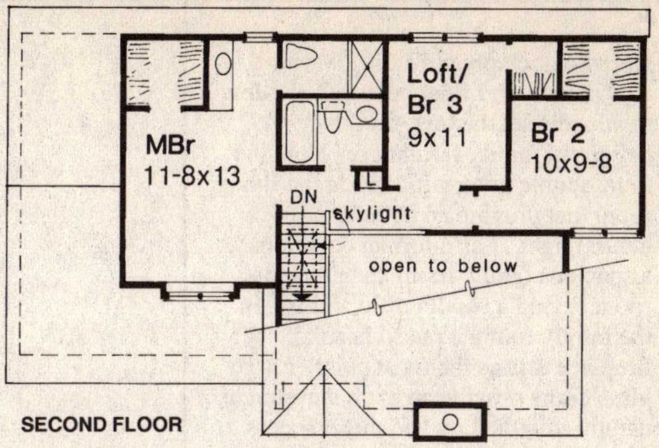

SECOND FLOOR

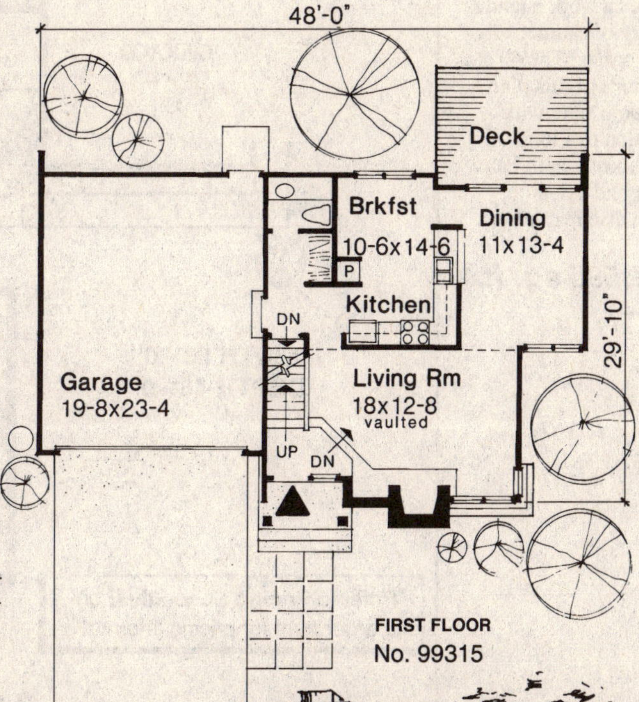

FIRST FLOOR
No. 99315

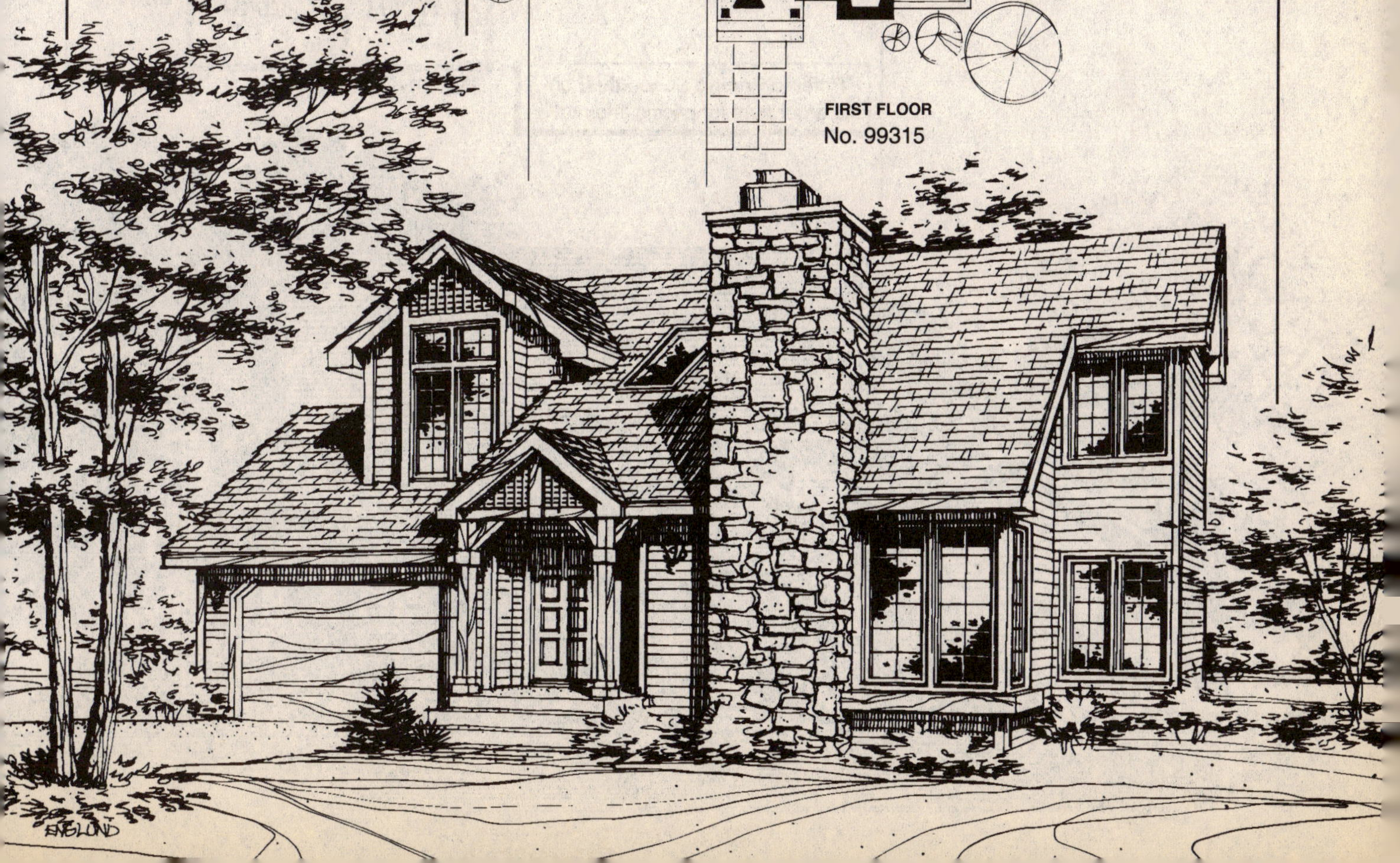

Farmhouse Favorite

Design 99262

Horizontal clapboard siding, varying roof planes, and finely detailed window treatments set the tone for this delightful family farmhouse. Note the four, double hung windows in the living room that provide an abundance of natural light. For informal occasions, a spacious family room and breakfast room extend a wealth of livability. In the family room, a raised hearth fireplace acts as the focal point. Large glass doors provide an extra measure of natural illumination and direct access to the rear terrace. The U-shaped kitchen, with a tile floor, utilizes a work island supplemented by plenty of cabinet, cupboard and counter space. The sleeping accommodations of this plan include a master bedroom suite with a walk-in closet in addition to a long wardrobe closet. The master bath has a tub plus a stall shower and a dual vanity. The main bath also features a dual vanity.

**First floor — 1,595 sq. ft.
Second floor — 1,112 sq. ft.**

Total living area: 2,707 sq. ft.

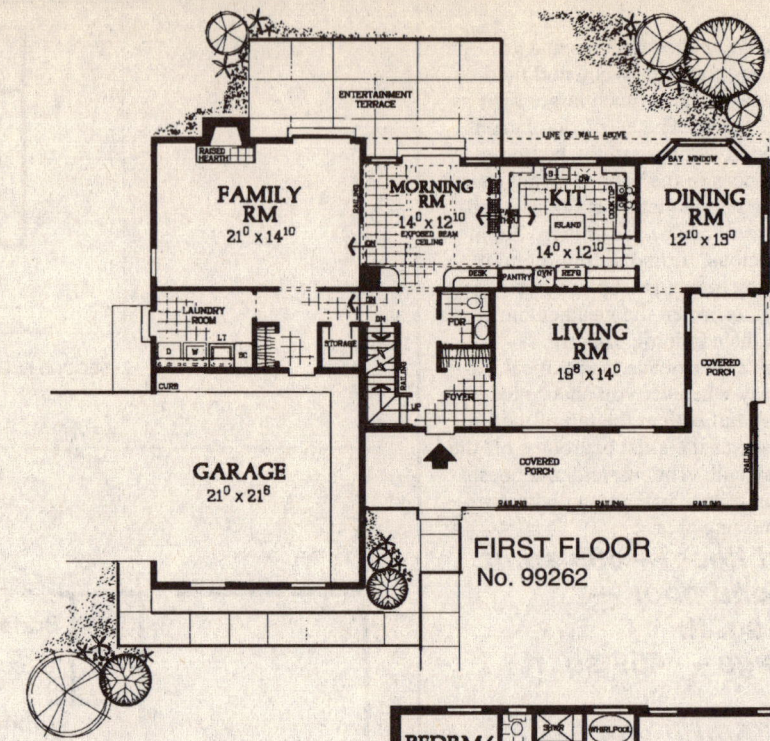

**WIDTH 63'- 0"
DEPTH 48'- 0"**

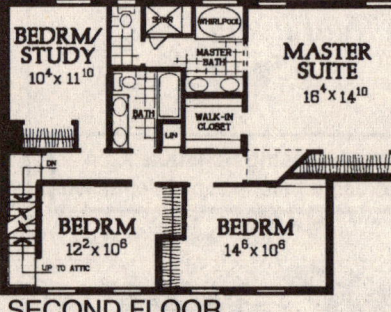

Refer to **Pricing Schedule E** on the order form for pricing information

ORDER TODAY! 1 - 800 - 235 - 5700

PRIVATE MASTER SUITE

Design 92238

This lovely brick elevation features segmented arches with sidelight and transom windows at the front entrance. The entrance leads to a roomy living room with a focal point fireplace and a wetbar. The dining area is open to both the living room and the kitchen. The efficient kitchen features an island, double sinks and a walk-in pantry. The bedrooms are situated to assure privacy for the master suite. A large walk-in closet and a compartmented bath are highlighted in the suite. The two additional bedrooms are located on the opposite side of the home in close proximity to the full hall bath. No materials list is available for this plan.

Main floor — 1,664 sq. ft.
Basement — 1,600 sq. ft.
Garage — 440 sq. ft.

Total living area:
1,664 sq. ft.

Refer to **Pricing Schedule B** on the order form for pricing information

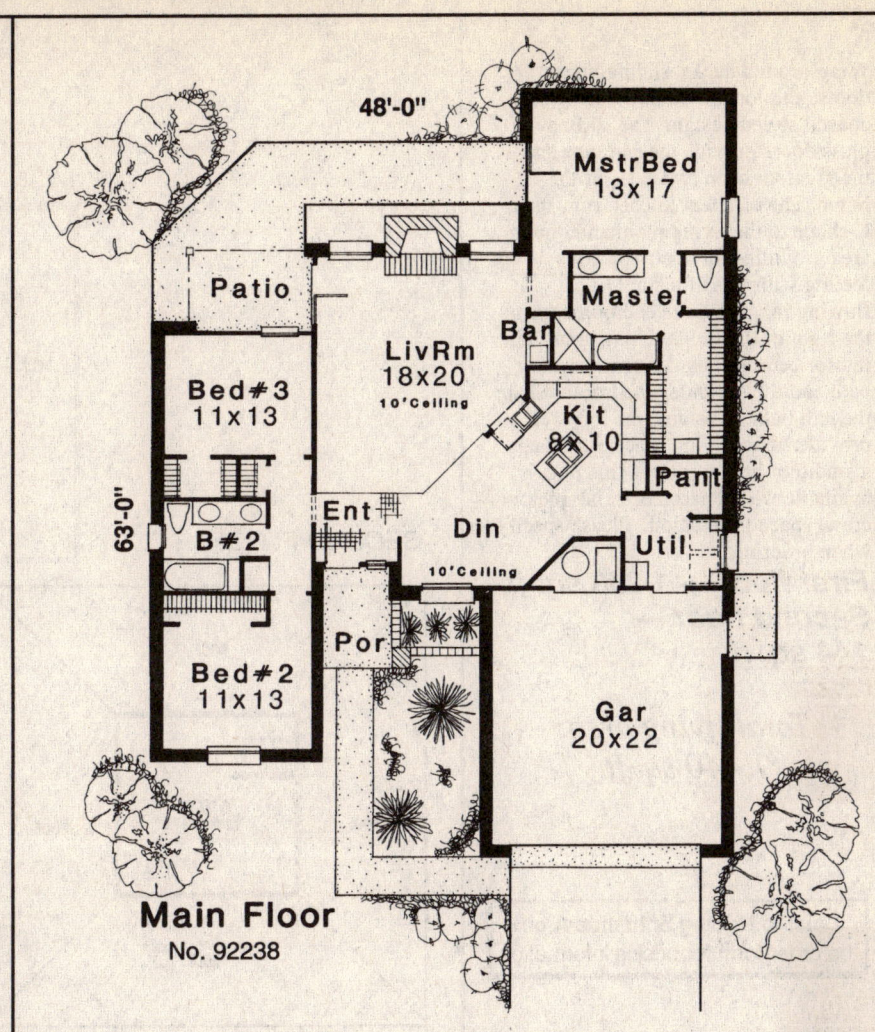

Main Floor
No. 92238

ORDER TODAY! 1-800-235-5700

Take ADVANTAGE OF THE VIEW

Design 92801

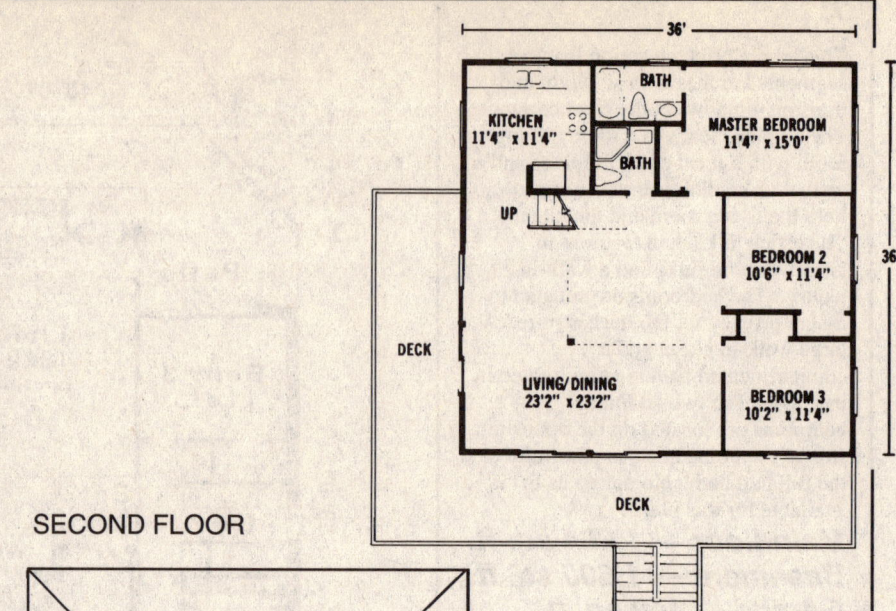

FIRST FLOOR
No. 92801

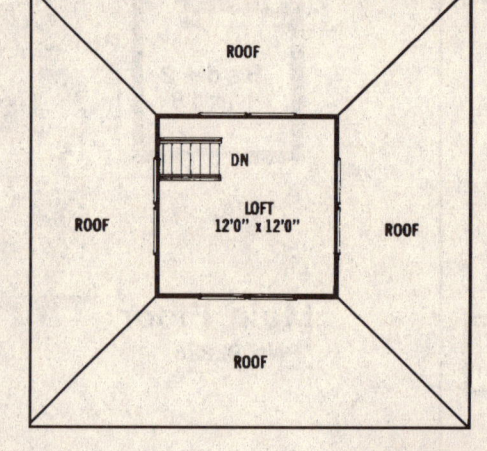

SECOND FLOOR

Wrap-around decks, sliding glass doors, and lots of windows accent this coastal styled design. The sliding glass doors provide the entrance and the great view on two sides of the home. The efficient kitchen runs in an L-shape to the living room and dining area providing an open, spacious feeling with lots of natural light flowing in. The three bedrooms are to the right of the living/dining area. The master bedroom has its own private bath and the secondary bedrooms share the hall bath. Upstairs, the loft area provides extra living space or perhaps a studio or hobby room. This plan is available with a basement, slab pier, or crawl space foundation. Please specify when ordering.

First floor — 1,296 sq. ft.
Second floor — 144 sq. ft.

Total living area: 1,440 sq. ft.

Refer to **Pricing Schedule A** on the order form for pricing information

ENHANCED EXTERIOR

Design 91063

A gabled roofline and arched front windows enhance the exterior of this modest sized home. Vaulted ceilings and an open interior design create a spacious feeling that this home is larger than its 1,207 sq. ft. The efficient floor plan offers a master bedroom with a generous closet and bath, while providing privacy from the other two bedrooms that share the second bath. The home is completed by a dining room and kitchen with much storage, many counter tops and a built-in pantry. This compact design is ideal for first time home buyers or the empty-nester. No materials list is available for this plan.

Main area — 1,207 sq. ft.
Garage — 440 sq. ft.

Total living area: 1,207 sq. ft.

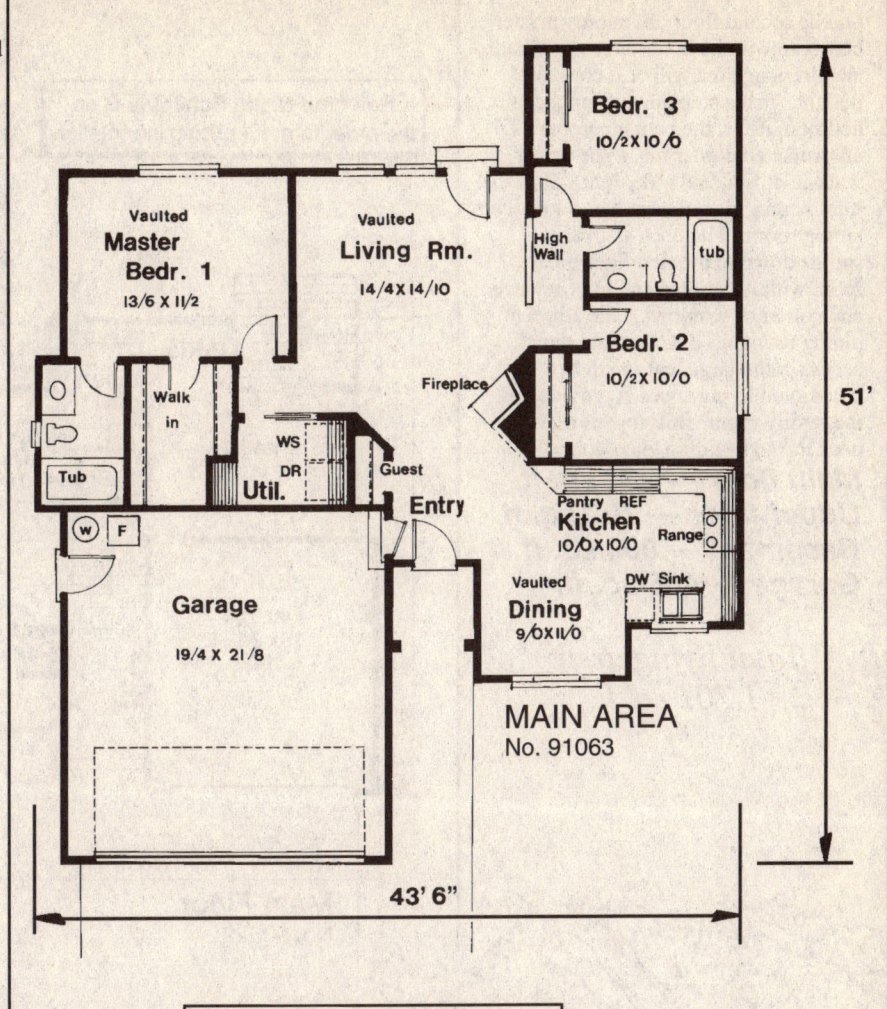

Refer to **Pricing Schedule A** on the order form for pricing information

Design 90329

DELIGHTFUL MASTER SUITE

On the second floor, the roomy master bedroom with its luxurious master bath and dressing area will be a constant delight. Just a step down from the bedroom itself, the bath incorporates an oversized corner tub, a shower, a walk-in closet, and a skylight. The third bedroom could serve as a loft or sitting room. The open staircase spirals down to the first floor great room with its vaulted ceiling, fireplace, and corner of windows. The adjacent dining room has a wetbar and direct access to the large, eat-in kitchen. Additional living space is provided by the family room which opens onto the deck through sliding glass doors.

Main floor — 904 sq. ft.
Upper floor — 797 sq. ft.
Basement — 904 sq. ft.
Garage — 405 sq. ft.

Total living area:
1,701 sq. ft.

Refer to **Pricing Schedule B** on the order form for pricing information

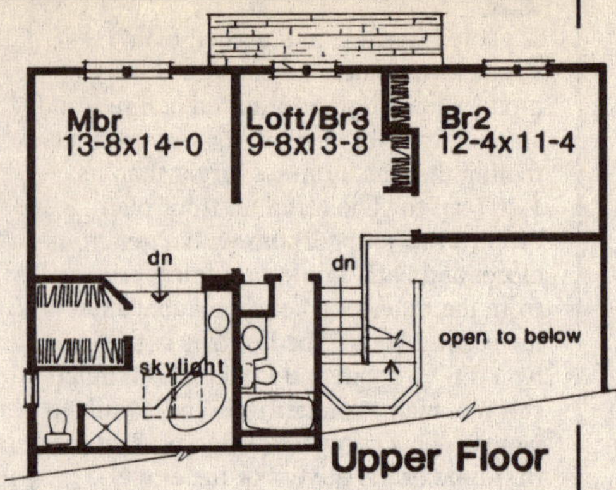

Upper Floor

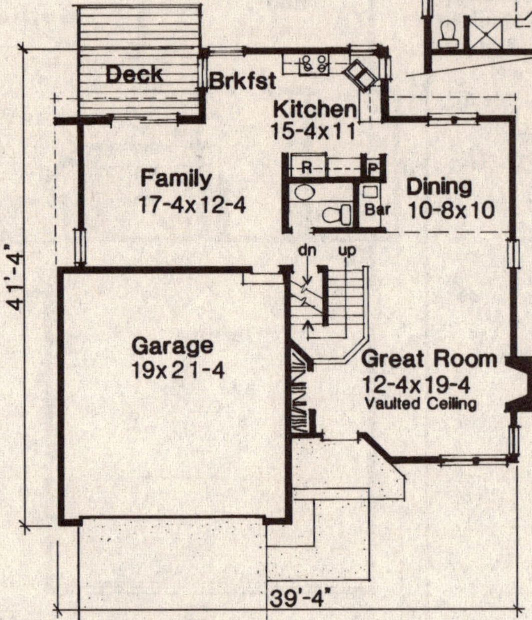

Main Floor
No. 90329

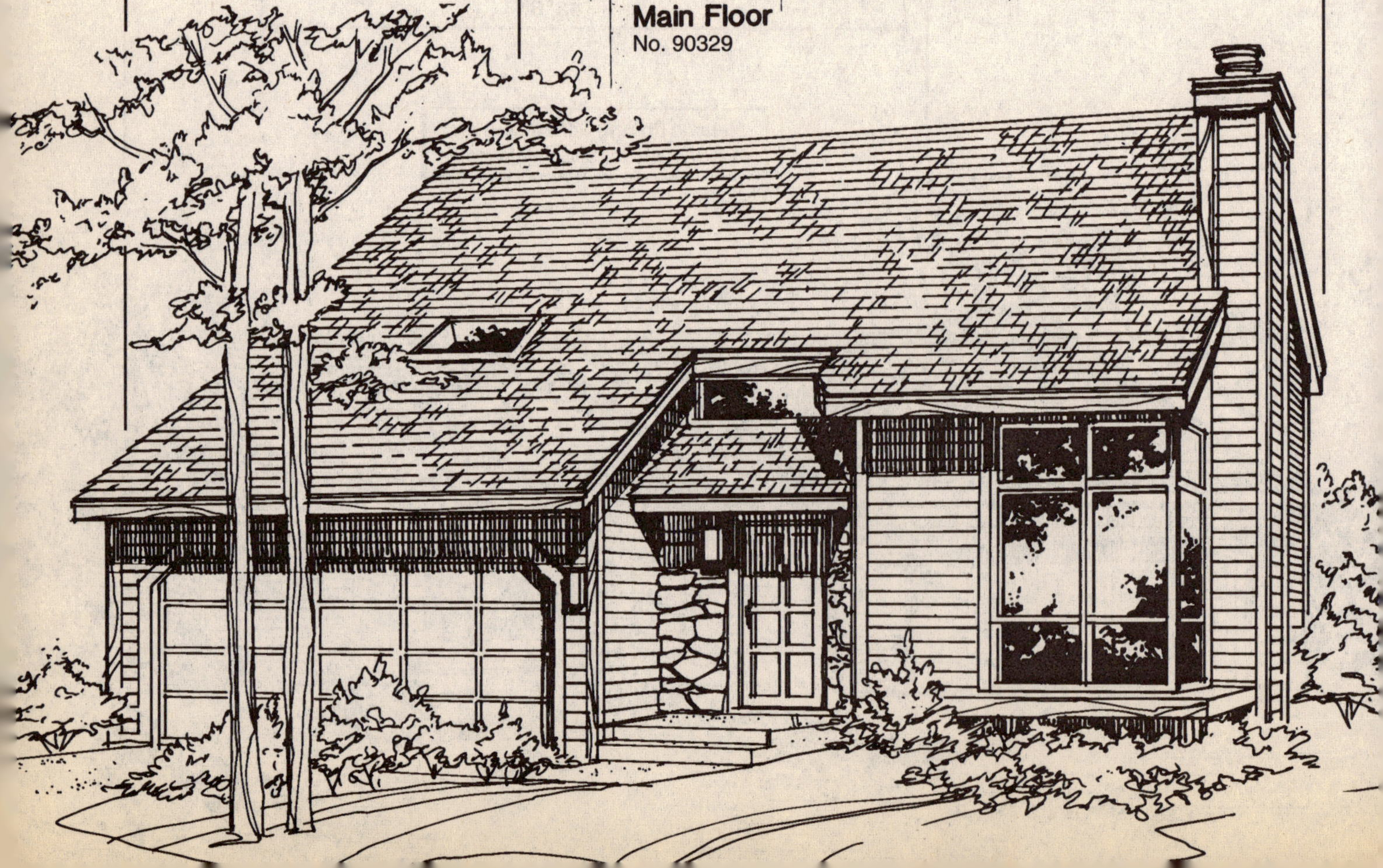

ORDER TODAY! 1 - 800 - 235 - 5700

Design 98502

SMALL SQUARE FOOTAGE, NOT VALUE

With only 1,965 sq. ft., this home has it all! The two living areas share a two-way brick fireplace. A formal dining room is located just off the entry. The convenient kitchen has a built-in pantry, and is open to the breakfast/family area. The master suite has a huge walk-in closet and a five-piece bath with a whirlpool tub. There are two other bedrooms and a full bath as well. A two-car garage and utility room complete this lovely home. With all these amenities, the only thing that this house needs is you and your family. This plan is available with a crawl space or slab foundation. Please specify when ordering. No materials list is available for this plan.

**Main floor —
1,965 sq. ft.
Garage — 441 sq. ft.**

*Total living area:
1,965 sq. ft.*

Refer to **Pricing Schedule C** on the order form for pricing information

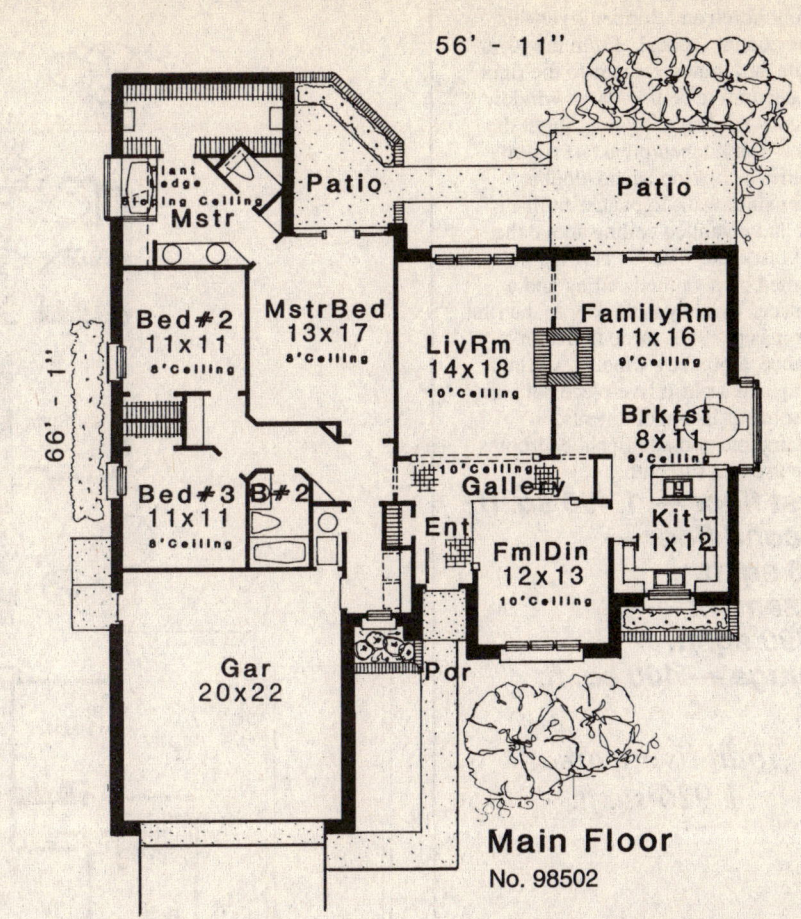

Main Floor
No. 98502

ORDER TODAY! 1-800-235-5700

First Floor Master Suite

Design 98357

A front porch and dormer gives this home country appeal. From the foyer, the elegant dining room is to the right. The decorative ceiling, large window and easy kitchen access highlight the room. The kitchen/breakfast room includes a cooktop island, double corner sink, walk-in pantry, built-in desk and a vaulted ceiling above the breakfast area. The Great room is accented by a vaulted ceiling and a fireplace. Privacy is the key to the first floor master suite. A double door entrance, a box bay window, vaulted ceiling and a plush five-piece bath are just some of its appointments. Upstairs, the two additional bedrooms share use of a full bath.

**First floor — 1,490 sq. ft.
Second floor — 436 sq. ft.
Basement — 1,490 sq. ft.
Garage — 400 sq. ft.**

Total living area: 1,926 sq. ft.

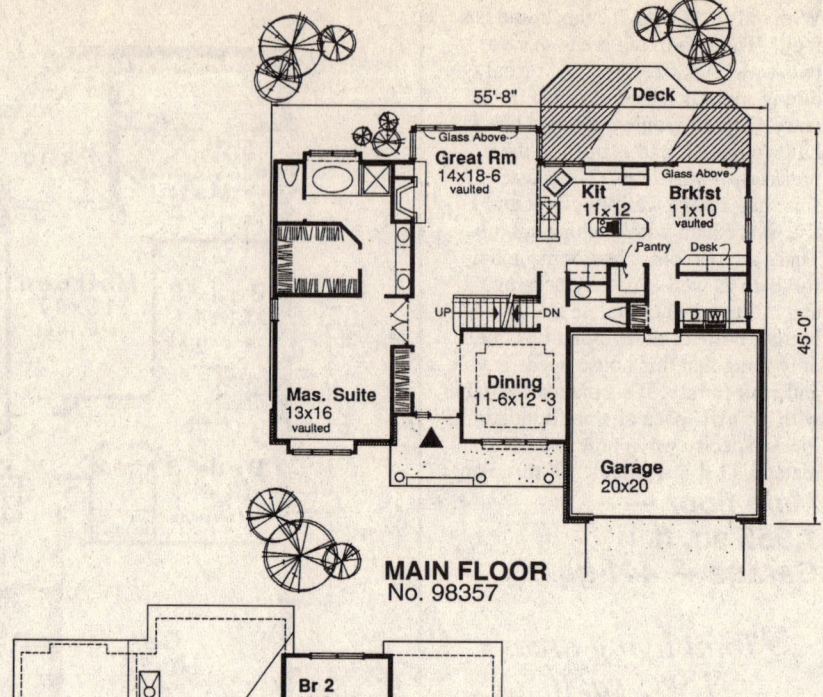

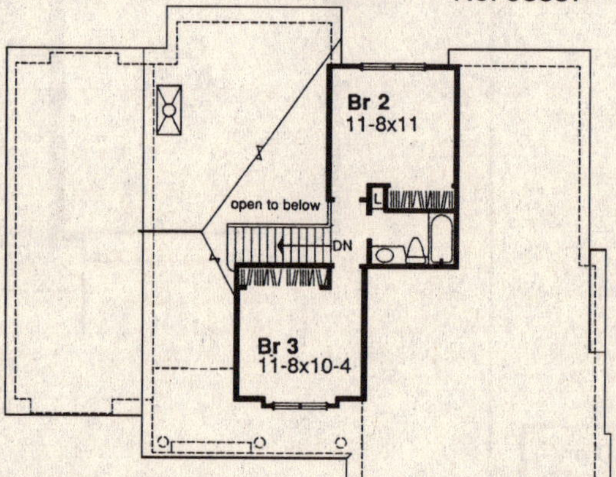

Refer to **Pricing Schedule C** on the order form for pricing information

HIGH CURB APPEAL

Design 93520

A stucco exterior and stone fireplace give this luxurious home a high curb appeal. The foyer features a two-story vaulted ceiling. Decks are featured off the dining room, family room and master bedroom. The kitchen offers two sinks, a large range island with eating bar, desk and walk-in pantry. The plush master suite includes a large walk-in closet sitting area, private deck and custom master bath. The pampering master bath features a jacuzzi tub, separate shower, and private room for the water closet.

First floor — 1,637 sq. ft.
Second floor — 1,559 sq. ft.

Total living area: 3,196 sq. ft.

Refer to **Pricing Schedule E** on the order form for pricing information

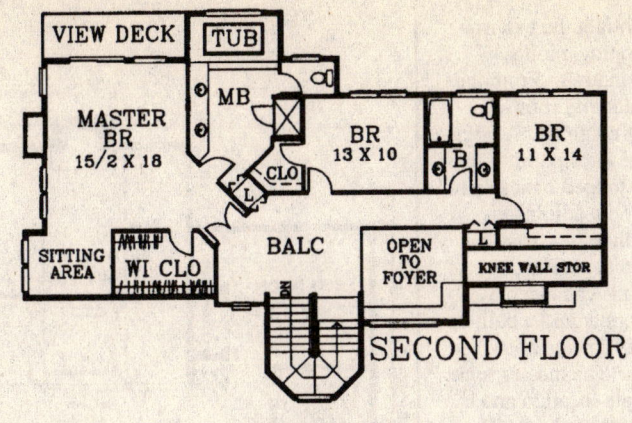

SECOND FLOOR

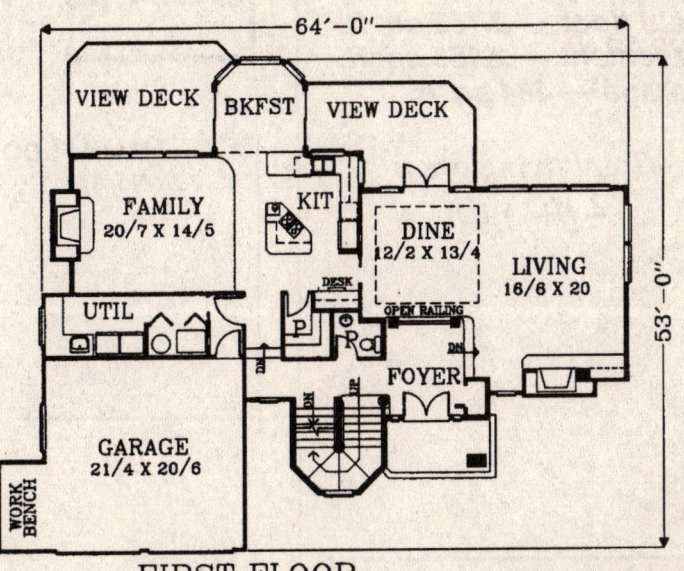

FIRST FLOOR
No. 93520

ORDER TODAY! 1 - 800 - 235 - 5700

DETAILS ARE KEY

Design 94811

Attractive details highlight the exterior of this home incorporating quoins, keystones and oval windows. From the entry, the expansive activity room is elegantly accented by columns. A large fireplace serves as the focal point of this living space which is topped by a sloped ceiling. The dining room adjoins the activity room and is directly across the short hall from the kitchen. The kitchen/breakfast area is enhanced by a cooktop island/serving bar and a built-in pantry. The laundry is conveniently placed off the kitchen. The master suite has been given a private location and is pampered by a grand master bath. The two secondary bedrooms are on the opposite side of the home and include ample closet space.

Main floor — 2,165 sq. ft.
Basement — 2,165 sq. ft.
Garage — 484 sq. ft.

Total living area:
2,165 sq. ft.

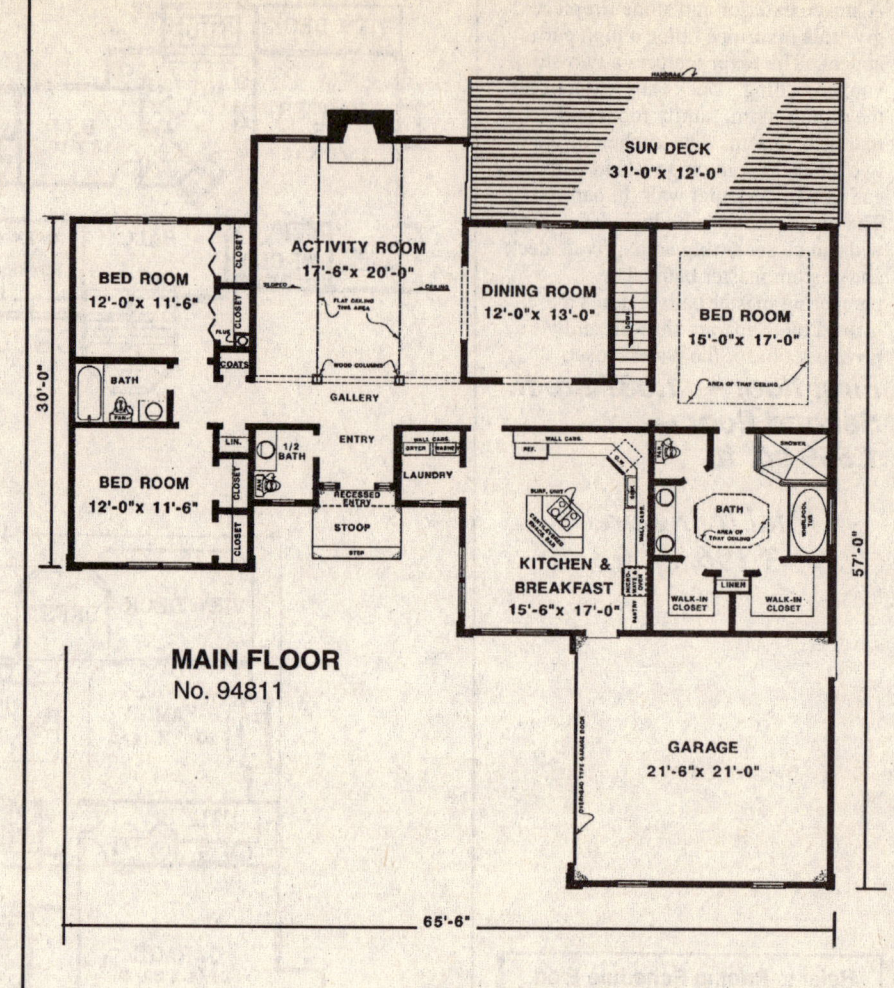

MAIN FLOOR
No. 94811

Refer to **Pricing Schedule D** on the order form for pricing information

ORDER TODAY! 1 - 800 - 235 - 5700

COUNTRY COTTAGE

Design 99804

We hardly wasted an inch creating a spacious interior for this dormered and gabled country cottage that lives much bigger than it looks. The front bedroom, master bedroom, and open Great room/kitchen gain vertical space from cathedral ceilings while the open foyer pulls the dining room and Great room together visually. A wrap-around front porch, a breakfast bay window, and a skylit back porch add charm and expand living space. The master bath pampers the owner with a whirlpool tub, a separate shower and a double vanity. A bonus room adds flexibility to the plan.

Main floor — 1,815 sq. ft.
Bonus room — 336 sq. ft.
Garage — 522 sq. ft.

Total living area: 1,815 sq. ft.

Refer to **Pricing Schedule C** on the order form for pricing information

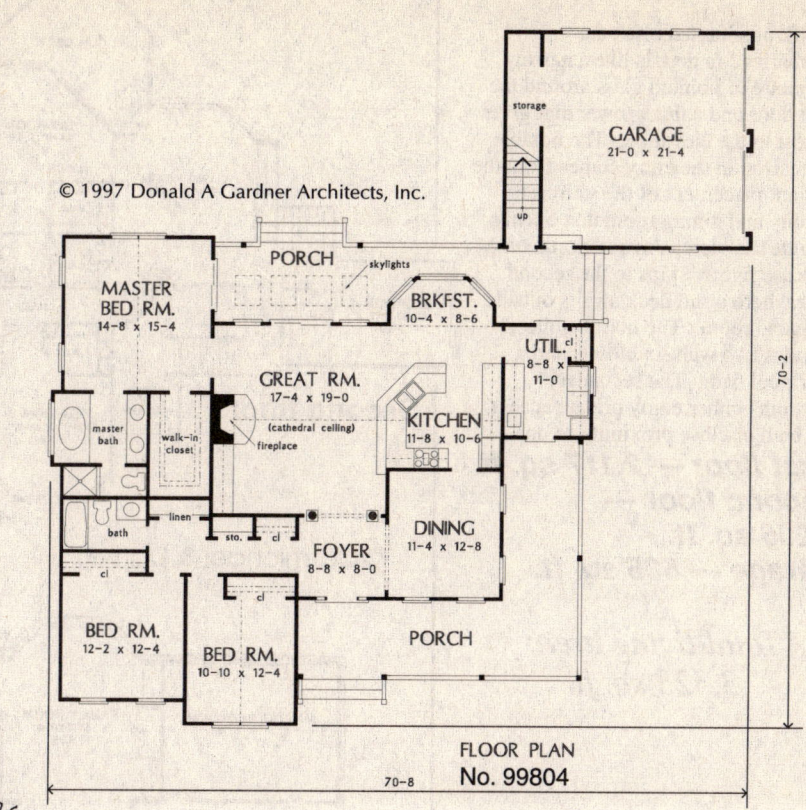

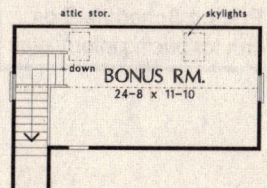

© 1997 Donald A Gardner Architects, Inc.

Design 99438

EYE-CATCHING TOWER

A look of softened brick are summarized in details like a narrow silhouette of pointed glass around the front door and a thick tower that gives a boost to the elevation. The notable impression in the entry comes from the brilliant placement of the staircase balcony and dining room that openly saturate the view. An additional back staircase lightly skips to the second floor where a sun deck awaits outside the game room. The master suite includes two walk-in closets and a whirlpool bath. The secondary bedrooms either enjoy private access to a bath or close proximity to one.

First floor — 2,117 sq. ft.
Second floor — 1,206 sq. ft.
Garage — 685 sq. ft.

Total living area: 3,323 sq. ft.

Refer to **Pricing Schedule E** on the order form for pricing information

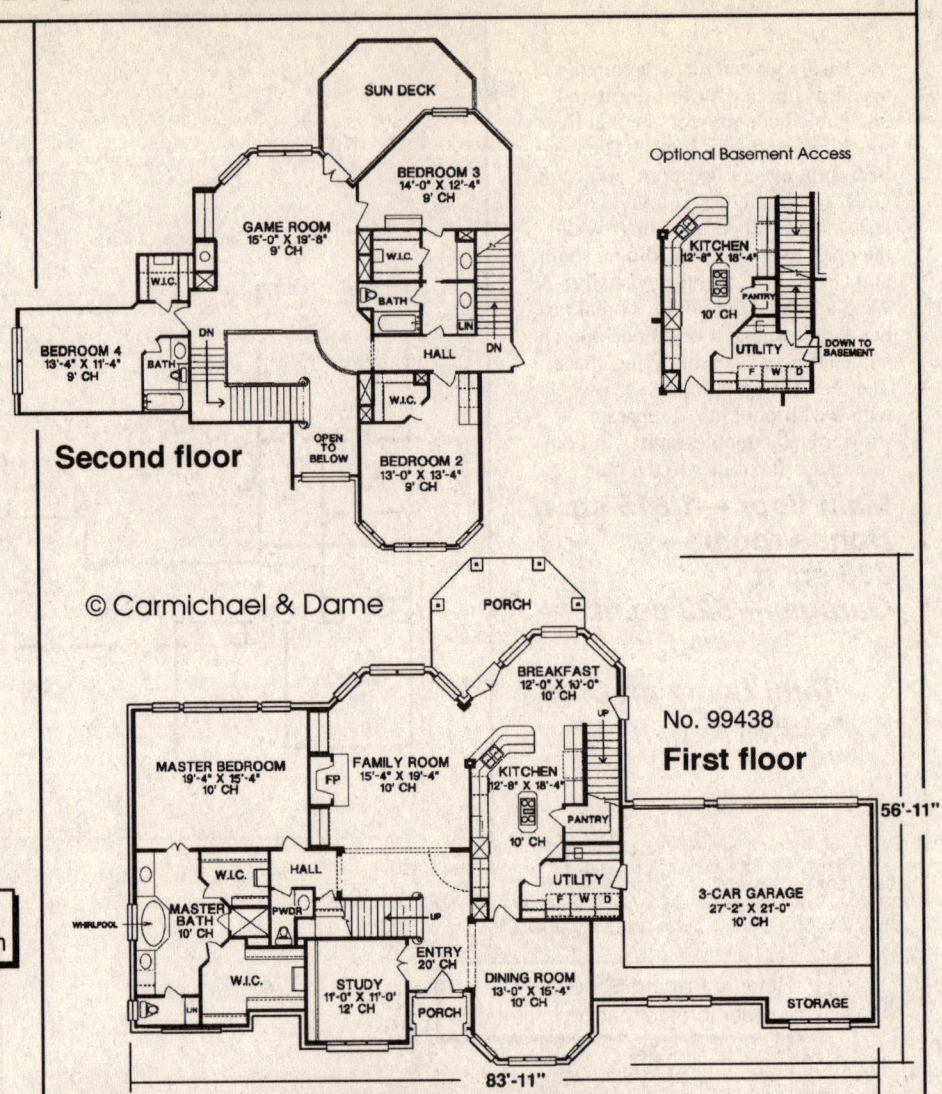

© Carmichael & Dame

Clever Design Has Plenty of Space

Design 24250

The design of this home allows for plenty of living space. This home makes use of custom, volume ceilings. The living room offers a sunken environment. The vaulted ceiling and fireplace give this room drama. The oversized windows framing the fireplace, enhance the drama with natural light. The kitchen features a center island and eating nook. There is more than ample counter space, a double basin sink and all the amenities you could ask for. The formal dining room adjoins the kitchen, allowing for easy entertaining. The spacious master suite enjoys a vaulted ceiling. Its lavish master bath allows for privacy and pampering. Cozy, comfortable, and peaceful is the feeling you get as you curl up on the window seat on a rainy afternoon to read your book. This suite is your own private get-away. The secondary bedrooms also have custom ceiling treatments and large windows that view the front porch.

Main area — 1,700 sq. ft.

Total living area: 1,700 sq. ft.

Refer to **Pricing Schedule B** on the order form for pricing information

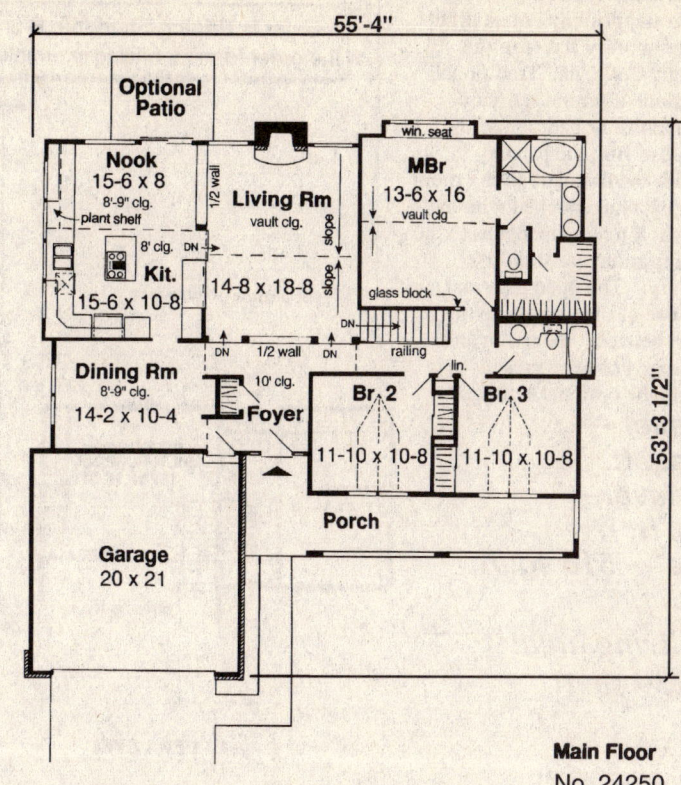

Main Floor
No. 24250

An EXCLUSIVE DESIGN
By Energetic Enterprises

CONTEMPORARY ENERGY-SAVER

Design 93501

Abundant windows, soaring ceilings, and a generous sprinkling of skylights lend a contemporary flavor to this updated Cape Cod plan. Traditional touches include a central staircase, two cozy main floor bedrooms, and two full baths. But, the balcony view from the loft, the dramatic living room dominated by a huge arched window, and the skylit kitchen that opens to the family/dining room are strictly contemporary. The open plan makes maximum use of the energy-saving wood stove between the living and family rooms. For even greater savings, add the optional sunspace.

Main level — 1,154 sq. ft.
Upper level — 585 sq. ft.
Garage — 516 sq. ft.

Total living area: 1,739 sq. ft.

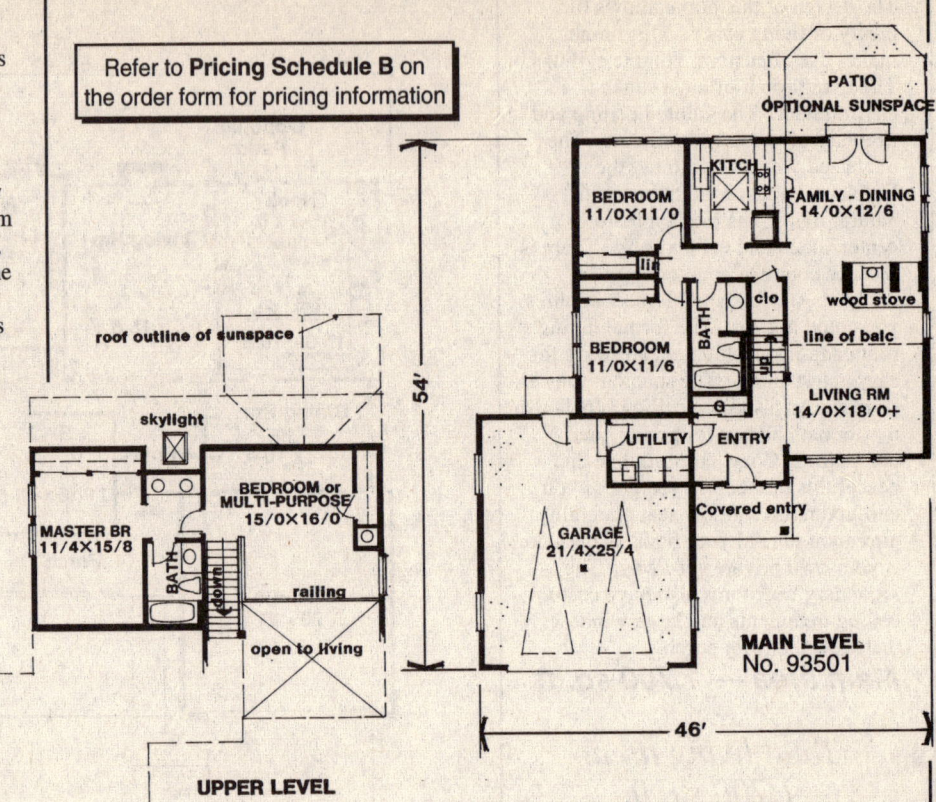

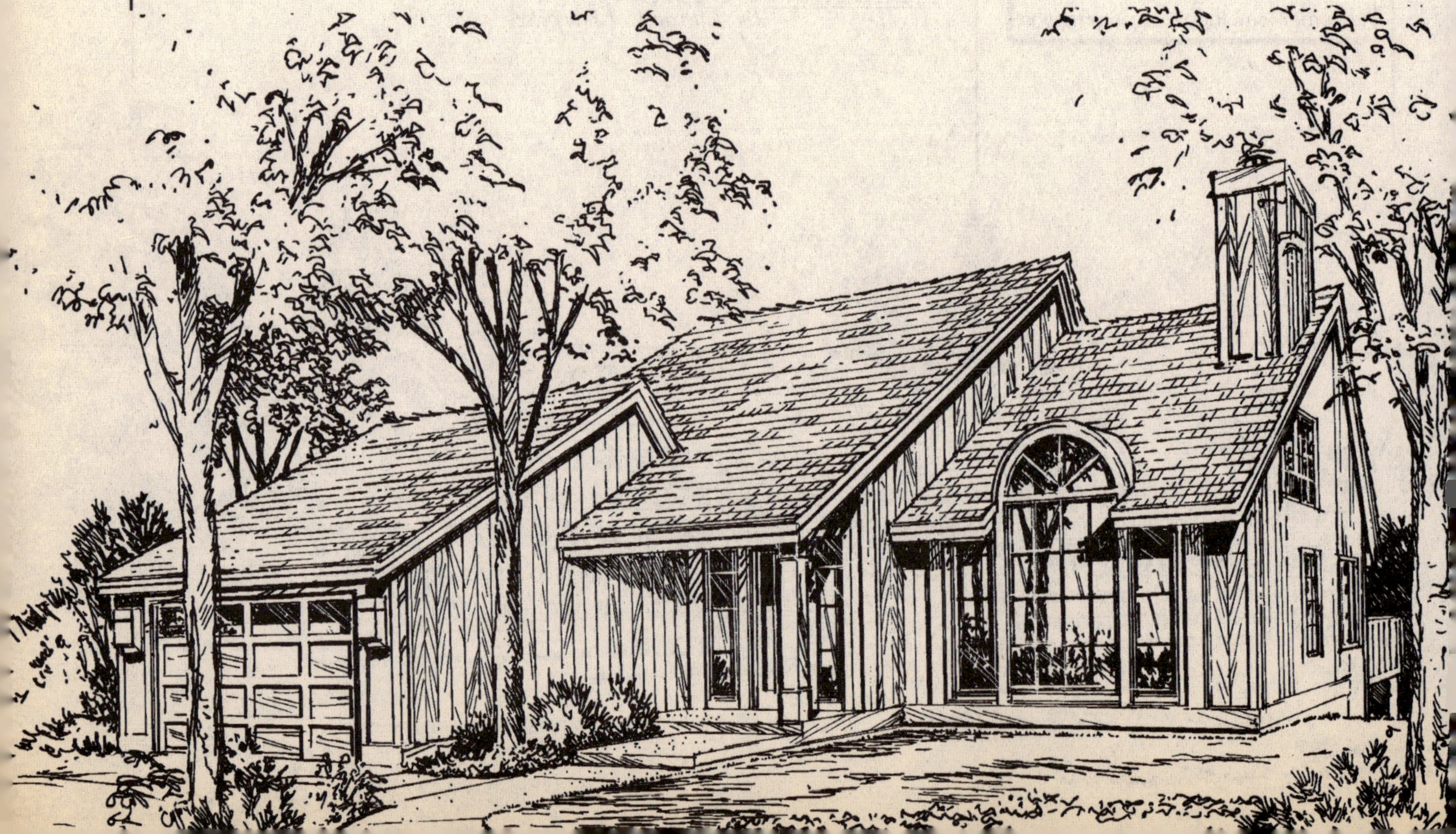

INVITING PORCH HAS DUAL FUNCTION

Design 91021

Here's a one-level home that's perfect for entertaining, rain or shine. The wrap-around porch provides an inviting entry for your guests and guarantees your outdoor parties will remain dry, even in a cloudburst. And, with sliding glass doors right in the bayed dining room, serving a picnic supper is a breeze. Don't worry about inviting a crowd. The openness of the family living areas helps traffic move easily. The bedrooms share a quiet part of the house, tucked behind the garage away from the noise of the street. This plan is available with a slab, crawl space or basement foundation option. Please specify when ordering.

Main area — 1,295 sq. ft.
Garage — 400 sq. ft.

Total living area:
1,295 sq. ft.

Refer to **Pricing Schedule A** on the order form for pricing information

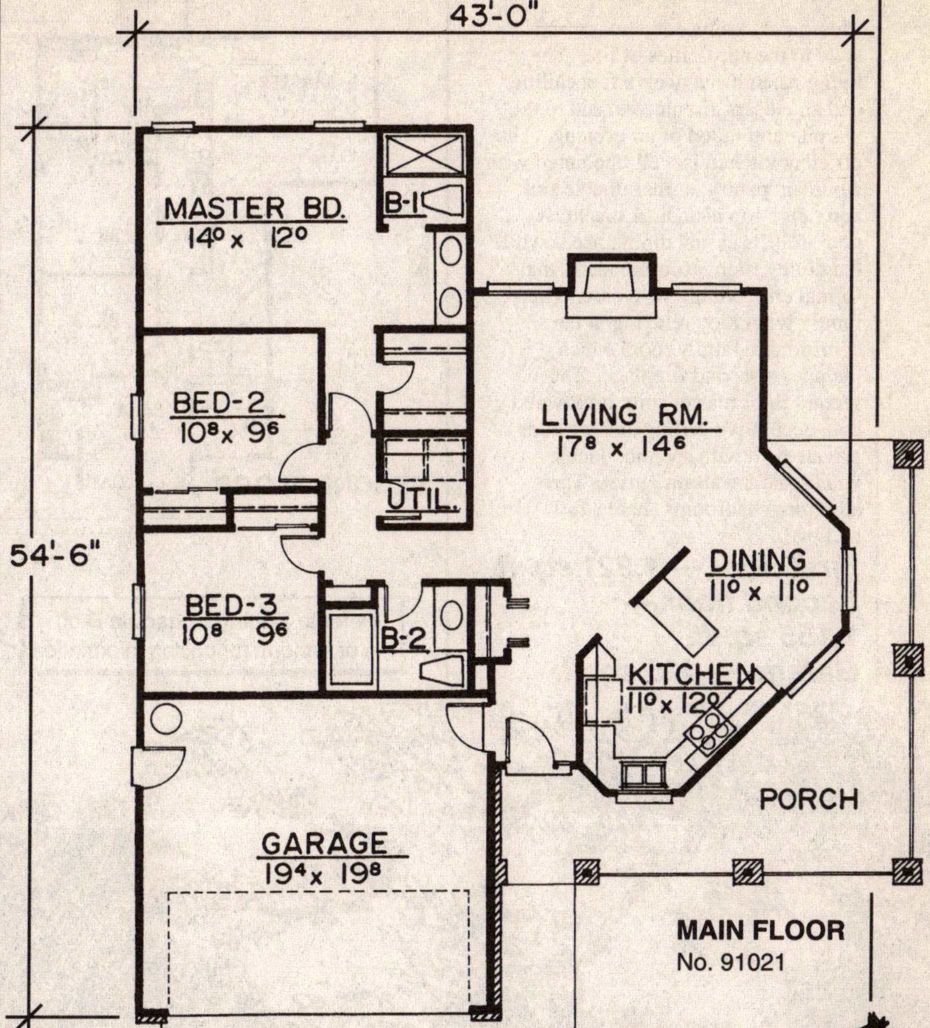

MAIN FLOOR
No. 91021

ORDER TODAY! 1 - 800 - 235 - 5700

Design 91526

LUXURIOUS TOUCHES

This stately home adds luxury and style to the necessities of life. The living room has a twelve foot ceiling and an elegant fireplace to add to the warmth and mood of an evening. The efficient kitchen is well-appointed with a built-in pantry, corner double sink and range-top island. A breakfast nook fulfills casual dining needs while the dining room accommodates the formal entertaining with ease. The family will enjoy relaxing in the comfortable family room which includes a second fireplace. The second floor master suite is crowned by a decorative ceiling and includes a private bath with spa tub, double vanity and a walk-in closet. Three additional bedrooms share a full hall bath.

First floor — 1,321 sq. ft.
Second floor — 1,155 sq. ft.
Garage — 420 sq. ft.

Total living area: 2,476 sq. ft.

Refer to **Pricing Schedule D** on the order form for pricing information

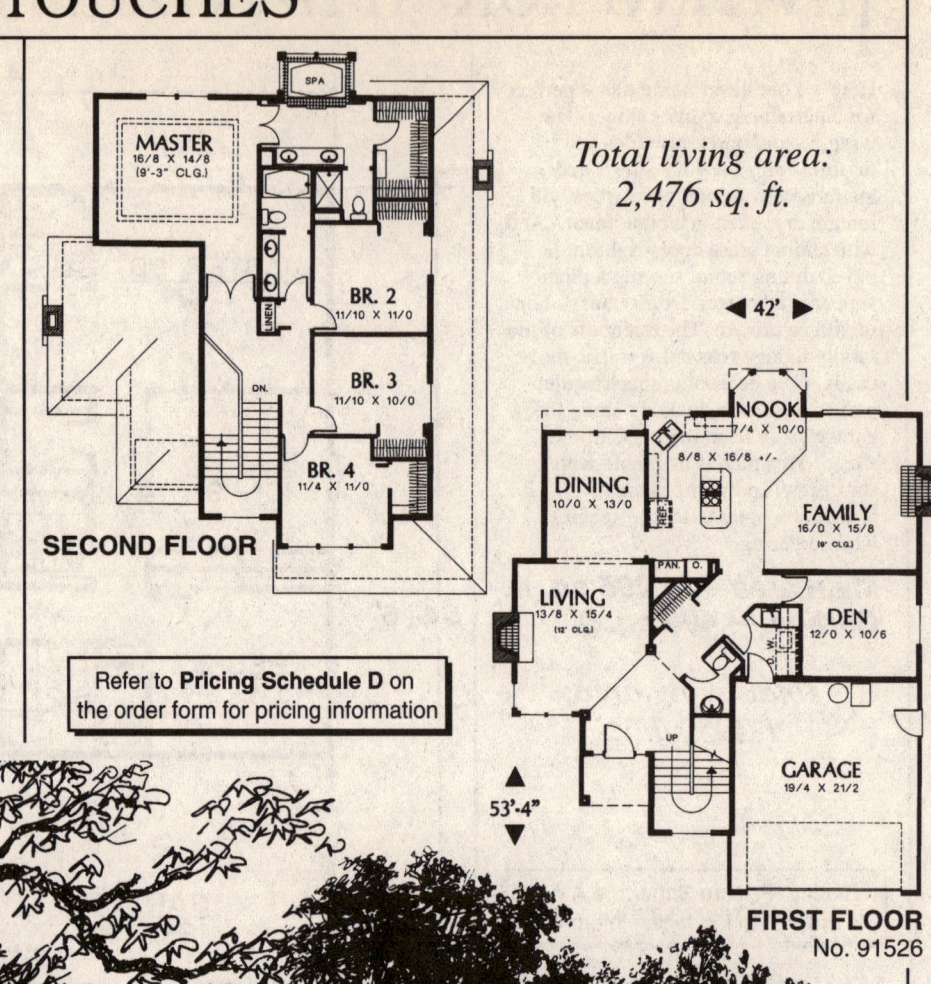

ORDER TODAY! 1-800-235-5700

WRAP-AROUND PORCH

Design 94138

The wrap-around porch on this home's facade gives a cozy homey feeling to the plan. The warm welcome continues within. The foyer leads into the living room and the adjoining dining room or straight to the rear of the home where the informal family living area is located. The kitchen includes a peninsula counter for extended work space. The family room features a fireplace and is open to the dinette which in turn is open to the kitchen. This open layout gives an airy spacious feel throughout the home. No materials list available for this plan.

**First floor — 900 sq. ft.
Second floor — 676 sq. ft.
Basement — 900 sq. ft.
Garage — 448 sq. ft.**

Total living area: 1,576 sq. ft.

Refer to **Pricing Schedule C** on the order form for pricing information

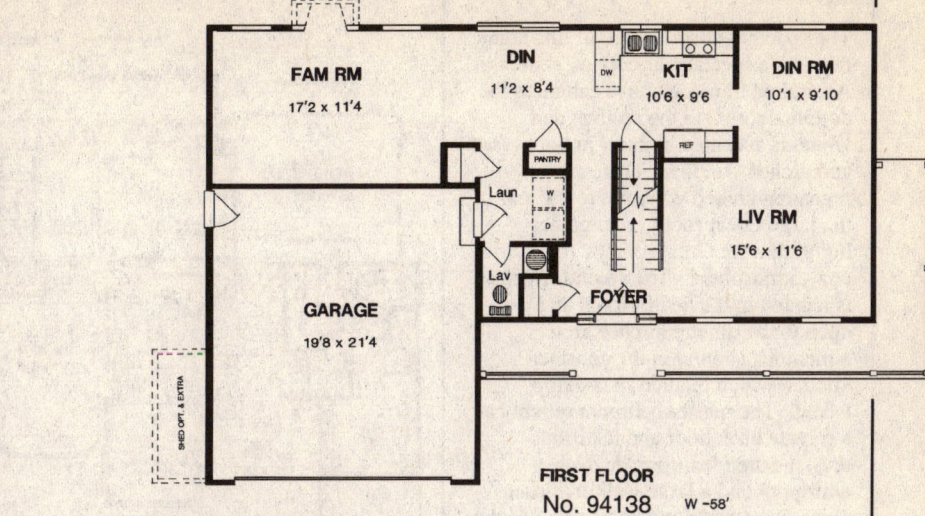

FIRST FLOOR
No. 94138   W–58' D–34'

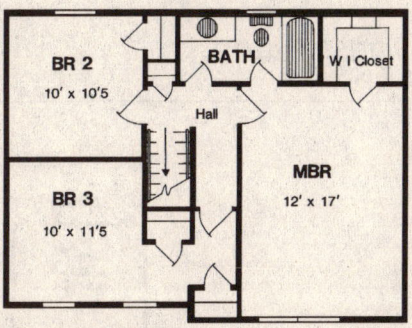

SECOND FLOOR

ORDER TODAY! 1-800-235-5700

Spectacular Curving Staircase

Design 94995

The spacious formal entry of this home features a spectacular curving staircase. An arched transom above enhances the double doors into the volume den which is accented by built-in bookcases and arched window. There are repeating arched windows to the rear of the large Great room. A fireplace highlights the Great room with a warm cozy atmosphere. The second fireplace is located in the hearth room and is open to the dinette/kitchen area. Amenities abound in the gourmet kitchen which includes a cooktop island. The master bedroom retreat has a private back door and luxurious dressing area featuring an oval whirlpool and a large walk-in closet. Generous closets and baths enhance the secondary bedrooms.

First floor — 2,252 sq. ft.
Second floor — 920 sq. ft.
Basement — 2,252 sq. ft.
Garage — 646 sq. ft.

Total living area: 3,172 sq. ft.

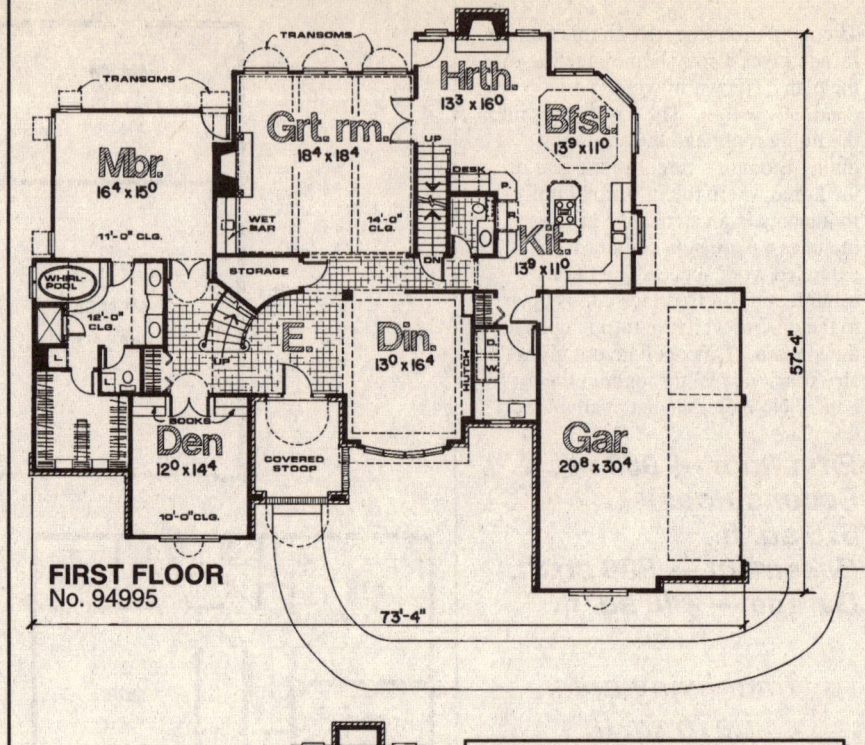

Refer to **Pricing Schedule E** on the order form for pricing information

© design basics, inc.

Spectacular Curving Staircase

Design 94995

The spacious formal entry of this home features a spectacular curving staircase. An arched transom above enhances the double doors into the volume den which is accented by built-in bookcases and arched window. There are repeating arched windows to the rear of the large Great room. A fireplace highlights the Great room with a warm cozy atmosphere. The second fireplace is located in the hearth room and is open to the dinette/kitchen area. Amenities abound in the gourmet kitchen which includes a cooktop island. The master bedroom retreat has a private back door and luxurious dressing area featuring an oval whirlpool and a large walk-in closet. Generous closets and baths enhance the secondary bedrooms.

First floor — 2,252 sq. ft.
Second floor — 920 sq. ft.
Basement — 2,252 sq. ft.
Garage — 646 sq. ft.

Total living area: 3,172 sq. ft.

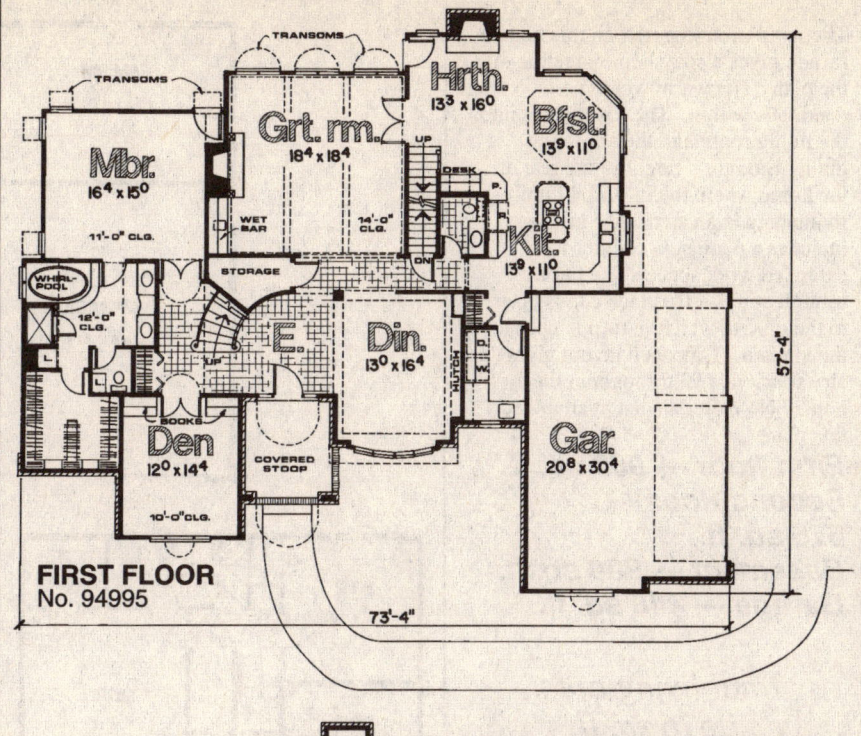

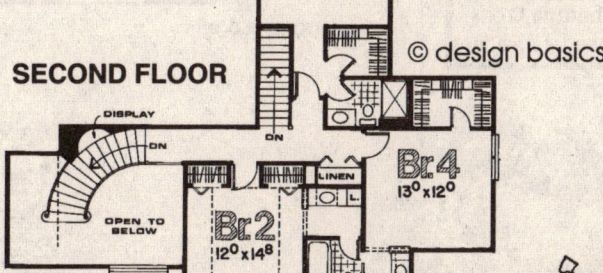

Refer to **Pricing Schedule E** on the order form for pricing information

© design basics, inc.

ORDER TODAY! 1 - 800 - 235 - 5700

WRAP-AROUND PORCH

Design 94138

The wrap-around porch on this home's facade gives a cozy homey feeling to the plan. The warm welcome continues within. The foyer leads into the living room and the adjoining dining room or straight to the rear of the home where the informal family living area is located. The kitchen includes a peninsula counter for extended work space. The family room features a fireplace and is open to the dinette which in turn is open to the kitchen. This open layout gives an airy spacious feel throughout the home. No materials list available for this plan.

First floor — 900 sq. ft.
Second floor — 676 sq. ft.
Basement — 900 sq. ft.
Garage — 448 sq. ft.

Total living area: 1,576 sq. ft.

Refer to **Pricing Schedule C** on the order form for pricing information

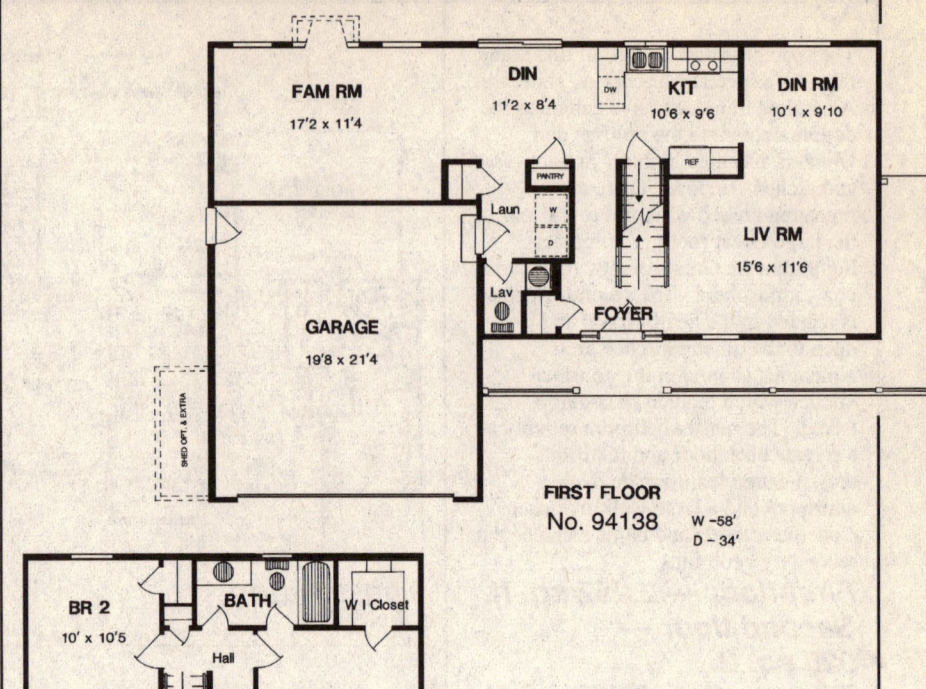

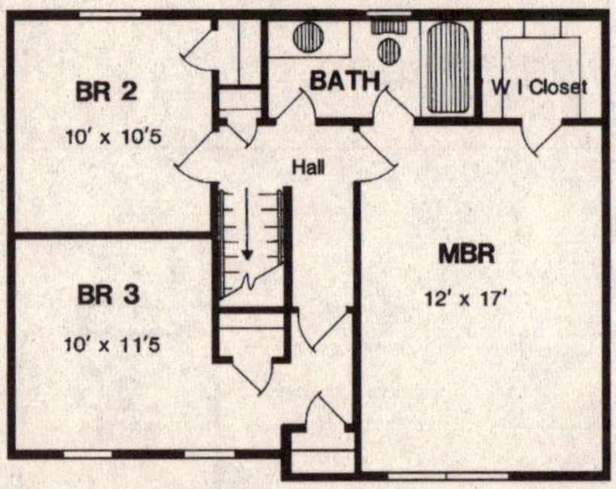

SOUTHERN TRADITION

Design 99641

An affordable, expandable house with a Southern Traditional flavor generates charm and warmth as one approaches the colonnaded front porch and enters the house. The foyer has a large coat closet and leads past the stairway to the second floor and to the main living space — a large living room with a 9-foot high ceiling. The living room flows gracefully into the dining room shaped by the angled pass-through into the kitchen. Two French doors lead from the dining room to a rear terrace. The kitchen, connecting to the left, provides another large space with plenty of countertop area, cabinet storage and bays out to form a dinette. Bedrooms flank both sides of the living room. On the left is the master suite that includes a large walk-in closet and master bath with a compartmentalized toilet, a separate stall shower, a whirlpool tub and two lavatories. Two identical bedrooms are located on the other side and share a full bath.

Refer to **Pricing Schedule B** on the order form for pricing information

First floor — 1,567 sq. ft.
Second floor (Bonus space) — 462 sq. ft.
Basement — 1,567 sq. ft.
Garage — 504 sq. ft.
Front porch — 152 sq. ft.

SECOND FLOOR PLAN

FIRST FLOOR PLAN
No. 99641

Total living area: 1,567 sq. ft.

ORDER TODAY! 1 - 800 - 235 - 5700

Graceful Home

Design 93611

The graceful facade of this beautiful home will impress all who come to visit. The open livable floor plan will impress you every day. The central living areas are open and airy. The split bedroom plan assures the utmost privacy. All major important areas look out the views at the rear of the home, and a sun room with glass on three sides brings in nature. Notice the laundry room, unusual for a home of this size. This design is a drive under, there is room for three vehicles, storage, a bedroom and hobbies below. There is even an optional loft above the kitchen for those who desire a higher view to the vista at the rear of this home. No materials list is available for this plan.

Main floor — 1,656 sq. ft.
Basement — 728 sq. ft.
Garage — 784 sq. ft.
Deck — 270 sq. ft.

An **EXCLUSIVE DESIGN** By Garrell Associates Inc.

WIDTH 54'-0"
DEPTH 45'-0"

up @ optional loft

DECK
SUNROOM BRFST. 10-2 x 9-2
MASTER BEDROOM 13-0 x 12-6
GRAND ROOM
KITCHEN 10-0 x 12-0
PAN
REF
BEDROOM 10-10 x 11-2
W.I.C.
DINING ROOM 14-0 x 11-0
FOYER
GALLERY
LNDRY.
BATH
BEDROOM 10-10 x 11-2
PORCH

MAIN FLOOR
No. 93611

Total living area: 1,656 sq. ft.

Refer to **Pricing Schedule B** on the order form for pricing information

Design 90356

BALCONY OVERLOOKS LIVING ROOM

Smaller houses are getting better all the time, not only in their exterior character and scale, but in their use of spacial volumes and interior finish materials. Here a modest two-story gains importance, impact, and perceived value from the sweeping roof lines that make it look larger than it really is. Guests will be impressed by the impact of the vaulted ceiling in the living room up to the balcony hall above, the easy flow of traffic, and abundant space in the kitchen and dining areas. Note too, the luxurious master suite with a window seat bay, walk-in closet, dressing area, and private shower.

Main floor — 674 sq. ft.
Upper floor — 677 sq. ft.

Total living area: 1,351 sq. ft.

Refer to **Pricing Schedule A** on the order form for pricing information

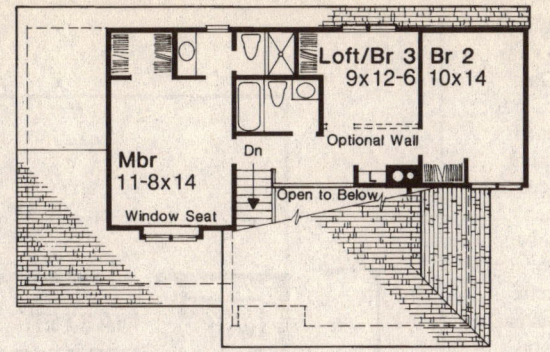

UPPER FLOOR PLAN

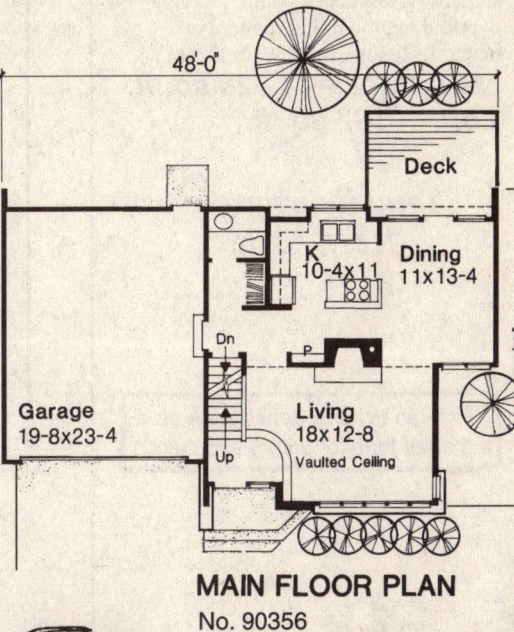

MAIN FLOOR PLAN
No. 90356

ORDER TODAY!   1 - 800 - 235 - 5700

Design 94309

Cozy Vacation Hide-Away

Highly windowed, the living room of this home offers an unrestricted view of your chosen surroundings. The spacious deck expands living space to the outdoors and includes a built-in grill for terrific outdoor entertaining. Inside, the cozy fireplace enhances the living room. The efficient kitchen includes a corner double sink and an eating bar. Two bedrooms are located on the main floor. The master suite is equipped with a walk-in closet and a private three-quarter bath. A spiral staircase gains access to the loft area overlooking the living room. No materials list is available for this plan.

Main floor — 1,028 sq. ft.
Loft — 187 sq. ft.

Total living area: 1,215 sq. ft.

Refer to **Pricing Schedule A** on the order form for pricing information

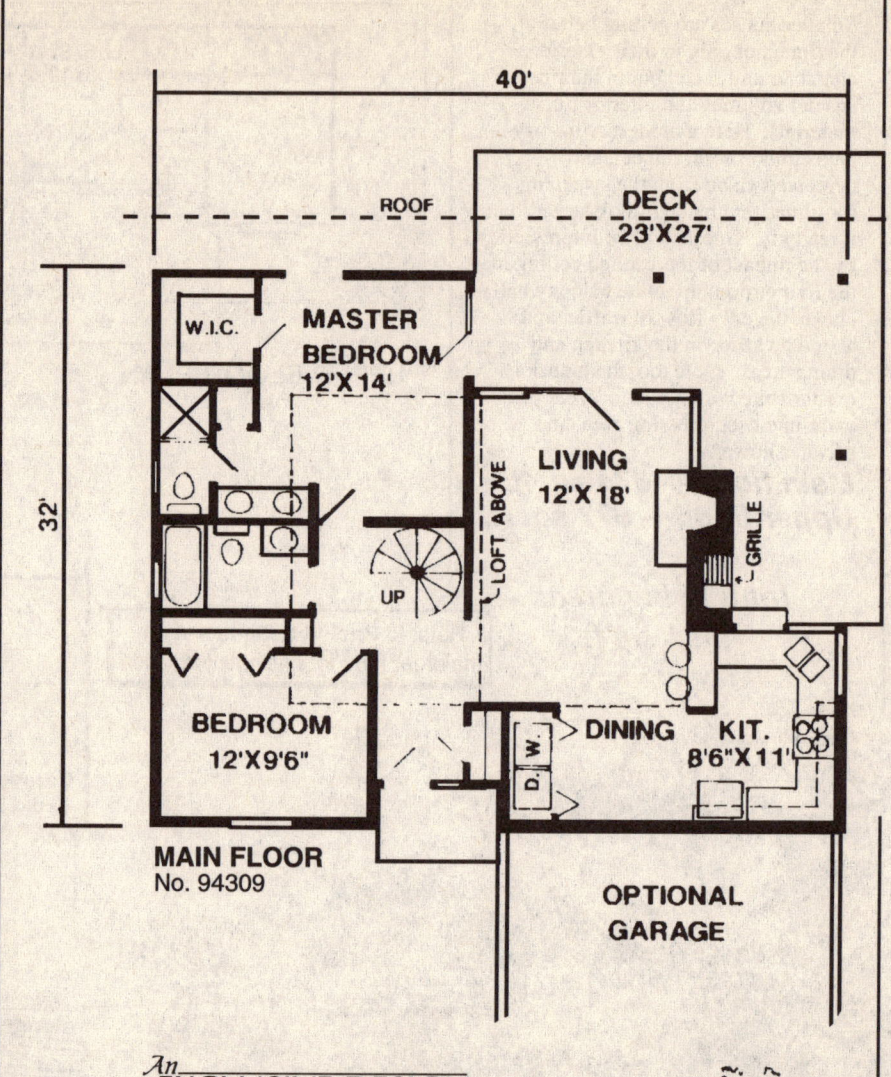

An **EXCLUSIVE DESIGN** *By Marshall Associates*

A LOT OF LIVING SPACE

Design 91081

There's a lot of living space in this four bedroom home with brick trim. Expansive windows in the vaulted living room allow for plenty of light, and the corner is the perfect place for a wood stove. The kitchen is generously sized and close to the garage for easy access. Two secondary bedrooms, one with a walk-in closet, share the main bath. There is a plant shelf above the staircase, which leads to the master suite and loft or optional bedrooms. The master suite bath features a skylight and walk-in closet. No materials list is available for this plan.

First floor — 1,076 sq. ft.
Second floor — 449 sq. ft.

Total living area: 1,525 sq. ft.

Refer to **Pricing Schedule B** on the order form for pricing information

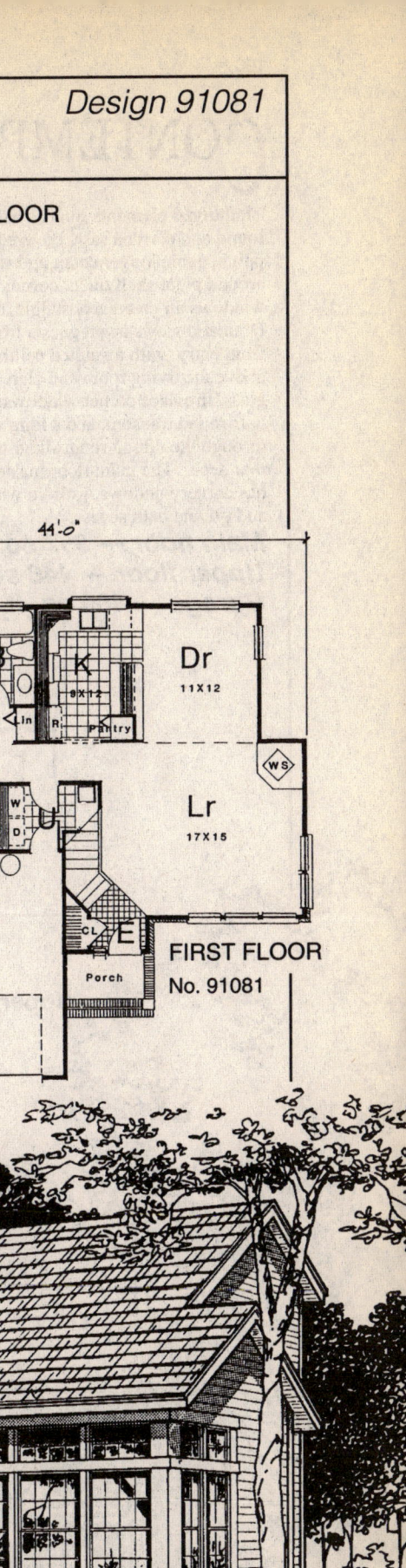

CONTEMPORARY TRADITIONS

Design 99339

Traditional elements such as half-round and divided sash, covered front porch, gable louver detail and wrap-around plant shelf under corner windows all create a nostalgic appeal. Dramatic views await guests from the front entry, with a vaulted ceiling above the living room and clerestory glass, fireplace corner windows with half-round transom, and a long view through the dining room slider to the rear deck. The main floor master suite has corner windows, walk-in wardrobe and private bath access.

Main floor — 857 sq. ft.
Upper floor — 446 sq. ft.
Garage — 400 sq. ft.

Refer to **Pricing Schedule A** on the order form for pricing information

Total living area: 1,303 sq. ft.

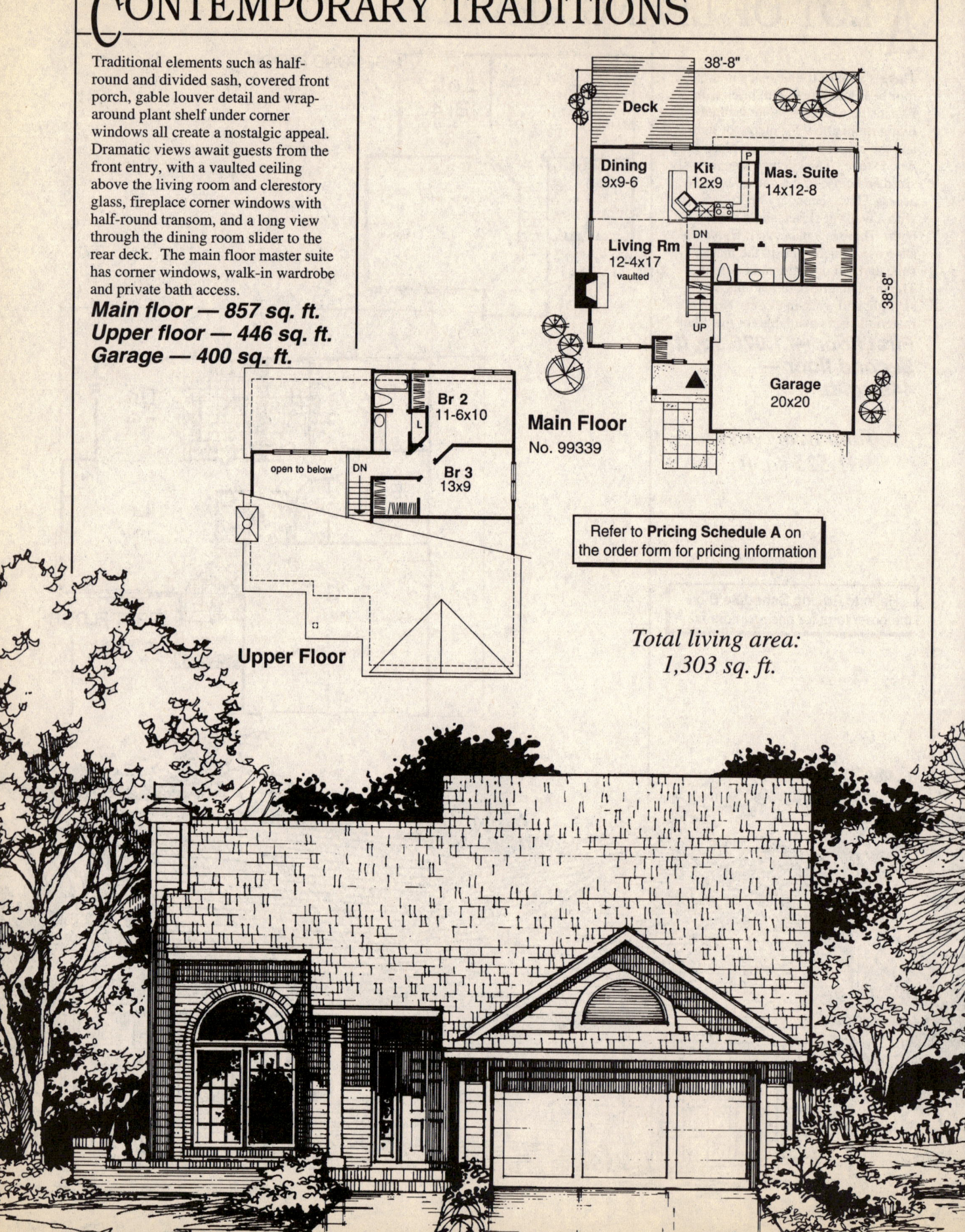

ORDER TODAY! 1-800-235-5700

Design 99812

Sunny Dormer Brightens Foyer

A sunny dormer brightens the foyer for a great first impression. This cozy home is full of today's comforts yet cost-effective to construct. The open Great room, dining room, and kitchen feature a cathedral ceiling that emphasizes a sense of spaciousness. An adjoining deck provides extra living or entertaining room. The front bedroom is expanded by a cathedral ceiling that shows off a double window with a circle top. The master suite is highlighted by a cathedral ceiling in the bedroom and includes a private bath with garden tub, double vanity, and walk-in closet. A skylit bonus room above the garage offers flexibility and opportunity for growth.

Main floor — 1,386 sq. ft.
Garage — 517 sq. ft.
Bonus room — 314 sq. ft.

Total living area: 1,386 sq. ft.

Refer to **Pricing Schedule B** on the order form for pricing information

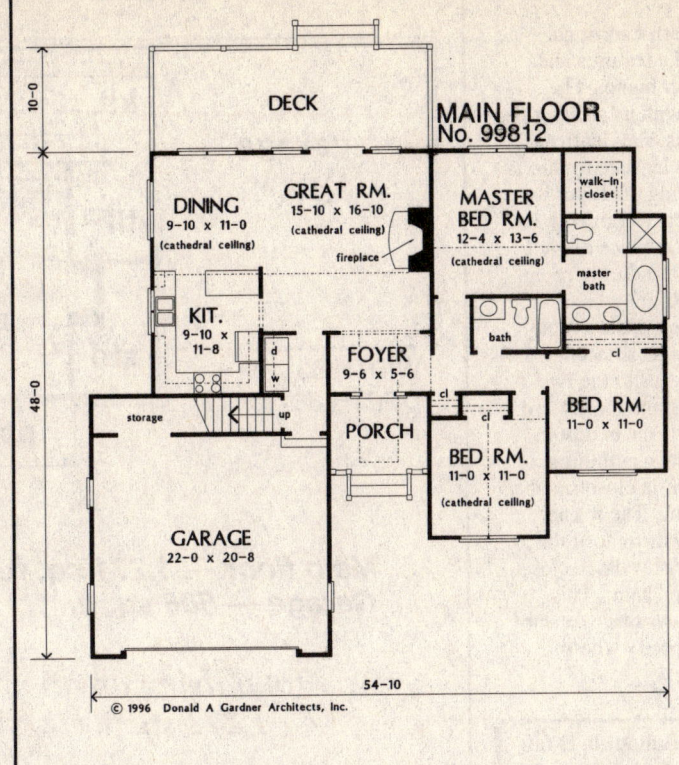

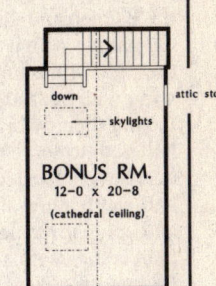

© 1996 Donald A Gardner Architects, Inc.

CHARMING SOUTHERN TRADITIONAL

Design 92503

This charming southern traditional styled home has all the features and looks of a much larger home. The covered front porch with its striking columns, brick quoins, and dentil moulding add a rich elegance to this stately design. Entering the foyer we find the spacious Great Room with its vaulted ceilings and fireplace as well as built in cabinets. The dining room is open to the Great Room which opens up to the whole middle of the plan. The utility room is adjacent to the kitchen and this leads to the two-car garage with its storage rooms. To the right of the foyer is the bedroom wing with bedrooms two and three having their own walk-in closets and a hall bath to serve them. The master bedroom is located to the rear of the hall and features a large walk-in closet and compartmentalized bath. This plan comes with a crawl space or slab foundation. Please specify when ordering.

Refer to **Pricing Schedule B** on the order form for pricing information

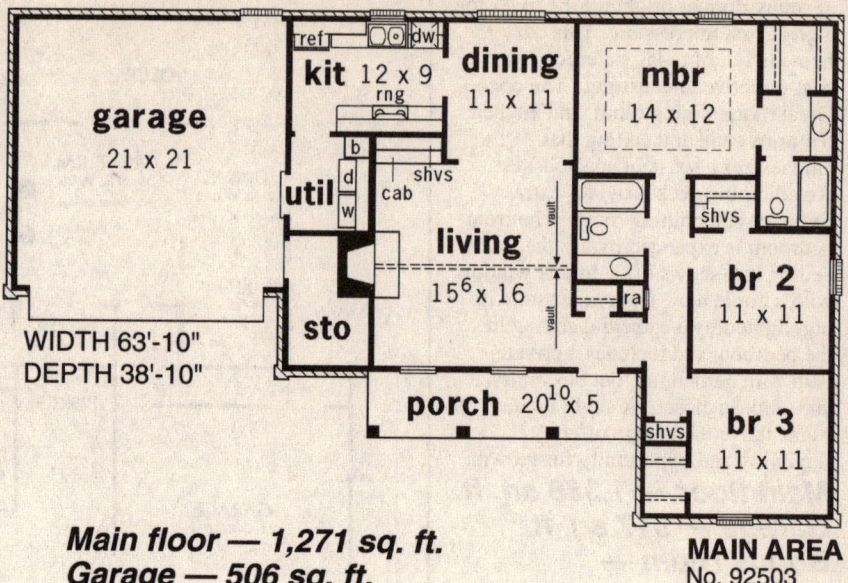

WIDTH 63'-10"
DEPTH 38'-10"

Main floor — 1,271 sq. ft.
Garage — 506 sq. ft.

Total living area:
1,271 sq. ft.

MAIN AREA
No. 92503

ORDER TODAY! 1 - 800 - 235 - 5700

Design 94314

Survey the Grand

An **EXCLUSIVE DESIGN**
By Marshall Associates

This home is definitely designed for a lot with a view. The rear of the home has cascading windows and decks. This arrangement allows for a terrific indoor/outdoor relationship. From the entry the visitor's views are into the Great room. The galley kitchen serves the dining area with ease. The Great room is enhanced by a fireplace and opens to the dining area. There is a main floor bedroom located next to a full bath. The rear wrap-around deck, wraps around the Great room. On the second floor, the master suite includes a private three-quarter bath and a private deck. A secondary bedroom and storage space completes the second floor. The lower level is a terrific place to relax. The recreation room includes a fireplace with sliding glass doors to the patio. A hot tub and built-in bar adds to the luxury of this home. No materials list is available for this plan.

Main level— 812 sq. ft.
Upper level —
653 sq. ft.
Lower level —
486 sq. ft.

Total living area:
1,951 sq. ft.

UPPER LEVEL
M. BEDROOM 14'X13'4"
BEDROOM - 2 12'6"X11'
STORAGE 8'X9'6"
WD. DECK

LOWER LEVEL
PATIO 17'X10'
RECREATION 17'X14'
HOT TUB
BAR
UTIL. 8'X10'

MAIN LEVEL
No. 94314
WOOD DECK
DINING 12'X8'6"
GREAT ROOM 17'X14'
KIT. 8'X10'
BEDROOM - 3 11'X11' + BAY
ENT.
GARAGE 13'X22'
WOOD DECK
36'
50'

Refer to **Pricing Schedule C** on the order form for pricing information

Openness Between Rooms Adds Space

Design 24269

The vaulted ceiling in the living room and the openness between rooms of this home make it feel larger than its 2,244 sq. ft. Once in the foyer, you must step down to enter either the living room, or the family room. The spacious living room flows into an elegant formal dining room. The family room is enhanced by a large fireplace. The efficient kitchen is convenient to both the formal dining room and the informal eating nook, which is brightened by a bay window and features a built-in pantry. The master suite, also with a vaulted ceiling, has a private luxurious master bath and two walk-in closets. The two additional bedrooms have use of a full hall bath that has an added convenience of a laundry chute. There is a loft area to be used as an extra bedroom or what ever the needs of the family are. No materials list is available for this plan.

Refer to **Pricing Schedule D** on the order form for pricing information

First floor — 1,115 sq. ft.
Second floor — 1,129 sq. ft.
Basement — 1,096 sq. ft.
Garage — 415 sq. ft.

Total living area: 2,244 sq. ft.

An EXCLUSIVE DESIGN *By Energetic Enterprises*

ORDER TODAY! 1 - 800 - 235 - 5700

Design 99650

COMPACT CONTEMPORARY

This compact contemporary exhibits a touch of country with its sheltering front porch, leading to a double door front entry and central foyer. Straight ahead is the large Great room, with a high ceiling and a corner fireplace. A right turn leads to the efficient U-shaped kitchen and adjacent eating space. The kitchen is open to the bayed window dining room. All these spaces flow together creating a feeling of spaciousness. The master bedroom has a large walk-in closet and a wonderful bath. Two additional bedrooms share the full bath in the hallway.

Main area — 1,507 sq. ft.
Basement — 746 sq. ft.
Garage — 432 sq. ft.

Total living area: 1,507 sq. ft.

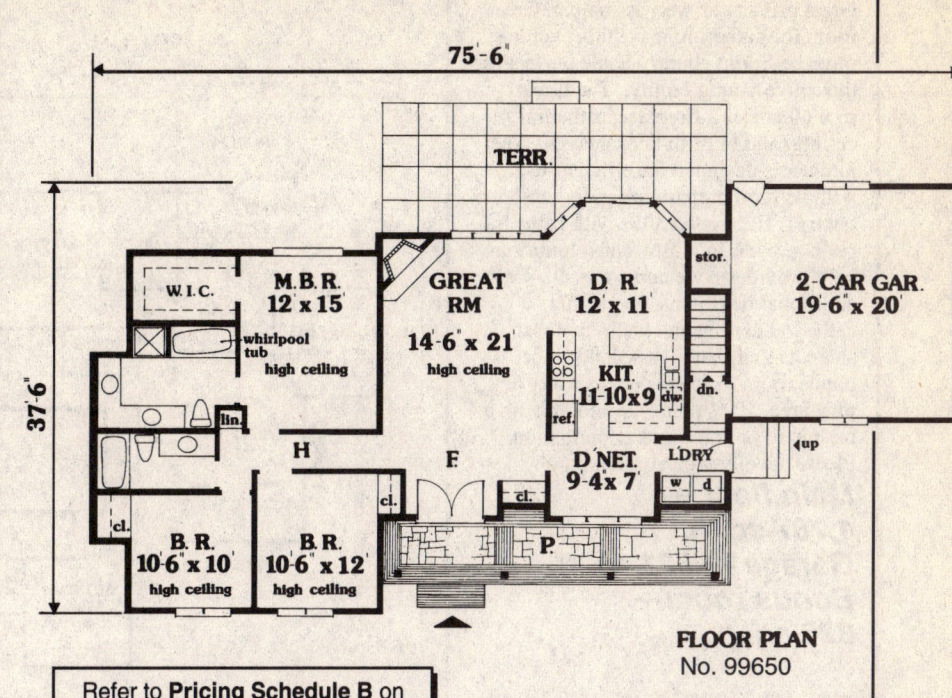

Refer to **Pricing Schedule B** on the order form for pricing information

ORDER TODAY! 1-800-235-5700

FOR THE ACTIVE YOUNG FAMILY

Design 99805

Great privacy as well as an open Great room for gathering make this exciting three bedroom country home perfect for the active young family. The Great room features a fireplace, cathedral ceiling, and built-in bookshelves. The kitchen is designed for efficient use with its food preparation island and pantry. The master suite with cathedral ceiling, walk-in closet, and a luxurious bath provides a welcome retreat. Two additional bedrooms, one with a cathedral ceiling and walk-in closet, share a skylit bath. A second floor bonus room makes a perfect study or play area. This plan is available with a basement or crawl space foundation. Please specify when ordering.

**Main floor —
1,787 sq. ft.
Garage — 521 sq. ft.
Bonus room—
326 sq. ft.**

*Total living area:
1,787 sq. ft.*

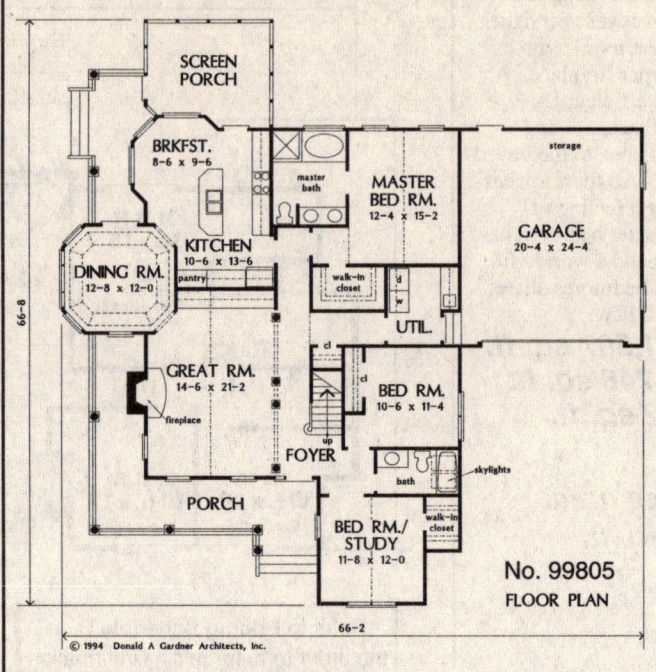

Refer to **Pricing Schedule C** on the order form for pricing information

© 1994 Donald A Gardner Architects, Inc.

YEAR ROUND RETREAT

ORDER TODAY! 1 - 800 - 235 - 5700

Design 90613

This compact home is a bargain to build and designed to save on energy bills. Large glass areas face south, and the dramatic sloping ceiling of the living room allows heat from the wood-burning stove to rise into the upstairs bedrooms through high louvers on the inside wall. In hot weather, just open the windows on both floors for cooling air circulation. Sliding glass doors in the kitchen and living room open to the deck for outdoor dining or relaxation. One bedroom and a full bath complete the first floor. A stair off the foyer ends in a balcony with a commanding view of the living room. Two spacious bedrooms are separated by a full bath.

First floor — 967 sq. ft.
Second floor — 465 sq. ft.
Basement — 811 sq. ft.

Total living area: 1,432 sq. ft.

Refer to **Pricing Schedule A** on the order form for pricing information

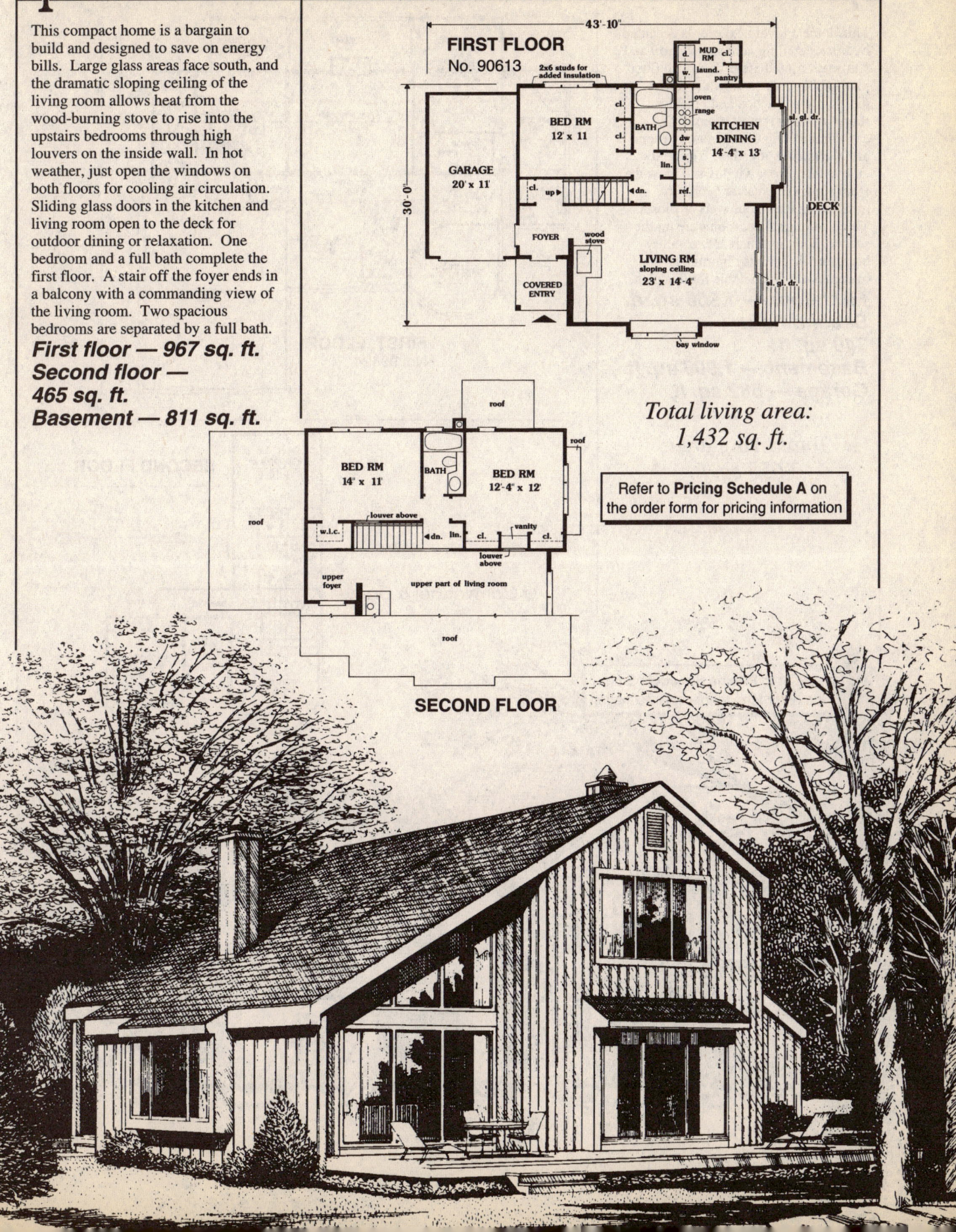

TURRETED ROOF WITH BRICK DETAIL

Design 99424

This home's lovely exterior is accented by brick detailing, a recessed entry and a turreted roofed area. The open floor plan enables one to view the study, dining room, kitchen and breakfast room from the family room. The cathedral ceiling ties the family room and the kitchen together. The study enjoys three front windows to view the front yard. The master bedroom includes an enormous walk-in closet. Three additional bedrooms are on the second floor and share a two vanity bath, terrific for busy mornings. No materials list is available for this plan.

First floor — 1,906 sq. ft.
Second floor — 749 sq. ft.
Basement — 1,906 sq. ft.
Garage — 682 sq. ft.

Total living area: 2,655 sq. ft.

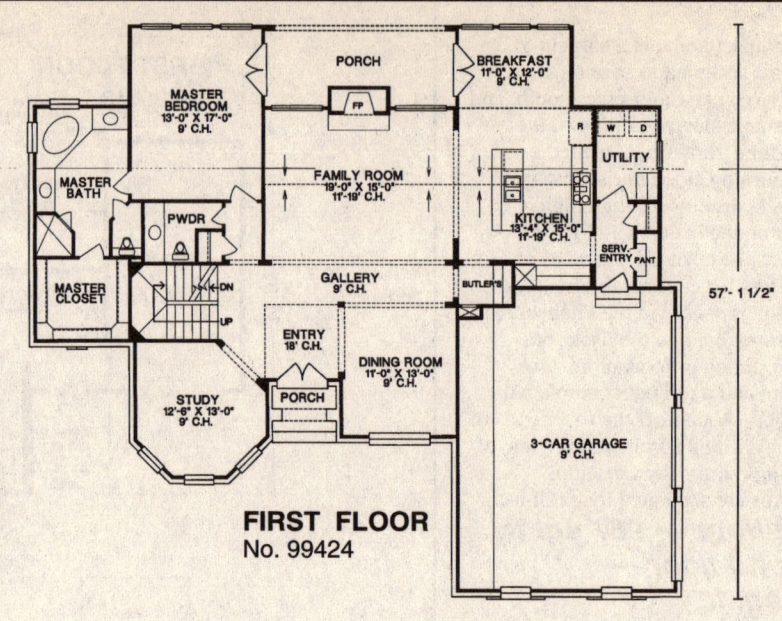

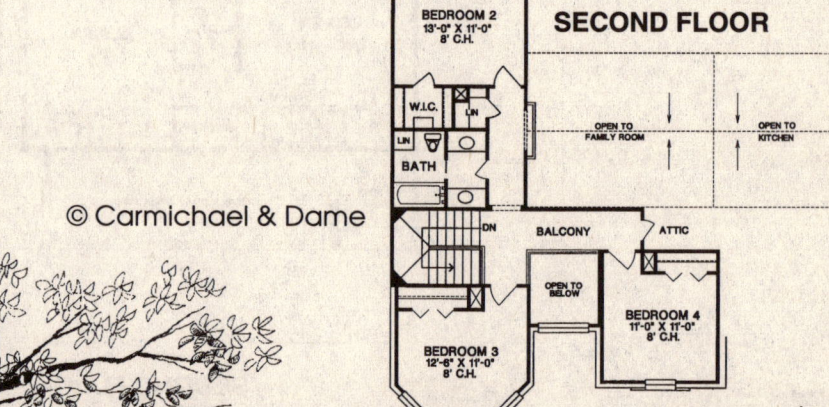

© Carmichael & Dame

Refer to **Pricing Schedule E** on the order form for pricing information

GREAT STARTER HOME

Design 24708

This functional, all on one level, home plan features a lovely country porch entry into a spacious living room that is accented by a fireplace. The efficient U-shaped kitchen has direct access to both the dining and the living room. A screened porch is accessed directly from the kitchen. The master bedroom includes a private double vanity bath with a whirlpool tub and separate shower. The two additional bedrooms share a full double vanity bath which has the added convenience of a laundry center. No materials list is available for this plan.

Main floor — 1,576 sq. ft.
Basement — 1,454 sq. ft.
Garage — 576 sq. ft.

Total living area: 1,576 sq. ft.

Refer to **Pricing Schedule B** on the order form for pricing information

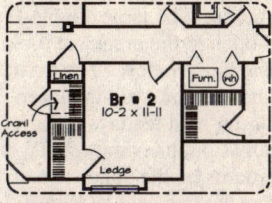

Alternate Crawl/Slab Plan

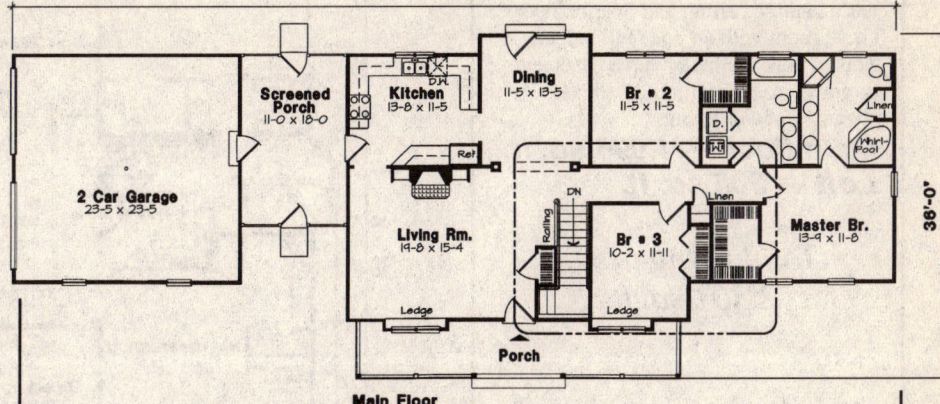

Main Floor
No. 24708

PERFECT FOR A CORNER LOT

Design 90444

This Ranch plan is ideal for a corner lot, with a rear garage that enters from the side. The focal point of this plan is the Great room with a vaulted ceiling, and loft above. The French doors on either side of the fireplace open onto a screened porch. The large double-L kitchen is open to the breakfast room, which has a bay window. The master bedroom has a large walk-in closet, and the master bath features a corner tub, as well as double vanities. Two other bedrooms on the opposite end of the house make this split-bedroom design popular. Each of these bedrooms has a walk-in closet, and a desk for school-age children. The loft has a vaulted ceiling and overlooks the Great room with an open rail balcony. This plan is available with a basement or crawl space foundation. Please specify when ordering.

Main floor — 1,996 sq. ft.
Loft — 305 sq. ft.

Total living area: 2,301 sq. ft.

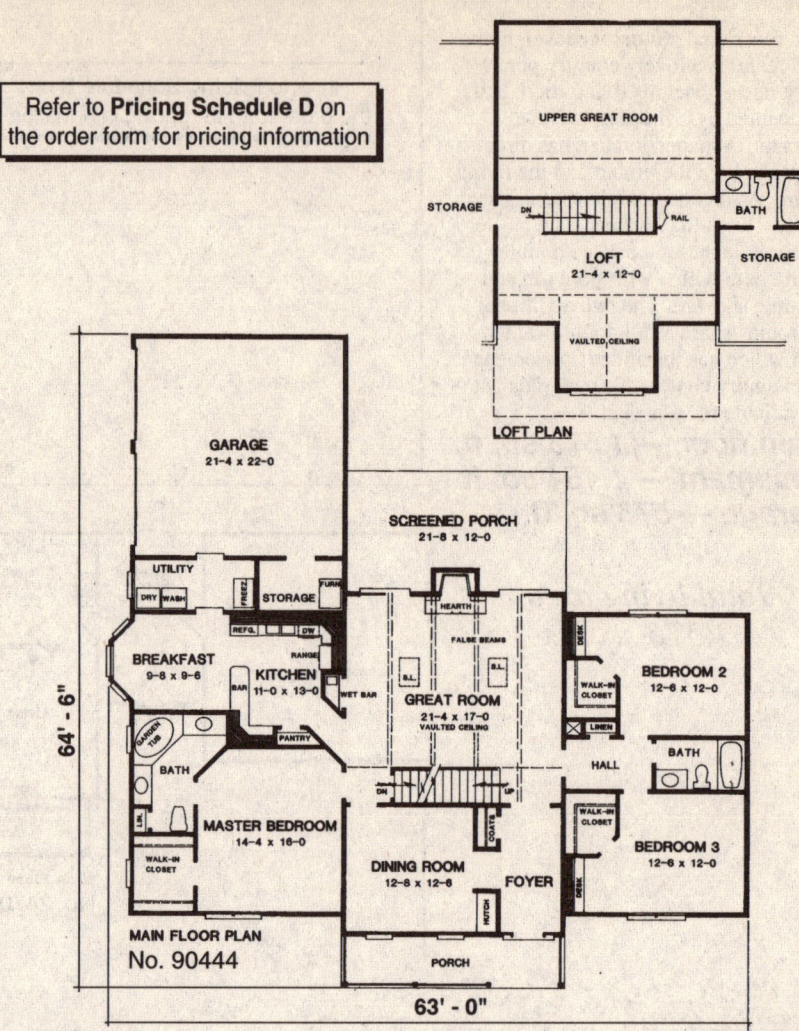

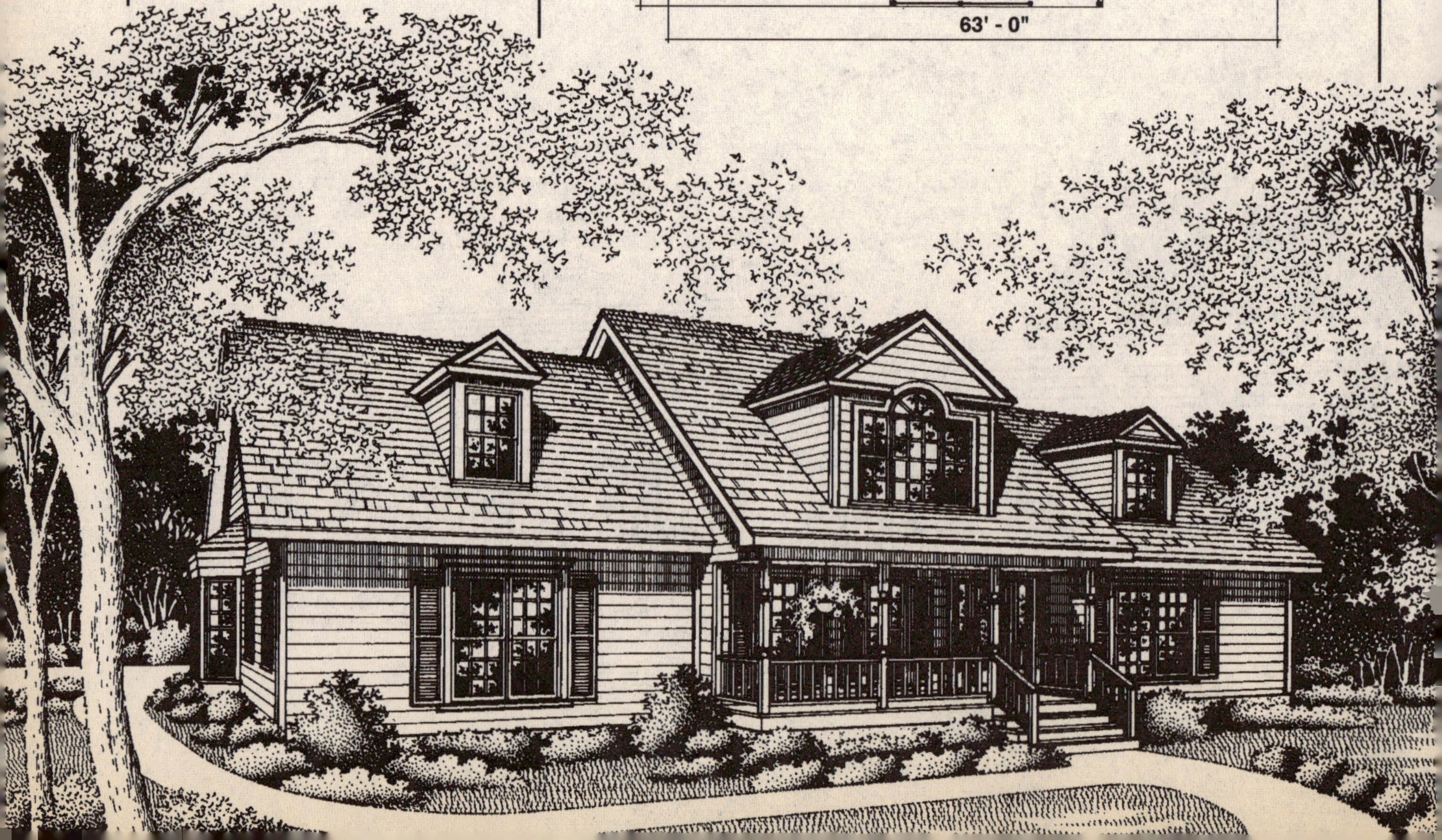

ORDER TODAY!   1 - 800 - 235 - 5700

Stunning Brick & Siding Exterior

Design 96414

This plan's stunning brick and siding exterior surrounds the well-planned living spaces to create a home where formal gatherings or casual family moments are equally pleasurable. The Great room is the center of attention, it is open to the breakfast bay, dining room, and foyer and provides nearby access to the bonus room. A bay window in the master bedroom creates a great master suite sitting area as well as a dramatic rear elevation. The master suite is also equipped with a spacious, pampering bath with corner shower, garden tub, enclosed toilet, and a huge walk-in closet.

**Main floor —
2,196 sq. ft.
Garage & Storage —
576 sq. ft.
Bonus room —
326 sq. ft.**

*Total living area:
2,196 sq. ft.*

Refer to **Pricing Schedule D** on the order form for pricing information

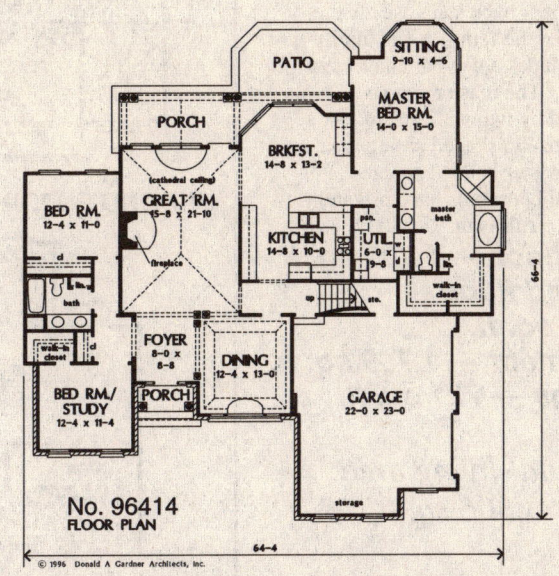

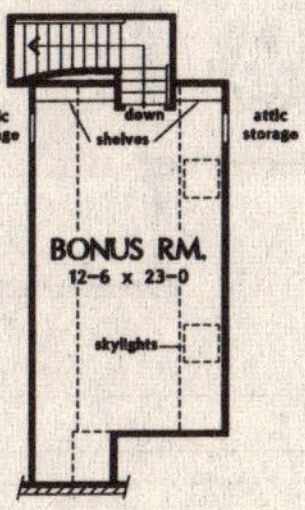

ORDER TODAY! 1-800-235-5700

Design 94933

REPETITIVE PEAKS

This gracious front facade is enhanced by the repetitive peaks of the roof line. The living room and the dining room combine for formal entertaining. The interesting T-shaped staircase highlights the entry. The gourmet kitchen includes a salad sink in the island as well as a snack bar. There is a convenient back staircase off the kitchen for the family. The family room includes a wet bar and a cozy fireplace. The master suite is pampered by two walk-in closets, a private gazebo shaped sitting area, and a skylit master bath. The three additional bedrooms have private access to a full bath.

First floor — 1,709 sq. ft.
Second floor — 1,597 sq. ft.
Basement — 1,709 sq. ft.
Garage — 721 sq. ft.

Total living area: 3,306 sq. ft.

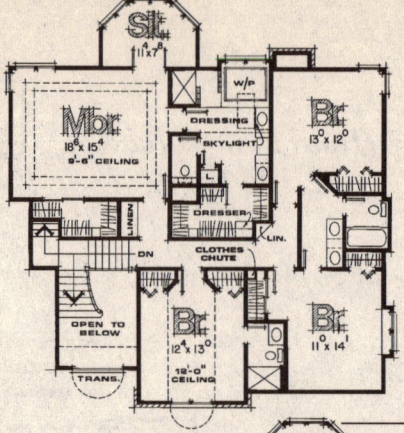

SECOND FLOOR

Refer to **Pricing Schedule F** on the order form for pricing information

© design basics, inc.

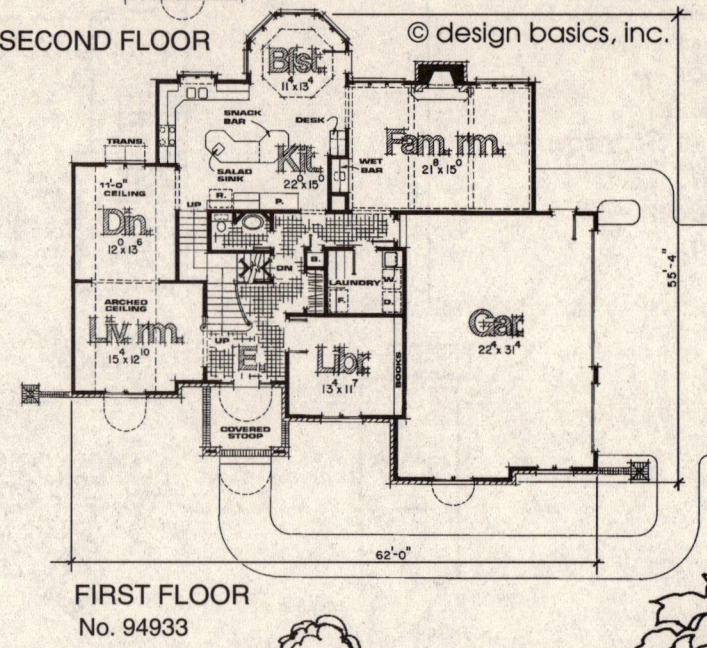

FIRST FLOOR
No. 94933

ORDER TODAY! 1-800-235-5700

Design 99851

DRAMATIC WINDOWS AND GABLES

Flanked by columns, the barrel vaulted entrance of this three bedroom home is echoed in its dramatic arched windows and gables. Interior columns add elegance while visually dividing the foyer from the dining room and the great room from the kitchen. The Great room is made even larger by its cathedral ceiling and bank of windows, including an arched clerestory window. A box bay window adds space to the formal dining room, while the kitchen features an angled center island with breakfast counter for the busy family. The master suite, secluded on the first floor, boasts his and her walk-in closets and a garden tub with a skylight. Two bedrooms upstairs share another skylit bath. This plan is available with a basement or crawl space foundation. Please specify when ordering.

First floor — 1,416 sq. ft.
Second floor — 445 sq. ft.
Garage & storage — 485 sq. ft.
Bonus room — 284 sq. ft.

Total living area: 1,861 sq. ft.

Refer to **Pricing Schedule C** on the order form for pricing information

© 1991 Donald A. Gardner Architects, Inc.

NOSTALGIA RETURNS

Design 99321

The return to a nostalgic exterior around contemporary volumetric interior spaces of the late 80's is reflected in this appealing 1,368 square foot ranch design. The half-round Great room transom window with quarter round detail makes for an interesting focal point inside and out. The vaulted ceilings inside make the rooms feel spacious, while the corner fireplace and side deck entered through the breakfast room sliders create an interesting entry impact.

Main area — 1,368 sq. ft.
Garage — 412 sq. ft.

Total living area: 1,368 sq. ft.

Refer to **Pricing Schedule A** on the order form for pricing information

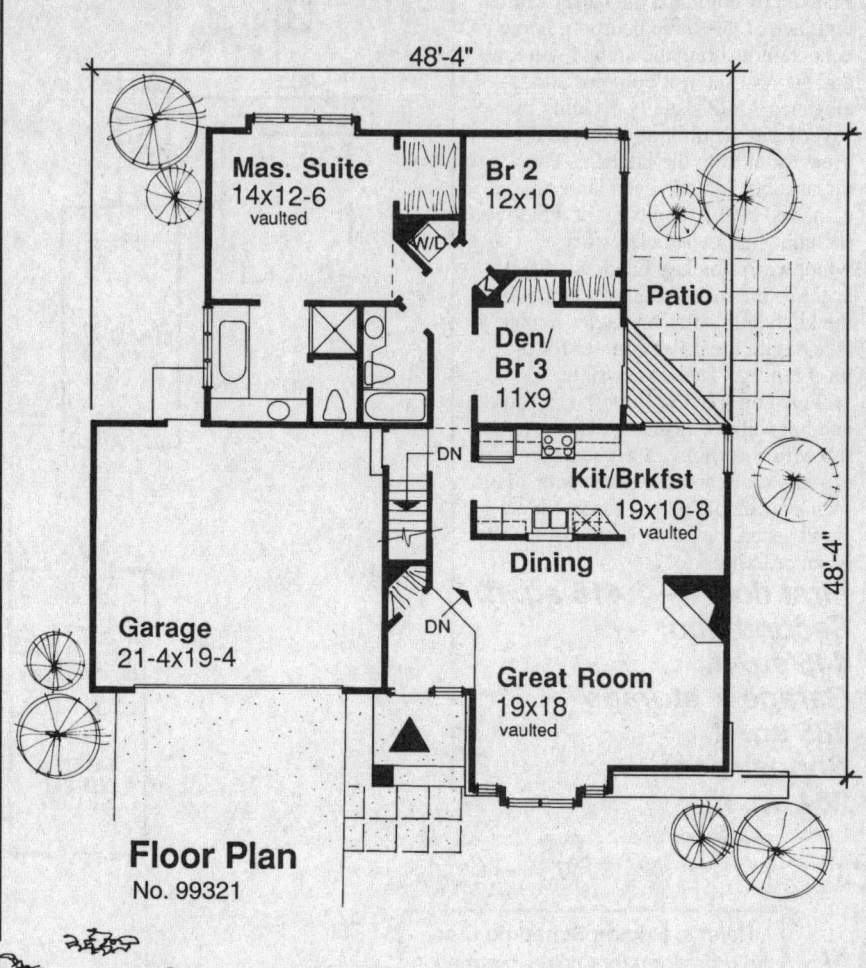

Floor Plan
No. 99321

Design 99410

MAGNIFICENT PRESENCE

The entry enjoys many different vistas. A curved staircase leads to an elevated study characterized by its arched opening, eighteen foot ceiling and very detailed block paneling. Looking forward there is a two-story living room with amazing glass to bring the outdoors in. A dramatic dining room is available for elegant entertaining. The expansive family room is open to the kitchen and breakfast bay, providing a vast informal family living area. Luxurious features and a spacious layout highlight this impressive home. No materials list is available for this plan.

First floor — 2,897 sq. ft.
Second floor — 1,603 sq. ft.
Basement — 2,897 sq. ft.
Garage — 793 sq. ft.

Total living area: 4,500 sq. ft.

Refer to **Pricing Schedule F** on the order form for pricing information

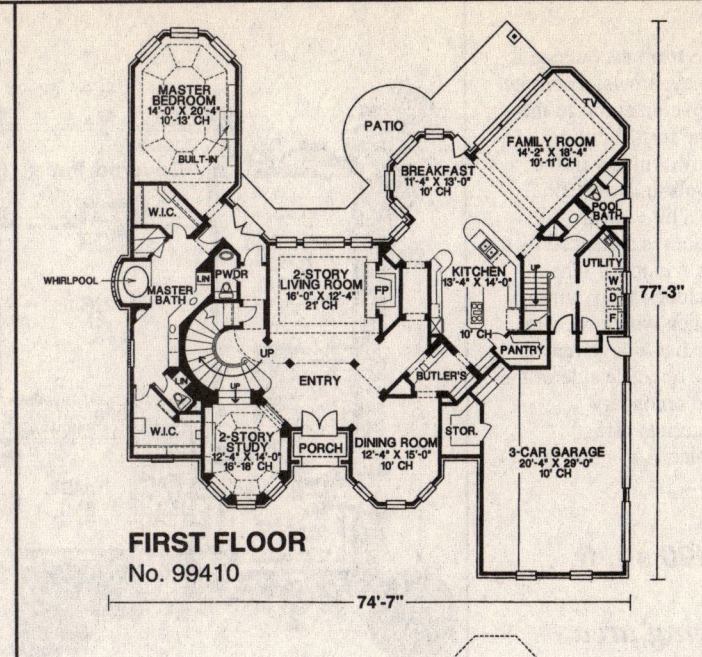

FIRST FLOOR
No. 99410

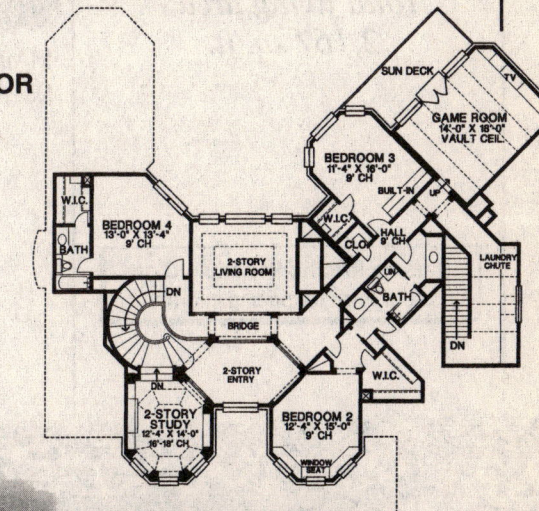

SECOND FLOOR

© Carmichael & Dame

ORDER TODAY! 1 - 800 - 235 - 5700

Arched Covered Entry

Design 98512

Viewing this home from the outside is sure to raise a few eyebrows. From its eyebrow arched covered entry, to the large window in the formal dining room to the eyebrow window in the master bedroom walk-in closet, this home is sure to be a hit. Inside, the enormous Great room is enhanced by a fireplace and large windows. The breakfast room includes a bay window and an angled kitchen with a built-in pantry. This home has a large master suite situated at the opposite side of the home from the two secondary bedrooms. No materials list is available for this plan.

**Main floor —
2,167 sq. ft.
Garage — 690 sq. ft.**

Total living area:
2,167 sq. ft.

Refer to **Pricing Schedule C** on the order form for pricing information

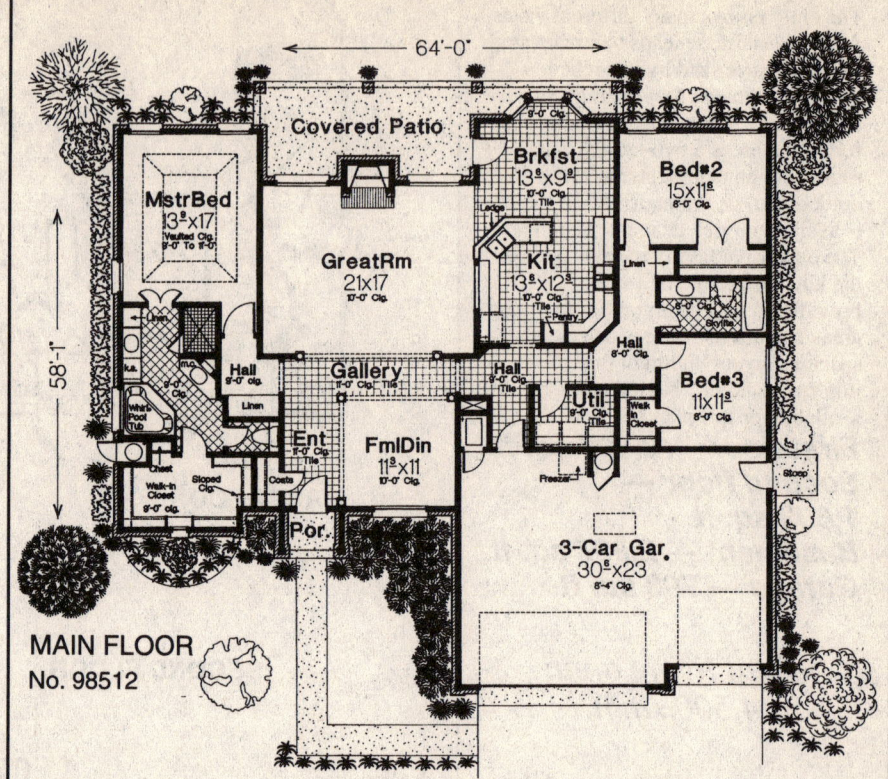

MAIN FLOOR
No. 98512

Design 92546

POSH EXTERIOR — FINE DETAIL

A distinguished front porch with columns defining the entrance, along with arched windows and stone quoins lend this home a stately appearance. A formal foyer gives way to the spacious den crowned in a decorative ceiling treatment and further enhanced by a fireplace. The formal dining room is to the right of the foyer. An efficient U-shaped kitchen, equipped with an extended counter/eating bar and an informal breakfast area, directly accesses the dining room. A decorative ceiling also tops the master suite. Adding to the suite's convenience and privacy, is a compartmented, private master bath and a large walk-in closet. Three additional, roomy bedrooms share the full hall bath. This plan is available with a slab or crawl space foundation. Please specify when ordering.

Main floor — 2,387 sq. ft.
Garage & storage — 505 sq. ft.

Total living area: 2,387 sq. ft.

Refer to **Pricing Schedule E** on the order form for pricing information

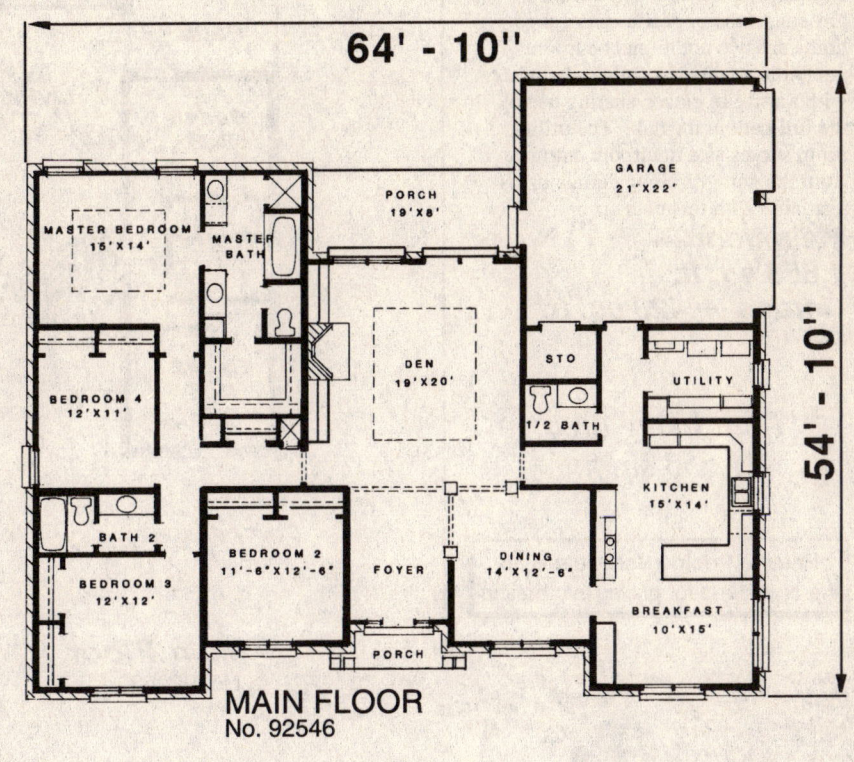

MAIN FLOOR
No. 92546

Three Bedrooms and More

Design 92283

A sheltered entrance leads to a tiled foyer. To the right is the dining and kitchen area. Straight ahead is the roomy living room with a cozy fireplace. The master suite, privately located, includes a vaulted ceiling, compartmented bath and a walk-in closet. At the opposite end of the home are two additional bedrooms, one with a cathedral ceiling the other with a walk-in closet, sharing use of the full bath in the hall. The utility room serves as a mudroom entrance from the garage. No materials list is available with this plan.

Main floor — 1,653 sq. ft.
Garage — 420 sq. ft.

Total living area: 1,653 sq. ft.

Refer to **Pricing Schedule B** on the order form for pricing information

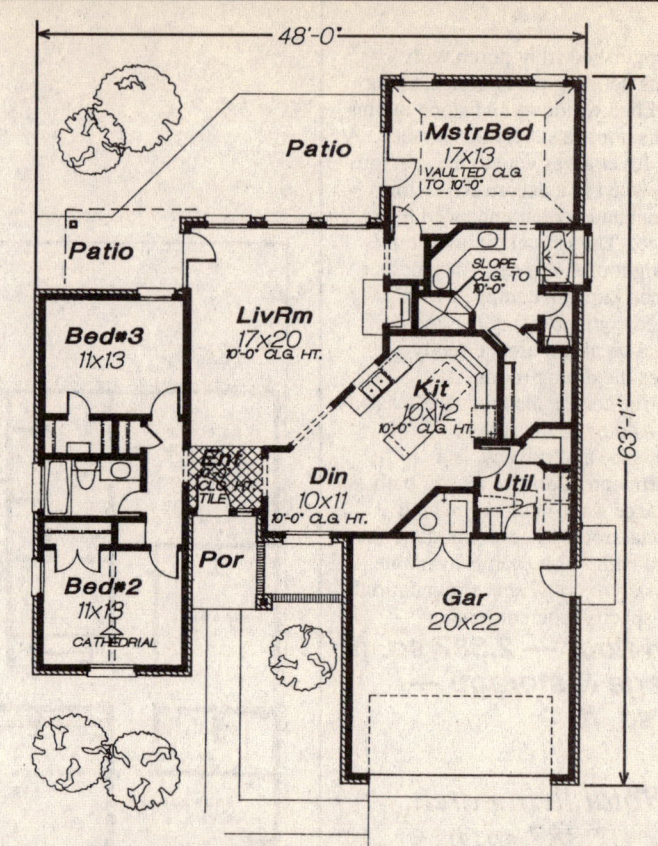

Main Floor
No. 92283

ORDER TODAY! 1 - 800 - 235 - 5700

CATHEDRAL CEILING OPENS INTERIOR

Design 99811

Two dormers add volume to the foyer, while a cathedral ceiling enlarges the Great room that is open to the kitchen and breakfast area. The foyer, Great room, kitchen, and breakfast area are defined by accent columns. The private master suite, located to one side of the house, features a tray ceiling in the bedroom. The master bath includes a garden tub, separate shower, and two skylights over a double vanity. The front bedroom, which also doubles as a study, features a tray ceiling that highlights a picture window topped off by a half-round window. The bonus room over the garage rounds out the plan.

Main floor — 1,699 sq. ft.
Garage — 498 sq. ft.
Bonus — 336 sq. ft.

Total living area:
1,699 sq. ft.

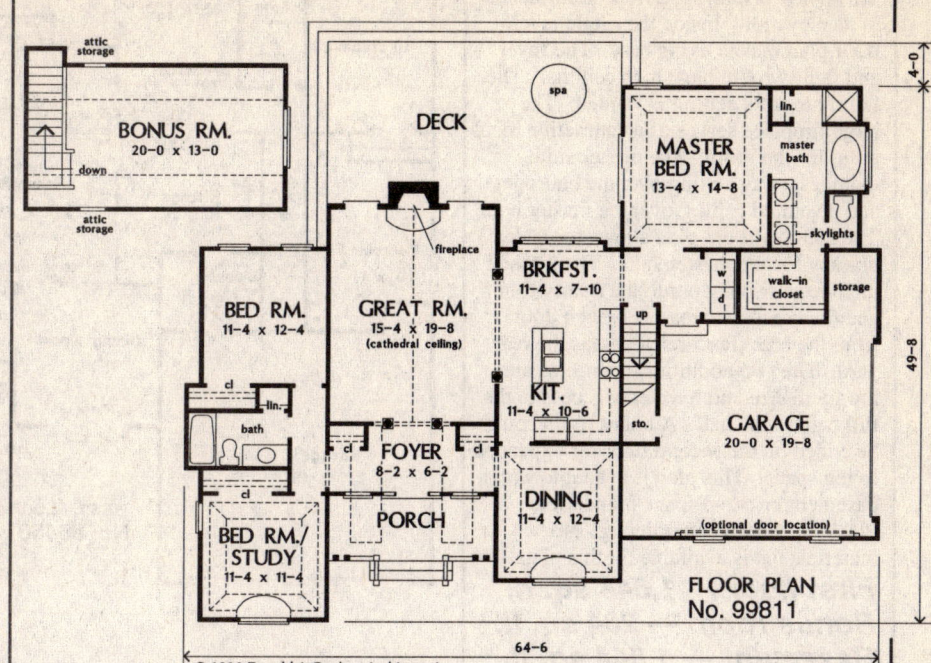

Refer to **Pricing Schedule B** on the order form for pricing information

© 1996 Donald A Gardner Architects, Inc.

Design 98460

WITH A EUROPEAN FLAIR

This home displays a European influence in its elevation. Inside the single level floor plan makes living easy. The foyer and family room have high ceilings. The family room's ceiling is vaulted. The large fireplace serves as an attractive focal point for the room. The master suite includes a tray ceiling over the bedroom and a vaulted ceiling over the master bath. The split bedroom plan allows for added privacy for the master suite. The kitchen includes a serving bar to the family room and the breakfast area. A French door from the breakfast area accesses the rear yard. The two additional bedrooms are roomy in size and have easy access to the full bath in the hall. A bonus room could be added on the second floor for expanded living space. This plan is available with a basement or crawl space foundation. Please specify when ordering. No materials list is available for this plan.

First floor — 1,544 sq. ft.
Bonus room — 284 sq. ft.
Basement — 1,544 sq. ft.
Garage — 440 sq. ft.

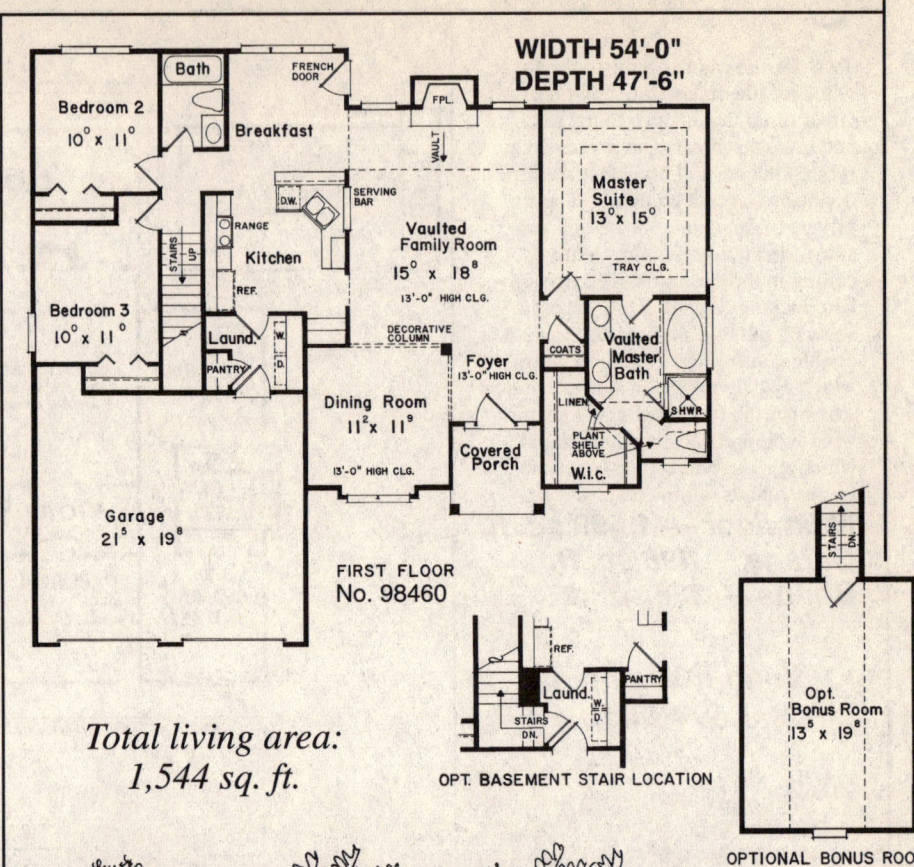

WIDTH 54'-0"
DEPTH 47'-6"

FIRST FLOOR
No. 98460

Total living area:
1,544 sq. ft.

OPT. BASEMENT STAIR LOCATION

OPTIONAL BONUS ROOM

Refer to **Pricing Schedule B** on the order form for pricing information

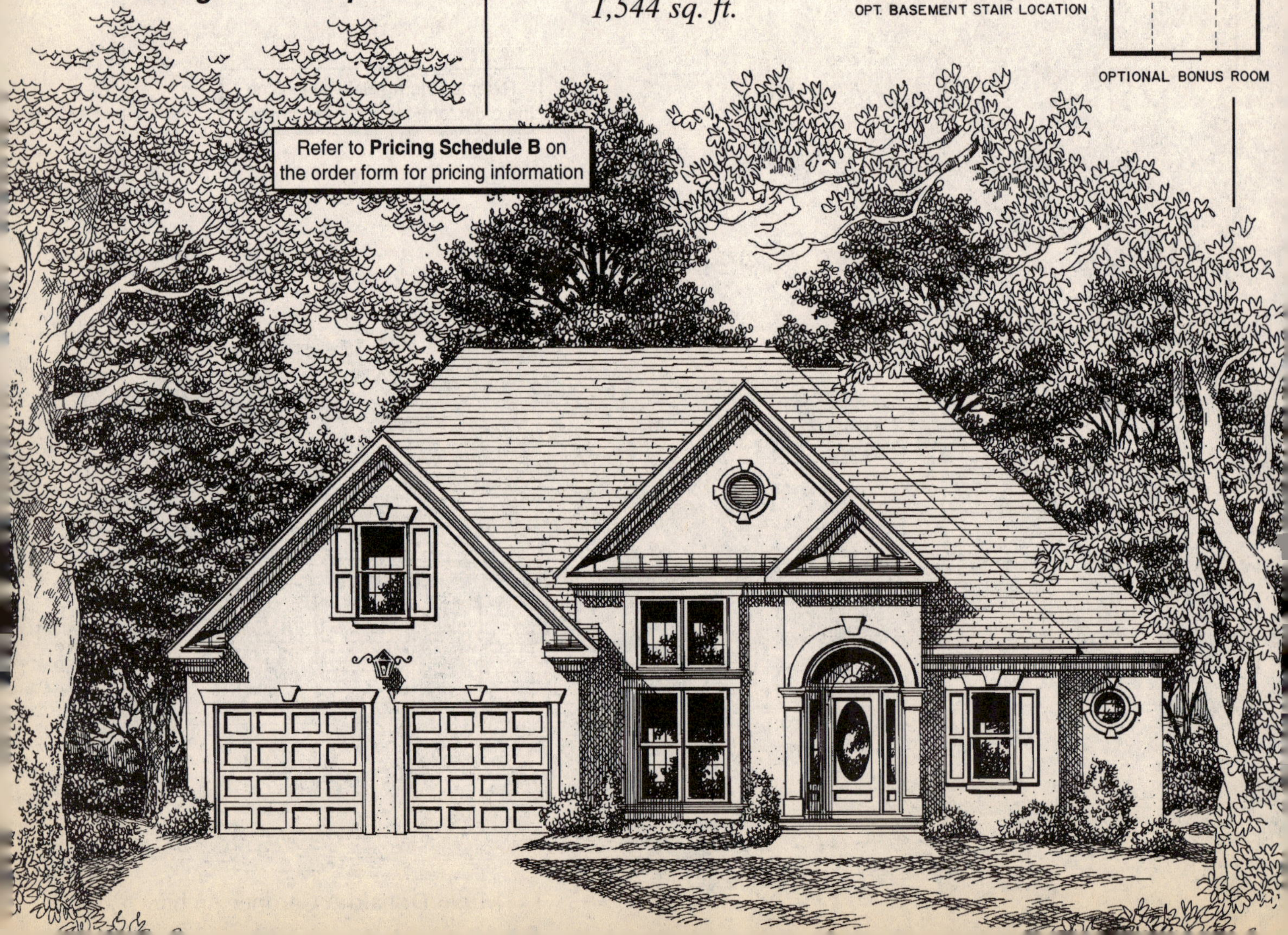

ORDER TODAY! 1-800-235-5700

Classic Colonial

Design 90469

This classic colonial can be built as a three or five bedroom. The large Great room, highlighted by a fireplace is the gathering room of the house. The formal dining room leads to the efficient and spacious kitchen, which is in easy proximity to the breakfast room with a bay window. Upstairs in the master suite, a large walk-in closet, a corner tub, a full sized shower and a dual vanity pamper the owner. Two other large bedrooms share the second full bath and complete the second floor. A telephone niche and reading nook provide private retreats. This plan is available with a basement or crawl space foundation. Please specify when ordering.

Main floor — 1,098 sq. ft.
Second floor — 1,064 sq. ft.
Garage — 484 sq. ft.

Total living area: 2,162 sq. ft.

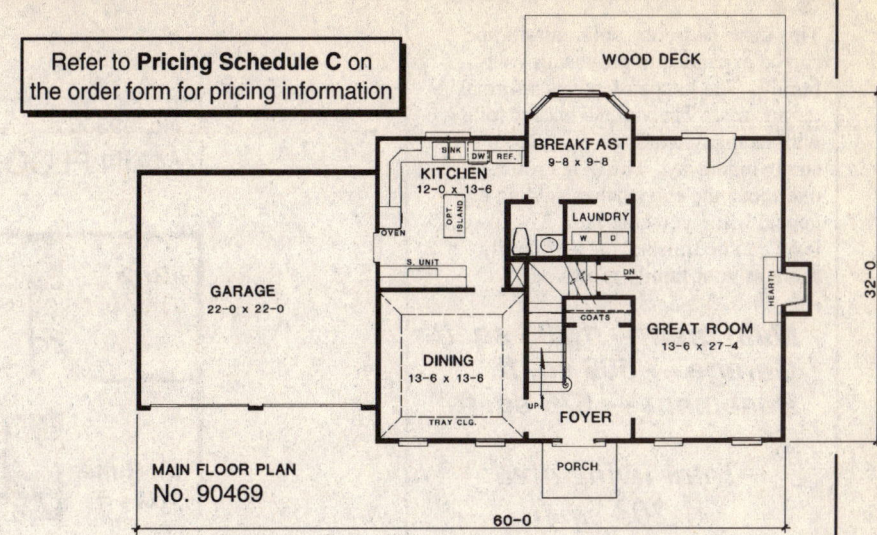

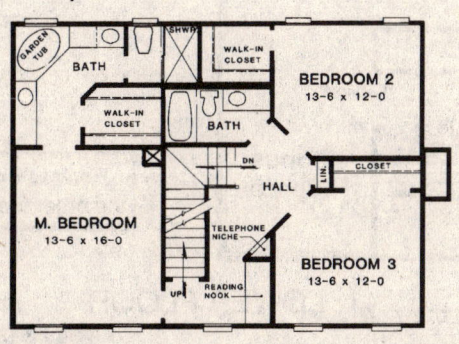

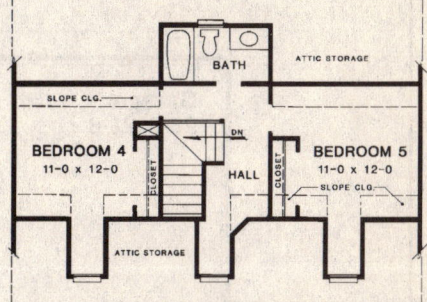

EXPAND WITH EASE

Design 99365

This three bedroom, split-entry home can be expanded to grow with your family. The kitchen features a formal dining area. The vaulted master suite with its many windows provides a sunny hideaway. The living room overlooks the entry below, adding eye appeal while you entertain. The lower level can be finished off as a family room as your family grows.

Main area — 1,203 sq. ft.
Garage — 509 sq. ft.
Basement — 676 sq. ft.

Total living area: 1,203 sq. ft.

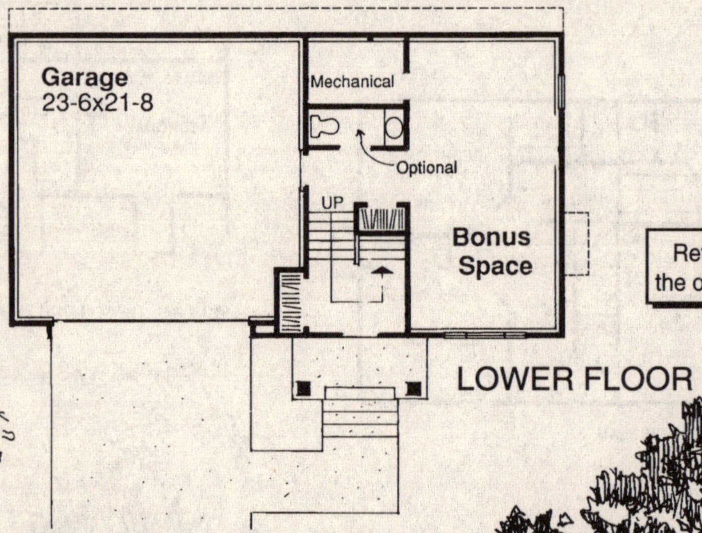

Refer to **Pricing Schedule A** on the order form for pricing information

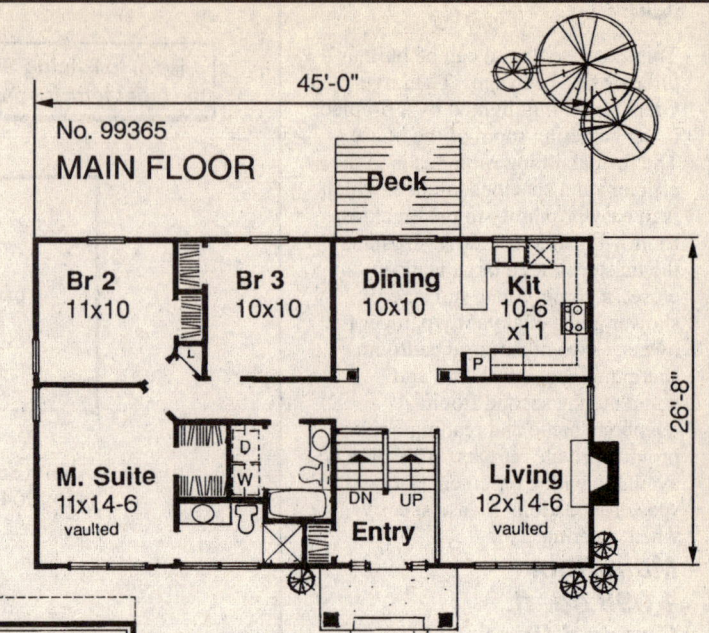

WARM AND INVITING

Design 24264

This warm and inviting home features a see-through fireplace between the living room and family room. The gourmet kitchen gives the cook in your family the added work space of an island, plus the all the amenities you've come to expect. Efficiently designed, the kitchen easily serves both the formal dining room and the nook. Upstairs, four bedrooms accommodate your sleeping hours. The master bedroom adds interest with a vaulted ceiling. The master bath has a large double vanity, linen closet, corner tub, separate shower, compartmentalized toilet, and huge walk-in closet. The three additional bedrooms, one with a walk-in closet, share the full hall bath. No materials list is available for this plan.

First floor — 1,241 sq. ft.
Second floor — 1,170 sq. ft.

Total living area: 2,411 sq. ft.

Refer to **Pricing Schedule D** on the order form for pricing information

An EXCLUSIVE DESIGN By Energetic Enterprises

ORDER TODAY! 1 - 800 - 235 - 5700

SMALL YET LAVISHLY APPOINTED

Design 98425

This home may be small in size, yet the attention to detail gives it a luxurious feel. The dining room, living room, foyer and master bath all boast high ceilings. The master bedroom includes a tray ceiling decoratively highlighting the suite. The master walk-in closet is huge for ample storage. The kitchen is open to the breakfast room enhanced by a serving bar and pantry. The living room includes a large fireplace and a French door to the rear yard. The secondary bedrooms are located on the opposite side of the home from the master suite, allowing for privacy for the owner. This plan is available with a basement, or crawl space foundation. Please specify when ordering.

**Main floor —
1,845 sq. ft.
Bonus room —
409 sq. ft.
Basement— 1,845 sq. ft.**

Total living area:
1,845 sq. ft.

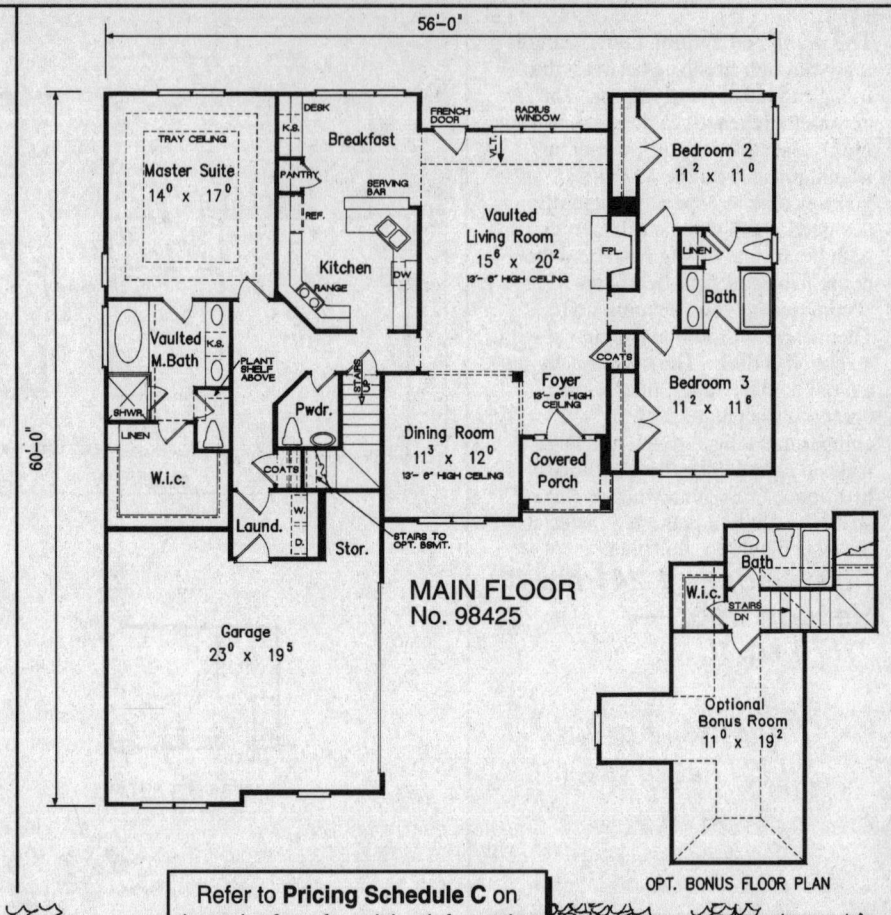

ORDER TODAY! 1 - 800 - 235 - 5700

Design 92539

STATELY AND DIGNIFIED

This plan gives a stately and dignified elevation yet, the plan encompasses all the conveniences a modern family requires today. The exterior is enhanced by multi-paned windows and a two-story arched entrance. The large master suite includes a private master bath with an oval tub, separate shower, compartmented toilet and double vanity. An expansive den is located to the rear with a ornate fireplace that includes built-in shelves on either side. The efficient kitchen has a large pantry, peninsula counter with double sink and eating bar, and a sunny breakfast area. An elegant evenings entertaining is sure to transpire in the formal dining room with the lovely bay window. On the second floor there are three additional bedrooms, each with a walk-in closet, that share the full double vanity bath. This plan is available with a crawl space or slab foundation. Please specify when ordering.

**First floor — 1,250 sq. ft.
Second floor — 783 sq. ft.
Garage — 555 sq. ft.**

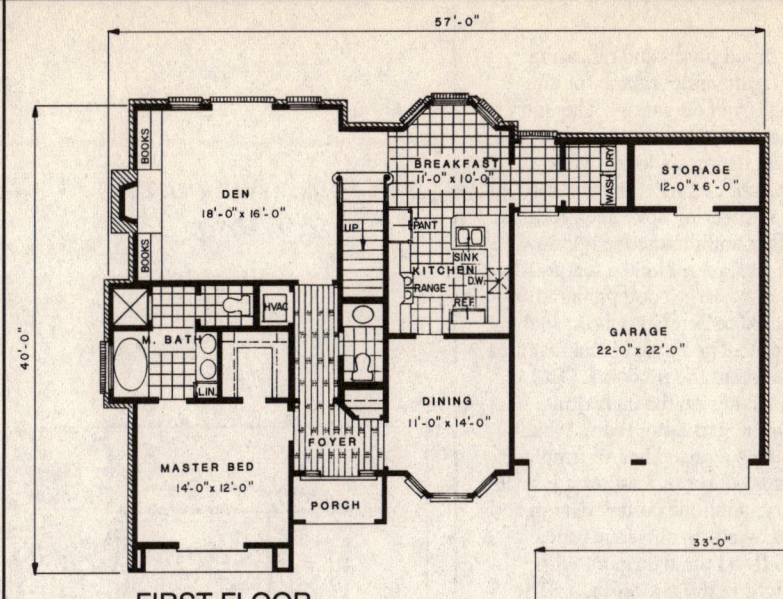

FIRST FLOOR
No. 92539

Total living area: 2,033 sq. ft.

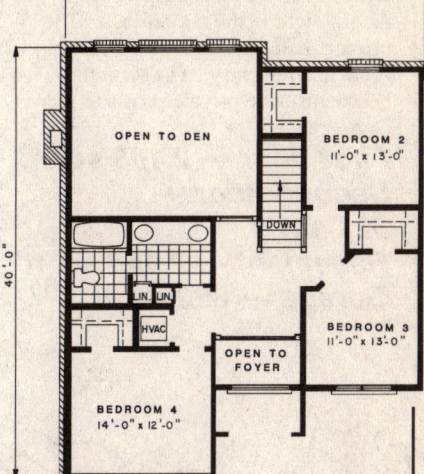

SECOND FLOOR

Refer to **Pricing Schedule D** on the order form for pricing information

ORDER TODAY! 1 - 800 - 235 - 5700

Traditional Home

Design 99452

A wood railed porch and repeating window treatment combine for a traditional front elevation. The entry offers views to the formal entertaining areas. The den has a lovely window and a ten foot ceiling. The Great room includes a towering seventeen foot ten inch ceiling and distinctive windows. The well-designed kitchen features two pantries and a large food preparation area situated to flow into the casual living areas. The bowed breakfast area has two exits to the outdoors. Tall windows center on the cathedral ceiling in the gathering room, which also includes a raised hearth fireplace. The master bedroom features a French door entry, a unique ceiling design and a spacious walk-in closet. Corner windows flood the whirlpool with natural light in the master bath. The upstairs balcony overlooks the Great room and the entry. The secondary bedrooms have private access to a bath.

Total living area: 2,979 sq. ft.

First floor — 2,158 sq. ft.
Second floor — 821 sq. ft.
Basement — 2,158 sq. ft.
Garage — 692 sq. ft.

Refer to **Pricing Schedule E** on the order form for pricing information

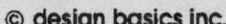

ORDER TODAY! 1 - 800 - 235 - 5700

Design 99404

CHARMING COUNTRY STYLE

This charming country style elevation has a wrapping porch and is accented by an oval window. The spacious Great room, directly accessible from the two-story entry and the breakfast area, is enhanced by a bowed window. An angled wall adds drama to the peninsula kitchen and creates a private entry to the master suite. The master suite contains a boxed nine foot ceiling, a compartmented whirlpool bath and a spacious walk-in closet. The second level balcony overlooks the U-shaped stairs and the entry. Twin linen closets located outside the upstairs bedrooms serve the compartmented bath.

First floor — 1,191 sq. ft.
Second floor — 405 sq. ft.
Basement — 1,191 sq. ft.
Garage — 454 sq. ft.

Refer to **Pricing Schedule B** on the order form for pricing information

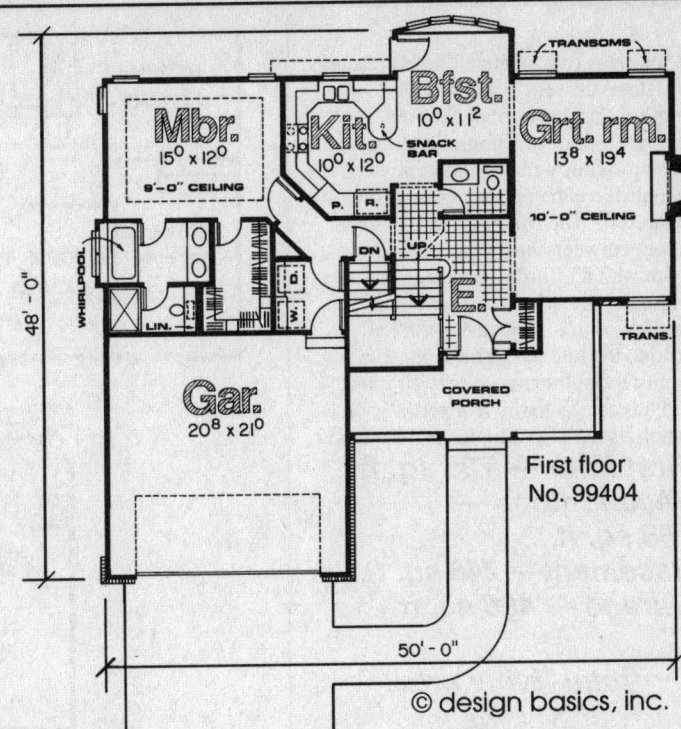

First floor
No. 99404

© design basics, inc.

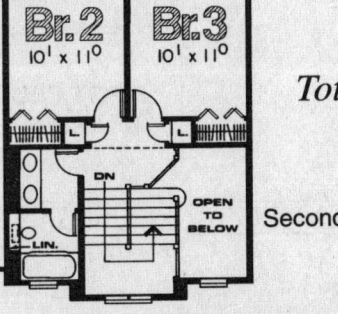

Total living area: 1,596 sq. ft.

Second floor

Four Bedrooms on Second Floor

Design 94316

ORDER TODAY! 1-800-235-5700

Floor plans that locate all bedrooms on one floor are very popular with families that have small children. The second floor of this home can give close proximity to the children, yet parents have the privacy of their own bathroom. The first floor has an open layout between the kitchen and living room which affords a spacious and airy feeling to the home. A convenient laundry center is located in the hall outside the kitchen. The expansive family room includes a cozy fireplace and has access to the rear patio. No materials list is available for this plan.

First floor — 736 sq. ft.
Second floor — 788 sq. ft.
Basement — 746 sq. ft.
Garage — 400 sq. ft.

Total living area: 1,524 sq. ft.

Refer to **Pricing Schedule B** on the order form for pricing information

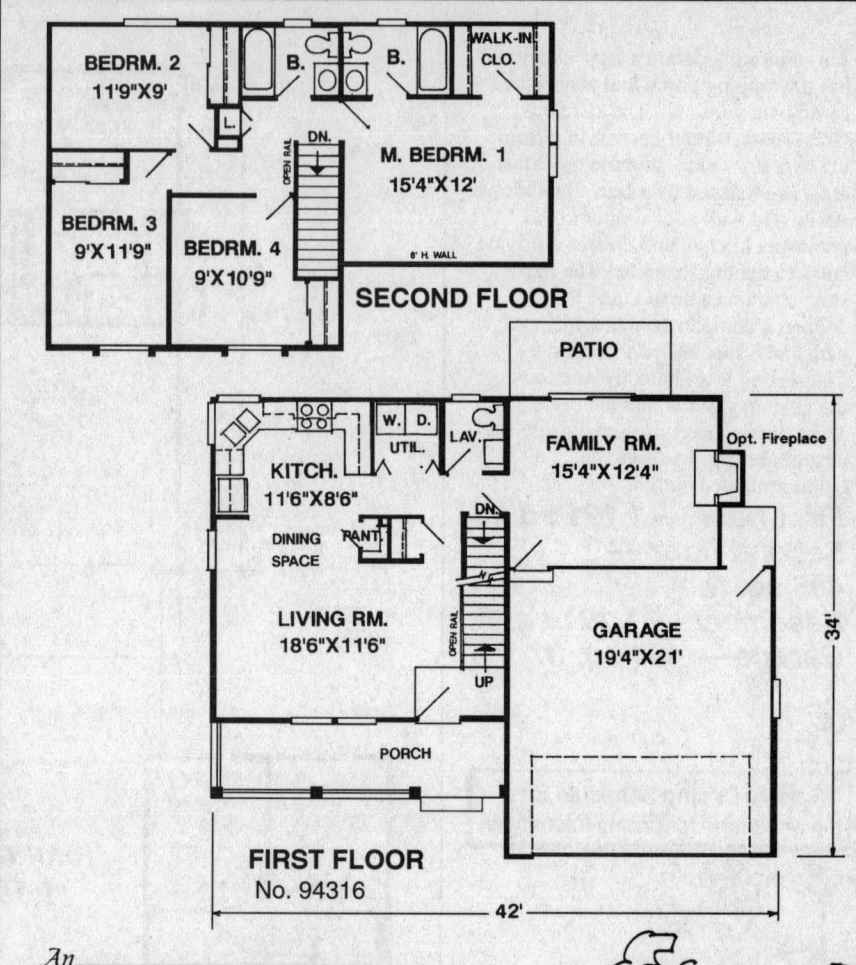

An **Exclusive Design** *By Marshall Associates*

A LARGE HOME WITH A COTTAGE FEEL

Design 24803

The heart of this home is certainly the Great room. A terrific gas fireplace and a decorative ceiling gives it a cozy, comfortable feeling. It is open to both the kitchen and the informal breakfast room. A screened in porch and a rear deck expand living space in the warmer weather. Formal dining takes place in the dining room accented by columns at each entrance. Privacy abounds in the master suite highlighted by a luxurious bath and a huge walk-in closet. On the lower level there are three additional bedrooms, one including a walk-in closet. A compartmented, double vanity bath is in close proximity to the bedrooms. There is also an expansive family room equipped with a gas fireplace. Ample storage space exists in two storage rooms. No materials list is available for this plan.

Main floor — 2,414 sq. ft.
Lower level — 1,533 sq. ft.
Basement — 881 sq. ft.
Garage — 816 sq. ft.

Total living area: 3,947 sq. ft.

Refer to **Pricing Schedule F** on the order form for pricing information

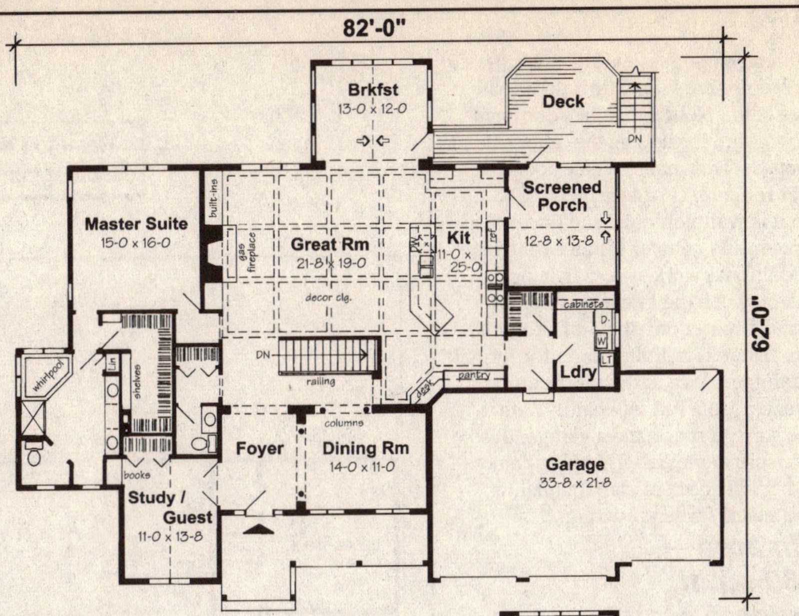

Main Floor No. 24803

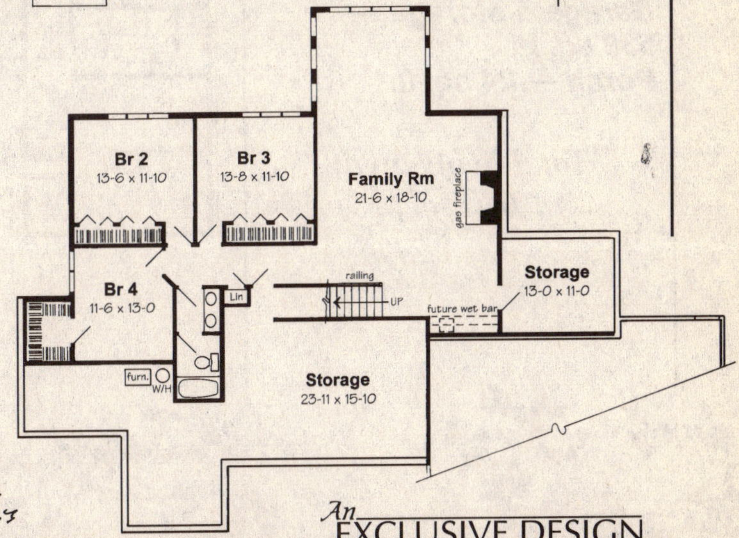

Lower Floor

An EXCLUSIVE DESIGN *By Britt J. Willis*

SECLUDED MASTER SUITE

Design 92527

This convenient one-level design offers a secluded master suite with a luxurious master bath. Notice that the additional bedrooms are located on the other side of the house. This makes a nice sound barrier for parents of teenagers. The kitchen is well-equipped and makes use of a peninsula counter for an eating bar and additional work space. The open layout between the kitchen, breakfast area and Great room gives a feeling of space. There is a dining room for formal entertaining. Two additional bedrooms have access to a full hall bath. With ample storage space and a garage, this plan is sure to please. This plan comes with a crawl space or slab foundation. Please specify when ordering.

Main area — 1,680 sq. ft.
Garage & storage — 538 sq. ft.
Porch — 24 sq. ft.

Total living area: 1,680 sq. ft.

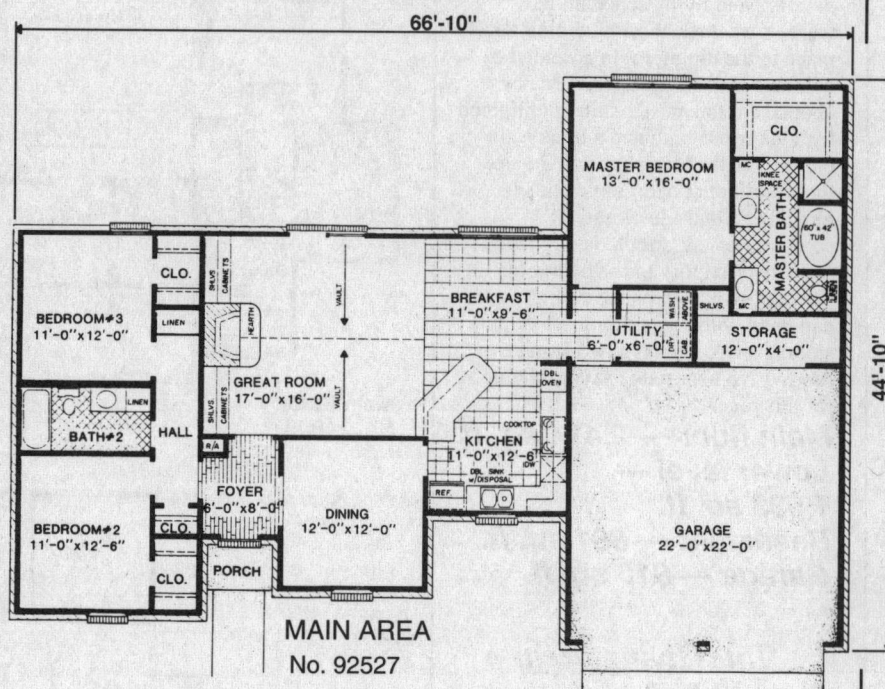

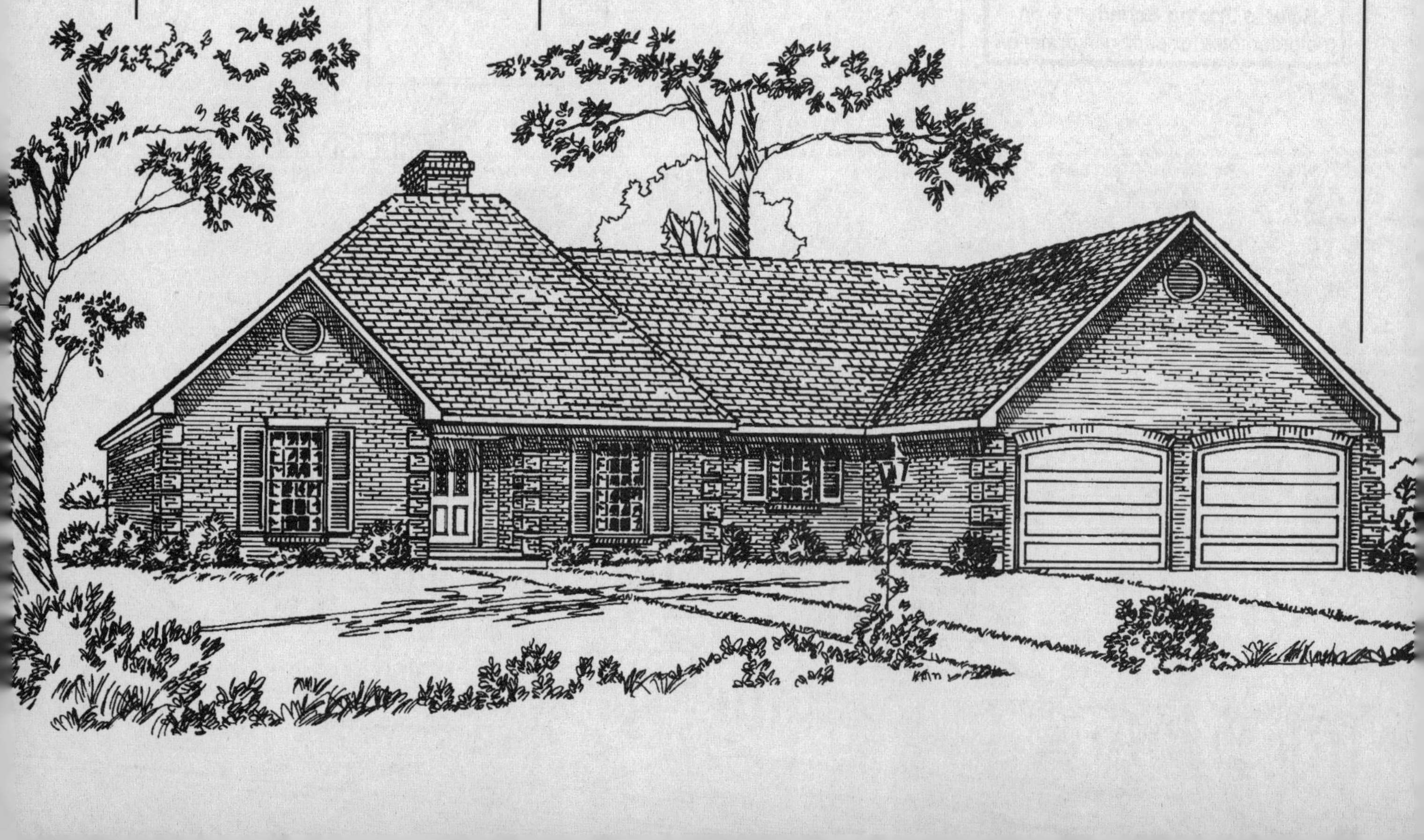

WINDOWS ADD WARMTH

Design 34011

Plenty of windows brighten this beautiful home with natural lighting and fresh air. More than enough closet space keeps clutter under control. A laundry room is located conveniently near all three bedrooms. The master suite features huge his-and-her walk-in closets and a private bath. Between the second and third bedroom is the second bathroom and linen closet. The family room is open to the dining area and kitchen. The kitchen is equipped with an island counter and has access to a garage.

Main area — 1,672 sq. ft.
Garage — 566 sq. ft.

Total living area: 1,672 sq. ft.

Refer to **Pricing Schedule B** on the order form for pricing information

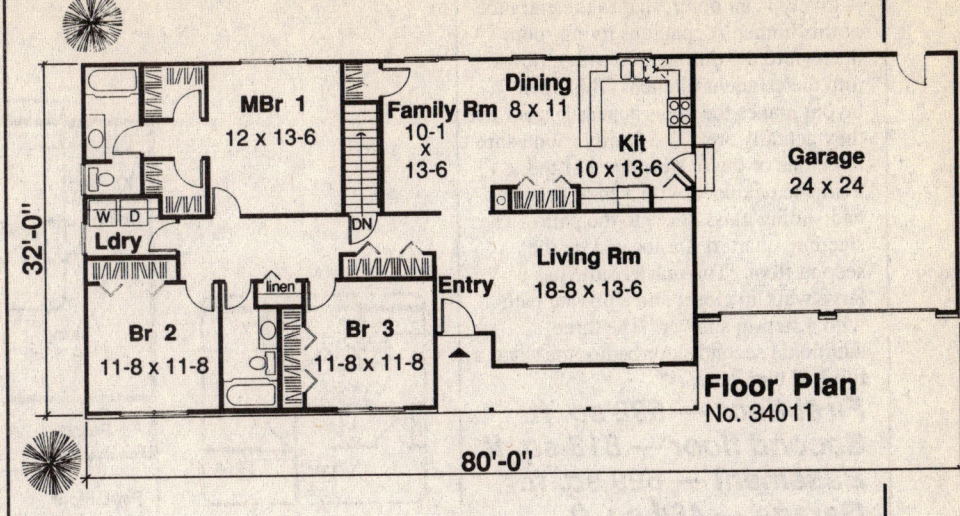

Floor Plan No. 34011

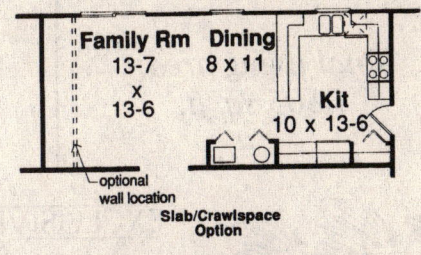

Slab/Crawlspace Option

Fireplace-Equipped Family Room

Design 24326

A lovely front porch shades the entrance of this home. A spacious living room opens into the dining area which flows into the efficient kitchen. This open layout makes the areas appear larger than they actually are. The family room, sure to be one of the busiest areas of the home, is equipped with a cozy fireplace and sliding glass doors to the patio. The sleeping quarters are located on the second floor. The master suite has a large walk-in closet and a private bath with a step-in shower. The three additional second floor bedrooms share a full hall bath.

First floor — 692 sq. ft.
Second floor — 813 sq. ft.
Basement — 699 sq. ft.
Garage — 484 sq. ft.

Total living area: 1,505 sq. ft.

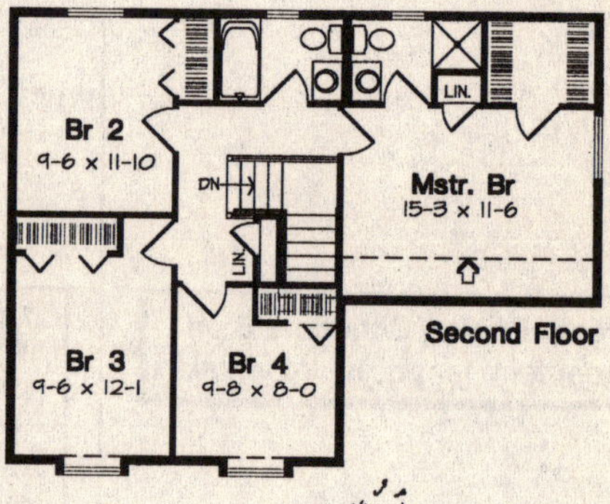

An EXCLUSIVE DESIGN *By Marshall Associates*

Refer to **Pricing Schedule B** on the order form for pricing information

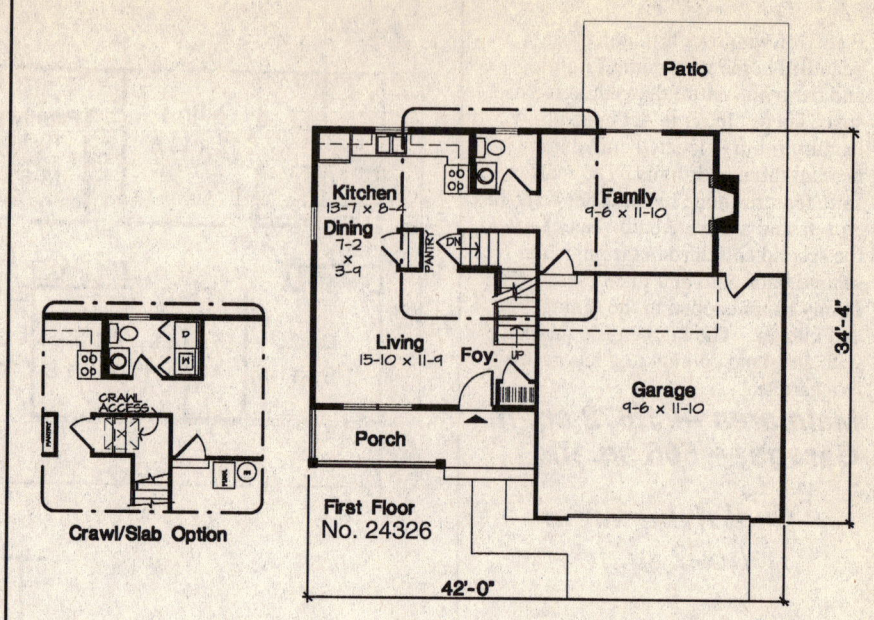

Special Touches Throughout

Design 93403

This compact home has many features that are usually found in larger homes. The vaulted ceiling in the kitchen/dining room is a nice touch that adds to the spacious feel. The efficient, U-shaped kitchen has double sinks under a bumped out window that views the front yard. The family room has a wood burning fireplace, giving the room a coziness. All three bedrooms are located at the rear of the home. The master suite has a vaulted ceiling, walk-in closet and a private bath with a double vanity. The two additional bedrooms share the use of a full hall bath. No materials list is available for this plan.

Main floor — 1,304 sq. ft.
Garage — 443 sq. ft.

Total living area: 1,304 sq. ft.

Floor Plan No. 93403

An Exclusive Design By Greg Marquis

Refer to **Pricing Schedule A** on the order form for pricing information

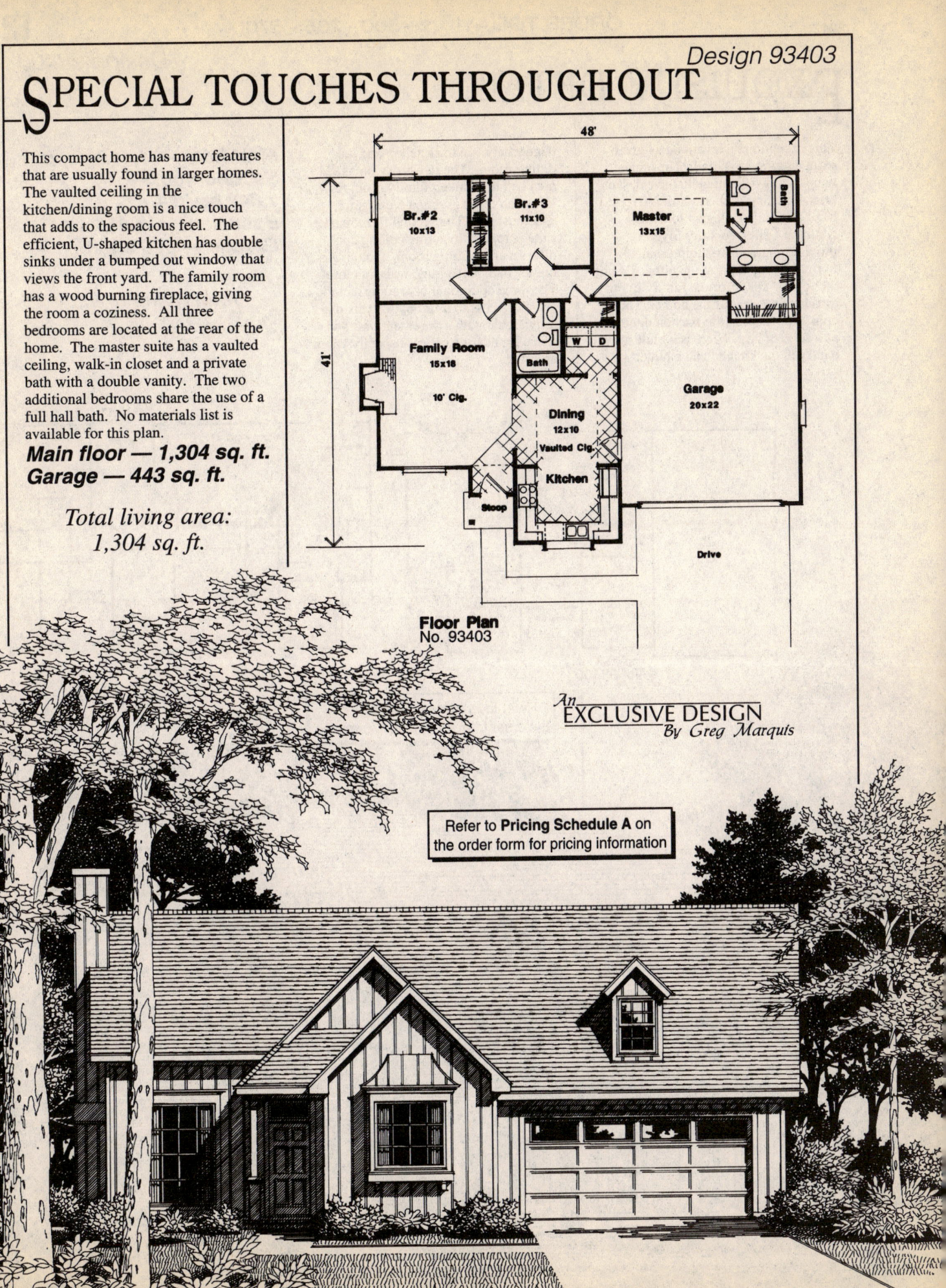

ORDER TODAY!   1 - 800 - 235 - 5700

EXQUISITE DETAIL

Design 98400

This exceptional elevation has given extra attention to detail. The arched windows have shutters to the sides and brick detailing with keystones overhead. Inside the elegant touches continue. The two-story foyer provides a grand first impression. Formal living areas are to either side of the foyer. The informal family living area is to the rear of the home. The cook top island in the kitchen doubles as a serving bar. There is a built-in pantry in the kitchen and a butler's pantry between the kitchen and the dining room. The two-story breakfast area and the sunken family room flow into each other giving a feeling of spaciousness. The second floor master suite is topped by a tray ceiling and offers a cozy sitting room, a luxurious master bath and a huge walk-in closet. The three additional bedrooms include private access to a full bath. This plan is available with a basement or crawl space foundation. Please specify when ordering.

First floor — 1,418 sq. ft.
Second floor — 1,844 sq. ft.
Basement — 1,418 sq. ft.
Garage — 820 sq. ft.

Total living area: 3,262 sq. ft.

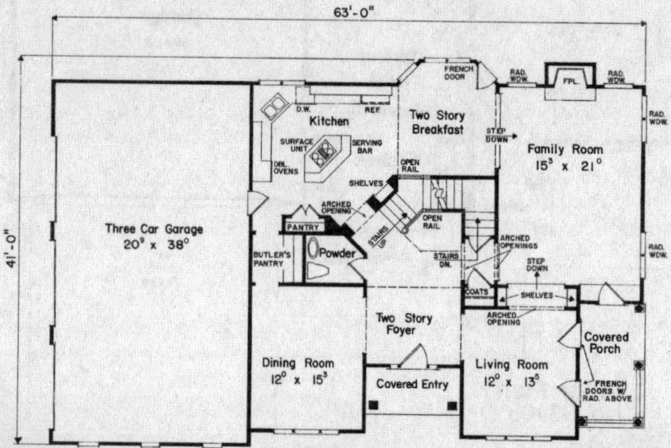

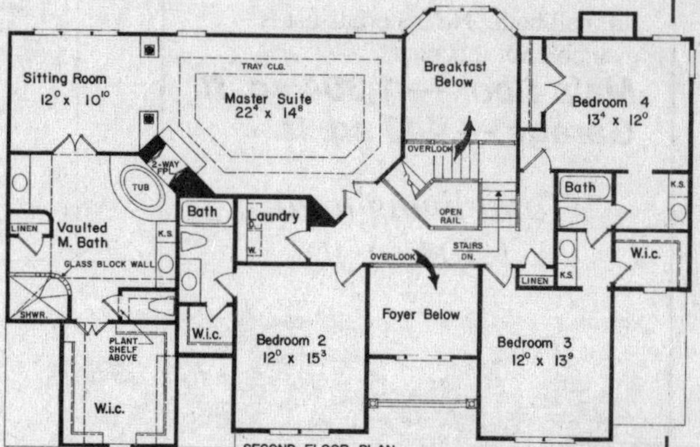

Refer to **Pricing Schedule F** on the order form for pricing information

IMPRESSIVE BRICK FACADE

Design 24550

This impressive brick home's decorative use of brick detailing around the windows creates a home with abundant curb appeal. The living room features a dramatic cathedral ceiling and a two-way fireplace. This room enjoys the natural light from the large front window. The dining room is complemented by a bay window. The fireplace in the family room adjoins a built-in entertainment center. This room is sure to be the hub of family life in the home. Notice the oversized kitchen island. This island can easily double as a snack bar. The kitchen boasts a pantry and built-in desk, as well as ample cabinet and counter space. The second floor has four bedrooms. The master suite has a vaulted ceiling, walk-in closet and luxurious master bath. The secondary bedrooms have ample closet space and share a hall full bath with dual basin vanity and linen closet. This is truly a home to be proud of.

First floor — 1,433 sq. ft.
Second floor — 1,283 sq. ft.
Basement — 1,433 sq. ft.
Garage — 923 sq. ft.

Total living area: 2,716 sq. ft.

An EXCLUSIVE DESIGN *By Britt J. Willis*

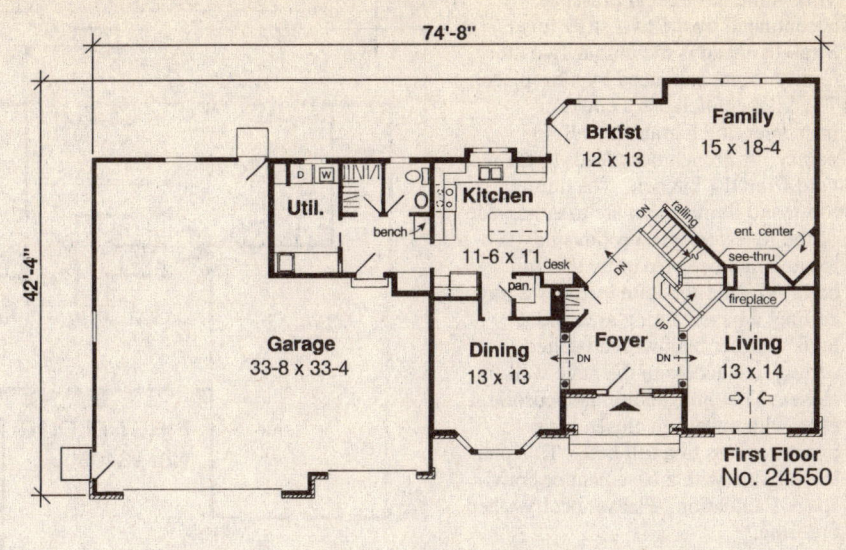

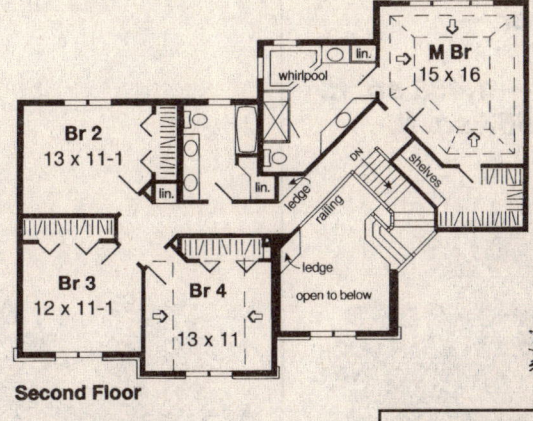

Refer to **Pricing Schedule E** on the order form for pricing information

ORDER TODAY! 1-800-235-5700

REGAL APPEAL

Design 98405

This home has a regal presence, accentuated by the two-story foyer. Straight ahead is the unique two-story family room, enhanced by a fireplace. The kitchen includes a cooktop island/serving bar and a walk-in pantry. A French door leads to the rear yard from the kitchen. The dining room and living room are to either side of the foyer. A guest room/study is located in close proximity to a full bath. The master suite includes a tray ceiling, a bayed sitting area and a lavish master bath with a vaulted ceiling and access to the huge walk-in closet. The three additional bedrooms, each with a walk-in closet, have private access to a full bath. This plan is available with a basement or crawl space foundation. Please specify when ordering.

Total living area: 3,039 sq. ft.

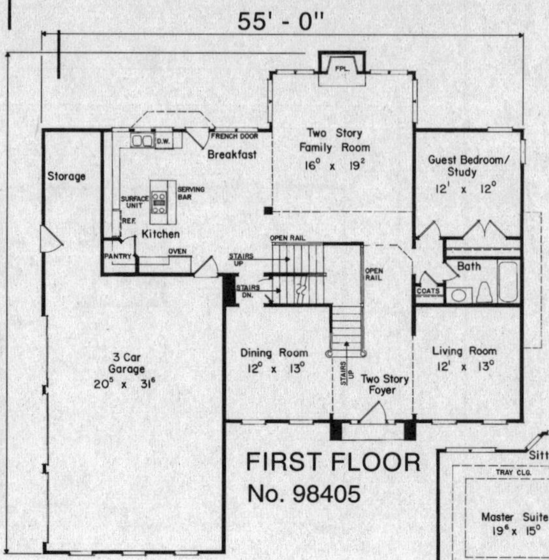

First floor — 1,488 sq. ft.
Second floor — 1,551 sq. ft.
Basement — 1,488 sq. ft.
Garage — 667 sq. ft.

FIRST FLOOR No. 98405

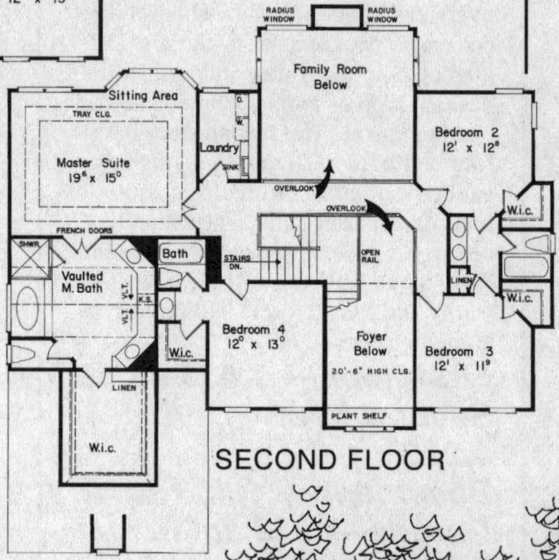

SECOND FLOOR

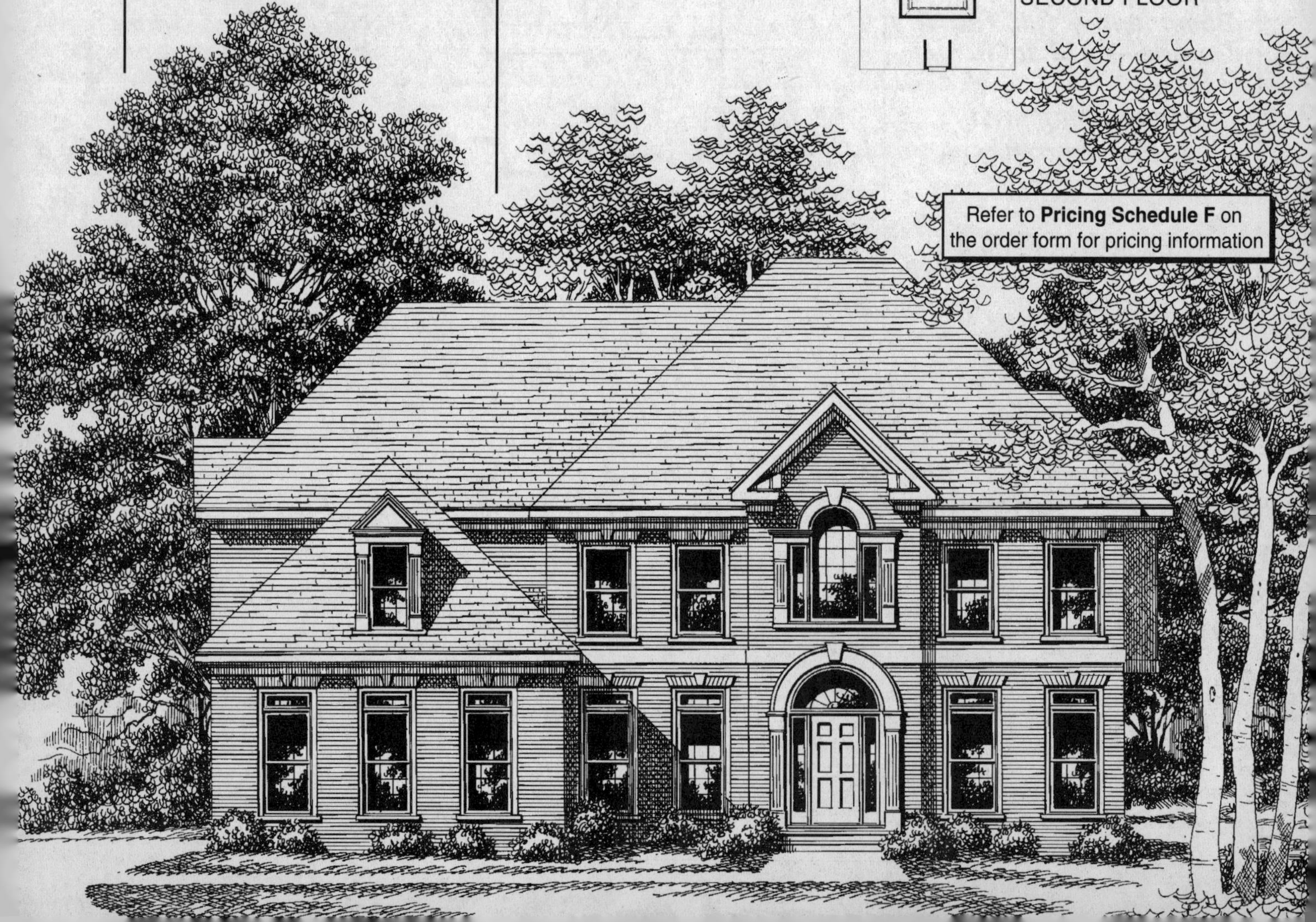

Refer to **Pricing Schedule F** on the order form for pricing information

Design 34054
RANCH PROVIDES GREAT KITCHEN

There's a lot of convenience packed into this affordable design. Flanking the kitchen to the right is the dining room which has a sliding glass door to the backyard, and to the left is the laundry room with an entrance to the garage. The master bedroom boasts its own full bathroom and the additional two bedrooms share the hall bath. An optional two-car garage plan is included.

Main area — 1,400 sq. ft.
Basement — 1,400 sq. ft.
Garage — 528 sq. ft.

Total living area: 1,400 sq. ft.

Refer to **Pricing Schedule A** on the order form for pricing information

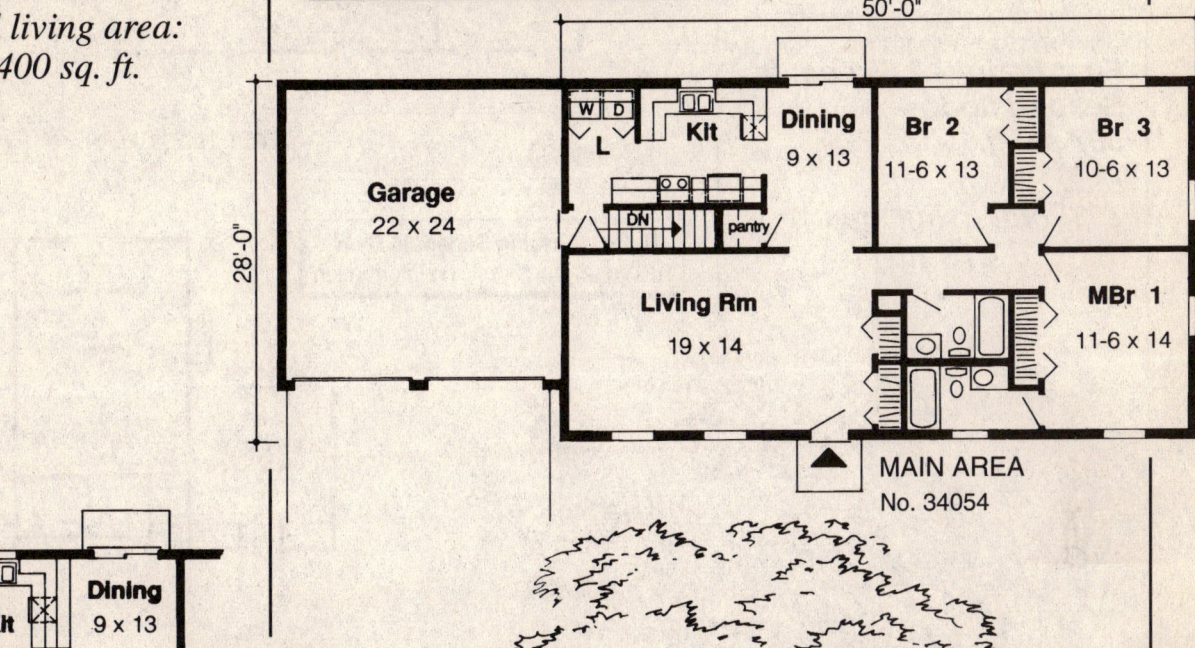

228   ORDER TODAY! 1 - 800 - 235 - 5700

CELEBRATE THE OUTDOORS

Design 96423

This country classic celebrates the outdoors with a wrap-around porch, sun room, and spacious rear deck. A palladian window in front, a grand arched window in rear, and skylights in the sun room let the sun shine in and add exterior drama. Inside, a second-level balcony overlooks the generous Great room with cathedral ceiling and clerestory. The large country kitchen has a pass-through to the Great room and a center island for easy food preparation. The private master suite has access to the sun room through a luxurious master bath with all the extras. This plan is available with a basement or crawl space foundation. Please specify when ordering.

First floor — 1,651 sq. ft.
Second floor — 567 sq. ft.

Total living area: 2,218 sq. ft.

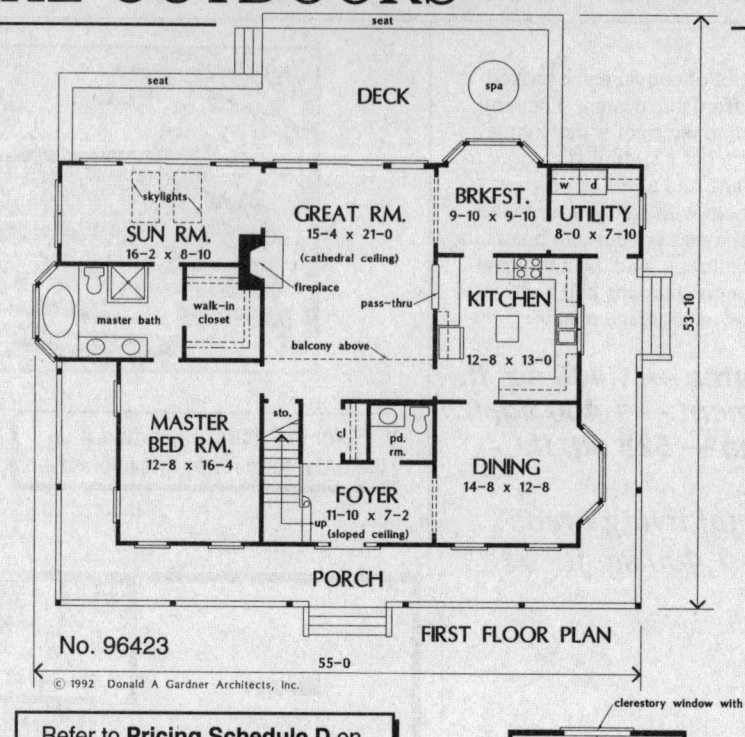

Refer to **Pricing Schedule D** on the order form for pricing information

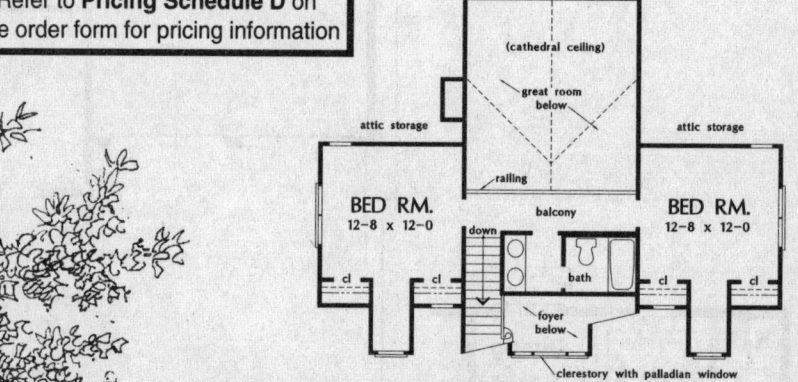

© 1990 Donald A. Gardner Architects, Inc.

ORDER TODAY! 1 - 800 - 235 - 5700

Easy Living Plan

Design 98406

This lovely home has been designed for modern living with an old-fashion feel. The cozy front porch protects guests from inclement weather while providing a warm welcome and great appeal. The two-story foyer has open access to the dining room to the left and the living room to the right. The kitchen, breakfast bay, and family room blend into a fantastic open living area. An angled, peninsula counter in the kitchen is the only barrier between the rooms. A convenient laundry center is tucked into the rear of the kitchen area. A luxurious master suite awaits the owner on the second floor. A tray ceiling crowns the bedroom and a vaulted ceiling tops the master bath. The two roomy, secondary bedrooms share the full bath in the hall. This plan is available with a basement, slab or crawl space. Please specify when ordering.

FIRST FLOOR
No. 98406

SECOND FLOOR

First floor — 828 sq. ft.
Second floor — 772 sq. ft.
Basement — 828 sq. ft.
Garage — 473 sq. ft.

Total living area: 1,600 sq. ft.

Refer to **Pricing Schedule B** on the order form for pricing information

ORDER TODAY! 1-800-235-5700

STUCCO ACCENTS

Design 99456

Stucco accents and graceful window treatments enhance the front of this home. The double doors open to the private den with brilliant bayed windows. The French doors open to a large screened-in veranda ideal for outdoor entertaining. The open living room and handsome curved staircase add drama to the entry area. The gourmet kitchen, spacious bayed dinette and voluminous family room flow together for easy living. The elegant bayed master bedroom with a ten foot vaulted ceiling is situated to the back of the home for privacy. Two walk-in closets, his-n-her vanity, corner whirlpool and compartment shower highlight the master dressing area. The three additional bedrooms have private access to full baths. This plan is available with a basement or slab foundation. Please specify when ordering.

First floor — 1,631 sq. ft.
Second floor — 1,426 sq. ft.
Basement — 1,631 sq. ft.
Garage — 681 sq. ft.

Total living area: 3,057 sq. ft.

FIRST FLOOR No. 99456

Refer to **Pricing Schedule E** on the order form for pricing information

SECOND FLOOR

© design basics inc.

Large Contemporary

Design 99794

At the heart of this home is a combined kitchen and family room with a sunny eating nook nestled into a bay window. The L-shaped center island, which houses both a range and a vegetable sink, also doubles as an eating bar. Plenty of counter and storage space is here to feed and serve a small platoon of family and friends. Sliding glass doors provide access to a deck that wraps around the entire back of the house, a natural for summertime entertaining. The master suite is downstairs, separate from the other bedrooms. It features a large walk-in closet and double vanity located outside the water closet. A raised nook could either hold a spa, or serve as a small, bright sitting room. The utility room has plenty of cupboards, counter space for folding clothes, and a fold-down ironing board. Clothing, bed linen and towels, from upstairs, arrive via a laundry chute.

First floor — 2,484 sq. ft.
Second floor — 972 sq. ft.
Basement — 2,440 sq. ft.
Garage/storage — 990 sq. ft.

Total living area: 3,456 sq. ft.

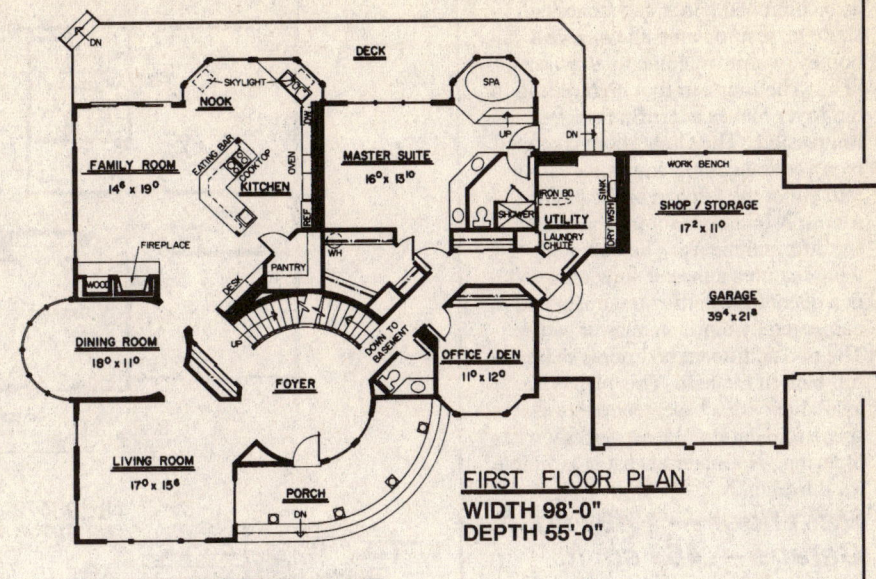

FIRST FLOOR PLAN
WIDTH 98'-0"
DEPTH 55'-0"

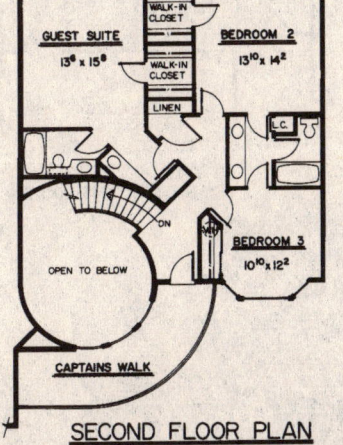

SECOND FLOOR PLAN
No. 99794

Refer to **Pricing Schedule F** on the order form for pricing information

BEAUTIFULLY ACCENTED DETAILS

Design 98472

The attention to detail on the elevation of this home achieves a striking style. The columned porch, keystones and shutters, just to name a few, give a homey, warm welcome to all who visit. The fourteen foot high ceiling in the foyer makes a terrific first impression. The Great room is topped by a vaulted ceiling and flows easily into either the kitchen or the dining room. A breakfast room is available for informal meals. The bedroom wing features a master suite crowned in a decorative ceiling treatment and pampered by a private master bath. The two additional bedrooms share the full bath in the hall. This plan is available with a basement or crawl space foundation. Please specify when ordering. No materials list is available for this plan.

Main floor — 1,492 sq. ft.
Garage — 465 sq. ft.

Total living area: 1,492 sq. ft.

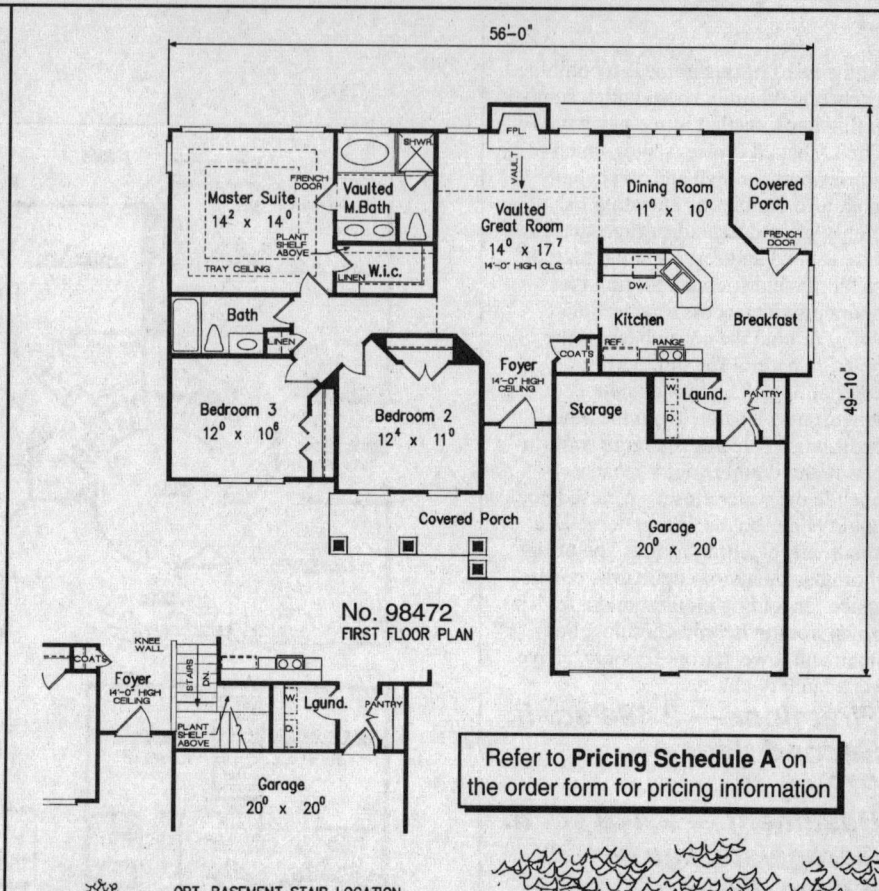

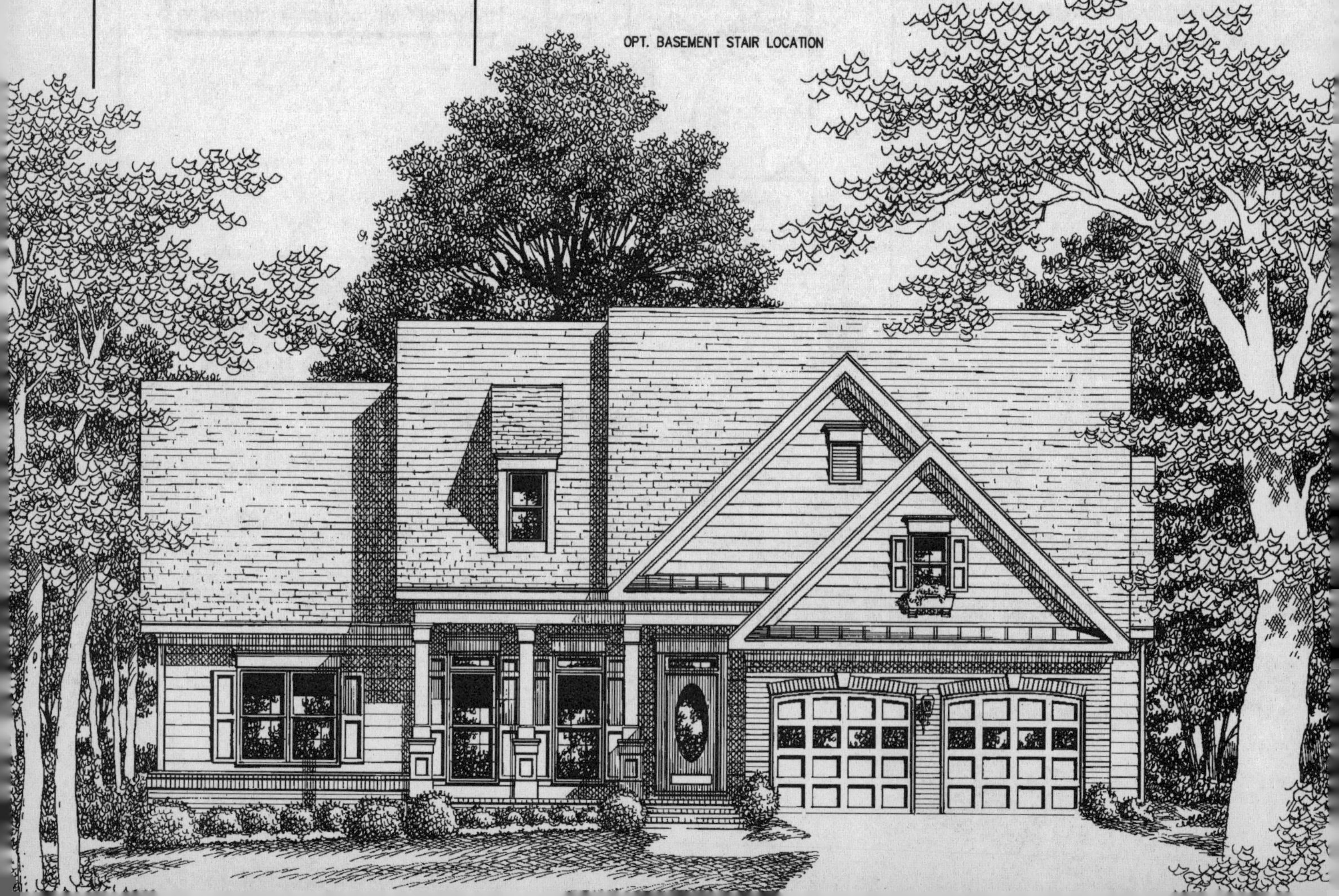

ORDER TODAY!   1 - 800 - 235 - 5700

Family Gathering Space

Design 84056

This classic Ranch features a large open Great room for family gatherings. The sunny kitchen sports a separate dining area. On the other side of the house three good-size bedrooms share two full bathrooms. A great hide-away laundry closet is located outside the large linen closet. A two-car optional garage attaches to this all inclusive home. No materials list is available for this plan.

**Main floor —
1,644 sq. ft.
Garage —
576 sq. ft.**

*Total living area:
1,644 sq. ft.*

Refer to **Pricing Schedule B** on the order form for pricing information

Alternate Plan w/ Crawlspace

- Breakfast 10-4 x 12-6
- Kit 10 x 15-2

MAIN FLOOR
No. 84056

- 52'-0" x 32'-0"
- Optional Garage 24 x 24
- Dining/Living 25-8 x 15
- Br 1   12 x 15-10
- Br 2   10-8 x 11-8
- Br 3   12 x 11-8
- Breakfast 10 x 12-6
- Kit 10 x 12-6

ORDER TODAY! 1-800-235-5700

WITH ROOM TO EXPAND

Design 98431

This home plan allows for future expansion using an optional bonus room. The first floor is introduced by a two-story foyer. The living room is to the right of the foyer and the dining room is to the left. The kitchen is positioned between the dining room and the breakfast bay, having ample cabinet space and counter space. The spacious family room flows from the breakfast bay. A fireplace and French door to the rear yard highlights the room. The second floor contains the master suite, topped by a tray ceiling, and two additional bedrooms. There is a private five-piece bath in the suite and the two additional bedrooms share the full bath in the hall. This plan is available with a basement or crawl space foundation. Please specify when ordering.

First floor — 882 sq. ft.
Second floor — 793 sq. ft.
Bonus room — 416 sq. ft.
Basement — 882 sq. ft.

Refer to **Pricing Schedule B** on the order form for pricing information

Total living area: 1,675 sq. ft.

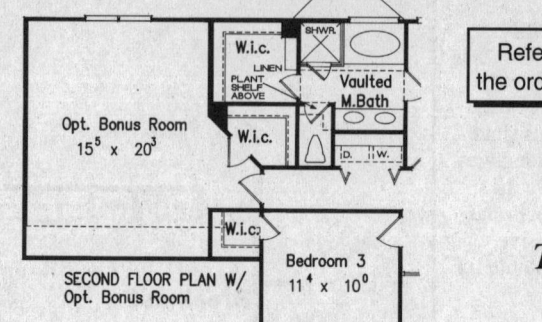

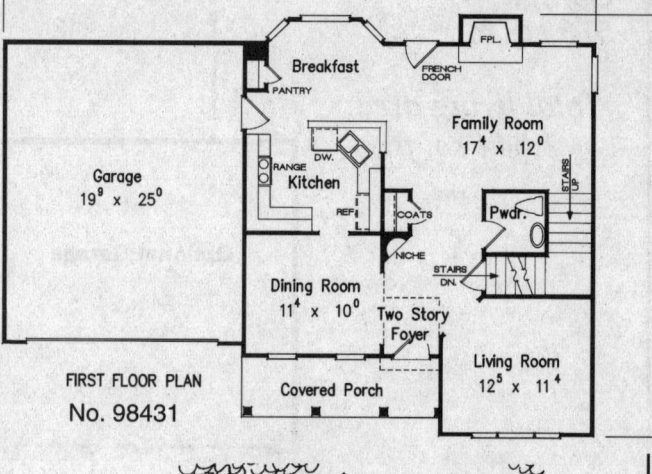

ORDER TODAY! 1 - 800 - 235 - 5700

Modern Slant on an Old Favorite

Design 98407

An old-fashioned Southern front porch gives a charming appeal to this lovely home. Inside, the two-story foyer is framed by the living room to the right and the dining room to the left. The family room is highlighted by a fireplace and a large window to the rear. The breakfast bay and kitchen blend into the family room for a large informal living area. An angled peninsula counter extends the work space of the kitchen. A study or secondary bedroom is privately located to the left rear of the home, giving direct access to the full bath. The lavish second floor master suite boasts a tray ceiling over the bedroom and a vaulted ceiling in the master bath. A large walk-in closet offers an abundance of storage space. The two additional bedrooms share the full bath in the hall. The bonus room will expand living space along with a family's needs. This plan is available with a basement or crawl space foundation. Please specify when ordering.

First floor — 1,135 sq. ft.
Second floor —
   917 sq. ft.

**Bonus room —
216 sq. ft.
Basement —
1,135 sq. ft.
Garage — 452 sq. ft.**

*Total living area:
2,052 sq. ft.*

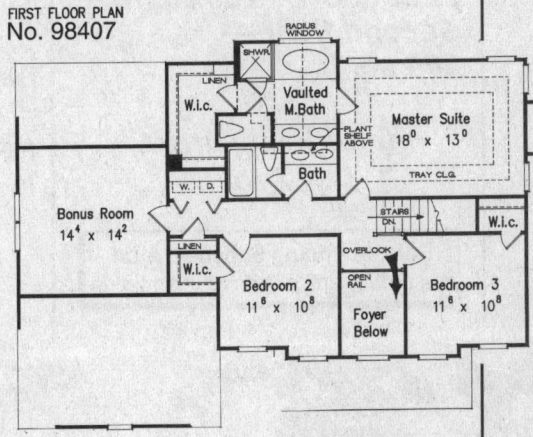

Refer to **Pricing Schedule C** on the order form for pricing information

ORDER TODAY!   1 - 800 - 235 - 5700

PERFECT FOR THE WOODS

Design 35007

A cozy, quaint atmosphere has been achieved in this two bedroom home. The living areas of living room, dining room/kitchen have been located at the front of the house. A sloped ceiling adds to the cozy feeling of the home while the built-in entertainment center adds convenience. The L-shaped kitchen includes a double sink and a dining area. A full bath in the hall is easily accessible from both bedrooms. The laundry center is tucked into the hall right next to the side door. A loft with a balcony overlooks the living room and dining area. There is a storage area to either side of the loft.

First floor — 763 sq. ft.
Second floor — 264 sq. ft.

Total living area: 1,027 sq. ft.

Refer to **Pricing Schedule A** on the order form for pricing information

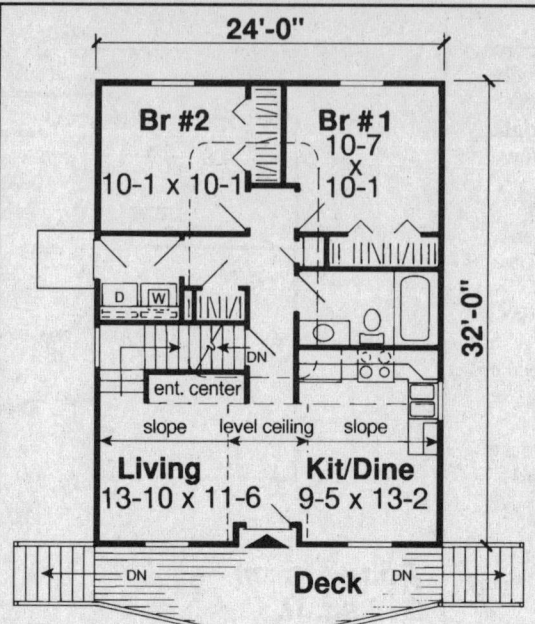

FIRST FLOOR
No. 35007

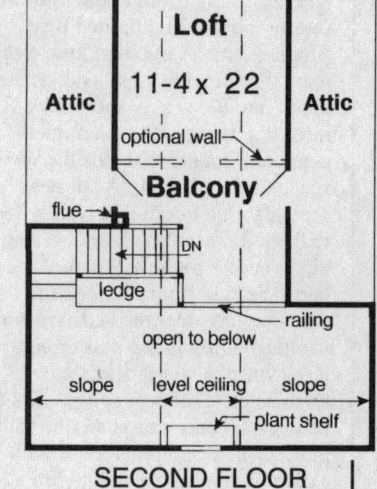

SECOND FLOOR

SLAB/CRAWL SPACE OPTION

Design 90620

FACE THIS HOUSE SOUTH

This modest ranch with generous rooms and passive solar features provides comfortable living for the family on a budget. The soaring, skylit central foyer provides access to every room. Straight ahead, the living room, dining room, and greenhouse form a bright, airy arrangement of glass and open space. The adjacent kitchen conveniently opens to a spacious, bay-windowed dinette. A separate wing contains three bedrooms and two baths, including an ample master suite.

Main area — 1,476 sq. ft.
Porch — 70 sq. ft.
Basement — 1,476 sq. ft.

Total living area:
1,476 sq. ft.

Refer to **Pricing Schedule A** on the order form for pricing information

MAIN FLOOR
No. 90620

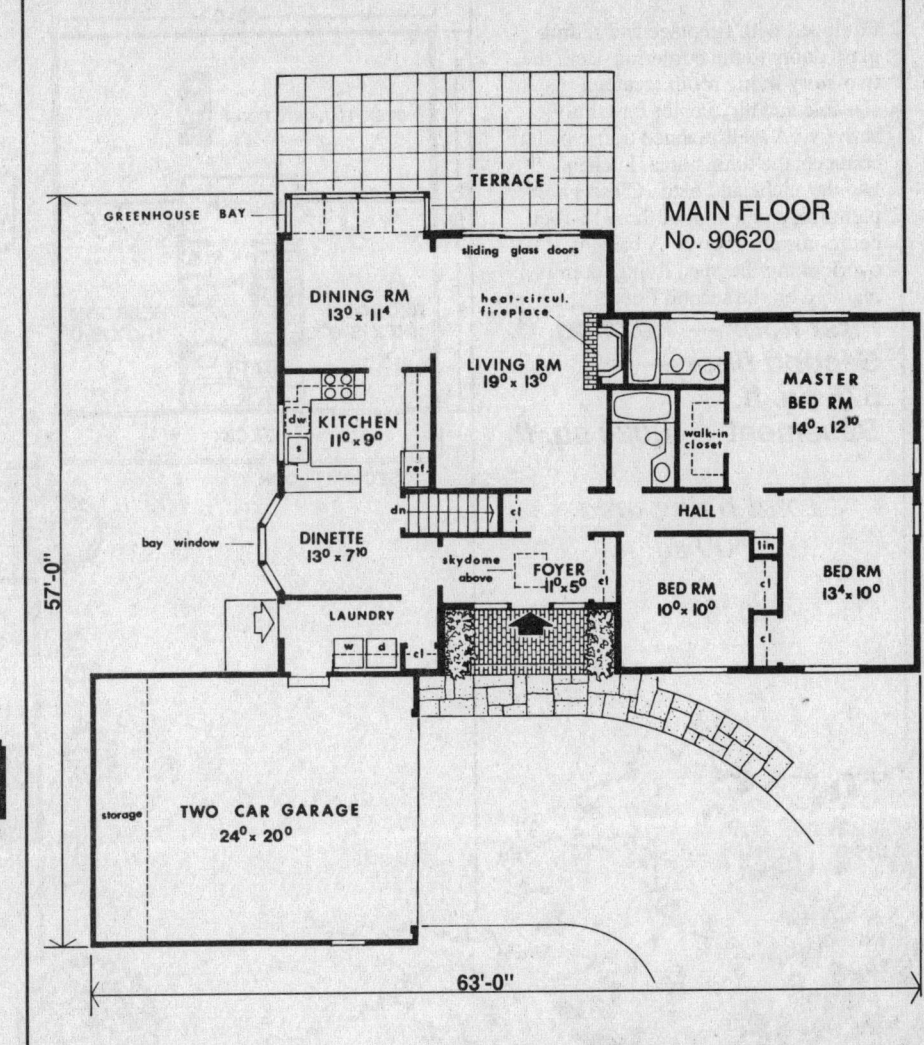

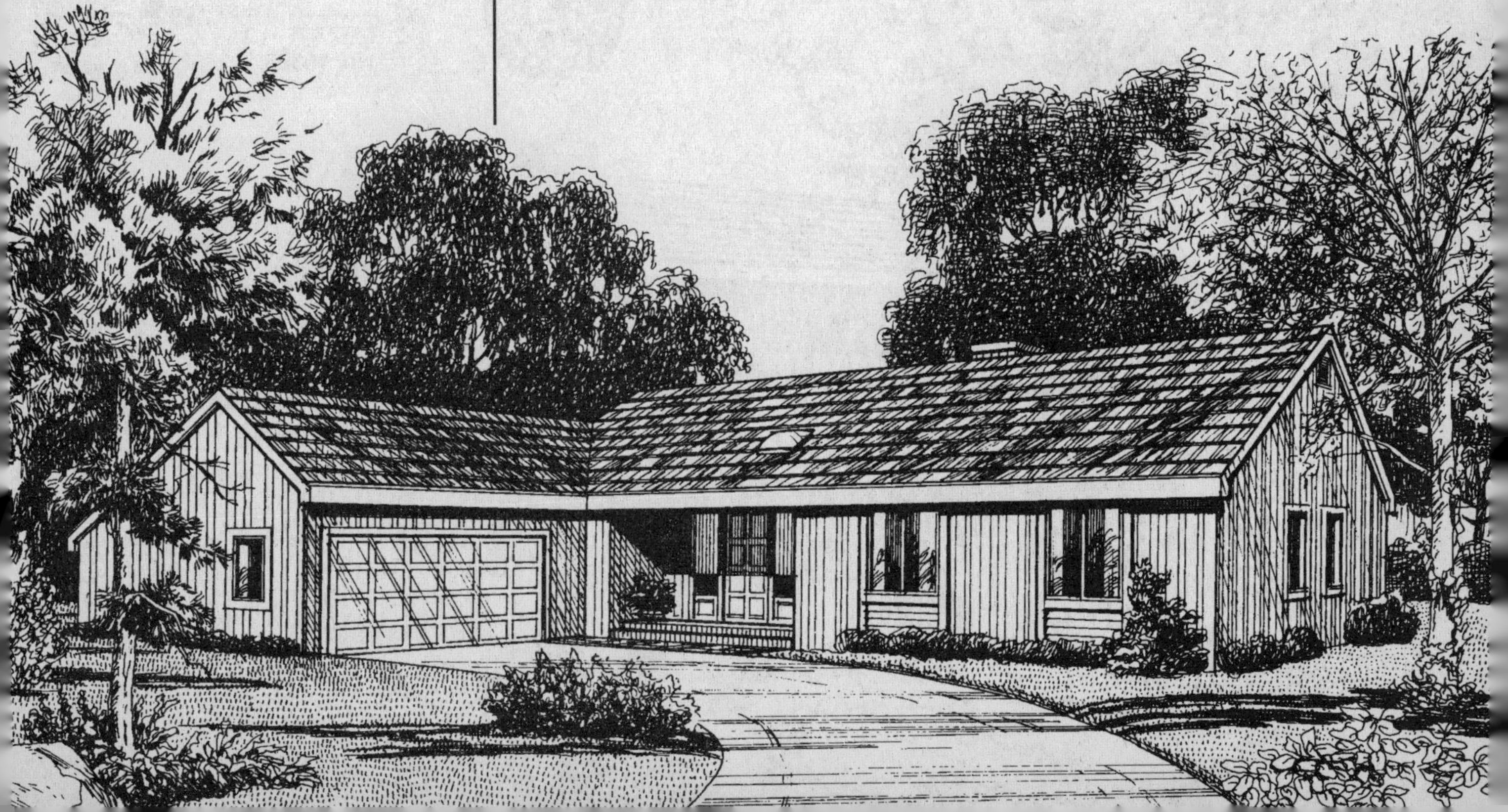

LIVING ROOM IS CENTRAL FOCUS

Design 10328

Equipped with fireplace and sliding glass doors to the bordering deck, the two-story living room creates a sizeable and airy center for family activity. A well-planned traffic pattern connects the dining area, kitchen, laundry niche and bath. Closets are plentiful, and a total of three 15-foot bedrooms are shown. A balcony overlooking the open living room is featured on the second floor.

First floor — 1,024 sq. ft.
Second floor — 576 sq. ft.
Basement — 1,024 sq. ft.

Total living area: 1,600 sq. ft.

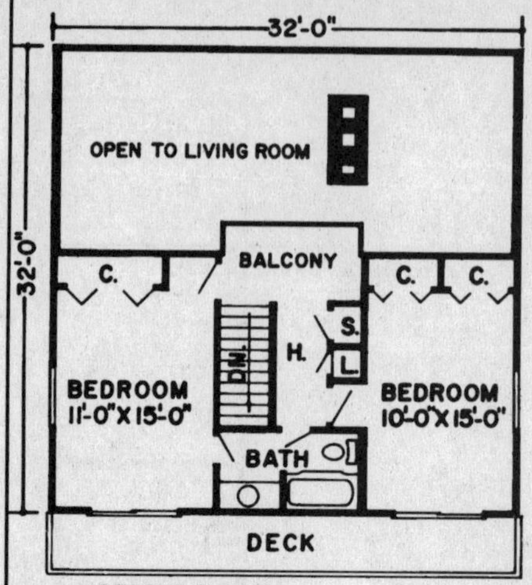

Refer to **Pricing Schedule B** on the order form for pricing information

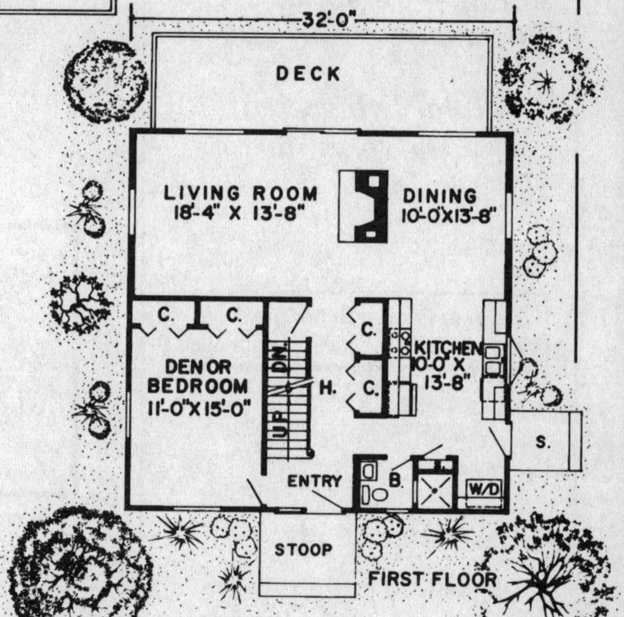

ORDER TODAY! 1-800-235-5700

ORDER TODAY! 1 - 800 - 235 - 5700

Design 96406

Roomy Yet Practical Home

A smart exterior and an economical use of interior space combine to create this roomy, yet practical home. The two-story foyer leads to a two-story Great room with fireplace, a wall of windows, and access to the back porch. Columns divide the Great room from breakfast room which is open to an angled kitchen with pantry. A handy utility room leads to a two-car garage with ample storage space. A split bedroom plan places the master suite with two walk-in closets on the first floor and two additional bedrooms, a full bath, and skylit bonus room on the second floor.

First floor — 1489 sq. ft.
Second floor — 534 sq. ft.
Garage & storage — 568 sq. ft.
Bonus room — 393 sq. ft.

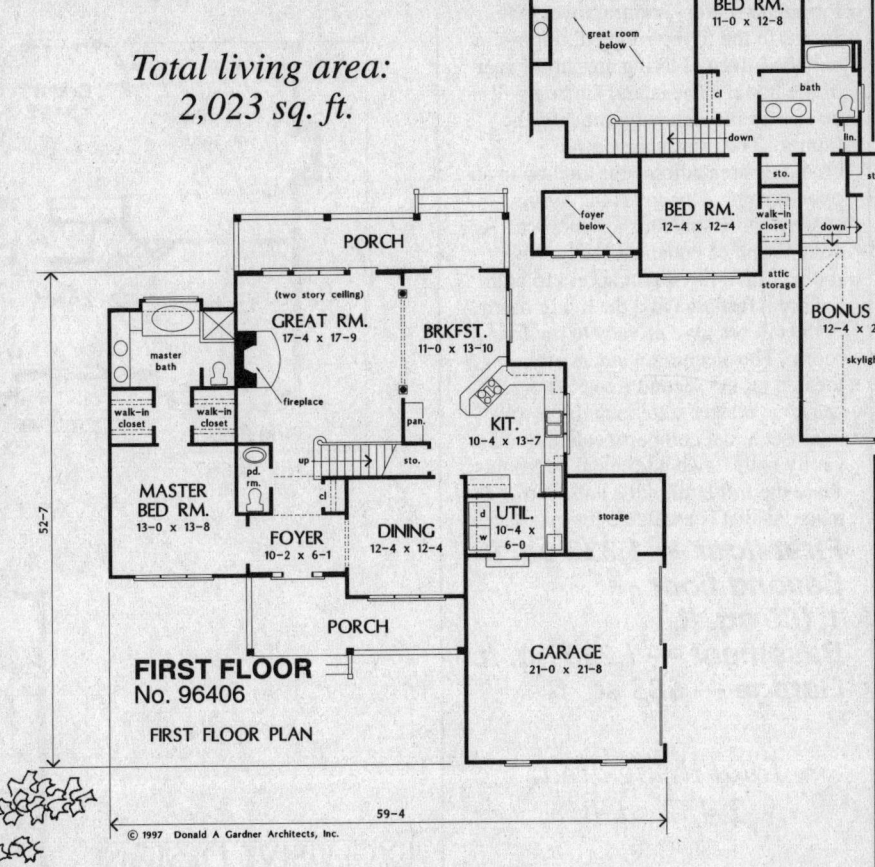

Total living area: 2,023 sq. ft.

Refer to **Pricing Schedule D** on the order form for pricing information

© 1997 Donald A. Gardner Architects, Inc.

Spacious Family Living Area

Design 24567

An attractive columned porch shelters the entrance of this stylish home. The formal, two-story, central foyer gives access to the living room, dining room and the informal living area at the rear of the home. The island kitchen will be sure to please the gourmet of the family. The highly windowed breakfast area adjoins the kitchen in an open layout. This gives the living space a more spacious appearance. A cozy fireplace enhances the family room, which has direct access to both the breakfast area and the living room. Pocket doors give privacy to the living room. The sleeping quarters are located on the second floor. The spacious master suite includes a walk-in closet and a compartmented, double vanity bath. Two additional bedrooms share the full bath in the hall. No materials list is available for this plan.

First floor — 1,332 sq. ft.
Second floor — 1,100 sq. ft.
Basement — 1,293 sq. ft.
Garage — 686 sq. ft.

Total living area: 2,432 sq. ft.

An EXCLUSIVE DESIGN By Britt J. Willis

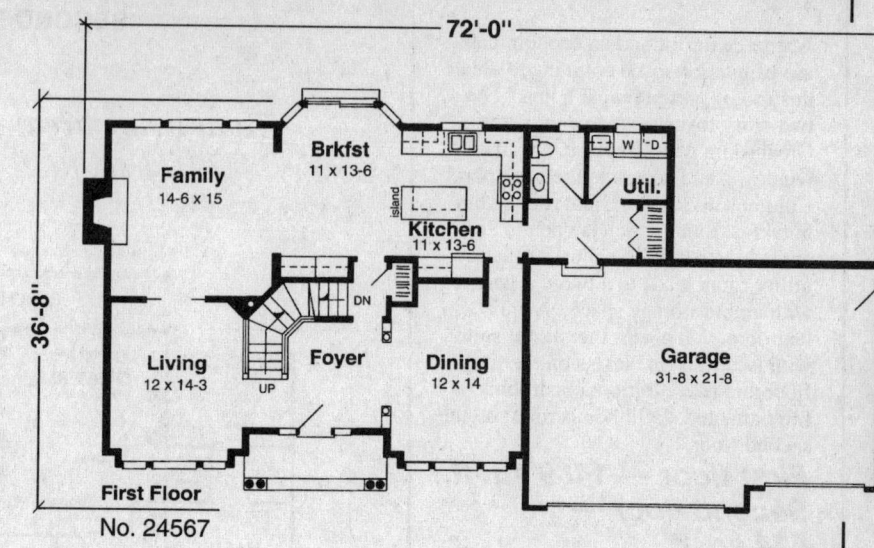

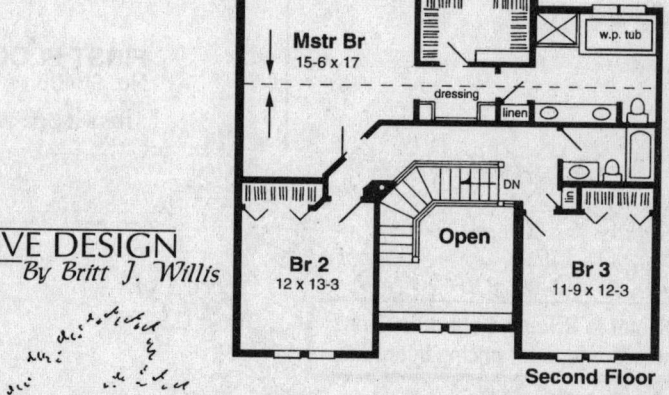

Refer to **Pricing Schedule D** on the order form for pricing information

TWO-SINK BATHS EASE RUSH

Design 90622

Save energy and construction costs by building this friendly farmhouse colonial. The inviting covered porch opens to a center hall, enhanced by the stairway leading to the four-bedroom second floor. Flanked by formal living and dining rooms, the foyer leads right into the open-beamed family room, island kitchen and bay window dinette. The rear porch adjoins both family and living rooms.

**First floor — 983 sq. ft.
Second floor — 1,013 sq. ft.
Mudroom — 99 sq. ft.
Garage — 481 sq. ft.**

Total living area: 2,095 sq. ft.

Refer to **Pricing Schedule C** on the order form for pricing information

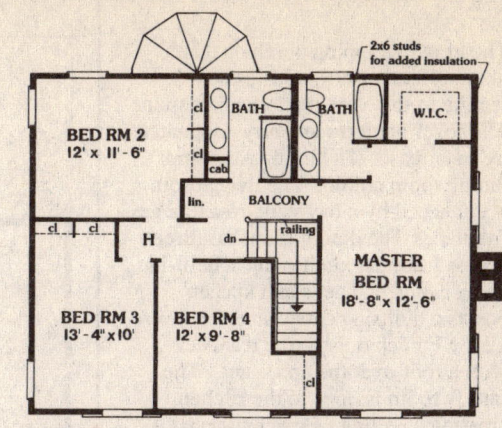

SECOND FLOOR PLAN

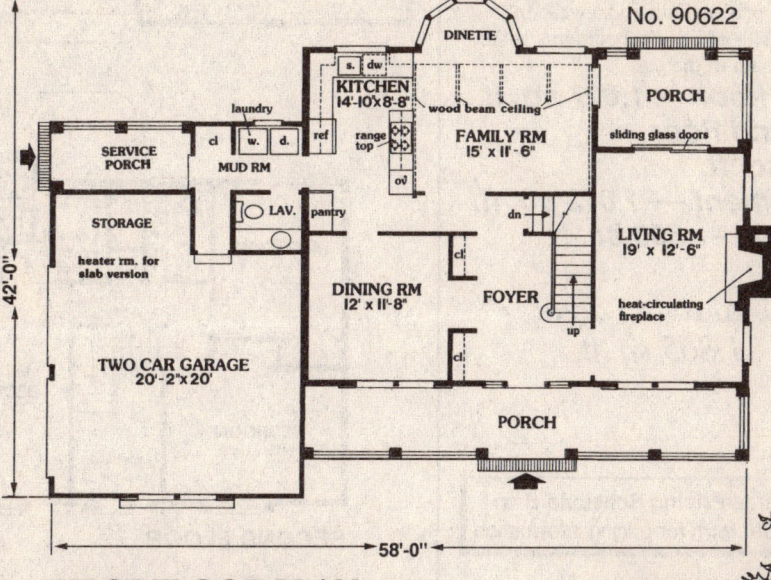

FIRST FLOOR PLAN

ORDER TODAY! 1 - 800 - 235 - 5700

ROOM FOR ALL IN THE FAMILY

Design 98815

The grand wrapping porch on this home offers a warm, old-fashion feeling to this very modern home plan. The foyer opens to an entry dominated by a staircase. The living room and dining room adjoin. The living room is enhanced by a bay window and a gas fireplace. The dining room has direct access from the kitchen and a built-in china cabinet. The island kitchen boasts a built-in pantry, an eating nook with a French door to the rear deck with a roof over the entry area. The family room is open to the kitchen, creating a feeling of spaciousness. A second gas fireplace accents the family room. Three bedrooms are located on the second floor. The master bedroom enjoys a private bath and a walk-in closet. The additional bedrooms share the full bath in the hall.

First floor — 1,027 sq. ft.
Second floor — 838 sq. ft.
Basement — 1,012 sq. ft.
Garage — 590 sq. ft.

Total living area: 1,865 sq. ft.

Refer to **Pricing Schedule B** on the order form for pricing information

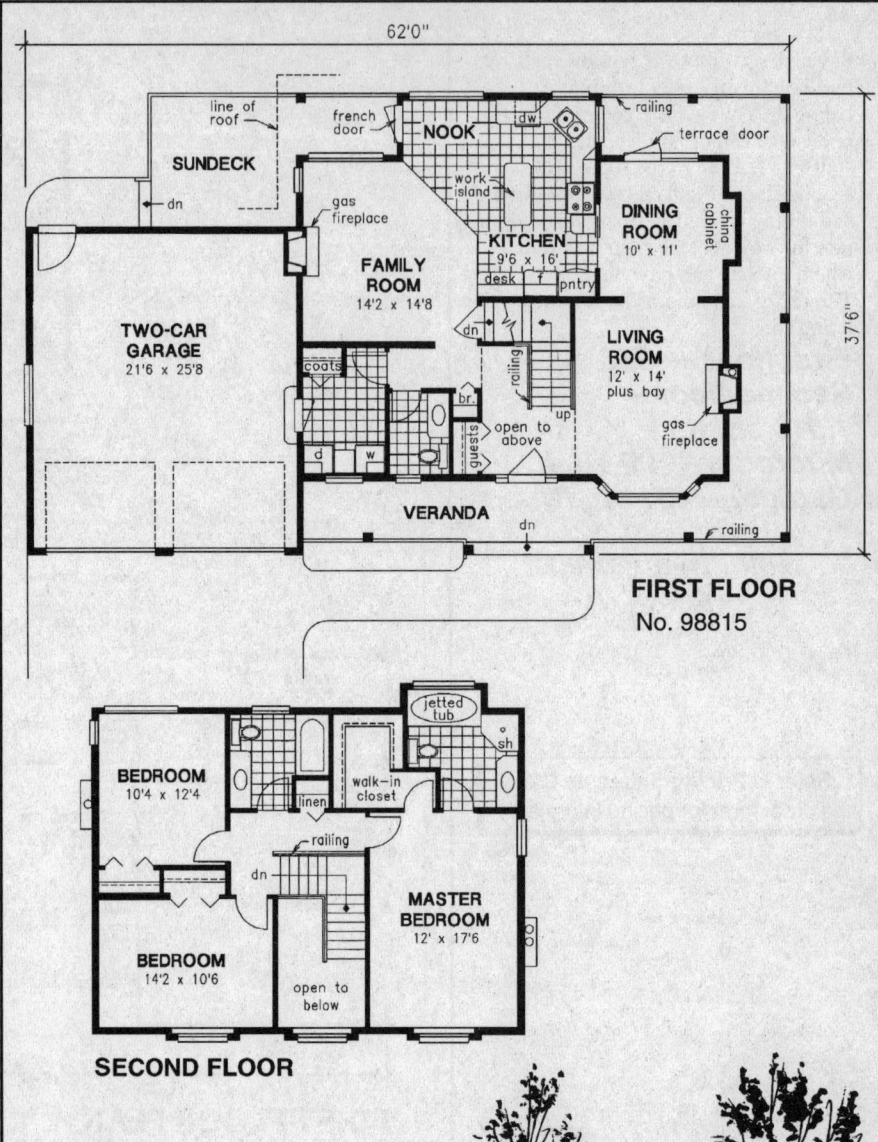

ORDER TODAY!   1 - 800 - 235 - 5700

Design 92531

ENHANCED BY A COLUMNED PORCH

The porch on this home is reminiscent of times gone by. Yet, this home is anything but old-fashioned. The Great room uses a modern decorative ceiling along with the fireplace. The amenities in the efficient kitchen/breakfast area will please the cook of your household. A dining room is available for formal entertaining. A private retreat, the master bedroom, has a master bath and walk-in closet. Walk-in closets are included in both bedrooms located at the other side of the house. A full bath is located in close proximity to both bedrooms. A garage, an additional storage area and a utility room complete this plan. This plan comes with a crawl space or slab foundation. Please specify when ordering.

Main living area — 1,754 sq. ft.
Garage & storage — 552 sq. ft.
Porch — 236 sq. ft.

Total living area: 1,754 sq. ft.

Refer to **Pricing Schedule C** on the order form for pricing information

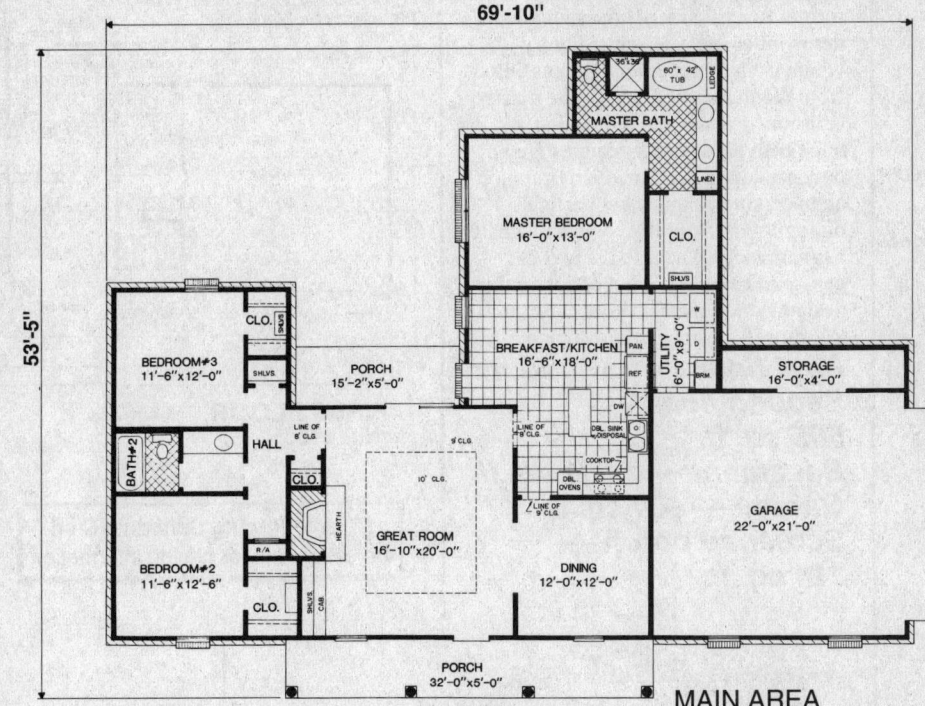

MAIN AREA
No. 92531

STUCCO AND STONE

Design 10555

This beautiful stucco and stone masonry Tudor design opens to a formal foyer that leads through double doors into a well-designed library which is also conveniently accessible from the master bedroom. The master bedroom offers a vaulted ceiling and a huge bath area. Other features are an oversized living room with a fireplace, an open kitchen and a connecting dining room. A utility room and a half bath are located next to the two-car garage. One other select option in this design is the separate cedar closet to use for off-season clothes storage.

First floor — 1,671 sq. ft.
Second floor — 505 sq. ft.
Basement — 1,661 sq. ft.
Garage — 604 sq. ft.
Screened porch — 114 sq. ft.

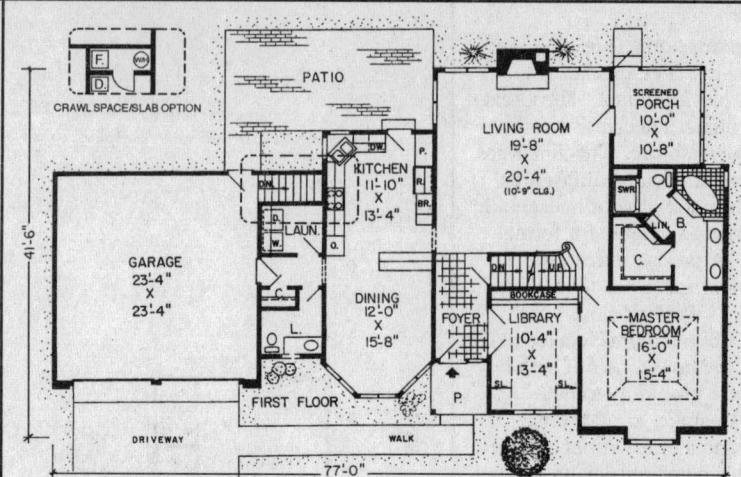

FIRST FLOOR
No. 10555

Refer to **Pricing Schedule C** on the order form for pricing information

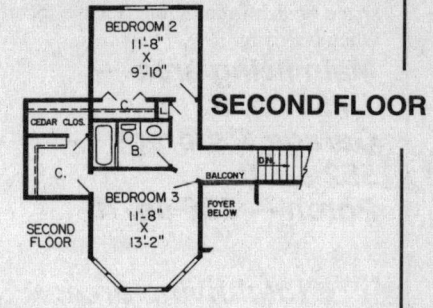

SECOND FLOOR

Total living area: 2,176 sq. ft.

ORDER TODAY! 1 - 800 - 235 - 5700

Skylight in Master Bedroom

Design 34029

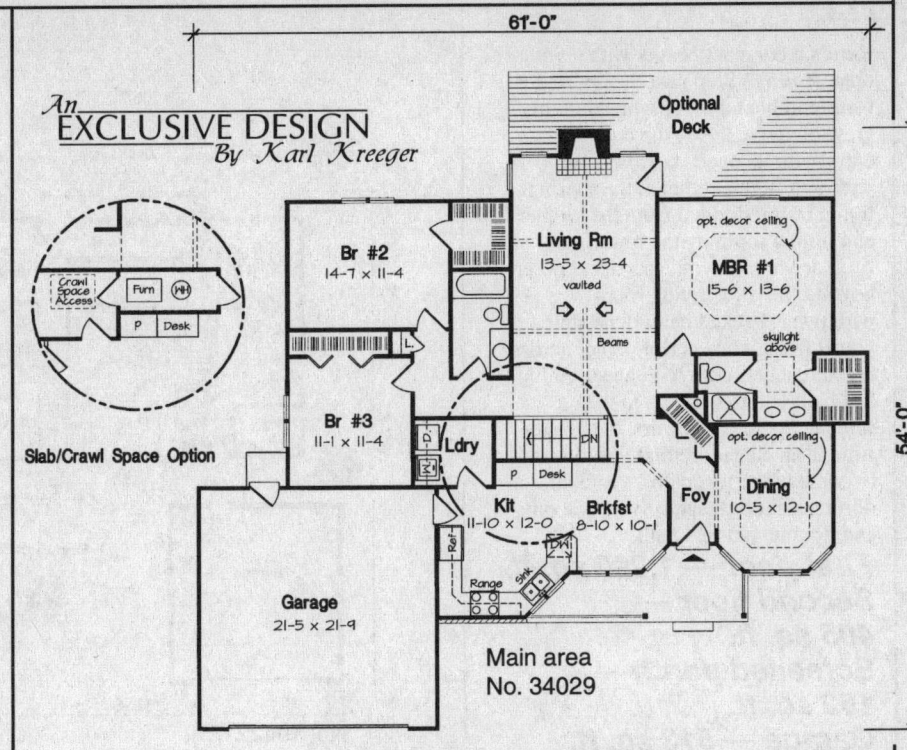

An Exclusive Design By Karl Kreeger

Slab/Crawl Space Option

Main area No. 34029

Keep dry during the rainy season under the covered porch entry way of this gorgeous home. A foyer separates the dining room with a decorative ceiling from the breakfast area and the kitchen. Off the kitchen is the laundry room, conveniently located. The living room features a vaulted beamed ceiling and a fireplace. A full bath is located between the living room and two bedrooms, both with large closet. On the other side of the living room is the master bedroom. The master bedroom has a decorative ceiling, and a skylight above the entrance of its private bath. The double-vanitied bathroom features a large walk-in closet. For those who enjoy outdoor living, an optional deck is offered, accessible through sliding glass doors off of this wonderful master bedroom.

**Main living area —
1,686 sq. ft.
Garage — 484 sq. ft.
Basement — 1,676 sq. ft.**

Total living area:
1,686 sq. ft.

Refer to **Pricing Schedule B** on the order form for pricing information

MASTER RETREAT AND SPACIOUS HOME

Design 19422

Here's a compact beauty with a wide-open feeling. Step past the inviting front porch, and savor a breathtaking view of active areas: the columned entry with its open staircase and windows high overhead; the soaring living room, divided from the kitchen and dining room by the towering fireplace chimney; the screened porch beyond the triple living room windows. Tucked behind the stairs, you'll find a cozy parlor. And, across the hall, a bedroom with an adjoining full bath features access to the screened porch. Upstairs, the master suite is an elegant retreat you'll want to come home for, with its romantic dormer window seat, private balcony, and double-vanitied bath.

**First floor — 1,290 sq. ft.
Second floor — 405 sq. ft.
Screened porch — 152 sq. ft.
Garage — 513 sq. ft.**

Total living area: 1,695 sq. ft.

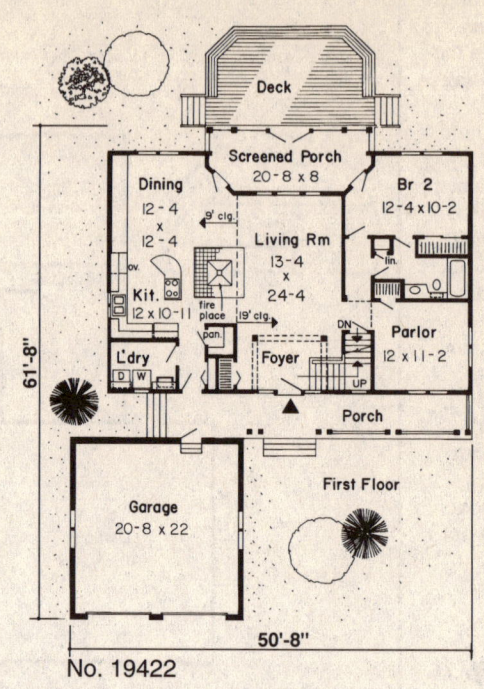

No. 19422

Refer to **Pricing Schedule B** on the order form for pricing information

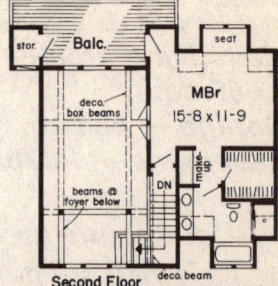

ORDER TODAY! 1 - 800 - 235 - 5700

MASSIVE CURB APPEAL, UNIQUE PLAN

Design 98517

Live like a king on a pauper's budget with this 2,175 square foot manor. With massive curb appeal and a unique floor plan, you'll feel pride each and every time you walk through the arched two-story covered entry. A formal dining room welcomes you as you enter. Just a few steps away, a massive Great room beckons one to rest a spell. The angled kitchen with large pass-through to the Great room will allow you to prepare meals with ease. A breakfast room will help start your day right after you awaken from your restful sleep in your cozy master suite. There are three bedrooms upstairs for the little ones. Don't forget the large storage area in the garage for all those family treasures. No materials list is available for this plan.

First floor — 1,472 sq. ft.
Second floor — 703 sq. ft.
Garage — 540 sq. ft.

Total living area: 2,175 sq. ft.

Refer to **Pricing Schedule C** on the order form for pricing information

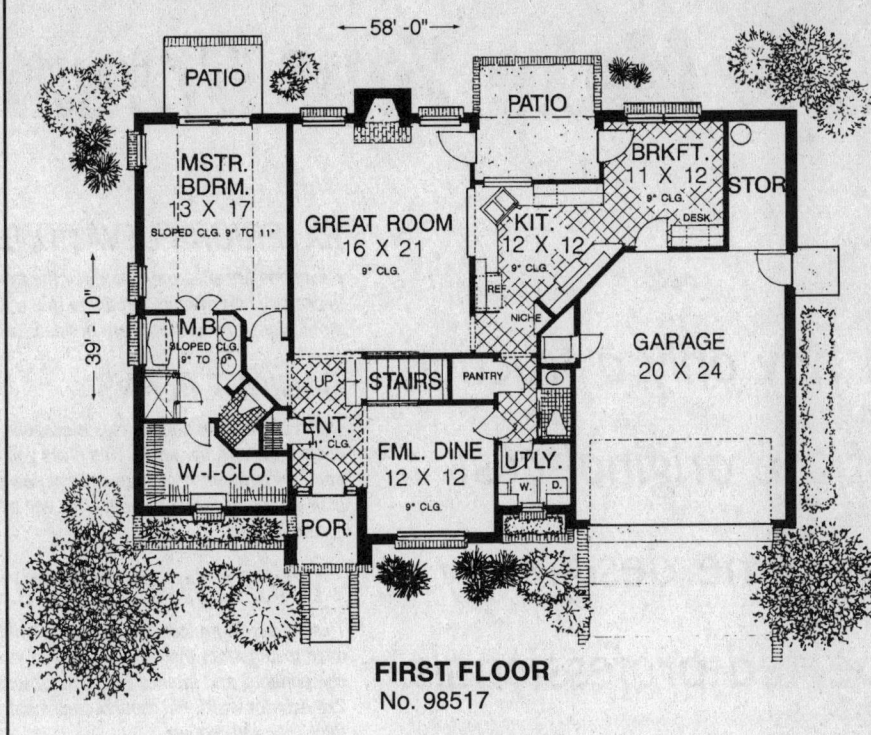

FIRST FLOOR
No. 98517

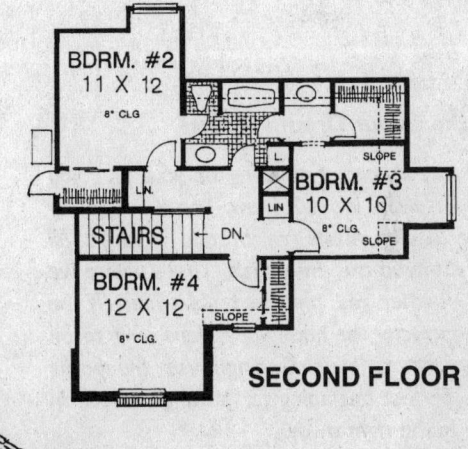

SECOND FLOOR

Everything You Need...
...to Make Your Dream Come True!

You pay only a fraction of the original cost for home designs by respected professionals.

You've Picked Your Dream Home!

You can already see it standing on your lot... you can see yourselves in your new home... enjoying family, entertaining guests, celebrating holidays. All that remains ahead are the details. That's where we can help. Whether you plan to build-it-yourself, be your own contractor, or hand your plans over to an outside contractor, your Garlinghouse blueprints provide the perfect beginning for putting yourself in your dream home right away.

We even make it simple for you to make professional design modifications. We can also provide a materials list for greater economy.

My grandfather, L.F. Garlinghouse, started a tradition of quality when he founded this company in 1907. For over 90 years, homeowners and builders have relied on us for accurate, complete, professional blueprints. Our plans help you get results fast... and save money, too! These pages will give you all the information you need to order. So get started now... I know you'll love your new Garlinghouse home!

Sincerely,

EXTERIOR ELEVATIONS
Elevations are scaled drawings of the front, rear, left and right sides of a home. All of the necessary information pertaining to the exterior finish materials, roof pitches and exterior height dimensions of your home are defined.

CABINET PLANS
These plans, or in some cases elevations, will detail the layout of the kitchen and bathroom cabinets at a larger scale. This gives you an accurate layout for your cabinets or an ideal starting point for a modified custom cabinet design. Available for most plans. You may also show the floor plan without a cabinet layout. This will allow you to start from scratch and design your own dream kitchen.

TYPICAL WALL SECTION
This section is provided to help your builder understand the structural components and materials used to construct the exterior walls of your home. This section will address insulation, roof components, and interior and exterior wall finishes. Your plans will be designed with either 2x4 or 2x6 exterior walls, but most professional contractors can easily adapt the plans to the wall thickness you require.

FIREPLACE DETAILS
If the home you have chosen includes a fireplace, the fireplace detail will show typical methods to construct the firebox, hearth and flue chase for masonry units, or a wood frame chase for a zero-clearance unit. Available for most plans.

FOUNDATION PLAN
These plans will accurately dimension the footprint of your home including load bearing points and beam placement if applicable. The foundation style will vary from plan to plan. Your local climatic conditions will dictate whether a basement, slab or crawlspace is best suited for your area. In most cases, if your plan comes with one foundation style, a professional contractor can easily adapt the foundation plan to an alternate style.

ROOF PLAN
The information necessary to construct the roof will be included with your home plans. Some plans will reference roof trusses, while many others contain schematic framing plans. These framing plans will indicate the lumber sizes necessary for the rafters and ridgeboards based on the designated roof loads.

TYPICAL CROSS SECTION
A cut-away cross-section through the entire home shows your building contractor the exact correlation of construction components at all levels of the house. It will help to clarify the load bearing points from the roof all the way down to the basement. Available for most plans.

DETAILED FLOOR PLANS
The floor plans of your home accurately dimension the positioning of all walls, doors, windows, stairs and permanent fixtures. They will show you the relationship and dimensions of rooms, closets and traffic patterns. The schematic of the electrical layout may be included in the plan. This layout is clearly represented and does not hinder the clarity of other pertinent information shown. All these details will help your builder properly construct your new home.

STAIR DETAILS
If stairs are an element of the design you have chosen, the plans will show the necessary information to build these, either through a stair cross section, or on the floor plans. Either way, the information provides your builders the essential reference points that they need to build the stairs.

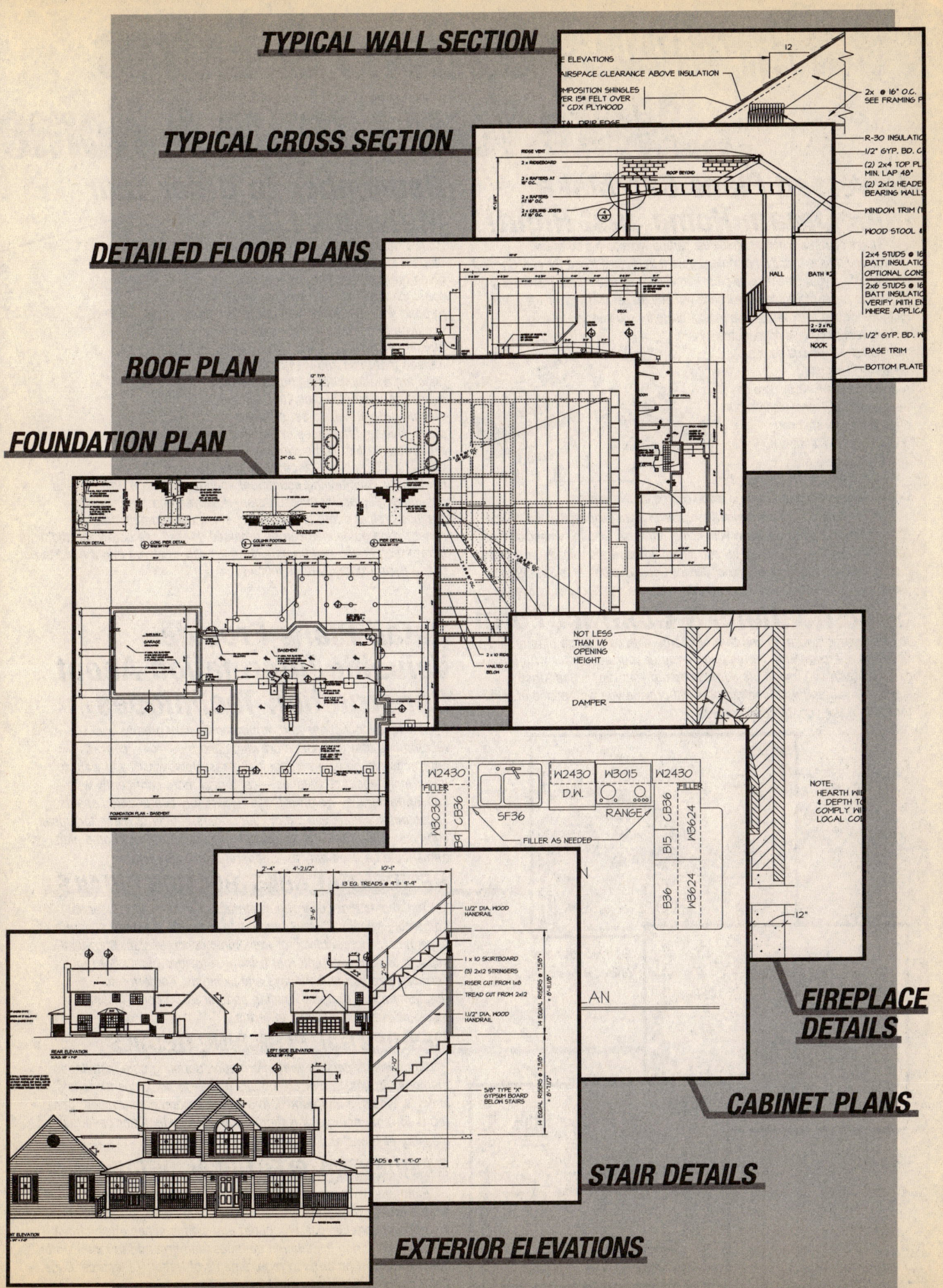

Garlinghouse Options & Extras ...Make Your Dream A Home

Reversed Plans Can Make Your Dream Home Just Right!

"That's our dream home...if only the garage were on the other side!"
You could have exactly the home you want by flipping it end-for-end. Check it out by holding your dream home page of this book up to a mirror. Then simply order your plans "reversed." We'll send you one full set of mirror-image plans (with the writing backwards) as a master guide for you and your builder.

The remaining sets of your order will come as shown in this book so the dimensions and specifications are easily read on the job site...but most plans in our collection come stamped "REVERSED" so there is no construction confusion.

We can only send reversed plans with multiple-set orders. There is a $50 charge for this service.

Some plans in our collection are available in Right Reading Reverse. Right Reading Reverse plans will show your home in reverse, with the writing on the plan being readable. This easy-to-read format will save you valuable time and money. Please contact our Customer Service Department at (860) 343-5977 to check for Right Reading Reverse availability. (There is a $125 charge for this service.)

Specifications & Contract Form

We send this form to you free of charge with your home plan order. The form is designed to be filled in by you or your contractor with the exact materials to use in the construction of your new home. Once signed by you and your contractor it will provide you with peace of mind throughout the construction process.

Remember To Order Your Materials List

It'll help you save money. Available at a modest additional charge, the Materials List gives the quantity, dimensions, and specifications for the major materials needed to build your home. You will get faster, more accurate bids from your contractors and building suppliers — and avoid paying for unused materials and waste. Materials Lists are available for all home plans except as otherwise indicated, but can only be ordered with a set of home plans. Due to differences in regional requirements and homeowner or builder preferences... electrical, plumbing and heating/air conditioning equipment specifications are not designed specifically for each plan. However, non-plan specific detailed typical prints of residential electrical, plumbing and construction guidelines can be provided. Please see below for additional information. If you need a detailed materials cost you might need to purchase a Zip Quote. (Details follow)

Detail Plans Provide Valuable Information About Construction Techniques

Because local codes and requirements vary greatly, we recommend that you obtain drawings and bids from licensed contractors to do your mechanical plans. However, if you want to know more about techniques — and deal more confidently with subcontractors — we offer these remarkably useful detail sheets. These detail sheets will aid in your understanding of these technical subjects. The detail sheets are not specific to any one home plan and should be used only as a general reference guide.

RESIDENTIAL CONSTRUCTION DETAILS

Ten sheets that cover the essentials of stick-built residential home construction. Details foundation options — poured concrete basement, concrete block, or monolithic concrete slab. Shows all aspects of floor, wall and roof framing. Provides details for roof dormers, overhangs, chimneys and skylights. Conforms to requirements of Uniform Building code or BOCA code. Includes a quick index and a glossary of terms.

RESIDENTIAL PLUMBING DETAILS

Eight sheets packed with information detailing pipe installation methods, fittings, and sized. Details plumbing hook-ups for toilets, sinks, washers, sump pumps, and septic system construction. Conforms to requirements of National Plumbing code. Color coded with a glossary of terms and quick index.

RESIDENTIAL ELECTRICAL DETAILS

Eight sheets that cover all aspects of residential wiring, from simple switch wiring to service entrance connections. Details distribution panel layout with outlet and switch schematics, circuit breaker and wiring installation methods, and ground fault interrupter specifications. Conforms to requirements of National Electrical Code. Color coded with a glossary of terms.

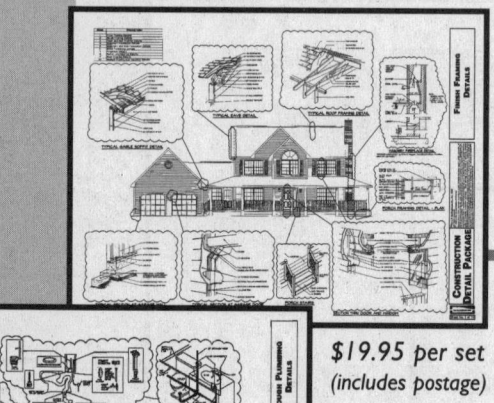

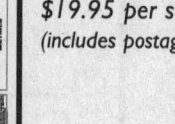

$19.95 per set
(includes postage)

Modifying Your Favorite Design, Made EASY!

OPTION #1
Modifying Your Garlinghouse Home Plan

Simple modifications to your dream home, including minor non-structural changes and material substitutions, can be made between you and your builder by marking the changes directly on your blueprints. However, if you are considering making significant changes to your chosen design, we recommend that you use the services of The Garlinghouse Co. Design Staff. We will help take your ideas and turn them into a reality, just the way you want. Here's our procedure!

When you place your Vellum order, you may also request a free Garlinghouse Modification Kit. In this kit, you will receive a red marking pencil, furniture cut-out sheet, ruler, a self addressed mailing label and a form for specifying any additional notes or drawings that will help us understand your design ideas. Mark your desired changes directly on the Vellum drawings. NOTE: Please use only a **red pencil** to mark your desired changes on the Vellum. Then, return the redlined Vellum set in the original box to The Garlinghouse Company at, 282 Main Street Extension, Middletown, CT 06457. IMPORTANT: Please **roll** the Vellums for shipping, **do not fold** the Vellums for shipping.

We also offer modification estimates. We will provide you with an estimate to draft your changes based on your specific modifications before you purchase the vellums, for a $50 fee. After you receive your estimate, if you decide to have The Garlinghouse Company Design Staff do the changes, the $50 estimate fee will be deducted from the cost of your modifications. If, however, you choose to use a different service, the $50 estimate fee is non-refundable.

Within 5 days of receipt of your plans, you will be contacted by a member of The Garlinghouse Co. Design Staff with an estimate for the design services to draw those changes. A 50% deposit is required before we begin making the actual modifications to your plans.

Once the preliminary design changes have been made to the floor plans and elevations, copies will be sent to you to make sure we have made the exact changes you want. We will wait for your approval before continuing with any structural revisions. The Garlinghouse Co. Design Staff will call again to inform you that your modified Vellum plan is complete and will be shipped as soon as the final payment has been made. For additional information call us at 1-860-343-5977. Please refer to the Modification Pricing Guide for estimated modification costs. Please call for Vellum modification availability for plan numbers 85,000 and above.

OPTION #2
Reproducible Vellums for Local Modification Ease

If you decide not to use the Garlinghouse Co. Design Staff for your modifications, we recommend that you follow our same procedure of purchasing our Vellums. You then have the option of using the services of the original designer of the plan, a local professional designer, or architect to make the modifications to your plan.

With a Vellum copy of our plans, a design professional can alter the drawings just the way you want, then you can print as many copies of the modified plans as you need to build your house. And, since you have already started with our complete detailed plans, the cost of those expensive professional services will be significantly less than starting from scratch. Refer to the price schedule for Vellum costs. Again, please call for Vellum availability for plan numbers 85,000 and above.

IMPORTANT RETURN POLICY: Upon receipt of your Vellums, if for some reason you decide you do not want a modified plan, then simply return the Kit and the unopened Vellums. Reproducible Vellum copies of our home plans are copyright protected and only sold under the terms of a license agreement that you will receive with your order. Should you not agree to the terms, then the Vellums may be returned, **unopened,** for a full refund less the shipping and handling charges, plus a 15% restocking fee. For any additional information, please call us at 1-860-343-5977.

MODIFICATION PRICING GUIDE

CATEGORIES	ESTIMATED COST
KITCHEN LAYOUT — PLAN AND ELEVATION	$175.00
BATHROOM LAYOUT — PLAN AND ELEVATION	$175.00
FIREPLACE PLAN AND DETAILS	$200.00
INTERIOR ELEVATION	$125.00
EXTERIOR ELEVATION — MATERIAL CHANGE	$140.00
EXTERIOR ELEVATION — ADD BRICK OR STONE	$400.00
EXTERIOR ELEVATION — STYLE CHANGE	$450.00
NON BEARING WALLS (INTERIOR)	$200.00
BEARING AND/OR EXTERIOR WALLS	$325.00
WALL FRAMING CHANGE — 2X4 TO 2X6 OR 2X6 TO 2X4	$240.00
ADD/REDUCE LIVING SPACE — SQUARE FOOTAGE	QUOTE REQUIRED
NEW MATERIALS LIST	$.20 SQUARE FOOT
CHANGE TRUSSES TO RAFTERS OR CHANGE ROOF PITCH	$300.00
FRAMING PLAN CHANGES	$325.00
GARAGE CHANGES	$325.00
ADD A FOUNDATION OPTION	$300.00
FOUNDATION CHANGES	$250.00
RIGHT READING PLAN REVERSE	$575.00
ARCHITECTS SEAL (Available for most states.)	$300.00
ENERGY CERTIFICATE	$150.00
LIGHT AND VENTILATION SCHEDULE	$150.00

Questions?
Call our customer service department at **1-860-343-5977**

"How to obtain a construction cost calculation based on labor rates and building material costs in <u>your</u> Zip Code area!"

ZIP-QUOTE!
HOME COST CALCULATOR

WHY?

Do you wish you could quickly find out the building cost for your new home without waiting for a contractor to compile hundreds of bids? Would you like to have a benchmark to compare your contractor(s) bids against? **Well, Now You Can!!**, with **Zip-Quote** Home Cost Calculator. Zip-Quote is only available for zip code areas within the United States.

HOW?

Our new **Zip-Quote** Home Cost Calculator will enable you to obtain the calculated building cost to construct your new home, based on labor rates and building material costs within your zip code area, without the normal delays or hassles usually associated with the bidding process. Zip-Quote can be purchased in two separate formats, an itemized or a bottom line format.

"How does **Zip-Quote** actually work?" When you call to order, you must choose from the options available, for your specific home, in in order for us to process your order. Once we receive your **Zip-Quote** order, we process your specific home plan building materials list through our Home Cost Calculator which contains up-to-date rates for all residential labor trades and building material costs in your zip code area. "The result?" A calculated cost to build your dream home in your zip code area. This calculation will help you (as a consumer or a builder) evaluate your building budget. This is a valuable tool for anyone considering building a new home.

All database information for our calculations is furnished by Marshall & Swift, L.P. For over 60 years, Marshall & Swift L.P. has been a leading provider of cost data to professionals in all aspects of the construction and remodeling industries.

OPTION 1

The **Itemized Zip-Quote** is a detailed building material list. Each building material list line item will separately state the labor cost, material cost and equipment cost (if applicable) for the use of that building material in the construction process. Each category within the building material list will be subtotaled and the entire Itemized cost calculation totaled at the end. This building materials list will be summarized by the individual building categories and will have additional columns where you can enter data from your contractor's estimates for a cost comparison between the different suppliers and contractors who will actually quote you their products and services.

OPTION 2

The **Bottom Line Zip-Quote** is a one line summarized total cost for the home plan of your choice. This cost calculation is also based on the labor cost, material cost and equipment cost (if applicable) within your local zip code area.

COST

The price of your **Itemized Zip-Quote** is based upon the pricing schedule of the plan you have selected, in addition to the price of the materials list. Please refer to the pricing schedule on our order form. The price of your initial **Bottom Line Zip-Quote** is $29.95. Each additional **Bottom Line Zip-Quote** ordered in conjunction with the initial order is only $14.95. **Bottom Line Zip-Quote** may be purchased separately and does NOT have to be purchased in conjunction with a home plan order.

FYI

An **Itemized Zip-Quote** Home Cost Calculation can ONLY be purchased in conjunction with a Home Plan order. The **Itemized Zip-Quote** can not be purchased separately. The **Bottom Line Zip-Quote** can be purchased separately and doesn't have to be purchased in conjunction with a home plan order. Please consult with a sales representative for current availability. If you find within 60 days of your order date that you will be unable to build this home, then you may exchange the plans and the materials list towards the price of a new set of plans (see order info pages for plan exchange policy). The **Itemized Zip-Quote** and the **Bottom Line Zip-Quote** are NOT returnable. The price of the initial **Bottom Line Zip-Quote** order can be credited towards the purchase of an **Itemized Zip-Quote** order only. Additional **Bottom Line Zip-Quote** orders, within the same order can not be credited. Please call our Customer Service Department for more information.

Zip-Quote is available for plans where you see this symbol. Zip-Quote will be available for plans 85,000 and above after Sept. 1, 1998.

SOME MORE INFORMATION

The Itemized and Bottom Line Zip-Quotes give you approximated costs for constructing the particular house in your area. These costs are not exact and are only intended to be used as a preliminary estimate to help determine the affordability of a new home and/or as a guide to evaluate the general competitiveness of actual price quotes obtained through local suppliers and contractors. However, Zip-Quote cost figures should never be relied upon as the only source of information in either case. The Garlinghouse Company and Marshall & Swift L.P. can not guarantee any level of data accuracy or correctness in a Zip-Quote and disclaim all liability for loss with respect to the same, in excess of the original purchase price of the Zip-Quote product. All Zip-Quote calculations are based upon the actual blueprint materials list with options as selected by customer and do not reflect any differences that may be shown on the published house renderings, floor plans, or photographs.

Ignoring Copyright Laws Can Be A $1,000,000 Mistake

Recent changes in the US copyright laws allow for statutory penalties of up to **$100,000** per incident for copyright infringement involving any of the copyrighted plans found in this publication. The law can be confusing. So, for your own protection, take the time to understand what you can and cannot do when it comes to home plans.

···WHAT YOU CANNOT DO···

You Cannot Duplicate Home Plans

Purchasing a set of blueprints and making additional sets by reproducing the original is **illegal**. If you need multiple sets of a particular home plan, then you must purchase them.

You Cannot Copy Any Part of a Home Plan to Create Another

Creating your own plan by copying even part of a home design found in this publication is called "creating a derivative work" and is **illegal** unless you have permission to do so.

You Cannot Build a Home Without a License

You must have specific permission or license to build a home from a copyrighted design, even if the finished home has been changed from the original plan. It is **illegal** to build one of the homes found in this publication without a license.

What Garlinghouse Offers

Home Plan Blueprint Package

By purchasing a multiple set package of blueprints or a vellum from Garlinghouse, you not only receive the physical blueprint documents necessary for construction, but you are also granted a license to build one, and only one, home. You can also make simple modifications, including minor non-structural changes and material substitutions, to our design, as long as these changes are made directly on the blueprints purchased from Garlinghouse and no additional copies are made.

Home Plan Vellums

By purchasing vellums for one of our home plans, you receive the same construction drawings found in the blueprints, but printed on vellum paper. Vellums can be erased and are perfect for making design changes. They are also semi-transparent making them easy to duplicate. But most importantly, the purchase of home plan vellums comes with a broader license that allows you to make changes to the design (ie, create a hand drawn or CAD derivative work), to make copies of the plan, and to build one home from the plan.

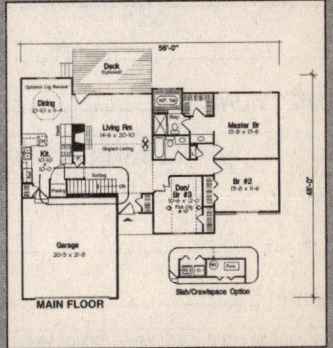

License To Build Additional Homes

With the purchase of a blueprint package or vellums you automatically receive a license to build one home and only one home, respectively. If you want to build more homes than you are licensed to build through your purchase of a plan, then additional licenses may be purchased at reasonable costs from Garlinghouse. Inquire for more information.

Order Code No. **H8NH1**

Order Form

Plan prices guaranteed until 8/1/99 —After this date call for updated pricing

___ set(s) of blueprints for plan #_____ $_____

___ Vellum & Modification kit for plan #_____ $_____

___ Additional set(s) @ $35 each for plan #_____ $_____

___ Mirror Image Reverse @ $50 each $_____

___ Right Reading Reverse @ $125 each $_____

___ Materials list for plan #_____ $_____

___ Detail Plans @ $19.95 each
  ❏ Construction ❏ Plumbing ❏ Electrical $_____

___ Bottom line ZIP Quote @ $29.95 for plan #_____ $_____

___ Additional Bottom Line Zip Quote
  @ $14.95 for plan(s) #_____
  _____ $_____

___ Itemized ZIP Quote for plan(s) #_____ $_____

Shipping (see charts on opposite page) $_____

Subtotal $_____

Sales Tax (CT residents add 6% sales tax, KS residents add 6.15% sales tax) (Not required for other states) $_____

TOTAL AMOUNT ENCLOSED $_____

Send your check, money order or credit card information to:
(No C.O.D.'s Please)

Please submit all United States & Other Nations orders to:
Garlinghouse Company
P.O. Box 1717
Middletown, CT. 06457

Please Submit all Canadian plan orders to:
Garlinghouse Company
60 Baffin Place, Unit #5
Waterloo, Ontario N2V 1Z7

ADDRESS INFORMATION:

NAME:_____

STREET:_____

CITY:_____

STATE:_____ ZIP:_____

DAYTIME PHONE:_____

Credit Card Information

Charge To: ❏ Visa ❏ Mastercard

Card # |__|__|__|__| |__|__|__|__| |__|__|__|__| |__|__|__|__|

Signature _____ Exp. ____/____

Payment must be made in U.S. funds. Foreign Mail Orders: Certified bank checks in U.S. funds only
TERMS OF SALE FOR HOME PLANS: All home plans sold through this publication are copyright protected. Reproduction of these home plans, either in whole or in part, including any direct copying and/or preparation of derivative works thereof, for any reason without the prior written permission of The L.F. Garlinghouse Co., Inc., is strictly prohibited. The purchase of a set of home plans in no way transfers any copyright or other ownership interest in it to the buyer except for a limited license to use that set of home plans for the construction of one, and only one, dwelling unit. The purchase of additional sets of that home plan at a reduced price from the original set or as a part of a multiple set package does not entitle the buyer with a license to construct more than one dwelling unit.

IMPORTANT INFORMATION TO READ BEFORE YOU PLACE YOUR ORDER

How Many Sets Of Plans Will You Need?

The Standard 8-Set Construction Package

Our experience shows that you'll speed every step of construction and avoid costly building errors by ordering enough sets to go around. Each tradesperson wants a set — the general contractor and all subcontractors; foundation, electrical, plumbing, heating/air conditioning and framers. Don't forget your lending institution, building department and, of course, a set for yourself. * Recommended For Construction *

The Minimum 4-Set Construction Package

If you're comfortable with arduous follow-up, this package can save you a few dollars by giving you the option of passing down plan sets as work progresses. You might have enough copies to go around if work goes exactly as scheduled and no plans are lost or damaged by subcontractors. But for only $50 more, the 8-set package eliminates these worries.
* Recommended For Bidding *

The Single Study Set

We offer this set so you can study the blueprints to plan your dream home in detail. They are stamped "study set only-not for construction", and you cannot build a home from them. In pursuant to copyright laws, it is _illegal_ to reproduce any blueprint.

Our Reorder and Exchange Policies:

If you find after your initial purchase that you require additional sets of plans you may purchase them from us at special reorder prices (please call for pricing details) provided that you reorder within 6 months of your original order date. There is a $28 reorder processing fee that is charged on all reorders. For more information on reordering plans please contact our Customer Service Department at (860) 343-5977.

We want you to find your dream home from our wide selection of home plans. However, if for some reason you find that the plan you have purchased from us does not meet your needs, then you may exchange that plan for any other plan in our collection. We allow you sixty days from your original invoice date to make an exchange. At the time of the exchange you will be charged a processing fee of 15% of the total amount of your original order plus the difference in price between the plans (if applicable) plus the cost to ship the new plans to you. Call our Customer Service Department at (860) 343-5977 for more information. Please Note: Reproducible vellums can only be exchanged if they are unopened.

Important Shipping Information

Please refer to the shipping charts on the order form for service availability for your specific plan number. Our delivery service must have a street address or Rural Route Box number — never a post office box. (PLEASE NOTE: Supplying a P.O. Box number _only_ will delay the shipping of your order.) Use a work address if no one is home during the day.

Orders being shipped to APO or FPO must go via First Class Mail. Please include the proper postage.

For our International Customers, only Certified bank checks and money orders are accepted and must be payable in U.S. currency. For speed, we ship international orders Air Parcel Post. Please refer to the chart for the correct shipping cost.

Important Canadian Shipping Information

To our friends in Canada, we have a plan design affiliate in Kitchener, Ontario. This relationship will help you avoid the delays and charges associated with shipments from the United States. Moreover, our affiliate is familiar with the building requirements in your community and country. We prefer payments in U.S. Currency. If you, however, are sending Canadian funds please add 40% to the prices of the plans and shipping fees.

An Important Note About Building Code Requirements:

All plans are drawn to conform to one or more of the industry's major national building standards. However, due to the variety of local building regulations, your plan may need to be modified to comply with local requirements — snow loads, energy loads, seismic zones, etc. Do check them fully and consult your local building officials.

A few states require that all building plans used be drawn by an architect registered in that state. While having your plans reviewed and stamped by such an architect may be prudent, laws requiring non-conforming plans like ours to be completely redrawn forces you to unnecessarily pay very large fees. If your state has such a law, we strongly recommend you contact your state representative to protest.

The rendering, floor plans, and technical information contained within this publication are not guaranteed to be totally accurate. Consequently, no information from this publication should be used either as a guide to constructing a home or for estimating the cost of building a home. Complete blueprints must be purchased for such purposes.

BEFORE ORDERING PLEASE READ ALL ORDERING INFORMATION

Please submit all Canadian plan orders to:
Garlinghouse Company
60 Baffin Place, Unit #5, Waterloo, Ontario N2V 1Z7
Canadian Customers Only: 1-800-561-4169/Fax #: 1-800-719-3291
Customer Service #: 1-519-746-4169

ORDER TOLL FREE — 1-800-235-5700
Monday-Friday 8:00 a.m. to 8:00 p.m. Eastern Time
or FAX your Credit Card order to 1-860-343-5984
All foreign residents call 1-800-343-5977

Please have ready: 1. Your credit card number 2. The plan number 3. The order code number ⇨ **H8NH1**

Garlinghouse 1998 Blueprint Price Code Schedule

Additional sets with original order $35

PRICE CODE	A	B	C	D	E	F	G	H
8 SETS OF SAME PLAN	$385	$425	$470	$510	$550	$595	$635	$675
4 SETS OF SAME PLAN	$335	$375	$420	$460	$500	$545	$585	$625
1 SINGLE SET OF PLANS	$285	$325	$370	$410	$450	$495	$535	$525
VELLUMS	$495	$540	$590	$635	$680	$730	$775	$820
MATERIALS LIST	$50	$50	$55	$55	$60	$60	$65	$65
ITEMIZED ZIP QUOTE	$75	$80	$85	$85	$90	$90	$95	$95

Shipping — (Plans 1-84999)

	1-3 Sets	4-6 Sets	7+ & Vellums
Standard Delivery (UPS 2-Day)	$15.00	$20.00	$25.00
Overnight Delivery	$30.00	$35.00	$40.00

Shipping — (Plans 85000-99999)

	1-3 Sets	4-6 Sets	7+ & Vellums
Ground Delivery (7-10 Days)	$9.00	$18.00	$20.00
Express Delivery (3-5 Days)	$15.00	$20.00	$25.00

International Shipping & Handling

	1-3 Sets	4-6 Sets	7+ & Vellums
Regular Delivery Canada (7-10 Days)	$14.00	$17.00	$20.00
Express Delivery Canada (5-6 Days)	$35.00	$40.00	$45.00
Overseas Delivery Airmail (2-3 Weeks)	$45.00	$52.00	$60.00

Option Key
- **ZIP** Zip Quote Available
- **R** Right Reading Reverse
- Duplex Plan
- Materials List Available

Index

Plan	Pg.	Price	Option	Plan	Pg.	Price	Option	Plan	Pg.	Price	Option	Plan	Pg.	Price	Option	Plan	Pg.	Price	Option
10328	238	B	X	90001	75	C	X	92106	166	E	X	94314	193	C		98539	93	F	ZIP
10483	2	A		90007	32	C		92237	163	F	ZIP	94316	218	B		98559	23	C	
10555	224	C	R ZIP	90008	150	D		92238	169	B		94811	176	D		98564	24	C	
10673	145	D		90011	65	C		92283	208	B		94933	202	F	ZIP	98714	121	C	X
10679	97	C	ZIP	90028	142	B		92503	192	C	X	94994	108	E		98801	42	B	
10686	156	F		90288	99	A		92527	220	C		94995	184	E		98804	146	A	
10787	123	C		90329	172	B		92531	243	C		96406	239	D		98806	80	A	
10839	56	B	R	90356	187	A		92539	215	D		96414	201	B		98810	144	F	
19422	246	A		90409	38	B		92546	207	E	X	96423	228	D		98815	242	B	X
20083	25	B		90420	46	D		92552	39	D		96459	36	D		98912	104	A	
20087	51	E		90441	77	C		92560	55	C		96494	11	D		99081	9	B	
20093	34	C		90444	200	D		92562	98	C		96505	113	D		99119	50	E	
20099	28	C	R	90449	86	D		92610	112	C	ZIP	97123	12	C		99129	96	C	
20108	157	C		90469	211	C		92622	82	C		97124	15	A		99132	128	C	
20111	81	D	ZIP	90613	197	A		92625	155	B		97201	14	A		99230	134	F	X
20128	135	C		90620	237	A		92630	102	B		97203	13	A		99238	149	A	X
20143	58	C		90622	241	E		92647	67	C		97701	16	C		99262	168	E	X
20148	92	B	R ZIP	90671	54	B		92649	126	B		97702	19	B		99315	167	A	
20179	139	A		90689	31	A		92660	127	C		97703	20	C		99321	204	A	
20198	43	B		90821	124	A		92695	110	A		98000	17	B		99339	190	A	
20205	47	A		90844	85	B		92801	170	A	X	98001	22	C		99365	212	A	
20220	91	A		90925	63	B		92804	103	B	X	98009	21	C	ZIP	99404	217	B	X
20363	72	D		90941	95	E		93000	70	C		98357	174	C		99410	205	F	
20368	161	D	R ZIP	90986	130	B		93015	79	A		98400	224	F		99424	198	E	R
24250	179	A	R ZIP	90990	147	A		93024	88	A		98403	60	F		99438	178	E	ZIP X
24264	213	D		91021	181	A		93030	131	C		98405	226	F		99452	216	C	
24269	194	D		91026	69	A		93055	40	E		98406	229	B		99456	230	A	
24326	222	B	ZIP	91063	171	A		93056	117	D	X	98407	225	F		99460	3	E	
24550	225	E		91077	120	B		93059	53	C		98408	106	C		99639	71	A	
24567	240	D		91081	189	B		93118	109	F	R	98410	41	D		99641	185	B	
24594	57	E		91082	151	E		93153	107	C		98411	138	A		99650	195	B	
24700	162	A		91083	152	E		93165	111	A		98423	133	B		99666	164	C	
24706	30	A		91089	154	E		93190	44	C	ZIP	98425	214	C		99794	231	F	
24708	199	B		91091	158	A		93193	26	C		98426	62	E		99801	118	D	ZIP X
24717	48	B		91111	101	E		93213	115	C		98431	234	B		99803	165	A	
24728	6	C		91319	84	E		93279	29	A	ZIP X	98438	140	F		99804	177	C	ZIP X
24803	219	F		91335	119	G		93287	153	C	X	98454	78	C		99805	196	C	
26112	4	A		91339	105	E		93319	143	E		98460	210	B		99811	209	B	
34005	83	A	R ZIP X	91340	49	A		93401	159	E		98472	232	A		99812	191	B	ZIP
34011	221	A		91342	52	A		93403	223	A		98487	18	A		99851	203	B	
34029	245	B	ZIP	91343	64	C		93442	7	A		98500	76	C		99856	5	B	
34047	33	E		91346	114	C		93501	180	B	X	98501	137	C		99871	256	F	ZIP X
34049	59	C		91411	116	C		93502	175	E		98502	173	C		99878	90	F	
34054	227	A	R ZIP X	91514	100	B	R	93611	186	A		98508	132	F	ZIP				
34150	45	A	R ZIP X	91517	129	C	R	94116	27	C	X	98512	206	C					
34154	74	B		91518	136	D		94130	122	C		98514	125	F					
34600	66	A		91526	182	C		94138	183	C		98517	247	B					
34602	87	B		91704	148	C		94146	160	D		98518	35	D	ZIP				
35007	236	B		91900	141	D		94261	8	C		98528	61	F					
35009	94	A	R	92026	68	A	X	94309	188	A		98534	37	E	ZIP				
84056	233	B		92048	89	F						98536	73	B	ZIP				

CHARM AND PERSONALITY

Design 99871

Charm and personality radiate from this country home. Interior columns dramatically open the foyer and kitchen to the spacious Great room which boasts an impressive cathedral ceiling and a fireplace. The master suite with tray ceiling accesses the rear deck through sliding glass doors, which the skylit bath has all the amenities you would expect in a quality home. Two generous bedrooms share a second full bath. Tray ceilings with roundtop picture windows bring special elegance to the dining room and front swing room. This plan is available with a basement, crawl space foundation. Please specify when ordering.

Main floor — 1,655 sq. ft.
Garage — 434 sq. ft.

Total living area: 1,655 sq. ft.

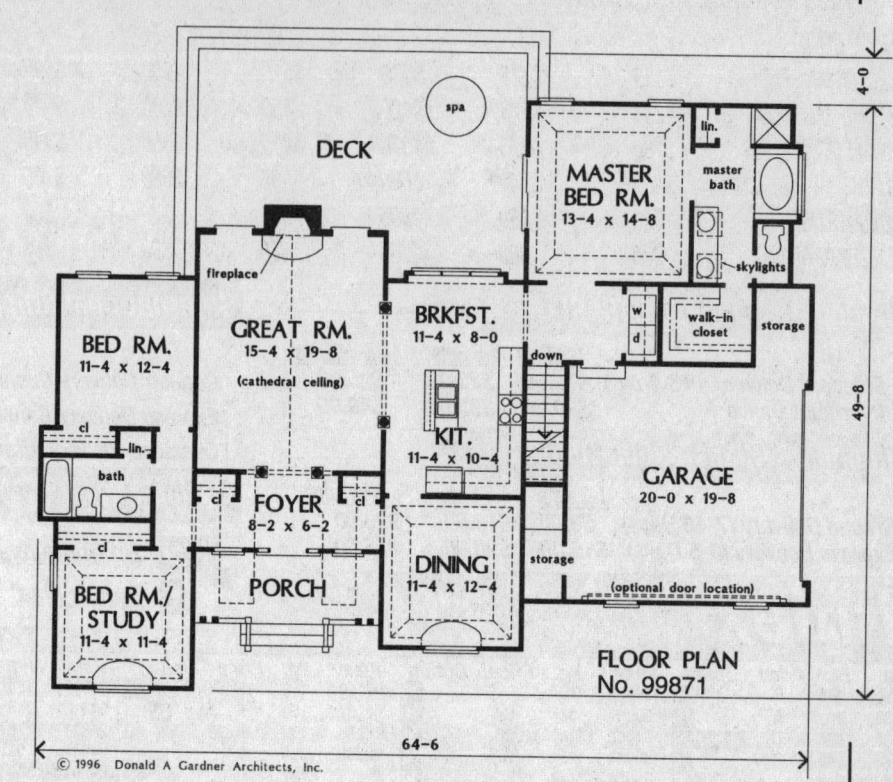

Refer to **Pricing Schedule C** on the order form for pricing information

© 1996 Donald A. Gardner Architects, Inc.